THE
ROAD FROM
COORAIN

THE
ROAD FROM
COORAIN

Jill Ker Conway

G.K.HALL&CO.
Boston, Massachusetts
1991

Published in Large Print by arrangement with
Alfred A. Knopf, Inc.

G.K. Hall Large Print Book Series.

Set in 18 pt. Plantin.

Library of Congress Cataloging-in-Publication Data

Conway, Jill K. , 1934–
    The road from Coorain / Jill Ker Conway.
      p. cm.—(G.K. Hall large print book series)
    ISBN 0-8161-5204-7 (lg. print)
    1. Conway, Jill K., 1934– —Childhood and youth. 2. Smith
College—Presidents—Biography. 3. Country life—Australia.
4. Large type books. I. Title.
[LD7152.7 1975.C66 1991]
378.1′11—dc20
[B]   91-8505

For John

THE
ROAD FROM
COORAIN

1

The West

The western plains of New South Wales are grasslands. Their vast expanse flows for many hundreds of miles beyond the Lachlan and Murrumbidgee rivers until the desert takes over and sweeps inland to the dead heart of the continent. In a good season, if the eyes are turned to the earth on those plains, they see a tapestry of delicate life— not the luxuriant design of a book of hours by any means, but a tapestry nonetheless, designed by a spare modern artist. What grows there hugs the earth firmly with its extended system of roots above which the plant life is delicate but determined. After rain there is an explosion of growth. Nut-flavored green grass puts up the thinnest of green spears. Wild grains appear, grains which develop bleached gold ears as they ripen. Purple desert peas weave through the green and gold, and bright yellow bachelor's buttons cover acres at a time, like fields planted with mustard. Closest to the earth is trefoil clover, whose tiny, vivid green leaves and bright flowers creep along the ground in spring, to be replaced by a harvest of seed-filled burrs in autumn—burrs which store within them the energy of the sun as concentrated protein. At the edges of pans of clay, where the topsoil has eroded, live waxy succulents bearing bright pink and purple blooms, spreading like splashes of paint dropped in widening circles on the earth.

Above the plants that creep across the ground are the bushes, which grow wherever an indentation in the earth, scarcely visible to the eye, allows for the concentration of more moisture from the dew and the reluctant rain. There is the ever-present round mound of prickly weed, which begins its life a strong acid green with hints of yellow, and then is burnt by the sun or the frost to a pale whitish yellow. As it ages, its root system weakens so that on windy days the wind will pick it out of the earth and roll it slowly and majestically about like whirling suns in a Van Gogh painting. Where the soil contains limestone, stronger bushes grow, sometimes two to three feet high, with the delicate narrow-leaved foliage of arid climates, bluish green and dusty grey in color, perfectly adapted to resist the drying sun. Where the soil is less porous and water will lie for a while after rain, comes the annual saltbush, a miraculous silvery-grey plant which stores its own water in small balloonlike round leaves and thrives long after the rains have vanished. Its sterner perennial cousin, which resembles sagebrush, rises on woody branches and rides out the strongest wind.

Very occasionally, where a submerged watercourse rises a little nearer the surface of the earth, a group of eucalyptus trees will cluster. Worn and gnarled by wind and lack of moisture, they rise up on the horizon so dramatically they appear like an assemblage of local deities. Because heat and mirages make them float in the air, they seem from the distance like surfers endlessly riding the plains above a silvery wave. The ocean they ride is blue-grey, silver, green, yellow, scarlet, and bleached gold, highlighting the red clay tones of the earth to provide a rich palette illuminated by brilliant sunshine, or on grey days a subdued blending of tones like those observed on a calm sea.

The creatures that inhabit this earth carry its colors in their feathers, fur, or scales. Among its largest denizens are emus, six-foot-high flightless birds with dun-grey feathers and tiny wings, and kangaroos. Kangaroos, like emus, are silent creatures, two to eight feet tall, and ranging in color from the gentlest dove-grey to a rich red-brown. Both species blend with their native earth so well that one can be almost upon them before recognizing the familiar shape. The fur of the wild dogs has the familiar yellow of the sunbaked clay, and the reptiles, snakes and goannas, look like the earth in shadow. All tread on the fragile habitat with padded paws and claws which leave the roots of grass intact.

On the plains, the earth meets the sky in a sharp black line so regular that it seems as though drawn by a creator interested more in geometry than the hills and valleys of the Old Testament. Human purposes are dwarfed by such a blank horizon. When we see it from an island in a vast ocean we know we are resting in shelter. On the plains, the horizon is always with us and there is no retreating from it. Its blankness travels with our every step and waits for us at every point of the compass. Because we have very few reference points on the spare earth, we seem to creep over it, one tiny point of conscious-ness between the empty earth and the overarching sky. Because of the flatness, contrasts are in a strange scale. A scarlet sunset will highlight grey-yellow tussocks of grass as though they were trees. Thunderclouds will mount thousands of feet above one stunted tree in the foreground. A horseback rider on the horizon will seem to rise up and emerge from the clouds. While the patterns of the earth are in small scale, akin to complex needlepoint on a vast tapestry, the sky is all drama. Cumulus clouds pile up over the center of vast continental spaces, and the wind moves them at dramatic pace along the horizon or over our heads. The ever-present red dust of a dry earth hangs in the air and turns all the colors from yellow through orange and red to purple on and off as the clouds bend and refract the light. Sunrise and sunset make up in drama for the fact that there are so few songbirds in that part of the bush. At sunrise, great shafts of gold precede the baroque sunburst. At sunset, the cumulus ranges through the shades of a Turner seascape before the sun dives below the earth leaving no afterglow, but at the horizon, tongues of fire.

Except for the bush canary and the magpie, the birds of this firmament court without the songs of the northern forest. Most are parrots, with the vivid colors and rasping sounds of the species. At sunset, rosella parrots, a glorious rosy pink, will settle on trees and appear to turn them scarlet. Magpies, large black and white birds, with a call close to song, mark the sunrise, but the rest of the day is the preserve of the crows, and the whistle of the hawk and the golden eagle. The most startling sound is the ribald laughter of the kookaburra, a species of kingfisher, whose call resembles demonic laughter. It is hard to imagine a kookaburra feeding St. Jerome or accompanying St. Francis. They belong to a physical and spiritual landscape which is outside the imagination of the Christian West.

The primal force of the sun shapes the environment. With the wind and the sand it bakes and cleanses all signs of decay. There is no cleansing by water. The rivers flow beneath the earth, and rain falls too rarely. In the recurring cycles of drought the sand and dust flow like water, and like the floods of other climates they engulf all that lies in their path. Painters find it hard to capture the shimmer of that warm red earth dancing in the brilliant light, and to record at the same time the subtle greens and greys of the plants and trees. Europeans were puzzled by the climate and vegetation, because the native eucalyptus trees were not deciduous. The physical blast of the sun is hot dry summers brought plants to dormancy. Slow growth followed in autumn, and a burst of vigorous growth after the brief winter rainy season. Summer was a time of endurance for all forms of life as moisture ebbed away and the earth was scorched. Winter days were like summer in a northern climate, and spring meant the onset of unbroken sunshine. On the plains, several winters might go by without a rainy season, and every twenty years or so the rain might vanish for a decade at a time. When that happened, the sun was needed to cleanse the bones of dead creatures, for the death toll was immense.

The oldest known humans on the continent left their bones on the western plains. Nomadic peoples hunted over the land as long as forty thousand years ago. They and their progeny left behind the blackened stones of ovens, and the hollowed flat pieces of granite they carried from great distances to grind the native nardoo grain. Their way of life persisted until white settlers came by bullock wagon, one hundred and thirty years ago, to take possession of the land. They came to graze their flocks of sharp-hooved sheep and cattle, hoping to make the land yield wealth. Other great inland grasslands in Argentina, South Africa, or North America were settled by pastoralists and ranchers who used forced labor: Indian peons, Bantus, or West African slaves. On Australia's great plains there were no settled native people to enslave. The settlers moved onto the plains long after the abandonment of transportation from Great Britain, the last form of forced labor available in the Antipodes. As a result, the way of life that grew up for white settlers was unique.

A man could buy the government leasehold for hundreds of thousands of acres of grassland at a modest price if he settled the land and undertook to develop it. Others, beyond the reach of government scrutiny, simply squatted with their flocks on likely-looking land. The scale of each holding was beyond European dreams of avarice. Each settler could look out to the vacant horizon knowing that all he saw was his. To graze the unfenced land required a population of sheepherders, or, as they came to be called, boundary riders. A settler would need twelve to fifteen hands for his several hundred thousand acres, but most would live out on the "run" (sheep run) at least a day's ride from the main settlement. The hands were solitary males, a freewheeling rural proletariat, antisocial, and unconcerned with comfort or the domestic pleasures. Their leisure went in drink and gambling, and their days in a routine of lonely and backbreaking work. The main house would be spare and simple also, its roof of iron and its walls of timber laboriously transported from the coast. The garden would be primitive and the boss's recreations would be little different from his hands'. If he shared his life with a wife and children, they lived marginally on the edge of his world of male activity. There was no rain for orchards, no water for vegetable gardens, and no society for entertaining. Women worked over wood stoves in 100 degree heat and heated water for laundry over an open fire. There was little room for the culinary arts, because everyone's diet was mutton and unleavened bread, strong black tea, and spirits. The ratio of women to men was as distorted in this wave of settlement as anywhere in the settlement of the New World.

The bush ethos which grew up from making a virtue out of loneliness and hardship built on the stoic virtues of convict Australia. Settled life and domesticity were soft and demoralizing. A "real man" despised comfort and scorned the expression of emotion. The important things in life were hard work, self-sufficiency, physical endurance, and loyalty to one's male friends, one's "mates." Knowledge about nature, the care of animals, practical mechanics was respected, but speculation and the world of ideas were signs of softness and impracticality. Religion and belief in a benevolent deity were foolish because daily life demonstrated beyond doubt that the universe was hostile. The weather, the fates, the bank that held the mortgage, bushfires—disaster in some form—would get a man in the end. When disaster struck what mattered was unflinching courage and the refusal to consider despair.

Very few women could stand the isolation. When a settler prospered, his wife and children moved to a distant but comfortable rural town, where there were schools for the children and companionship for their mother. If he did not prosper, she was likely to be overwhelmed by loneliness. Nothing interrupted the relentless routine of hard labor, the anxiety of illness far from hope of help, the certainty of enervating summer heat, frosty winter cold, and the pervasive anxiety of disaster looming. Disaster could strike swiftly—some little-understood disease might wipe out the investment in the flock or the herd; a man or a child could die from snakebite, a tetanus-infected wound, a fall from a horse. Or disaster could set in slowly with the onset of drought. It was ever-present and a woman at home alone all day had time to think about it. Some took despairingly to drink, some fell into incurable depression, others told their husbands they could not endure it and left for the city.

The ideal woman was a good manager—no small task with only wood stoves, kerosene lamps, inadequate water, and the nearest store for canned goods fifty to a hundred miles away. She was toughened by adversity, laughed at her fears, knew how to fix things which broke in the house, and stifled any craving she might once have had for beauty. She could care for the sick, help fight a bushfire, aid a horse or cow in difficult labor, laugh and joke about life's absurdities and reverses, and like a man, mock any signs of weakness or lack of stoicism in her children. Everyone knew the most important gift to a child was an upbringing which would toughen him (her) up so as to be stoic and uncomplaining about life's pains and ready for its reverses. The sons of the outback made great soldiers in modern wars because they had been prepared for them since infancy. The daughters lacked such a calling.

The pattern of the year followed the seasons. If the rains came, they fell in the winter. Lambing was planned for the spring, when the grass was at its best, and the last winter showers might have left some tender growth for young lambs to nibble before their teeth developed. If seasons cooperated, the lambs were well grown, able to walk great distances for their food and water by the time the summer set in. In February, before the summer reached its peak, the lambs were shorn, and the faces and withers of the grown sheep were trimmed so that flies could not infest the places where sweat and urine soiled their fleeces. In June, in midwinter, when it was less harmful to move the animals over distances and hold them penned in yards, the grown sheep were brought to a shearing shed and shorn. If there had been an uninterrupted supply of nourishment through the year, their fleece would be seven inches thick, unstained by dust, and carrying an unbroken staple that meant it could be easily combed to spin the finest yarn. If the land they grazed did not carry enough herbage throughout the year, the staple of their fleeces would show a break to mark the point where the food supply had faltered. When the staple was broken it could not be so easily combed, and the yarn it produced, being of less high quality, sold for less. If there were too many breaks it might not repay the cost of producing it.

A pastoralist could follow several economic strategies. Fewer sheep could be grazed over a set area of land, moved to fresh pasture whenever their nourishment required, and thus produce smaller amounts of more valuable wool. More sheep could be grazed over land they would crop bare in a year, for a larger volume of less valuable wool. The land which was grazed out each year succumbed quickly to drought. The land which was grazed in careful rotation might not succumb for as long as four or five years, for the unbroken root systems of the plants would hold the ground. One thing was certain. If the drought was long enough, sheep and cattle would, in their hunger, drag up the roots of the herbage, their sharp hooves would loosen the topsoil, and it would begin to blow away in the wind. The grasslands the earliest settlers saw had never been cropped by ruminant animals. No sharp hooves had ever disturbed the soil. It looked rich and indestructible, but in reality it was one of the most delicately balanced environments on the planet.

Cattle require much larger supplies of protein than sheep. They could not prosper on the plains except where pockets of heavy soil and low-lying land allowed for more luxuriant grass and the reliable saltbush. They, too, were bred to calve in the spring, nursed through their first summer, and then shipped away to some richer land where they could be fattened for the butcher. The calculus of risk in raising them was simple. It might not rain enough in the winter to produce the long grass they required. If it did not, the cows would be only marginally fertile, their calves stunted, and few would survive the heat of summer. Those that did would be less valuable because of the scrawny muscles built ranging long distances to find nourishment. They would be sold to meat canners at a marginal price. Moreover, in their struggle for life they would degrade the land in one progression of seasons. Sometimes the saltbush they chewed to the roots did not return for decades. Sometimes the land eroded so badly that the treasured saltbush was gone for good. No matter how one planned to coax an increase from the land,

14

it was a gamble in which the odds could suddenly change drastically.

The first generation of settlers took up vast tracts of land. Two hundred and fifty thousand acres, three hundred thousand, half a million acres; such tracts allowed an owner to graze thirty to forty thousand sheep, and a good-sized herd of cattle, while still possessing some room to rotate the grazing of the flocks and herds. Wool was light in relation to its value, easy to transport to distant markets, and after the invention of refrigeration, meat was also a profitable export to densely populated Europe. Those who planned their enterprises well grew rich enough to see out the lean years of losses or low earnings during recurring cycles of drought. Even so, many gambled on the wrong hunches about the seasons, and saw their lands fall into the hands of the land and finance companies who had been their bankers and mercantile agents. As much as forty percent of the plains was held by banks and land companies after the great drought of the 1890s and the fearful agricultural depression which accompanied it. There it remained until after 1900, when politicians in the newly federated Australia had to wrestle with the concentration of land ownership.

One of the recurring themes in Australian political life was the longing of the landless for the independence of the family farm, and their hatred for the privilege they saw accruing to the owners of huge grazing properties. While the nature of the land and the economics of its exploitation required large holdings and considerable capital investment, voters clung to the myth that small-scale farming was possible and they regularly elected state governments committed to breaking up and reallocating large holdings. By 1914, much of the richer land in more fertile and well-watered areas had been broken up into smaller holdings, and all that remained were the great grazing leases on the western plains. In 1919, a grateful country turned to allocating land from these leases to the soldiers who had made the Australian name legendary for valor during the First World War.

In 1919, land and grazing was the traditional source of wealth for a nation which had achieved one of the highest per capita incomes in the world from the growth and export of wool and wheat. Land ownership was the principal source of status. Families that had grown rich in commerce progressed quickly to the life of gentlemen farmers. The large acreages of graziers carried more status than the struggling family farms of wheat farmers. The work of the grazier might be lonely and arduous, but he was seen as living life on a heroic scale, while the settled life of the wheat farmer returned less profit and seemed domestic and lacking in adventure. The great sheep and cattle stud properties where the best bloodlines were preserved and the greatest breeding animals were carefully tended carried the names of ancient great estates in England and Scotland, and hinted at pretensions to the life of the English country gentry.

The soldier settlers carried with them a strange mixture of feelings about the England the Australian rich emulated so sedulously. They scorned "the bloody brass hats," the English military leadership they correctly blamed for the suffering and slaughter of war in the trenches in France. They laughed at Mayfair accents but spoke fondly of Blighty. Piccadilly, Leicester Square, and Westminster were the center of the political world for them. Horrible as the experience of battle had been, the journey from Australia, the experience of England and the Continent, and the sense of epic participation in momentous world events filled them with pride and inspired a collective and treasured sense of history.

Whenever they gathered together for the working bees that became a way of life as each new western land lease acquired a house, or sheepyards, or sheds for shearing, they talked about the 1944–1918 War. Sometimes solemn, sometimes ribald, they refought the battles. Each one learned where the other had been at Ypres, at Passchendaele, at Vimy, on the Menin Road, or with what outfit at Gallipoli. Heads would nod about tactical blunders that had cost lives needlessly. Arguments would break out about which regiments had been to the right or left in the line. Maps would be drawn in the red soil and places marked where this man was wounded or that friend died. There would be bursts of sardonic laughter about the stupidity of the high command and the inefficiency of the desk types who lived in luxury far from battle and spent their lives drawing up ridiculous military regulations. Generally they respected the Germans, despised the French ("the bastards wouldn't fight"), condescended to the inability of the British ("the poor bloody Poms") to manage a hard and dangerous life in a harsh environment, and reserved judgment on the Americans.

The chance to acquire title to a western land lease was the chance of a lifetime. In the expansive environment of the 1920s, men who felt lucky to be alive looked at the plains and dreamed about finally achieving economic independence. Perhaps, if things went well, their children could live the life of Australia's pastoral elites. For the returned soldiers, class consciousness was more or less set aside, but most knew they wanted private schools for their children, fashionable clothes for their wives to wear to the races, a fancy horse or two in the stables, and freedom from worry about money.

The voices that exclaimed over the follies of brass hats or swore poetically about the stubborn ways of sheep and cattle did so in a mélange of accents. Some carried a Scots burr, some a trace of a Yorkshire flat *a;* some spoke grammatically and displayed the manners produced by attendance at one of Australia's private schools. Most spoke broad Australian: picturesque in image, laced with the rhyming slang of Cockney London and the poetic black humor of the Irish. Their manners and their clothes were deliberately working-class. At night when they sat with their wives beside their crackling static-blurred radios, they waited for Big Ben to chime and then heard the impeccable British accents of the BBC announcer reading the news. With that voice they absorbed a map of the world which placed their near neighbor, Japan, in the Far East, and located distant Turkey in the Near East. So far as Australia was concerned its map was also clear and idiosyncratic. There were Sydney, Melbourne, and Adelaide on the southeast coast, and the bush. Other places existed— small country towns, the new federal capital planned at Canberra, the Snowy Mountains with their huge areas of snow and ice, industrial seaports like Newcastle, near the coalfields. They did not register because there were really only two places in the westerner's consciousness: the bush, and the metropolis at the end of the railway line where the wool was sold.

The city was a place of unaccustomed leisure for people who labored hard seven days a week. For the men there were cheerful drinking occasions before the wool sales or the agricultural shows. For the women there were the shops, the doctors and dentists for the children, and the luxury of restaurants, fresh fruit and vegetables, seafood, flower stands. For the children there were the marvels of electric lights, neon signs, moving pictures, and unlimited candy stores. These were balanced but not outweighed by the ministrations of the dental and medical professions and the ominous crowds. For everyone there were the sore feet and aching legs which came from wearing one's best shoes on hard pavements, and the unaccustomed feel of city clothes.

Everyone much preferred the rare occasions of leisure and festivity at home. There were picnic races, a bush festivity which involved horse racing by day, cheerful and alcoholic gambling and dances by night. A district might band together to stage a gymkhana, where the jockeys were not professionals and the horses were local products. Every half-dozen stations would have somewhere a vestigial race track, barely a trace in the soil, with some rickety shelters from the sun and some kind of access to water. Bookmakers throve as people cheerfully gambled away the year's profits in big bets, unconsciously recognizing that there were few other really satisfying diversions. Old lumber and battered corrugated iron would be pieced together to make a community hall in the middle of nowhere, and dances would be arranged by the Country Women's Association, or the Returned Soldiers' League. Musicians would materialize, and the men would appear in unaccustomed suits accompanied by wives in long dresses. People starved for company danced happily till dawn, reluctant to go home. Supper would be a feast at which every woman's prowess in the kitchen was assessed, and none of the hardworking revelers needed to worry about dieting.

Before they set out in the lightening sky, they stood to attention for "God Save the King," and if the evening had become an occasion for remembering 1914–1918, they sang "Land of Hope and Glory," evoking the memory, not so much of England, but of her mighty Empire, of which Australia was the proudest part. Anyone who mocked these loyalties learned quickly that he or she did not belong.

The cars would sweep home over the dusty roads, their lights visible like pillars of fire across the plains. If one arrived home first, one could stand on one's veranda and watch the other departures, visible for twenty miles or so. On regular nights there were only the stars, the cry of a fox, and the sound of the wind. Then if a car traveled very late at night it meant an emergency. Distant watchers would crane their heads to see where it went, and wonder what had gone wrong.

2

Coorain

Every penny of my father's savings was invested on taking up his block of land in the Western Division of New South Wales, granted him as a soldier settler in 1929. With them he built a house set foursquare to the points of the compass. The living room and bedrooms looked out to the rising sun, the kitchen saw it sink in a sudden blaze of flaming color. The side verandas received the occasional cooling southerly breeze or the hot winds from the north. My mother's savings, accumulated during her nursing career, equipped the house with furniture, linen, china, and silver bought at auctions in Sydney in 1930. She had impeccable taste, as well as great thrift and practicality. Her purchases were items of quality discarded by city dwellers in favor of the fashions of the twenties. The ample oak furniture, delicate curtains, and old-fashioned china gave the place the solid comfort of an earlier era, and belied the true nature of the family finances. The cool, airy comfort of the house with its expanses of highly polished linoleum and generously proportioned furniture suggested an easy inheritance from the past. In fact, the house, the land, the spotless equipment, and the well-groomed horses in the stables represented an act of will, a gamble on which two natural risk takers had staked everything they had.

They had come to see the land in the summer of 1929 in the midst of a drought that was to become legendary. The eighteen thousand acres of the block, a ninety-nine-year lease from the Western Lands Commission of New South Wales, had been carved out from earlier leases of hundreds of thousands of acres. Occasional fences marked the vast paddocks of the earlier owner and indicated the boundary of the new block. That year the drought was so severe that the topsoil was drifting, engulfing any obstacle in its path. The new owners thus drove not through the gate but over the silted-up boundary fence. My father was elated as he surveyed the realization of his dream to own land and to raise his own flocks of sheep and cattle. For my mother, not born to the bush, my father's long-dreamed-of property was a nightmare of desolation.

She had grown up in a comfortable Queensland country town where the hills along the coastal range captured plentiful rain, the gardens were lush, and the rich soil suited small-scale agriculture. Until her marriage to my father at the age of twenty-eight, she had lived by choice in cities. Their married life had begun in considerable style on the rich and well-established sheep station my father managed for one of Australia's great landholders. That homestead was situated on a river and overlooked a lake. The Chinese gardener grew sumptuous vegetables and flowers for the cook, whose kitchen fed twelve to fourteen people daily. The place hummed with sociability and activity, for the overseer and jackeroos (men of education and good family) dined with the manager and his wife. The lady of the house oversaw the station store for the hands, supervised the domestic help, and oversaw the care of anyone injured on the property.

The eighteen thousand acres they rattled across in their T-model Ford had no surface water, and only a few isolated and scraggy clumps of eucalyptus trees. It seemed flatter and more barren than any land she had ever seen. She saw no landmarks to identify directions, only emptiness. My father saw strong fertile soil, indications of grazed-out saltbush, dips and changes in the contours of the land and its soils, landmarks of all kinds. The contours of the isolated trees indicated the prevailing winds. The sand drifts told him the path of the dust storms which boiled out of the inland desert in a drought. In his mind's eye he had already taken possession of the earth and it was already blooming after the next rain. My mother, nursing her infant son, felt the flying sand become grit in her mouth and eyes and was temporarily daunted.

On the one-hundred-and-fifty-mile drive back to comfort and the constraints of being someone else's employee they struck a bargain. He would attempt the gamble for independence only if she gave it her whole-hearted assent. He was too much in love to contemplate the standard bush marriage where the wife and children lived in relative comfort in some distant country town. Half measures were not part of the vocabulary of either partner, and so it was agreed. They would go together, run the risks, and reap the benefits. He would move ahead of her to oversee the building of the house. She would make the journey to Sydney to equip it.

Neither of them could explain to curious children where their urge to get ahead and make something of life came from. Different as their backgrounds were, both were driven to excel, to run the best station, breed the best sheep, raise the brightest children, run the most efficient house. Yet they approached their new venture from entirely different perceptions of what was involved.

My father was born in the early 1890s, close to the South Australian coastal town of Port Pirie. Orphaned in early childhood, he and a younger brother were raised in the large and outgoing family of an uncle and aunt on Berta Station, near Broken Hill, a large acreage lost to the perennial debts and poor seasons of woolgrowing on the plains. They had no patrimony from dimly remembered parents and few opportunities in the sluggish pre-World War I Australian economy. At sixteen he began working for the mining company that was the only large employer besides the pastoral industry, Broken Hill Proprietary Limited. He was tall, with blazing blue eyes, a mercurial temperament, and a wicked sense of humor that won men and women friends with ease. The Roman

Catholic Church was an important center of emotional and social life for a lonely young man with few prospects. He had the manners and style of a man born to inherit land and husband it well. His education had been the lore of raising sheep and cattle, breaking horses, knowing how to command men. All his life he would be moved to rage when lesser men gained land he knew he could have managed better. There was no prospect of any for him so it was as natural as breathing to seek adventure by enlisting in 1914. He cherished, like all his family, ties of affection and family mythology to his Lowland Scottish heritage. The Scottish virtue of unswerving loyalty meant unreflecting acceptance of Great Britain as the font of all that mattered in the world besides the bush Australian ethos of strength and endurance.

What began as an adventure ended in horror too profound for speech. The farewells, the adoring young ladies, the troopship, England, and training on Salisbury Plain were in line with all the British Empire tales heard in childhood. The daily slaughter of the trenches never ceased to be a part of his nightmares. A childhood spent hunting kangaroos made him an excellent shot and earned him the post of sharpshooter, the man sent ahead alone to pick off the enemy. About this he could not speak, except to describe the common experience of the trenches, a kind of fellow feeling for the opponent. His worst memories were the screams of wounded horses, and the sight of men being driven back to the trenches at rifle point. An injury to the sight of one eye and trench feet, feet swollen with rheumatism and infected from long stretches standing in water, put an end to sharpshooting and marching. After taking part in the Battle of Passchendaele, he was sent home.

The homecoming was bittersweet. It rankled that married men who had served overseas qualified for grants of land, but he, as a single man, did not. He took a job as the overseer of a large western sheep station, and quickly progressed to manager for another of the great properties of an absentee owner. There he met my mother and embarked upon the marriage that made him eligible for land.

By all accounts, my mother, always handsome, was then an extraordinary beauty. She was tall, slender, and graceful in carriage, and blessed with a coloring of skin and hair which made her memorable. Her abundant, curling hair was deep auburn highlighted with gold, but instead of the redhead's tender skin she had an olive complexion which tanned to a fine rosy color without a hint of a freckle. This natural beauty was accompanied by boundless physical and intellectual energy. She was a "new woman," a professional trained nurse, used to independence and responsibility, and in her late twenties she was already running her own country hospital. She was the child of a feckless British immigrant family. Her father was the type of Micawberish character whose failure to get ahead in England took him to the colonies. Her mother, a generous-hearted woman, lacked the education to make a success of the endless household businesses she undertook to support her burgeoning family. Soon after the family arrived in Queensland, my mother's father quietly disappeared in the Australian contingent to the Boer War, a volunteer who neglected to mention his family when enlisting, and who was thereafter merely a shadowy presence to his eight children. My mother never forgave nor forgot the desertion, the casual sexual exploitation of her mother, and the humiliations of the economically marginal family.

Her resentment of men was fueled by the

conventional sex roles assigned in her family, where the daughters were expected to wait on the males and to defer to the judgment of the older sons, who encouraged their mother to enter one economic venture after another. At fourteen my mother left school, began to work in an office, and to study bookkeeping at night. She resented the earnings which went to support unemployed older brothers, or to compensate for easily avoided economic failures. At seventeen she left. Claiming to be eighteen, she began her nurse's training at a general hospital in Rockhampton, a bustling country town and port, three hundred miles north of Brisbane. She was never homesick for a moment. She loved the order and discipline of hospital life, the starched and shining order of the medical world, and the chance to be in charge. She was a natural healer. No effort was too great to make a patient comfortable. No reward was sweeter than the total dependence of the very sick or the helplessness of an infant. She reveled in blessed independence: money to invest in clothes and outings, a chance to explore the world.

She finished her training while still in her teens, and she set to work to use it to educate herself. She took nursing posts in all the worlds about which she was curious. In this way she sampled life on one of the great inland cattle stations, where the household still dressed for dinner and the style of life was baronial. She explored the life of a young professional in a big city hospital and took nursing posts in the households of the fashionable rich in Sydney during the twenties. By the time she came to run the hospital in Lake Cargelligo, the town nearest the sheep station my father managed, she had been an independent single woman for almost ten years, and she was used to being in charge.

The hospital was much needed, its matron and nurses much appreciated, and the opening year a high-spirited and sociable one for the matron and her friend Eva, who had come along on the adventure as head nurse. Near the end of that first year, my father brought an injured station hand to the hospital and was much taken by the beautiful matron, and she by him. For two stiff-necked, cautious individuals they took very little time to decide on life together. They were married within a month of meeting, before my mother's doubts about men could assert themselves, and before my father's anxiety about establishing a family without a solid economic base could take hold. One possible bone of contention was quickly brushed aside as of no account. My mother was a modern feminist, a loyal follower of Marie Stopes and Havelock Ellis. Their views on sex and marriage were her bible, and through them she knew that the Roman Catholic faith was anathema. She had delivered unwanted children of Catholic mothers, watched the mother's life ebb out after botched abortions, and she would have nothing to do with a faith she equated with the irresponsible male domination of women she resented so bitterly. At that point in his life, my father's Catholic faith occupied the background, not the forefront, of his mind. He had not lived in a serious Catholic community since his departure for the front in 1914. The experience of modern war had shaken his faith and left him lackadaisical in its observance. They settled for a Protestant marriage service, and there let the matter rest.

Nine months later, their first son, Robert, was born, and in the third year of their married life, their second son, and as they planned it, their last child, Barry, was born. My mother's nursing training and her natural habits of order allowed her to enjoy raising her own children without the usual worries of young brides. Her infants were toilet trained before they were toddling, clean and radiant with health, dressed in neat starched clothes no matter how hot the weather. Their infant ills were speedily cared for, and they occupied a stable environment which made for regular sleep and predictable behavior. It is hard to speculate about what these two driven achievers might have done if the fates had presented them with a sickly child, or a slow learner. Might they have learned to bend a little before the harshness of fate? In any event, the first scenes in the founding of the family unfolded auspiciously. The boys were strikingly handsome, intelligent, models of good manners, and the envy of all who saw them. It was this young family of four which set out in 1930 to take up a soldier settler's block on the western plains.

They called the new property Coorain, an aboriginal word which means windy place. The house they built was of weatherboard, with the ubiquitous corrugated iron roof of bush houses. It was a low-spreading bungalow, surrounded by verandas on all sides to catch the cooling breezes of summer when the thermometer would settle in over 100 degrees for weeks at a time. My father's bush sense made him site the house out in the open blazing sun, because wherever there were trees for shelter was where the water gathered after heavy rain. Visitors mocked his decision and asked why he had not taken advantage of the shade offered by the low-lying clump of trees just behind the site of the house. He was proved wise when the next wet year came. Other houses were flooded, but Coorain was not.

They were desperately short of water. The only supply came from the rain which was collected on the broad, gently sloping roof of the house. Optimistically, they planted a line of sugar gums along the east, north, and south of the house, and to the west, fast-growing pepper trees which were drought resistant and would soon shade the house from the afternoon heat. Climbing vines were planted to shade the verandas and a few geraniums decorated small beds by the front entrance. It was extremely hard to grow any-thing when the only water to be had was bailed out of the bathtub after the children were bathed in the evening. There was water deep underground, but it was costly to bore down to it, and the first investment had to be made in good water for sheep and cattle.

So there was no garden, no fresh fruit or vegetables, and no way to mitigate the red baked soil, the flatness, and the loneliness.

Seven miles to the north was a tiny post office in the old coaching town of Mossgiel. In coaching days the stages had changed teams there; there was a hotel, a store, and a scattering of houses. After the automobile all that remained was the post office, the remnants of a hotel, and a ramshackle hall. There was a telephone exchange at Mossgiel, but Coorain had no telephone because the cost of seven miles of line to link up to the Mossgiel exchange had to be postponed until the sheep were producing wool and there was income from the property.

When my father left in the morning to work on the fences, or on one of the three bores that watered the sheep and cattle, my mother heard no human voice save the two children. There was no contact with another human being and the silence was so profound it pressed upon the eardrums. My father, being a westerner, born into that profound peace and silence, felt the need for it like an addiction to a powerful drug. Here, pressed into the earth by the weight of that enormous sky, there is real peace. To those who know it, the annihilation of the self, subsumed into the vast emptiness of nature, is akin to a religious experience. We children grew up to know it and seek it as our father before us. What was social and sensory deprivation for the stranger was the earth and sky that made us what we were. For my mother, the emptiness was disorienting, and the loneliness and silence a daily torment of existential dread.

Had she known how to tell directions she would have walked her way to human voices. As it was, once she traveled any distance from the house she would be swept by fear that she could not find it again. Each morning my father would ask her to drive him to a corner of the property where the sheep were and the horses were running. With the ease of one accustomed, he would catch a horse, saddle it, swing easily into the saddle, wave, and tell her when to expect him home. She would drive home desperately hunched over the wheel of the T-model Ford, peering for the tracks the car had made on the way out. She could tell no one place on the property from the other, and she was afraid to admit it to him.

At home, faced with the drudgery of cooking over a wood stove, laundering clothes in a copper heated by a wood fire, and baking bread after the day's work was over, her mind turned sadly to her starched white nurse's uniforms and the pleasures of being off duty. But she was no quitter. Her greatest strengths were an iron will and great powers of endurance. No standard of cleanliness or nicety of domestic arrangements was sacrificed because of the limited supply of water, the outdoor privy, and the never-ending red dust. By six in the evening the children were bathed, the struggling geraniums watered, the dinner table set with starched linen and well-polished silver, and she was dressed immaculately for dinner. My father, freshly shaven and dressed for leisure, would join her, and they would dine as though there were a cook and a maid in the kitchen.

After dinner the kerosene lamps, shiny crystal with freshly polished glass chimneys, were lit. My father turned to his stock records, his day book and accounts. My mother began to read. She was acutely aware that she had no formal education. Lacking society, she made a virtue of necessity and began a program of self-education. Books traveled to her in parcels of twelve from a lending library in Sydney five hundred miles away. She read systematically: nineteenth- and twentieth-century English fiction, biographies of great men, the best commentaries she could find on current events. One evening a week was surrendered reluctantly to mending and sewing. Otherwise the hours after dinner were sacred to her reading. When the night closed out the wilderness, and her husband and children were beside her in the simple but charming house, she found contentment uniquely suited to her nature. They were hers alone. This was her world, responding to her sense of order. No hint of the complications of other human relationships need be considered except within the pages of a book.

My parents had begun their venture at the least propitious time possible. Sheep grazing is capital-intensive in its start-up and slow to yield returns even under the best climatic conditions. Their venture at Coorain began in a period of intense drought and coincided with the onset of the Great Depression, a time when the return on a pound of wool often did not meet the cost of producing it. They were desperately short of cash and had to live as self-sufficiently as the property would allow. My mother made everyone's clothes and cut everyone's hair. They ate the standard bush diet of meat (homegrown) and potatoes and pickles (inexpensive when bought in bulk). Chickens were kept for eggs, butter was homemade, and after a good rain there would be wild spinach to pick for greens. Everyone was carefully dosed with cod-liver oil and lime juice to make up for the lack of fresh fruit and vegetables.

After three years of such effort, the annual wool sale produced a surplus. It was possible to make a trip to Sydney for dental and medical care, and for the luxury of buying some stylish and well-cut clothes. My mother discovered to her astonishment that the three years had made her a countrywoman. The hard pavements hurt her feet. The noise seemed unusually bothersome. The crowds were psychologically oppressive. She would actually be pleased to go home.

Her medical checkup produced an unexpected moral dilemma. She had benign uterine growths so large that they could cause a life-threatening hemorrhage. The same week she realized that despite her usual careful precautions, she was pregnant. Her response was characteristic rebellion. In no time, those stylish new clothes would be unwearable. Worse still would be the new economic burden just when the family finances promised relief from grinding parsimony. She tried all the methods to induce abortion she knew without success. Her medical advice swung her rebellion in another direction. She was told she must terminate the pregnancy at once and undergo a hysterectomy. Her usual resentment at male dominance flared up. No doctor was going to railroad her into an abortion. Determined to have her child, she returned to Coorain.

Her decision certainly placed her in some danger. The nearest medical care was seventy-five miles away, and primitive at best. If her gynecologist's predictions were fulfilled, help would be minimal and very slow in coming. She would be alone for many hours each day, with no one to send for help. I do not know how much of the story she told my father. In later years, it was a tale she was fond of telling me. She did not seem to understand that I was troubled to know that on the one hand I had been unwanted, and on the other brought into the world at considerable hazard to my mother. In any event, she proved her medical advisers wrong, and I was born without incident, in the small cottage hospital in the town of Hillston, some seventy-five miles away from Coorain.

My parents had wanted a daughter in the

vague way people think about the gender of a child. Neither stopped to ponder what possible role a female child could play in the setting in which they lived. The out-of-doors world was exclusively male. The domestic world was exclusively under my mother's control. She did not like to share it with other women, even domestic servants, or the governesses who now lived with us to teach my brothers elementary school. She preferred the help of immigrant Irish and Scottish youngsters who came to us from Dr. Barnardo's Homes in England. They could be taught to do things exactly as she wished.

About the time of my arrival, my father could also afford help for the property. Beside the house there now appeared a cluster of outbuildings. Stables and a cow shed, a garage, and a cottage for the station hand. Housing for drays, farm carts, and a lightweight sulky used for fast travel over country roads when rain had made them impassable for cars. My impending birth had also added a telephone line as a necessary precaution against medical emergency. The place now resounded to other human voices and one could pick up the telephone whenever one wanted contact with the outside world.

My first steps were taken in a household

in which the hard domestic chores were performed by men under my mother's eagle-eyed supervision. Because of my mother's orderliness, the household had an unbreakable routine so that I can tell from this early memory what day of the week it was. On Monday the laundry was done. White things were boiled in the copper and starched. Colored things were scrubbed by hand and rinsed in blue. Care was taken in hanging them out to dry lest the sun bleach the colored fabrics white. On Tuesdays the ironing was done with flatirons heated on the top of the kitchen stove. As the household grew, the whole of Wednesday was needed for sewing and mending. Thursday was for baking. Scones, cupcakes, sponge and pound cakes for tea, tarts and flans for desserts, meat pies to use up leftovers. All were baked in the oven of the wood stove, with a quick test of the hand to determine whether the oven temperature was "just right" to brown pastry or make a sponge cake rise. Friday was for cleaning house. Every room was swept and dusted thoroughly, every floor was washed, wax polish was applied to the linoleum floors, and then they were shone by hand. On the Friday of my first steps, this task was being done by Jimmie Walker, a cheerful and willing Irish lad in his late teens. Jimmie had been sent out by an emigrants' welfare organization to find his fortune in Australia. He was desperately homesick when he came to Coorain, and loved to play with us children because we reminded him of his brothers and sisters at home. We were entranced with a new playmate and were always by his side as he worked. His metabolism was attuned to gentler climates and we children were astonished and fascinated by the extent of his perspiration compared with that of the hard-bitten Australians we knew. On this Friday I was assisting the floor polishing by crawling backwards in front of him ever alert to the point when a river of perspiration would drop from his forehead and nose and smear the beauty of the floor he was polishing. While we were thus engaged, he on hands and knees, and I crawling backwards intently observing his forehead, I suddenly stood erect and went to fetch a fresh towel for dealing with the flood. I don't recall the steps, but I have a clear picture of the excited faces of my mother and brothers summoned by Jimmie's shout.

Another of my earliest memories is of my mother singing me to sleep seated on a cane chair on the front veranda of the house. She and I, and the governess instructing my brothers in a nearby room, were a tiny island of women in a world that revolved around male activities. Her voice was cheerful, positive, and relaxed as she hugged me warmly. I recall the comfort and security of being sung to sleep and also some tentative efforts to struggle out of the warm embrace. I was born with a different type of skin and hair from the rest of the family. Their hair grew luxuriantly and curled. Mine was fine and limply straight. They tanned in the sun. I freckled and grew scarlet. The tweed coat my mother was wearing as she cradled me scratched and prickled so that mixed in with the security was a sense of being ill at ease. The memory is symbolic of the way our relationship was to unfold.

We did not see my father until he came home from the run in the late afternoon or early evening. As we saw the car on the horizon or his figure on horseback silhouetted on the skyline, we would rush to finish whatever task or game was under way to be ready to greet him by the gate to the stableyard. He would stable the horse, or put the car away, and then make his way to the house carrying me on his shoulders, with the two boys circling around, our questions about his day tumbling out helter-skelter. Had he seen any snakes? Were there any lambs yet? Was there much water in the dam at Brooklins (one of the largest and most distant paddocks), part of the recent addition to the property, a second grant, which brought its acreage to thirty-two thousand acres. Occasionally we would have news of our own to offer. We had found an emu's egg on a walk. Jimmie had shot a hawk with a wing-span of four feet. Bob had reached the top of one of the climbable trees nearby. Our world revolved around the land and its creatures, the weather, and our parents. After my father had bathed and changed he and my mother would sit in the shade, on the edge of the front veranda, drinking a glass of ice-cold beer before dinner. We were instructed to keep our distance and to remain quiet during their one moment of relaxation in the day. We would watch from a distance as they sat, close together, enjoying a stirring evening breeze. Their feet rested on the large nardoo stone which formed the front step, and as they talked they would gaze out over their land, discussing this project, or that pipedream. My mother's conversation would be intense and serious, but before long my father's way with words, puns, and storytelling would have her laughing. They would look out on their world with high good humor. They seemed content.

3

Childhood

Because of my parents' thrift, hard work, and ingenuity, the sheep station of my early childhood became a more and more delightful place to live. Each year after the wool sales, some new comfort was added. A kerosene refrigerator appeared to replace the old burlap drip safe, bringing ice water into our lives. My mother acquired a 1934 Ford V-8 sedan, with leather upholstery and unbelievably comfortable springs. Our clothes now came from mail-order catalogues, and an occasional case of crisp red apples would arrive from the irrigation area orchards several hundred miles to the east. A small pond was made for the poultry yard, and my mother added ducks to the chickens we had to protect each night from the foxes.

In the year of my fifth birthday, the totally unexpected happened. It rained five inches in one night, and we woke in the morning to see our homestead sitting on a comfortable island. The clump of trees behind the house was half submerged. The chickens were clucking nervously on their perches in the night poultry yard, sitting just above the water, and the ducks were sailing magisterially around a vastly enlarged pond. The sheepdogs sat on top of their kennels gazing at the water swirling by, and an army of ants, beetles, scorpions, and other insects milled about at the water's edge driven before the slowly advancing flood.

In the next few weeks it continued to rain more, so that an unheard-of eight inches had fallen within less than a month. The transformation of the countryside was magical. As far as the eye could see wild flowers exploded into bloom. Each breeze would waft their pollen round the house, making it seem as though we lived in an enormous garden. Everywhere one looked the sites of old creek beds became clear as the water gathered and drained away. Bullrushes shot up beside the watercourses, and suddenly there were waterfowl round about, erupting into flight as one approached. We saw the sky reflected in water for the first time. Stranger still, the whole countryside was green, a color we scarcely knew. Evidences of the fertility of the soil were all about us. Trees sprang up as the waters receded around our house, and before long a new clump of eucalyptus saplings was well launched in life. On walks we would find enormous mushrooms, as large as a dinner plate, but perfectly formed. These we would gather to take home to grill on top of the wood stove, filling the house with a wonderful aroma. Walks became adventures of a new kind because they were likely to reveal some new plant or flower not seen before, or show us why the aboriginal ovens were located where they were, close to what was once a stream or a water hole. We made a wooden raft and poled it cheerfully around the lake near the house, alighting on islands that were old sandhills, now suddenly sprouting grass.

Everywhere one went on the property was a vision of plenty. Dams brimmed with water. Sheep and cattle bloomed with health and nourishment. It was clear that there would be an abundant crop of wool, whiter and longer than any we had ever grown. On the heavier land, tall strong grasses grew resembling the pampas grass of Argentina. My father looked at it dubiously. When it dried it would be a fire hazard, and so a fresh herd of cattle was bought to eat it down and fatten for the market. Best of all, my father planned a late lambing season that year, and the young lambs, nourished by their mothers' ample milk, frisked away like creatures in a child's picture book.

My parents were jubilant. My mother was forty-one, my father in his early fifties. I recall them then, in the prime of life, surrounded by their young family, full of plans for the future. Success did not make them complaisant, for in one very important respect they were not like other people in our part of the world. They did not simply concern themselves with local affairs. Their dwelling might be remote but they were conscious of living in a world touched by important political and economic events. They took the Sydney newspapers, even though they came a week late. My mother read avidly about the rise of fascism in Europe. We heard them discuss when war would break out, and what the conflagration would be like this time. My mother, ever passionate in her opinions, was scathing after listening on the crackling radio to Chamberlain's speech about "peace in our time." My father, remembering the Somme and Passchendaele, was less certain. Every evening after we children were sent to bed, they sat, by the fire in winter, or in summers on the veranda, while she told him what she had been reading. My bedroom was close to both, so that I have dim memories of her describing the earliest reports of the persecution of the Jews, of Mussolini's Blackshirts and their use of castor oil. The most heated discussions concerned the rise of Japan as an industrial power. My mother was an avid reader of Pearl Buck's novels and had a strong sense from them of international rivalries in our Asian Pacific world. She predicted that after Hitler provoked war in Europe, the Japanese would begin to expand in the Pacific. Such conversations always ended with my father reminding her of the might of the British navy and the impregnability of bases like Singapore. Very shortly we were all gathered around the radio straining to hear Churchill's great speech after Dunkirk, my mother weeping, my father looking very grave.

I hero-worshiped my older brother Bob, six years older than I, and the leader of our childhood expeditions. He was tall for his age, blond, with vivid blue eyes. From an early age, he impressed people with his sense of composure and unusual emotional and physical energy. When you were with him you *knew* interesting things would happen. He was just enough older than I and our brother, Barry, to be allowed to ride the biggest horses, shoot the best rifles, carry out commissions to do this or that on the place alone. There were enough years between him and me for him to treat me gently as his baby sister, whereas I scuffled and occasionally quarreled with my brother Barry, four years my senior. Of our family, Barry's was the sunny disposition, and the gentlest of temperaments. Both boys were generous in playing with me, reading to me, entering into my various forms of make-believe. When we were older, both were ready to take me along on the projects I longed to be part of. We rode fences together, often too deep in conversation to pay more than passing attention to the state of the fences. We explored, stopped to climb trees, investigated eagle's nests, and out of sight of the house, broke the rules against the galloping of horses. As a trio, we were so close to one another that each knew without speech what the other was thinking and feeling.

Mindful of her own childhood, my mother encouraged a strict equality between us. As I played more with my brothers, I was inclined to run to her when the going got too rough. It was not tolerated. "Don't come running to me," she said. "If he hits you, hit him back." On the next occasion when my brother Barry hit me, I had a cricket bat in my hands. Remembering the injunction, I struck out furiously and broke the two newly grown front teeth, previously part of Barry's customary sunny smile. My parents were shocked, but my mother kept her part of the bargain. "I told her to do it," she said. "No one must scold her." Later, away from the heat of the moment, she explained that she had meant hitting back with one's fists, not more dangerous weapons.

I learned to read sitting under the table where my brothers were being taught school. Miss Grant, their governess, a short, stocky young woman of limited imagination, was perpetually attempting to establish what she thought the proper schoolroom discipline. Hers was a taxing job. Her young charges were both of energetic and inquiring minds which quickly moved well beyond the store of knowledge she had acquired in her country high school. English lessons were simple drills in grammar. Arithmetic was also a question of rules, and geography a matter of memorizing maps. My brothers were diligent enough but quickly became bored with their daily drilling in facts and recitation of rules. Sensing the potential for rebellion, I would often choose such a moment to tease them, tie their shoelaces together, tickle their feet, or engage in other provocations to get them in trouble with Miss Grant. To keep me quiet, I was usually given letters and numbers to trace, and then to copy. My mother, on her endless afternoons ironing in the kitchen, found I knew my letters and set me to reading aloud to her. She told me it was to entertain her and relieve the boredom, but she had me reading proudly before I knew I was being taught. Then, as an encouragement, she would discuss with me which children's book we should order from her lending library. Thereafter, the weekly parcel brought eleven books for her and one for me. Her teaching was always carried out so imaginatively that her pupils simply had fun gratifying their curiosity. Poor Miss Grant, perpetually afraid of being challenged, tried to rule by threats. "Drink your milk, or you'll never grow big and tall like your mother," she would say to still my mutiny at being made to drink children's milk instead of adult tea at mealtimes. My mother quietly filled a teacup with milk, added a faint dash of tea, and the problem was solved. Inexorably, Miss Grant became a figure of fun for us children. When playing, we would imitate her threats to one another. My brothers, perfect mimics, would set about teaching me something in precisely her tone of voice. Hers was a lonely life, devoid of recreation outside school hours. She left after eighteen months. She was, however, the very best type of the country governess, and her limitations made my parents advance their plans for sending the boys away to school.

So our idyllic routine was interrupted in 1940 by my brother Bob's departure for boarding school in Sydney. We had never been parted before and the wrench was as though we were being physically severed. My mother, who adored her handsome first-born son, was particularly stern with Barry and me as we went to leave Bob at his new Sydney boarding school, five hundred miles and a day and a night's train journey from home. "If either of you cry, or so much as let out a whimper, I'll never forgive you," she said. We obeyed and she fought back her tears till we were out of sight of the school.

My parents now paid the price of having taught us all to be self-reliant and to make our own minds up about things. Bob would not stay in school. He left many times, even going so far as to prepare to ride ticketless on the eighteen-hour train ride back home. After trying several alternatives, my parents dispatched Barry with him the next year to a new school and the two kept one another company so that there were no more breaks for home.

The boys were sent to the oldest and most prestigious boys' boarding school in Sydney —the King's School, a school where many sons of the old landed families went. It was, like all boys' boarding schools, modeled on Thomas Arnold's muscular Christianity. My parents were intent on giving their children the best of the world they knew. They didn't realize that it was hard for bush children to make the transition to the city, and that the contingent of country boys in the school, many of them sons of landed rich, saw no reason to work hard intellectually. They expected to go back home to a cheerfully horsey life on the land. My mother cherished dreams of her sons becoming lawyers or doctors. My father wanted them to find a secure place in the world, and dreamed that one of them would take over a much enlarged Coorain from him. Intent on establishing their sons securely within Australia's class-conscious society, they pined at the separation, but knew it was for the best.

The combination of the 1939–1945 War and my brothers' departure for boarding school meant that I was alone at Coorain with my parents. Single young men from the backcountry were always the first to volunteer for military service. By 1940, the few station hands available worked on the larger stations where there was company and some after-hours sociability. After Japan joined the Axis powers and entered the war in 1941, all able-bodied men were drafted, and there was total manpower control of all adult women and men. My father, a war veteran, with injuries and heart problems we were told resulted from being gassed in the 1914-1918 War, could have requested help for an essential primary producing industry. He and my mother were intensely patriotic and it was a matter of pride for them to manage alone. Each of us contributed to the war effort as best he or she could. Our contribution would be to work longer and harder. The job of running Coorain itself became harder as we began to experience the effects of the war. Australia produced no gasoline, and the produce of the oil wells and rubber plantations of Southeast Asia was diverted to Europe to meet the wartime priorities of motorized armies. After gasoline rationing was introduced, we went back to an earlier transportation era. Everything took more time. Picking up the twice-weekly mail on the dusty main highway four miles from the house took several hours. Going to the post office seven miles away was a morning's expedition. Traveling the twenty-odd miles to work with sheep or tend the bores and water troughs at the far end of our odd-shaped property meant rising at 4:00 A.M. to put in the hours of riding necessary to get there to start work before the heat of the day. We saved our meager ration of gasoline for essentials, going forty miles to the nearest store in the railroad town of Ivanhoe, meeting the train when the boys came home from school. A reserve was necessary for emergencies: bushfires, a broken arm, a wound needing stitches.

After the first shock of the boys' departure, my loneliness was moderated by the arrival of a fascinating new companion. The expanded size of Coorain meant that my father could hire a man who was a mine of bush lore and knowledge to put down a bore to provide a plentiful water supply for the Coorain homestead. Bob McLennan, universally known as old Bob, was not fazed by the lack of gasoline to power his well-drilling equipment. He had drilled many bores by hand in his long lifetime, and was quite ready to begin again. I watched intently as his auger was produced, the hole begun and steadily deepened as old Bob paced around in a circle, like some medieval figure on a treadmill. Since his task required slow movement, he had plenty of breath left to answer the questions of a curious child. We would find the first water at twenty feet, he said. It would be salty, and useless for our purposes. As each layer of soil came up, he explained about its place in the formation of the earth. We should find good water after about one hundred and twenty feet, he thought—that was unless we struck stone, which would mean the sweet, fresh water was deeper underground. We both tasted the water at twenty feet, and agreed that it was very salty. At forty-eight feet, another stream was crossed, equally metallic in taste. Soon after, very interesting things began to come up with each return of the drilling equipment to the surface: gravel, shale, slimy black oily-looking mud. Bob began to look troubled.

The going was getting harder, and the chances were increasing that he would hit rock. At ninety feet, there it was, solid and desperately hard to drill. Bob was philosophical, pacing steadily, but his auger now made a few inches a day. My parents joked that perhaps he would be in residence with us till retirement. Months of work and wages had been invested and it was too late to abandon this effort and choose another site. Many weeks later Bob was through his six feet of granite, and the water found at one hundred and twenty feet was sent away for testing. He and I had done a lot of tasting and shaking our heads over it. It was not very clear, and after we had carefully measured the flow, it was less than a hundred gallons an hour. Bob said it wouldn't do, but my father, hoping the job, now much more extended than he'd planned, would be completed, sent the water to the assayers anyway. The answer proved Bob's point. It was not fit for human consumption. It contained too much salt, traces of gold, a minute quantity of lead sulfate. So Bob resumed his slow pacing. He was a slight bony man, small in stature, slow and deliberate in all his movements, endlessly talkative. He kept the same pace in heat or cold, and he respected the earth he worked with. He called the earth "she," and he personified the hole he was drilling, now of epic proportions, and his auger. "Now we'll see what the bastard has to offer," he would say, winding his winch furiously to pull up the next load of earth. The mechanics of drilling were endlessly interesting to me. As the hand drill ate away the earth, metal casing was pushed down inside the hole. As the hole deepened, casing of a smaller and smaller size was pushed down inside the original. This provided the firm outer casing for the bore, within which piping and a water pump would eventually be installed. Bob began with casing of a monumental size "in case the bugger's really deep," he explained cheerfully. As each new piece of casing was driven into the earth and the next piece attached, a few inches of the original would protrude, requiring slicing off to make the joins even. These round wheels of metal became my toys, each succeeding size being delivered to me as a gift by Bob. It seemed that I had a family of them, all in neatly descending ages and sizes. I knew too few people to name them after actual acquaintances, but eventually I hit upon calling them after the various leaders of the Allies, both political and military. I knew who all of them were because I went regularly with my father to collect the mail, and he had me read the front page of each issue of the *Sydney Morning Herald* to him on the slow return journey from the mailbox. I named the amplest and most impressive circle of metal Winston Churchill, and a smaller but nonetheless impressive one, General de Gaulle.

Possessing in these toys a perfect symbolic system for representing hierarchy, I named a very modest one after the Prime Minister of Australia, thereby recognizing a set of power relationships I could not then have articulated. These pieces of metal were assembled to mimic the Quebec Conference, and a new character, larger than de Gaulle but noticeably smaller than Churchill, was introduced, President Roosevelt. The fortunes of war had already required regular reorganization of the rank order, my need after the battle of El Alamein being for a General Montgomery, second in size only to Churchill.

One day, more than six months after old Bob began his labors, my father and I returned from an afternoon expedition to see old Bob, a beatific smile on his face, rolling a sample of water around in his mouth as though it were vintage claret. As we approached, he spat it out and said, "It's beautiful water, Mr. Ker, and she'll pump thirty thousand gallons a day." The assayers agreed on the quality, and time proved him right about the flow, which never faltered in the driest seasons. We never knew how many hundreds of miles he had tramped in his months of labor, but he wore out three pairs of boots and one steel auger. The equipment for the windmill and storage tank had already been purchased in anticipation of the moment. Shortly, a fifty-foot steel windmill tower and a forty-thousand-gallon tank on a thirty-foot stand towered beside our house.

The arrival of the water wrought miracles. My mother, freed of cooking for two hungry boys and a governess, raced through the household chores to work for three or four hours after lunch in her garden. The soil was fertile, there was ample fertilizer from the horses, cattle, and sheep, and the blessed water proved to contain only a little limestone which most plants flourished on. My father built a high windbreak, made of cane grass which grew on the property, to shield her seedlings from the hot winds. Inside it she produced a vision of paradise fit for a sultan's courtyard. In front of the house were perennial beds, lining the verandas. Two perfectly balanced rectangles of green lawn were laid out, framed by long, thin rectangular beds for annuals. To the south of the house was the vegetable garden, and to the north the citrus orchard. The northern side of the cane windbreak became a trellis for grapes, and a little to the northwest was the potato bed.

She had a fine sense of color, and a passion for scented flowers. Soon I would drift off to sleep in the evening bathed in the perfume of stocks, wallflowers, and heliotrope in summer, the crisp aroma of chrysanthemums in autumn. A whole bed was given over to Parma violets, and great fistfuls of them would sit in the middle of the round table on which we dined in summer on the southern screened veranda.

The fruits and vegetables were as marvelous to a child raised on canned vegetables and dried apples. The scent of orange and lemon trees, the taste of fat green grapes, and the discovery of salads were marking points of that first year of water.

Because it was clear that I was educating myself through reading everything within reach—a topsy-turvy mixture of children's books, my mother's books on current affairs, war correspondents' accounts of the war, my father's books on stock breeding—my parents decided not to bother with elementary school by correspondence for me the year my brothers left for boarding school. Instead, I became my father's station hand. He needed help with mustering sheep, something which needed two people on horseback to accomplish easily. I rode out with him to check the state of fences, always in need of careful attention if bloodlines were to be kept clear. We went together to clean watering troughs, carry out the maintenance of windmills, trim and dress the fly-infested spots which developed around the crutch of sheep where flies would lay eggs in the hot summer months. Dressing fly-blown sheep was hard, hot work because one had to round up the particular flock, get the sheepdogs to hold them, and then dive suddenly into the herd to tackle the one animal whose fleece needed attention. An agile child was better at doing the diving than an adult, and in time I learned to do a kind of flying tackle which would hold the animal, usually heavier than I was myself, until my father arrived with the hand shears and the disinfectant.

Much of the work with sheep involved riding slowly behind them while moving them from one paddock to another, traveling at a pace which was a comfortable walk for the animals. Often we dismounted and strolled along, horse's reins looped over an arm. Occasionally something might startle the sheep, requiring my father to shout commands to the dogs, but otherwise it was not demanding work, and it was a perfect setting for extended conversation. Why did God allow the crows to pick out the eyes of newborn lambs, I asked, as we passed a bloody carcass. My father never treated such questions as idle chatter, but tried seriously to answer. He didn't know, he replied. It was a puzzle. The world seemed set up so that the strong preyed on the weak and innocent. I would ask endless questions about the weather, the vegetation, the transmission of characteristics through several generations of sheep. How to breed to eliminate that defect, or promote this desirable characteristic. When the lambs were a year old, we would bring the sheep into the nearest sheepyards, or make a temporary one, so that we could cull the flocks, selecting the discards which would be sent for immediate sale or used for our own food.

I did reasonably well as a station hand while in sight of my father. He could shout directions, or notice that I was having trouble getting the dogs to work for me and arrive quickly to solve the problem. I didn't always do so well when we worked in the large paddocks, twelve or fifteen thousand acres in size, where we would separate, one going clockwise, one counterclockwise, turning the sheep into the middle, to be gathered into one flock and moved as a whole to a new spot. I was a long-legged seven-year-old, but not quite tall enough to remount my horse if I got off to kick some lazy sheep into motion, or to investigate a sick or lame one. Then there would be no getting back on till the next fence, or the rare occasional stump. At first I was not quite secure enough in ego to cope with the space, the silence, and the brooding sky. Occasionally I would find myself crying, half in vexation at my small size and the pigheadedness of sheep, half for the reassurance of a sound. By the family's code it was shameful to weep, and I was supposed to be too grown-up for such babyish behavior. Once the wind carried the sound to my father on the other side of the paddock. By the time we were reunited, I had reached a fence, climbed on my horse, and become secure again by seeing him in the distance. "I thought I heard someone crying," he observed to me as we met. I looked him in the eye. "I didn't," I said. There he let the matter rest.

The sheepdogs were always a trial to me. They were trained to respond to a series of calls. Their trainers were station hands and drovers whose calls were usually poetic, blasphemous, and picturesquely profane. I would try to make my voice deep, and sound as though I really meant to flay them alive when I got home if they didn't go behind or get around or whatever other command was needed, but I didn't believe it and neither did they. My father would laugh at me shouting to the black kelpie whose pink tongue and nose I loved, "You black bastard, I'll flay the hide off you if you don't go around." "You don't sound as if you mean it," he said. "Why not just try whistling, that's easier for you to do." He tried to teach me the series of whistles used to command sheepdogs. I did better at that, but they would never obey me perfectly, as they did my father.

As we did our day's work, theological questions kept cropping up. "Isn't it wrong to kill?" I would ask, as we drove home with a fat young sheep, feet tied together, who would be slaughtered when we arrived at the wooden block near the dog kennels used for such purposes. I always felt a sneaking fellow feeling for the creature as its neck was slit and its blood ebbed away to be drunk voraciously by the dogs. Skinning a sheep was a lengthy process, so there was plenty of time to explore the question. God made the creatures of the earth for man's use, my father responded. It was wrong to kill needlessly for sport, the way some people hunted kangaroos, but it was moral to kill what we needed to eat. Besides, he said, what would happen to the sheep if we never culled them. Their wool would deteriorate, their body types grow weaker, and they would all starve because we couldn't feed them all and all their natural increase. "Did you kill people during the war?" I would ask, meaning the 1914–1918 War. "Yes," he would respond. Killing in self-defense was moral also, and the war had been a generalized version of that situation. But no war was ever really just because of the pain and suffering inflicted not only on soldiers, but on civilians. We should work for a world where there were other ways of settling conflicts. It was wrong for so many generations of young men to be killed, as had happened in 1914–1918, and was happening now. He prayed the war

71

would be over before Bob was old enough to go.

After the water supply was provided for the house, we built our own shearing shed. It was built of Oregon pine and galvanized iron, by an eccentric and talented carpenter named Obecue. Mr. Obecue, my parents said, was a secret ladykiller, who had had a series of young and wealthy wives. This information made me gaze at him with more than usual curiosity. I could not fathom his attractions, but I admired intensely the way his fingers flew about, appearing to fabricate things so fast the result seemed to be achieved by sleight of hand. I would sit on the frame for the woolshed floor watching as he laid it, his mouth full of long nails, his hammer striking home exactly right each time, and the result a smooth floor with nails driven in in an unwavering straight line. He was an excitable man, easily upset if anyone appeared to criticize his work, and equally easily made happy by praise. He was a fast worker. The shed was up before we knew it, changing our skyline permanently.

Once the shed was built, a new excitement came into life because instead of our sheep being driven overnight to the woolshed at Mossgiel Station, our neighbor to the north-east, to be shorn, the shearing team came to Coorain. There would be six or eight shearers, a "rouseabout"—the odd-job boy perpetually being set in action by the shouts for the shearers' needs: disinfectant for a cut sheep, a count-out for a full pen of shorn animals (anything that would speed the shearers at their piece work), a wool classer and his assistant, and a cook. I had never seen so many people on Coorain before, and I never tired of watching the throbbing bustle of the woolshed operating at full speed, the shearer's blades powered by an impressive black engine. Everyone's movements were so stylized that they might have been the work of a choreographer. A really good shearer knew just how to touch a sheep so that it relaxed and didn't kick. Bodies bent over the sheep, arms sweeping down the sides of the animal in long graceful strokes to the floor, the shearers looked like participants in a rite. The rouseabout would pick up each fleece as it finally lay in a pure white heap on the floor, walk with it to the classer's table, then he would fling his arms wide as if giving benediction, and let it fall. The fleece would descend to the table, laid perfectly flat, and the classer, hardly lifting his eyes from the table, would begin dividing it

73

into sections, throwing it into bins organized by spinning classifications. Everyone's hands looked fresh and pink because of the lanolin in the wool. The shed was permeated by the smell of engine oil, from the engine which powered the shearers' blades, and by the smell of lanolin.

Beyond the classer's bins were the wool press and the storage area, where the bales of wool would be pressed to reduce the wool's bulk, carefully weighed, numbered, branded, and then piled to await the contractor who hauled it to the nearest railroad station. Large woolsheds had mechanical presses, but ours, being small, had a hand press operated by an athletic giant of a man, naturally nicknamed Shorty. Shorty was six feet six, weighed one hundred and ninety pounds, all of it muscle; there was no spare flesh on his body. He pressed the wool into bales by sheer muscle, operating the system of weights and ratchets which could compress four hundred and fifty pounds of wool into the size of a small bale. Then he would take metal grappling hooks and fling the bales about the storage area as though they were weightless. I loved to watch him work, and whenever I wasn't needed in the sheep-yards outside, I would come into the shed, climb to the highest point on the pile of bales, and talk to Shorty. He had a wife and family of his own, farther south, whom he missed terribly, since his team began shearing in Queensland in January and worked its way south until it got to us in June. Each year when he came back, he would exclaim over how I had grown, look purposely blank for a moment, and then with exaggerated cries of absence of mind, recall that he had brought me some candy.

In quiet moments, when he had caught up with the supply of wool and had time to sit down, we exchanged confidences. On some Mondays, he would confess to having had too much to drink over the weekend. Once, deeply troubled and exasperated with himself, he talked of going to see "the girls." I knew in a general way that this was not the best conduct for a married man, so I tut-tutted with as much wisdom as I could summon up and said once didn't matter. It seemed to offer him some relief.

Twice a day, the whistle blew for "smoko" time. The cook would bring over billies of tea and mounds of sweet pound cake and biscuits. Everyone would relax, consume vast supplies of tea from tin mugs, and roll the inevitable cigarette. Sometimes, a shearer might get what Shorty thought was too friendly with me. "The kid's a girl," he would say warningly. That would end the matter. It was easy to see how people might be mistaken, because I wore my brother's cast-off clothes for work outdoors and had my hair tucked away under the usual Australian felt hat.

Each year I waited eagerly for Shorty and the rest of the team to return. Yet I also knew that there were class boundaries to all our dealings with one another. In the evening during the two weeks of shearing, Mac, the wool classer, being an educated person, was always invited to dinner at the house. We were all eager to see Mac, a witty and ironic Scot, whose friendship my parents valued. I loved to see him because he was a great storyteller, and the hour by the fire before dinner would be filled with jokes and laughter. Because he saw the Coorain wool clip each year, he could offer valuable advice about its good and bad characteristics, and make suggestions about qualities that should be introduced into the breeding lines. Best of all for my parents, because he had been traveling from station to station year after year, he was a fount of gossip, and news about distant friends, comical happenings,

76

marriages and divorces, signs of changes in the cycle of wet and dry years. My parents were hungry for talk with other adults, and they would stay in animated conversation till long after I had drifted off to sleep.

The war brought another form of sociability into the routine of our lives. My mother, a shy woman, and a nervous driver over country roads, nevertheless felt that in addition to the work of Coorain, she should undertake some further form of war work. Our district contained not much more than thirty families within its fifty-mile radius. My mother recruited the women of these families into a local branch of the Red Cross. The twenty-five or so members of the branch held very formal meetings in the creaky old Mossgiel village hall. The minutes of meetings were recorded in my mother's neat handwriting, and the branch set to work to raise money for comforts for soldiers, and to produce the standard khaki socks, scarves, sweaters, and balaclavas which Sydney headquarters of the Red Cross said were needed. Thereafter, my mother's evening reading was accompanied by the click of needles, and I was taught to knit the simple squares which were crocheted together to make scarves. The best part of the Red Cross activity was undoubtedly the fund raising. This was done by means of organizing dances in the Mossgiel hall, to which people came from hundreds of miles around. The floor would be prepared the day before. Sawdust was sprinkled about liberally. Candles were then cut up and scattered about over the sawdust, and any children fortunate enough to be around were asked to sit on clean burlap bags on which they were towed in wildly exciting circles about the floor. When the floor was pronounced just right for dancing, the sawdust was swept up to reveal a gleaming floor. My mother's garden provided a sizable part of the decorations for the hall. Garlands of flowers and streamers were wound around the posts and beams, transforming the old hall from its workaday self. On the actual day, musicians arrived, and my mother and her committee members carried mountains of delicious food into the supper room at the back of the hall. The actual money for the Red Cross came from raffles, a variety of party games, such as a dart board in the shape of Hitler's face, which people fought to compete at. At the end of the evening, the cakes uneaten at supper would be auctioned off to the highest bidder. Often the cheerful winner would present the cake back to the organizers for another round of bidding, so that many cakes had accounted for thirty or forty pounds before the evening concluded.

These occasions gave me a fresh vision of my parents. I had never seen my mother in evening dress before, and rarely saw my father in his well-cut navy pinstripe suits. They were a handsome and lively pair, and full of fun and laughter. My father's gift for storytelling made him always the center of a laughing group, while my mother would dance happily without remembering the hard day of preparations. There being no one to sit with me at home, I came in my best clothes to these functions, and was tucked into bed in the backseat of the car, at what my mother deemed an appropriate hour. It was all very exciting. The sound of "When you come down Lambeth way, any evening, any day" usually indicated that the party was warming up. The music was from the thirties, untouched by any hint of jazz or swing. I thought it quite wonderful. Sometimes the mood of the evening would persist while we drove home, my father's beautiful tenor voice singing the popular songs of the moment until the lights of our car shone on the windows of Coorain.

It was no surprise to me that my mother's

little Red Cross branch regularly won awards for raising more money than branches five and six times its size. The dances gave pleasure to everyone, and the fund raising gave people a chance to express their loyalty to the Allied cause. My mother was in her element, using her powers of organization for a cause she revered. She could brook no opposition, however, and her efforts ceased as abruptly as they had begun because she disagreed with the easy bush habit of looking the other way when minors bought drinks at the bar. Negotiation not being a part of her mentality, she left the Red Cross work she had launched just as she and my father sadly needed recreation and distraction.

Our other great expeditions were to the town of Hillston, seventy-five miles to the east of Coorain. It was a railroad town, on the banks of the Lachlan River, and it was the seat of our vestigial local government. My father served on the Pastures Protection Board, a body that concerned itself with the control of vermin, the eradication of dangerous plant materials such as Bathurst burrs which destroyed a sheep's fleece, or certain poisonous plants which were a hazard. It also supervised the public stock routes over which anyone could drove sheep or cattle, and took responsibility for the maintenance of watering places and holding yards along the stock routes. Its meetings were occasions for us all to visit Hillston. The town looked like a stage set for a western town. It had a wide, dusty main street lined with rundown hotels, a dilapidated store, and one stock and station agent's office announced by a tilting sign from which the paint was peeling. A night spent at one of the hotels was bedeviled by fleas and the days offered few diversions for an adult. The town contained a milk bar and coffee shop which represented unbelievable luxury to me. One could have milk shakes and ice cream, and at the back of the café there was a garden, with a pond full of goldfish, overlooking the Lachlan River and its stately gum trees. If I was lucky, we would meet my father's friend and our neighbor, Angus Waugh, on the street, and he, a bachelor, would decide to see how many milk shakes a child my size could drink. Angus was a member of the same board my father sat on, and often we would take lunch or dinner together at one of the two rickety hotels which faced one another on Main Street. If Angus had enjoyed more than enough beer before or during lunch, he was likely to take me back to the milk bar and buy out the entire stock of chocolates just for the fun of watching my expression.

He was the archetypal Scot, short, stocky, peppery in manner, loyal and warmhearted to his friends, and a formidable enemy. His sense of humor was legendary. In our household, we all remembered with glee overhearing his voice on the telephone to the local store in Ivanhoe, an institution which exploited its monopoly position to overcharge shamelessly. "Is that Ned Kelly and Company," Angus said, naming Australia's most famous armed bandit. "What are you going to rob me most for today?" Our telephone lines were often tangled with those of other stations, but we children always hoped we would pick up the phone and overhear that familiar voice from Clare, Angus's vast family property, fifty miles to the west. He often stopped a night with us on the way back from Hillston, and that was always a special time. Knowing how much our parents liked and admired him, we adopted him as an honorary uncle, and were eager to sit while he talked about life and the bush, using pungent and vivid language that was always memorable. I liked to watch his face when he told a story. A gingery mustache, which partially concealed his mouth, would give a telltale wiggle as he, otherwise deadpan, told some ridiculous tall story. His deep-set brown eyes literally sparkled with mirth, and his laughter was wholehearted and satisfying. His sense of fun was particularly appealing to children, whom he always treated as though they were his exact contemporaries.

All in all, what might on the surface appear like a lonely childhood, especially after the departure of my brothers, was one filled with interest, stimulation, and friends. It lacked other children, and I was seven before I even laid eyes on another female child. Yet this world gave me most of what we need in life, and gave it generously. I had the total attention of both my parents, and was secure in the knowledge of being loved. Better still, I knew that my capacity for work was valued and that my contributions to the work of the property really mattered. It was a comprehensible world. One saw visible results from one's labors, and the lesson of my mother's garden was a permanent instruction about the way human beings can transform their environment. My memories of falling asleep at night are to the comfortable sound of my parents' voices, voices which conveyed in their tones the message that these two people loved and trusted one another. After the windmill was built, I would wake in the morning as the early dawn wind began to turn the sails to the familiar clinking sound of the pump working. Magpies used to perch on the windmill's stand and sing every morning at first light. This sound would mingle in my waking with the early morning smell of flowers in the garden. It was an idyllic world.

4

Drought

After the great rain of 1939, the rainfall declined noticeably in each successive year. In 1940, the slight fall was of no consequence because our major worry was that the accumulation of growth on the land would produce serious bushfires. These did occur on land quite close to us, but my father's foresight in getting cattle to eat down the high grass preserved Coorain from that danger.

In 1941, the only rain of the year was a damp cold rain with high wind which came during the lambing season in May and June and carried off many ewes and their newborn lambs. After that there were no significant rainfalls for five years. The unfolding of a drought of these dimensions has a slow and inexorable quality. The weather perpetually holds out hope. Storm clouds gather. Thunder rolls by. But nothing happens. Each year as the season for rain approaches, people begin to look hopefully up at the sky. It mocks them with a few showers, barely enough to lay the dust. That is all.

It takes a long time for a carefully managed grazing property to decline, but three years without rain will do it. Once the disaster begins it unfolds swiftly. So it was with us.

My parents, buoyed up by the good year of 1939, the results of that good year returned in the 1940 wool sales, the new water supply, and the new woolshed, remained hopeful for a long time. By 1942, it was apparent that the drought could be serious and their levels of anxiety began to climb. I was conscious of those anxieties in a variety of ways. That year, 1942, my eighth, was my first one of correspondence school. There was no governess, nor was there any pretense that I would keep a daily school schedule. On Friday afternoons, from 2:00 P.M. until I finished (usually around 4:30 P.M.), I did my week's school. My mother made it a pleasant occasion for me by saying, "Today, you don't have to work out of doors. You can sit in the shade [or if it was winter, in the sun] on the veranda, have your own pot of tea, and do your schoolwork." Thus I was introduced to study as a leisure activity, a gift beyond price. When I was close to finishing, my mother would arrive to glance quickly over the work. Then she questioned me closely about the state of each paddock, what my father had said about it when we were there last, and then, ever so discreetly, she would lead me to talk about how he had seemed as we worked together that week. I needed no instruction not to mention these conversations. I knew why she was anxious.

My father and I would set out to work on horseback as usual, but instead of our customary cheerful and wide-ranging conversations he would be silent. As we looked at sheep, or tried to assess the pasture left in a particular paddock, he would swear softly, looking over the fence to a neighbor's property, already eaten out and beginning to blow sand. Each time he said, "If it doesn't rain, it will bury this feed in a few weeks." It was true and I could think of nothing consoling to say.

His usual high spirits declined with the state of the land, until the terrible day when many of our own sheep were lost because of a sudden cold rain and wind when they had too little food in their stomachs. Although my mother produced her usual ample meals, he began to lose weight his bony frame could ill afford. He lost his wonderful calm, and deliberation in planning, and would be excited by the slightest sign of trouble. A few years ago, a bore losing water flow would have meant there was a problem with the pump, requiring some days' labor to repair it. Now he would instantly worry about whether the water supply was running dry. We would fall to work on raising the pump and assessing the problem as though disaster were at hand.

My mother was impatient with this excitability and in my father's presence, would try to deflate it. But I knew from her questions that she too was worried. When the work to be done on the run didn't need two people, my father would say, "Stay home and help your mother, she needs help in the house." My mother would let him set out for the stables or the garage and then say to me, "I don't need help. Run quickly and go with your father. See if you can make him laugh." So I would set out, and begin to play the child I no longer was. I would think up nonsense rhymes, ask crazy questions, demand to be told stories, invent some of my own to recount. Sometimes it would have the desired effect, but it was hard to distract a man from the daily deterioration of our land and flocks. Every time we stopped to look at the carcass of a dead sheep and dismounted to find out why it had died, it became more difficult to play my role.

My brothers would return home from boarding school to a household consumed with anxiety. Coming, as they did, from the totally enclosed world of a school, with its boyish high spirits, it was hard for them to change emotional gear and set immediately to work on whatever projects had been saved for a time when there were several extra pairs of strong hands available. Mealtimes were particularly difficult because inevitably their world contained many points of reference beyond Coorain. Much of what they reported seemed frivolous to parents who had never attended a fashionable school and had struggled for the considerable learning they possessed. In better times they might have entered enthusiastically into this new world of their sons, but my father in particular jumped to the conclusion that his sons were not working hard at school. In fact they were, but they now lived in a culture in which it was a serious *faux pas* to indicate that one worked hard at study. The two worlds were not easy to mesh. As a result, the boys tended to work together; or we three made our recreations as unobtrusively as possible away from the adult world. Bob's passion was electronics. We spent hours together winding coils and puzzling our way through the diagrams which guided the construction of his first shortwave radio. He instructed me patiently in the characteristics of radio waves, and explained elementary concepts in physics by duplicating many of the demonstrations in his school textbooks. Barry took me with him on his early morning trips to collect the rabbits and foxes he trapped to help control these populations, which were hazards to our sheep. The skins provided him pocket money for investment in a wide variety of projects. While he was home from school, guides on writing short stories, books on muscle building, magazines about automobiles lent the mail bag an excitement lacking at other times.

There was not much room in the household routine for the mood swings and questioning of adolescence. Discipline was strict, and departures from it earned immediate punishment. The cloud of parental disapproval could be heavy when there was no escaping to other society. At sixteen, Bob let slip his religious doubts during a lunchtime conversation. Though these were a logical consequence of his heavily scientific school program, my parents were outraged. They had expected that by sending him to a high Anglican school, his religious education was ensured. Religious belief was a touchy subject in the family because my father adhered to his Catholicism while my mother was outspoken in her criticism of Catholic ideas on sexuality and the subordination of women. There was little occasion for the expression of these differences because there was no place of worship in either faith within seventy to a hundred miles of Coorain. Still, the differences slumbered under the surface. Poor Bob was treated as an unnatural being for his doubts and accused of being ungrateful for the sacrifices made to send him to a religious school. I was glad when the boys returned safely to school a week later without more explosions of discord. I was puzzled about the whole question of religion myself, since my parents both seemed highly moral people to me. As both faiths seemed to produce excellent results, I did not know what to make of the difference. When we made one of our rare visits to Sydney, and my parents separated for the day, my mother to shop, my father to visit banks and wool merchants, I usually went with him, since I got tired and vexed my mother by complaining while she rushed to do a year's shopping in a matter of days. At the end of the day, before setting out for our hotel or flat, my father would stop at St. Mary's Cathedral for vespers. I liked the ritual and the Latin chant. I also understood when he said it would be better not to mention these visits to my mother.

The routine of the academic year required that the boys return to school at the end of the summer vacation before the periods of most intense activity on the property: crutching time in February (when only the withers of the sheep were shorn to limit fly infestation in hot weather) and shearing in early June. Crutching time in 1943 was particularly worrisome. It was a fearfully hot summer. The sheep were poorly nourished and the last season's lambs weak. They needed to be moved slowly, held in paddocks close to the sheepyards, crutched quickly, and returned to their sparse pastures before heat exhaustion took its toll. In addition, to speed the whole process, someone needed to be at the woolshed, counting each shearer's tally of sheep, and pushing the supply of animals into the shed, so that not a moment was lost. It was always an exhausting business, because speed required constant running about in the 100 degree weather. This year, it was clear that my father found it hard to bear the pace.

At home in the evening, I found my mother feeling his pulse, administering brandy, and urging him to lie down. The heat and anxiety had combined to revive the irregular heartbeat that had been one of the factors occasioning his discharge from the army in 1917. My mother was at her best caring for the sick. She radiated calm. The errant pulse was checked regularly and diagnosed as palpitations, but not a serious arrhythmia.

The next day, we went a little more slowly at the work in the yards, advised by my mother that we could still afford to keep the team an extra day or two, or lose a few sheep, provided that my father was in sound health. I now found myself volunteering for jobs I was not quite sure I could do, in order to be sure that he had more time to rest. The next afternoon, after the close of work at the shed, there was a lot of riding still to be done. "These sheep need to go to Rigby's, that mob to Denny's," my father began, about to give me an assignment to return sheep to their paddocks. "I can do both," I said rashly, having never moved so many sheep on my own. "Mind you, move them slowly, and don't let them mix with the rams. Take the dogs, and don't open the gate until you have the dogs holding them at the fence." He had forgotten that I couldn't remount easily, and that the dogs didn't work very well for me. I was half pleased at completing the two assignments, half astonished that anyone had left me to handle them alone. Too much is being asked of me, I thought privately, forgetting that it was I who had volunteered. There was no getting around that the work was there and had to be done, and so I fell early into a role it took me many years to escape, the person in the family who would rise to the occasion, no matter the size of the task.

Shortly afterwards, the first terrible dust storm arrived boiling out of the central Australian desert. One sweltering late afternoon in March, I walked out to collect wood for the stove. Glancing toward the west, I saw a terrifying sight. A vast boiling cloud was mounting in the sky, black and sulfurous yellow at the heart, varying shades of ocher red at the edges. Where I stood, the air was utterly still, but the writhing cloud was approaching silently and with great speed. Suddenly I noticed that there were no birds to be seen or heard. All had taken shelter. I called my mother. We watched helplessly. Always one for action, she turned swiftly, went indoors, and began to close windows. Outside, I collected the buckets, rakes, shovels, and other implements that could blow away or smash a window if hurled against one by the boiling wind. Within the hour, my father arrived home. He and my mother sat on the back step, not in their usual restful contemplation, but silenced instead by dread.

A dust storm usually lasts days, blotting out the sun, launching banshee winds day and night. It is dangerous to stray far from shelter, because the sand and grit lodge in one's eyes, and a visibility often reduced to a few feet can make one completely disoriented. Animals which become exhausted and lie down are often sanded over and smothered. There is nothing anyone can do but stay inside, waiting for the calm after the storm. Inside, it is stifling. Every window must be closed against the dust, which seeps relentlessly through the slightest crack. Meals are gritty and sleep elusive. Rising in the morning, one sees a perfect outline of one's body, an afterimage of white where the dust has not collected on the sheets.

As the winds seared our land, they took away the dry herbage, piled it against the fences, and then slowly began to silt over the debris. It was three days before we could venture out, days of almost unendurable tension. The crashing of the boughs of trees against our roof and the sharp roar as a nearly empty rainwater tank blew off its stand and rolled away triggered my father's recurring nightmares of France, so that when he could fall into a fitful slumber it would be to awake screaming.

It was usually I who woke him from his nightmares. My mother was hard to awaken. She had, in her stoic way, endured over the years two bad cases of ear infection, treated only with our available remedies, hot packs and aspirin. One ear was totally deaf as a result of a ruptured eardrum, and her hearing in the other ear was much reduced. Now her deafness led to a striking reversal of roles, as I, the child in the family, would waken and attempt to soothe a frantic adult.

When we emerged, there were several feet of sand piled up against the windbreak to my mother's garden, the contours of new sandhills were beginning to form in places where the dust eddied and collected. There was no question that there were also many more bare patches where the remains of dry grass and herbage had lifted and blown away.

It was always a miracle to me that animals could endure so much. As we checked the property, there were dead sheep in every paddock to be sure, but fewer than I'd feared. My spirits began to rise and I kept telling my father the damage was not too bad. "That was only the first storm," he said bleakly. He had seen it all before and knew what was to come.

In June, at shearing time, we hired one of the district's great eccentrics to help in the yards. I could not manage mustering and yard work at the same time, and my father could not manage both either without too frenetic a pace. Our helper, known as Pommy Goodman, was a middle-aged Englishman with a perfect Mayfair accent, one of the foulest mouths I ever heard, and the bearing of one to the manner born. He was an example of the wonderful variety of types thrown up like human driftwood on the farther shores of settlement in Australia. One moment he would be swearing menacingly at a sheep that had kicked him, the next minute addressing me as though he were my nanny and about to order nursery tea. I resented being called "child," and noticed that Pommy did more leaning on the fence and offering advice than hard work. But it was good to have a third person on hand, and especially someone who could drive a car, something I could not do, my legs not yet being long enough to disengage a clutch. Pommy could drive ahead and open a gate, making the return of sheep to a paddock a simple task. He could shuttle between the house and woolshed on the endless errands that materialized during the day, and he could count out the sheep from the shearers' pens, something I was not good at because my mathematical labors by correspondence were always done slowly and deliberately. The sheep raced for freedom at a furious pace, leaping through the gate in twos and threes, so that my counts were often jumbled. The shearers, by now old friends, knowing that my father was not well, tolerated my efforts and secretly kept their own tally, so the records were straight at the end of the day.

After helping at crutching time, Pommy, by now a friend to me, took the job of postmaster at our little post office and manual telephone exchange in Mossgiel. There he was as bossy as he had been to me in the

98

sheepyards, listening to everyone's conversations, offering his own comments at crucial points in people's communication, and opening and closing the service at arbitrary hours. It soon became clear that he was drinking heavily, alone every night in the postmaster's cramped quarters. His slight frame grew emaciated and when I came with my father to the post office he barely had the spirit to correct my grammar. One morning, about three months after he left us, the exchange was dead. No one paid much attention, thinking that he was taking longer than usual to sober up. His first customer of the day found him swinging from the central beam of the post office, fully dressed in suit and tie. He had been sober enough to arrange the noose efficiently and kick the chair he stood on well across the room. I could never go there again without eyeing the beam and wondering about his thoughts that night. What old sorrows had overwhelmed him? Or was he simply a victim of loneliness and depression? I wondered whether his inner dialogue that night was in the voice of a cultivated Englishman, or in that of a foul-mouthed drover. He came to be one of my symbols for our need for society, and of the folly of believing that we can manage our fate alone.

I was used to worry about my father's health and state of mind, but it was a shock in the spring of 1943 to learn that my mother must go to Sydney for a hysterectomy, surgery that, in the current state of Australian medicine, still required months of recuperation. She left for Sydney shortly before the boys arrived home from school for the Christmas holidays. I was sent for an anticipated month's stay with friends who lived thirty miles away from us on a station with the poetic name Tooralee. My hosts had an only child, a daughter, then about five years old, and slow to speak for lack of the talkative child company my visit was to supply. My mother was, in fact, away for eight weeks. She had caught a cold the day before entering the hospital for her surgery, and that infection had progressed quickly to pneumonia, a dangerous infection in the period before antibiotics or sulfa drugs. When she returned, stepping off the silver-painted diesel train in Ivanhoe into a temperature of 108 degrees, she was startlingly pale and thin. My father began to order us to lift packages, to jump to do the household chores, and to work in our amateurish way at tending her garden. She refused all well-intentioned efforts to make her an invalid. "My surgeon says his stitches are very strong," she said. "I can lift anything. I will have all my energy back in three months." So she did; but we never again saw the rosy-cheeked, robust woman of our childhood. She remained painfully thin.

As we entered the late summer of 1944, we had about half our usual stock of sheep, now seriously affected by inadequate nourishment. It was clear that they would not make it through the summer unless it rained, or we began to feed them hay or grain to supplement their diet. The question which tormented my parents was whether to let them die, or invest more in maintaining them. If they died, fifteen years of careful attention to the bloodlines was lost. Yet even if fed supplements they might die anyway, for the dry feed would not supply the basic nutrients in fresh grass and herbage.

Now the nighttime conversations were anguished. Both of them had grown up fearing debt like the plague. It hurt their pride to mortgage the land, just like more feckless managers. Furthermore, the feeding would require more labor than my father and I could manage. In the end, it was resolved to borrow the money, buy the wheat, and hire the help. But these actions were taken with a heavy heart. My father was plagued by doubts about the wisdom of the decision. My mother, once settled on a course of action, was imperturbable. Their basic difference of temperament was that she lacked imagination and could not conceive of failure, while my father's imagination now tormented him with ever darker visions of disaster. She regarded this fevered imagination dourly and thought it should be controllable. He tried to keep his worst fears to himself.

Our help came in the wonderful form of two brothers, half aboriginal, half Chinese. The elder brother, Ron, in his early twenties, was light-skinned and slightly slant-eyed; the younger, Jack, looked like a full-blooded aboriginal. They came from the mission station in Menindee, one hundred and seventy miles away. They were as fine a pair of station hands as one could ever hope for. Ron could fix engines and manage all things mechanical. He was quiet, efficient, and totally dependable. Jack could talk to animals, soothe a frightened horse, persuade half-starving sheep to get up and keep walking. Jack could pick up a stone and toss it casually to knock down out of the sky the crows gathering around a foundered animal. He could track anything: snakes, sheep, kangaroos, lizards. Jack's only defect so far as station management was concerned was that at any time he might feel the aboriginal need to go "on walkabout." He was utterly reliable and would always reappear to complete the abandoned task he'd been at work on when the urge came. But he could be gone for days, or weeks, or months.

Feeding the sheep was hard work. Feed troughs made of metal could not be considered because the drifting sand would quickly cover them. If the weaker sheep were to get their nourishment, the expanse of feeding troughs must be large so that every animal would have its chance at the grain. So we settled on burlap troughs hung on wire— light enough for the wind to blow beneath when empty, cheap enough to produce in hundred-foot lengths. Replacement lengths became available each time we emptied a hundredweight bag of wheat. With a bag needle and a hank of twine at hand anyone could mend the troughs, or with a little wire and some wooden pegs, create new ones.

When we began our feeding program in the troughs placed by major watering places, the sheep seemed only slowly to discover the grain. Within a few weeks the hungry animals would stampede at the sight of anyone carrying bags of wheat, and someone had to be sent as a decoy to draw them off in search of a small supply of grain while the major ration was being poured into the troughs. Since I could carry only twenty pounds at a fast run, I was the decoy while the men carried forty- and fifty-pound bags on their shoulders to empty into the feeding troughs. At first the sheep were ravenous but measured in following the decoy. Soon they would race so hard toward the grain that they would send the decoy flying unless he or she outraced them. Then they would pause, wheel on catching the scent of the ration in the troughs, and stampede back toward the food.

Our principal enemies as we carried out this daily process were the pink cockatoos and crows, which tore the burlap to pieces in search of the grains of wheat left behind. Soon the mending of the troughs was a daily task, a task made miserable by the blowflies, the blistering sun, the blowing sand, and the stench of the bodies of the sheep for whom the wheat had arrived too late.

For my father each death was a personal

blow, and he took himself to task for the suffering of the animals. Our conversations as we rode about the place took on a grimmer tone. "When I'm gone, Jill, sell this place. Take care of your mother. Make sure she goes to the city. There's nothing but heartbreak in fighting the seasons." Or, "If anything happens to me, promise me you'll take care of your mother. Make her sell this place. Don't let her stay here." I would promise anything to change his mood and get the conversation on another topic. But I rarely succeeded. Usually he would go on to talk about my future, a future in which he clearly did not expect to share. "Work hard, Jill," he'd say. "Don't just waste time. *Make something of yourself.*" Reverting to his idée fixe that my brothers did not try hard enough at their schoolwork, he would continue, "Don't be like your brothers. Don't waste your time in school. Get a real education and get away from this damn country for good." I would promise, choking back tears at the thought of his death and a future away from Coorain. But even I could see that he was right about the battle with the seasons. Without discussing the subject with anyone, I concluded that the God who was supposed to heed the fall of the sparrow had a lesser morality than humans. Each clap of dry thunder and each vista of starving animals made the notion of a loving God a mockery. I kept my father's words about impending death to myself. I was used to being the listener to fears and worries my parents needed to express, but did not want to worry one another about. It seemed too monstrous a possibility to speak about, and in a primitive way I feared that naming it might make it happen.

One troublesome aspect of the frustration of my parents' dreams was the extent to which they transferred their ambitions to their children. My brothers, being five hundred miles away, were not readily available as vehicles for ambition. Being at hand, I became the focus of all the aspiration for achievement that had fueled both parents' prodigious energies. My correspondence school required little of my time and less energy. My teacher's reports were always positive and my work praised. Naturally, it should have been, for I had heard the same lessons discussed in the schoolroom by my brothers and their governess.

I read omnivorously, everything that came to hand, and through reading my mother's books I asked questions about politics and history which both parents took for signs of high intelligence. Lacking playmates, I would retreat from the adult world to my swing, set away in the eucalyptus trees a hundred yards or so from the house. There I would converse at length with imaginary companions, usually characters from some recently read novel or war correspondent's report, which I only dimly understood. I would kick furiously in order to rise up higher and see a little farther beyond the horizon. In the midst of my dreams of glory drawn from highly glamorized accounts of war and feats of heroism, I would sometimes stop crestfallen and wonder if I would ever get away from Coorain. Sometimes, needing to be alone, I would walk for hours, scanning the ground for aboriginal ovens, collecting quartz fragments, observing the insect life—anything to be away from the house and its overwhelming mood of worry.

The nighttime conversations now made me nervous because they frequently settled on what a remarkable child I was, and how gratifying it would be for parents to observe my progress. I had no way of assessing their judgments, but I was certainly uncomfortably aware that I and my performance in life had become the focus of formidable emotional energies.

Like all children, I was occasionally mischievous and misbehaved. In more carefree times my pranks, like my brothers', met with swift punishment from parents who believed that sparing the rod was certain to spoil the child. The occasional token chastisement was easy to resist psychologically. One had only to refuse to apologize and express contrition for enough hours to gain the upper hand on parents who were tired in the evening and wanted to go to bed. Now, however, I encountered more subtle, and to me more terrifying, punishments. If I misbehaved, my parents simply acted as though I were not their child but a stranger. They would inquire civilly as to who I was and what I was doing on Coorain, but no hint of recognition escaped them. This treatment never failed to reduce me to abject contrition. In later life my recurring nightmares were always about my inability to prove to people I knew quite well who I was. I became an unnaturally good child, and accepted uncritically that goodness was required of me if my parents' disappointments in life were ever to be compensated for.

That June most of our older sheep were too weak to be shorn. My father took the few whose wool was worth shearing and who could stand the journey to a neighboring station, since the numbers were too small to warrant bringing a shearing team to Coorain. On the first day of his absence, my mother also left in the afternoon to pick up the mail and carry out some other errands. I had time to fulfill an often neglected promise to my brother Bob that I would listen on his shortwave radio every afternoon and record the stations and countries I heard. That day, the sixth of June, I turned the dial to the point where we had discovered that we could hear the uncensored news being dictated to General MacArthur's headquarters. To my astonishment, I heard the impassive announcer's voice report the news of the Allied landing in Normandy, and the establishment of beachheads beyond Utah and Omaha beaches literally only a few hours earlier. By the time my mother returned in the late afternoon, I was gibbering with excitement and almost incoherent with my news. She listened carefully, sorted out the story, and promised to tell my father when he telephoned that evening. This she did, although the evening Australian news contained no report of the landing. I was not vindicated until the six o'clock news the following night, when the Australian censors decided to release the news of the successful landings. Thereafter, no matter what the circumstances on Coorain, I could always distract my father by reading him reports of the campaign on the various fronts in Europe as we jolted about Coorain in our sulky, traveling to clean watering troughs or mend our feeding troughs. I could supplement the newspaper accounts by the more accurate reporting which I heard on my brother's radio, where the actual figures of casualties were reported rather than the bland announcements made for civilian consumption. Reading about the invasion in Europe was reassuring because our own situation in Australia had grown more precarious as the war in the Pacific unfolded.

We had been jolted out of complacency by the fall of Singapore, the supposedly impregnable British naval base, fortified with guns which pointed only out to sea. My mother and I had been on a brief trip to Sydney when Singapore fell. The newspaper headlines covered the whole front page of the afternoon dailies. So great was the shock that Australians, the most taciturn of people, had actually been moved to speak about the news to total strangers. Handfuls of refugees began to arrive from Hong Kong, but there were none from Singapore, except the Australian commander, Major-General Gordon Bennett, who we were ashamed to learn had deserted his men. Many of our friends and sons of friends had been in the Australian contingent at Singapore, including our fondly remembered Jimmie Walker. We had his smiling picture in his A.I.F. uniform sent just before his departure. The news of Japanese treatment of prisoners and the atrocities committed upon the civilian population of the Philippines made the increasing likelihood of the invasion of Australia seem more threatening.

My parents' conversations on this possibility were chilling but practical. Australia was drained of able-bodied men, away fighting in Europe and the Middle East. These two proudly loyal subjects of the British crown had thrilled to the sound of Churchill's speeches hurling defiance at Hitler, invoking the glory of the British Empire to inspire the defense of England. They were correspondingly shaken to realize that Australia was expendable in Britain's war strategy, and that the Australian government had

had great difficulty in securing the return of the battle-scarred Ninth Division from Tobruk to take part in the defense of Australia. Once this was clear they turned soberly to consideration of what to do in the event of an invasion. They calculated correctly that the continent was too vast to be easily overrun, that the Japanese would concentrate on the ports and the food supplies. We, who were hardy backcountry people, could disappear if need be into the great outback desert and live off the land like aborigines. There were various plans for getting the boys home, and discussions about how that might be achieved in a time of likely national panic. When the call came for civilians to turn over all their hunting rifles to the government to help arm the militia, a pitifully small group of men who had refused to serve overseas when drafted, my father kept back one of his rifles and hid it with a supply of ammunition. If we were ever in danger of capture, he and my mother had calmly agreed that he would shoot his wife and children first and then himself. In preparation for such dire possibilities, we hid supplies in a remote part of Coorain. The gasoline was described as a cache to be reserved for emergencies, and we never spoke about the need for a weapon.

We had very realistic expectations about the defense of Australia, because it was patently apparent that there was a failure of leadership in the country, symbolized by Major-General Gordon Bennett's ignominious flight, the flustered performance of the first wartime leader, the United Australian Party Prime Minister Robert Menzies, and the short-lived Country Party government which followed. The task of defending the country was impossible for Australians alone, and the old empire mentalities of our leaders left them, without the protection of Great Britain, as paralyzed as the defenders of Singapore. My parents were rugged individualists who scorned socialism and the Labor Party as the political recourse of those who lacked initiative. Nonetheless, their spirits soared when the Labor Prime Minister, John Curtin, took office, candidly acknowledged our situation, and called for American assistance. They recognized an Australian patriot, and I learned for the first time that loyalty to Great Britain and love for Australia were not synonymous. It was an important lesson.

After the June shearing of 1944, we knew that if it did not rain in the spring our gamble was lost. The sheep would not live through until another rainy season. There were so few to feed by September 1944 that our friends and helpers, Ron and Jack Kelly, left for another job. We on Coorain waited for the rain which never came. The dust storms swept over us every two or three weeks, and there was no pretending about the state of the sheep when we traveled around the property. The smells of death and the carrion birds were everywhere. The starving animals which came to our feed troughs were now demented with hunger. When I ran off as decoy to spread out a thin trail of grain while the troughs were filled, they knocked me over and trampled me, desperate to tear the grain from the bag. Their skeletal bodies were pitiful. I found I could no longer bear to look into their eyes, because the usually tranquil ruminant animals looked half crazed.

We lost our appetite for meat because the flesh of the starving animals already tasted putrid. I was never conscious of when the smell of rotting animals drowned out the perfumes from my mother's garden, but by early December, although it still bloomed, our nostrils registered only decaying flesh. By then the sand accumulating on the other side of the windbreak was beginning to bend the cane walls inward by its weight, and we knew it was only a matter of time before it too was engulfed.

My mother, as always, was unconquerable. "It has to rain some day," she told my father. "Our children are healthy. We can grow our food. What does it matter if we lose everything else?" She did not understand that it mattered deeply to him. Other memories of loss from his childhood were overwhelming him. He could not set out in mid-life to be once more the orphan without patrimony. As he sank into deeper depression, they understood one another less. She, always able to rouse herself to action, could not understand how to deal with crippling depression, except by a brisk call to count one's blessings. This was just what my father was unable to do.

My brothers were summoned home two weeks early from school, though to help with what was not clear. There was pitifully little to do on Coorain. There were the same burlap troughs to mend, the same desperate animals to feed, but the size of the task was shrinking daily. The December heat set in, each day over 100 degrees. Now so much of our land was without vegetation that the slightest breeze set the soil blowing. Even without the dust storms, our daily life seemed lived in an inferno.

My mother's efforts to rouse my father were indefatigable. One Saturday in early December was to be a meeting of the Pastures Protection Board in Hillston. Early in the week before, she set about persuading him to drive the seventy-five miles with his close friend Angus Waugh. Reluctantly, he agreed. The Friday before, a minor dust storm set in, and he decided against the drive. It was fearfully hot, over 108 degrees, and we passed a fitful evening barricaded in against the blowing sand.

The next morning I awoke, conscious that it was very early, to find my father gazing intently at me. He bent down to embrace me and said good-bye. Half asleep, I bid him good-bye and saw his departing back. Suddenly, I snapped awake. *Why is he saying good-bye? He isn't going anywhere.* I leapt out of bed, flung on the first clothes to hand, and ran dry-mouthed after him. I was only seconds too late. I ran shouting after his car, "I want to come. Take me with you." I thought he saw me, but, the car gathering speed, he drove away.

Back in the house, my mother found me pacing about and asked why I was up so early in the morning. I said I'd wanted to go with my father, and wasn't sure where he went. He was worried about the heat and the adequacy of the water for the sheep in Brooklins (a distant paddock), she said, and had gone to check on it. It was a hot oppressive day, with the wind gaining strength by noon. I felt a leaden fear in my stomach, but was speechless. To speak of my fears seemed to admit that my father had lost his mental balance. It was something I could not say.

His journey should not have taken more than two hours, but then again he could have decided to visit other watering places on the property. When he was not home by two, my mother and Bob set out after him. Neither Barry nor I, left behind, was inclined to talk about what might have happened. Like a pair of automatons, we washed the dishes left from lunch and settled in to wait. When no one returned by four, the hour when my mother stoked the stove and began her preparations for dinner, we went through the motions of her routine. The potatoes were peeled, peas shelled, the roast prepared, the table laid.

Eventually, Bob arrived home alone. There had been an accident, he said. He must make some phone calls and hurry back. We neither of us believed him. We knew my father was dead. Finally, at six o'clock, the old grey utility my father drove hove into sight driven by my brother Bob; my mother's car followed, with several others in its wake. She took the time to thank us for preparing dinner before saying she had something to tell us alone. We went numbly to our parents' bedroom, the place of all confidential conversations. "I want you to help me," she said. "Your father's dead. He was working on extending the piping into the Brooklins dam. We found him there in the water." My eyes began to fill with tears. She looked at me accusingly. "Your father wouldn't want you to cry," she said.

We watched woodenly as my father's body was brought to rest in that same bedroom. We were dismissed while she prepared it for the funeral which would take place in two days. In the hot summer months, burials had to be speedy and there was no need for anyone to explain why to us children. We had been dealing with decaying bodies for years.

Because of the wartime restrictions on travel and the need for haste, there was little time to summon family and friends. Telegrams were dispatched but only my mother's brother and sister-in-law, close to us in Sydney, were actually expected. Eventually, we sat down to dinner and choked over our food, trying desperately to make conversation with the kindly manager from a neighboring station who had come to help. The meal seemed surreal. The food on the plate seemed unconnected to the unreal world without my father in it in which I now lived. I was haunted by the consciousness of his body lying close by in the bedroom, which my mother had sternly forbidden me to enter.

After we went sleeplessly to bed, we heard a sound never heard before, the sound of my mother weeping hopelessly and inconsolably. It was a terrible and unforgettable sound. To moderate the heat we slept on a screened veranda exposed to any southern breeze which might stir. My brother Barry's bed was next to mine. After listening to this terrible new sound, we both agreed that we wished we were older so that we could go to work and take care of her. We tossed until the sun rose and crept out of bed too shocked to do more than converse in whispers.

My mother soon appeared, tight-lipped and pale, somehow a ghost of herself. Dispensing with all possibility of discussion, she announced that Barry and I were to stay with friends for a few days. She did not want us to see our father buried, believing that this would be too distressing for us. Though we complied without questioning the plan, I felt betrayed that I would not see him to his last rest. She, for her part, wanted to preserve us from signs of the body's decay. As we set out, driven by the kindly Morison family, who had cared for me during my mother's illness, we passed the hearse making its way toward Coorain. Its black shape drove home what had happened.

How my father's death had actually come about we would never know. He was a poor swimmer, and had attempted to dive down in muddy water to connect a fresh length of pipe so that the pump for watering the sheep could draw from the lowered water level of the dam. It was a difficult exercise for a strong swimmer, and not one to undertake alone. Why he had chosen to do it alone when my two brothers, both excellent swimmers, were at home, we could not understand. I did not tell anyone of his early morning visit to me. I realized that we would never know the answer to the question it raised.

Everyone expected that my mother would sell Coorain, move to the city, and allow a bank or trust company to manage our finances. In our part of the world this was what widows did. Our circle of friends and advisers did not bargain for my mother's business sense and her strong will. She would not sell the property when it was worth next to nothing. She planned instead to run it herself, wait for the rains which must come, and manage our one asset for our maximum benefit. The boys were to return to school according to the usual schedule. She would hire some help, and she and I would remain at Coorain. Presented with this plan and a request to finance it, her startled woolbrokers remonstrated with her about the hazards of a woman taking charge of her own affairs. Seeing her resolve, they acquiesced, and offered her a loan secured by our now virtually nonexistent sheep. So she returned resolute to preserve and enhance the enterprise she and my father had built.

He had not been a man to give much thought to transferring property to wife or children, and so my mother, as his sole heir, became liable for sizable death duties. Some of my first lessons in feminism came from her outraged conversations with the hapless valuation agent sent to inventory and value the assets of the estate for probate. She was incensed to discover that her original investment in furniture, linen, silver, and household equipment was now merged in my father's estate. No value was attributed either to the contributions she had made to the enterprise through the investment of her capital fifteen years before, or to the proceeds of her fifteen years of twelve- and fourteen-hour days of labor. Her outspoken anger cowed the man into some concessions, but her rumblings about this economic injustice continued for years, and instructed me greatly.

Heroic as she was, we would not have fared so well in her defiance of the fates had we not been given the affection, support, and physical presence of my mother's younger brother and his wife. Both worked in essential wartime occupations in Sydney, my uncle as an engineer and my aunt as the senior nurse in a munitions factory. Informed of my father's death, both requested leave to attend his funeral and to help his widow cope with her loss, and both were refused any more than forty-eight hours' absence. In characteristic Australian fashion, they defied the manpower authorities, talked their way onto the train for the west despite the restrictions on civilian travel, and arrived to stay shortly before my father's funeral.

Once they took in the situation my mother faced, they decided to defy the orders they promptly received to return to their respective jobs. Instead, they elected to see her through the harsh first months of bereavement. Their warm hearts, wonderful common sense, and comforting physical presence reassured us children, as my mother grew suddenly thinner, her abundant hair grey almost overnight, and her moods, normally equable, swung to every point of the compass. We struggled through Christmas, trying to celebrate, but at every point in the day we met memories of my father's presence the previous year. At the end of January, the boys left for school, and in late February, my uncle finally obeyed the accumulating pile of telegrams and official letters requiring him to return at once to his wartime post. My aunt remained another month, a calming presence, full of life force, cheerfully sustaining our spirits by her questions about our way of life in a remote part of the country she had never visited. Before my uncle left, our former helper Ron Kelly returned, leaving a much better job to take care of Coorain and us once again.

By the time he arrived, we were feeding only seven or eight hundred sheep in two paddocks, and working to preserve the various improvements, bores, wells, sheepyards, and fences from the encroaching sand. Each day, the three of us went out with our loads of wheat, and to work on the now hated burlap troughs. They were hateful because they had become tattered with much use, and required daily attention with patches, twine, and bag needle. There was no way to make the repairs except to sit down in the dust, thread one's needle, and go at it. With the sun beating down, no hands free to drive away the flies, and the sounds of the ever-hungry and opportunistic cockatoos waiting to tear apart our handiwork, we could not escape awareness of the repetitious and futile nature of our labors.

Each afternoon, Ron set out for another tour of fences: to dig out those standing up, to treat posts being attacked by white ants under the sand, and to oil and care for all the working parts of the windmills and pumping equipment. At night after the lamps were lit, the silence in the house was palpable. My mother and I read after dinner, but as the time approached for going to bed she would become unaccustomedly nervous and edgy. She found sleeping alone a nightmare, and after a few weeks of sleepless nights she said she needed my company in her bed. After that it was I who had trouble resting, for she clung to me like a drowning person. Alone, without my father, all her fears of the wilderness returned, and she found the silence as alienating as when she first arrived on the plains. She would often pace the verandas much of the night. Both of us would be grateful for the dawn.

Once a week our friend and neighbor Angus Waugh drove the fifty miles to visit us. He would talk over the state of the sheep and the land with my mother, offer sound advice, and try to make her laugh. I longed for his visits so that for even a few hours the care of this silent and grieving person would not rest only on my shoulders. He could always make me laugh by telling wild nonsense stories, or wickedly funny accounts of the life and affairs of distant residents in the

125

district. My mother, in fact, knew in great detail every aspect of the management of a sheep station. Angus knew this very well, but his weekly presence gave her some adult company, and enabled him to keep a watchful and sensitive eye on how we both were faring.

In February, although my mother was uncertain whether she could afford it, the shearing contractor and his team arrived to crutch our sheep. They followed the bush code of helping those in trouble, and told my mother to pay them when she could, or never if it wasn't possible. Help appeared from all quarters at crutching time, and our few poor sheep were back in their paddocks before we knew it. My friends on the team never spoke of our bereavement, but they were even more than usually kind about my efforts to keep on top of everything that was happening at the shed.

By the time the boys came home for their holidays in May it was clear that very few of the animals would survive even if it rained within a few weeks. My brothers shot the few remaining large animals we could not feed—the Black Angus bull, formerly the rippling black embodiment of sexual power and energy, now a wraith; the few poor cows;

some starving horses. And then in the next weeks the last sheep began to die by the hundreds. We would pile up the carcasses of those that died near the house, douse them with kerosene, and set them alight, to reduce the pervasive odor of rotting flesh. The crows and hawks were fat, and the cockatoos full-breasted on their diet of wheat, but one by one all other forms of life began to fade away.

After the boys went back to school in June, there was little to do on the place. No amount of digging could prevent the silting-up of fences, and the maintenance of equipment did not require much oversight. Once we were alone again, I was more than usually worried about my mother, because she ate next to nothing, fell to weeping unexpectedly, and seemed much of the time in a trance. The effort expended in getting up and carrying on each day exhausted her. This was combined with the effort expended in refusing to accept the possibility that our enterprise at Coorain might go under. Because this fear was repressed, she was fearful of lesser things. Once when I went riding without telling her, her fury startled me. Once when I went to work on a bore with Ron, an individual who would have died to secure our safety, she gave me a tongue-lashing about never again working alone with him.

Shortly after these explosions, Angus arrived for one of his visits. He took a walk with me and asked how we were doing. As I shook my head, uncertain about how to say what was on my mind, he supplied the words for me. "You're worried about your mother, aren't you," he said. I nodded. "She doesn't eat?" "That's right," I said. "She's depressed?" I nodded. "You ought to leave here," he said. "There's not a bloody thing you two can do here now. The pair of you look like something out of Changi and it's to no purpose. Would you like to leave, live like a normal child and go to school?" I felt a great wave of relief. "Yes," I said.

That night Angus talked to my mother as they took a walk around the house and grounds. I heard snatches, and realized that he was playing the other side of the argument skillfully. "You can't keep Jill here forever. It's not right. She should be in school. Neither of you can do anything here. Look at her. She's so skinny she could come from a concentration camp. It's time to leave and go to Sydney, and let her get on with her life. You can hire a manager to take care of this place, and I'll watch over it for you."

The next morning my mother eyed me as though I were a stranger. I was certainly a sight. I was in my eleventh year, so underweight my clothes for an eight- or nine-year-old hung on me, and as Angus said, I looked worried enough to be an old woman. Once she noticed my appearance the matter was settled for my mother. She began to make plans for us to leave.

With Angus's help we found a splendid manager. Geoff Coghlan was a thoroughly knowledgeable man about sheep and cattle, and the ways of our western plains country. He had been too young to participate in the 1914–1918 War, and a few years too old to join the armed forces in the 1939–1945 War, then wending toward Allied victory in Europe, and more slowly toward the defeat of Japan in the Pacific. Margaret, his wife, was the daughter of near neighbors, and Coorain offered them a home of their own. Given that my mother would live in Sydney, where I could attend a good school, our new managers would have relative independence to run things their way. It was agreed that they would move to Coorain early in August 1945, and we would depart close to the end of the month.

The actual prospect of departure evoked complicated emotions. The house, the garden, the vistas of space were the only landscape I knew. The ways of the backcountry were second nature, and I associated Sydney with stiff formal clothes, sore feet, and psychological exhaustion from coping with unaccustomed crowds. Yet I knew I could not deal unaided with my mother's grief and despair. As time passed, the energy she had summoned to manage the immediate details of life after my father's death was dissipated, and she sank into a private world of sorrow from which I could not detach her. I was lonely and grief-stricken myself. I had come to hate the sight of the desolate countryside, the whitening bones, and the all-pervasive dust. I, too, was consumed with anxiety because the experience of cumulative disaster had darkened my mood, and made me see the fates as capricious and punishing.

Yet to leave Coorain was almost beyond my comprehension. Each day I prepared myself for the departure by trying to engrave on my memory images that would not fade —the dogs I loved best, the horse I rode, the household cat, the shapes of trees. Ever since my father's death I had called his figure and voice to mind each morning as I woke, determined not to let it fade. Now I did the same with each familiar detail of life. It was strange to hear my mother and Mrs. Coghlan discuss what equipment should stay at Coorain, what china and glass should go with us. The familiar shapes of pots and pans, the patterns on the china—all took on a life of their own. Hitherto they had been simple aspects of the world that was.

Before we left, we made a visit to Clare Station, some fifty miles to the west, to spend two nights with Angus, his sister Eileen, and his younger brother Ron. Their parents had taken up a vast acreage in the 1880s, moving out onto the plains driving their sheep before them, transporting their belongings in bullock wagons. Clare, as they had named their property, had once been larger than its current five hundred thousand acres. It had been so large it was virtually a small town, with such extensive stables and accommodations that it could comfortably serve as a stop for the Cobb and Company coaches which traveled the west before the railroad and the automobile. The second generation of the Waughs were a formidable Scottish clan, thrifty, hardworking, generous, excellent businessmen. I had never seen anything at once so large and at the same time so haphazard. The station homestead was organized around a courtyard, three sides of which were bedrooms and bathrooms, arranged in no order I could discern. One walked across a second courtyard to the vast dining room, itself a good five-minute walk from the kitchens, set well away in case of fire. Everyone laughed about the fact that this inconvenient distance made the meals always lukewarm, but no one seemed to mind. The furniture was massive, leather-covered sofas and oak chairs surrounded the fireplaces in two adjoining sitting rooms. Huge gilt-framed landscapes of Scottish scenes adorned the walls. These I studied carefully, having never seen real paintings on canvas, let alone pictures of such unfamiliar highland sheep and cattle. Scattered over the faded linoleum floors were Oriental rugs. Things were well worn but clearly no one fretted over polishing them the way my mother did. Before dinner, everyone drank Scotch neat. Water was regarded as harmful to the taste. Angus told me his parents had still toasted "the king over the water" in his childhood, and that he remembered the rooms decorated with tartans. The woolshed was massive, like the house and its contents. The shed was large enough to shear what had once been a herd of forty thousand sheep. Everything—quarters for station hands, stables, yards, sheds for farm equipment—seemed on a gargantuan scale to me, just as the vast paintings of highland landscapes seemed to dwarf the people in the living rooms. I loved to hear Angus tell stories about the pioneering days of his parents, and the way of life before railways and cars made such city comforts as store-bought canned goods accessible. Clare had experienced the same disasters as we had at Coorain, but ten lean years made little difference to the family fortune. On a station of this size, one could wait out the seasons with relative composure.

When the time came for us actually to pack for the train journey, I began to feel a strange emptiness in the pit of my stomach. My consciousness departed to some relatively distant point above my body, and I looked down at what seemed almost pygmy-size figures going about the business of departure. My mother, faced with a practical task, was her systematic self. Suitcases and trunks were packed. Boxes of china and linen, a few books, our clothes. But everything else remained, and I realized that we were going into the world outside relatively lighthanded. She broke down over the packing of my father's clothes. I, for my part, refused to pack any toys or dolls. I knew that in most important ways my childhood was over.

When the day of our departure dawned, it arrived as both a relief and a sentence. I wanted the break over, yet I could not bear to say good-bye. I was up and dressed early, uncomfortable in my town clothes. I took one last walk and found I had no heart for it. We drank the inevitable cup of morning tea as the bags and boxes were loaded. Suddenly, we were in the car driving away from Coorain. I looked back until it sank from sight beneath the horizon. My mother gazed resolutely ahead. In ten minutes it was all over.

Departures for Sydney by train took place at the small railroad station at Ivanhoe, some forty miles north of Coorain. There was little to the town but a cluster of railroad maintenance workers' huts, some shunting yards, and a set of stockyards for loading sheep and cattle. A store, a garage, a road haulage company, and a few more ample houses lined the dusty main street. The train itself was the most impressive part of the landscape. The passenger train we rode on for half the journey to Sydney was one of our few chances to encounter modernity. It was diesel-powered, streamlined, air-conditioned, painted a dazzling silver to evoke the site of its origin, Broken Hill, an inland silver mining center. When the boys rode it to school, my father had always tipped the porter so that the boredom of their journey could be broken by an exciting ride in the engine cabin, actually watching the needle of the speedometer climb past eighty miles an hour. When the diesel engine had built up speed, it purred along effortlessly while the countryside outside raced by at a bewildering rate. The Diesel, as we called it, announced itself twenty or more minutes before its arrival by the huge column of red dust it churned up as it tore across the plains. We spent the twenty minutes in careful goodbyes, and then piled quickly into the train which stopped only a merciful three minutes in the station. We both now wanted this ordeal over.

As the train pulled out and gathered speed, my mother and I stood at the door waving. We both choked with tears a little as we passed the system of points just outside the station where the train always slowed a little. Once my father, too preoccupied with giving advice to his sons to notice the time, had been obliged to jump from the moving train at that point.

Yet in counterpoint to my grief was overwhelming relief. It was true that we had been cast out from our paradise. But that paradise had become literally purgatorial for us. My mother had seen the product of fifteen years of unremitting labor disappear. She had lost a partnership of work and love which had made her utterly fulfilled. Without it she was at sea. I felt that my heart was permanently frozen with grief by what had happened to both my parents. I feared even greater disasters were we to remain at Coorain. I had lost my sense of trust in a benign providence, and feared the fates. My brother Bob had taken to reading me his favorite Shakespeare plays while home on his last vacation, and I had been transfixed by the line from *King Lear:* "As flies to wanton boys are we to the gods,/ They kill us for their sport." I did not understand the nature of the ecological disaster which had transformed my world, or that we ourselves had been agents as well as participants in our own catastrophe. I just knew that we had been defeated by the fury

136

of the elements, a fury that I could not see we had earned. In the life that lay ahead, I knew I must serve as my father's agent in the family and muster the energy to deal with such further disasters as might befall us. For the moment, we were down on our luck and had to begin all over again.

5

Schooling

The familiar train journey to Sydney was unusually trancelike as we traveled away from Coorain for good. My mother and I seemed disconnected from time and space, moving between worlds. The Silver City Comet quickly left behind the heat and the shimmering red light of the Western Division. Its cars hummed with efficient air-conditioning machinery. Its seats, upholstered in light blue, and its wide windows covering the whole upper half of its streamlined carriages, combined to suggest movement to a new world. Such mundane belongings as suitcases were stored in racks in the vestibule to each car. Just as the lines of the train suggested effortless ease, the passengers also seemed to be moving easily, uncluttered by such intractable things as baggage and parcels. My mother and I, aware of psychic baggage, sat silently, struggling with the conflicting emotions of relief, grief, and fear, emotions we were well schooled not to discuss.

The train's windows presented a striking panorama of Australian life. At first, nothing was visible but open plains with pitiful railroad workers' settlements crouched beside the railway line. The train stopped to dispense mail to them, and in this emergency caused by the drought, supplies of water. We who rode in comfort looked out at the ragged children and tired women who inhabited the burlap and tin shacks, as though we were comfortable spectators of the action in a Dickens novel, the forlorn waifs gazing in upon us merely signs of some other person's social imagination. Much later, at Sydney University, I learned about the social scientist's concept of social distance. To me it always recalled the cool carriages and the hot plains, the desolate shacks, and the uplifted faces of the undernourished children.

As the day wore on we came to more substantial railway stations, with signs of solid-looking towns behind them. Once we passed the line of rainfall where wheat could be grown, silos dominated the horizon, and the homesteads came closer together. Later we crossed substantial watercourses, and saw towns with solid-looking buildings, and such signs of civic pride as schools and churches. As the afternoon progressed toward sunset, the sun's rays drew new colors from the earth and etched new shapes in relief. Now the fields of wheat shone, green or bleached gold, a strange and romantic sign of plenty after the arid plains. On past journeys, I had looked condescendingly at wheat farms and their inhabitants. Now I looked with fresh curiosity. Who was behind the walls of the homesteads? What was life like there? Was it easier to survive drought here?

Finally, after five to six hours' travel, we came to the town of Parkes, to a substantial railway terminal with several platforms and a commotion of steam trains and people illuminated in unfamiliar electric light. Here, as always, we were flustered by an unaccustomed sense of hurry because there was less than an hour to eat quickly in the dining room and see the luggage transferred to the Forbes Mail, an express train for Sydney. It was a steampowered, red-plush-upholstered, and red-carpeted train which recalled the grand aspirations of train travel before the automobile. Its sleeping compartments glittered with polished brass, and smelled of freshly laundered linen. We children always fought to climb the green velvet ladder which carried one to the upper berth where we could lie dreaming and waking as the train labored all night over the mountains, and brought us twelve hours later to the outskirts of Sydney.

Those night train journeys had their own mystery because of the clicking of the rails, the shafts of light pouring through the shutters of the sleeping compartment as we passed stations, and the slamming of doors when the train stopped to take on passengers. In the morning there was the odd sight of green landscape, trees, grass, banks of streams—and an entirely different palette of colors, as though during the night we had journeyed to another country. Usually I slept soundly, registering the unaccustomed sounds and images only faintly. This time I lay awake and listened, opened the shutters and scanned unknown platforms, and wondered about the future.

By seven the next morning we stood in the lurching corridors gazing out at the intimidating sight of crowded city streets, slums with ramshackle houses, more substantial suburbs with brick houses and prim gardens, all marked with the soot the trains dispensed evenhandedly on poverty and respectability alike. Most startling were the factories, acres of roofs, gleaming lights, and burgeoning steam. We were in time to see the hordes of workers entering for the morning shift. The confluence of machinery, steam power, and people led me to shudder inwardly because of a sudden sense of primitive energy which I feared. Beyond the factories, the train gathered speed, hooted importantly, and rushed into Sydney's Central Station, to a platform so long one couldn't see the end of it, crowded with people, porters, luggage carts, and shouting newsboys.

In the past when making these journeys, I had savored the panorama of the countryside, vaguely resented the discomfort of town clothes, and enjoyed the prospect of ice cream sundaes, being spoiled by my grandmother, uncle and aunt, seeing the ocean, riding on ferries in the Sydney Harbor and in trams. All had been punctuation points before returning home. Now there was no home to go to, and our arrival at the cheerful house my uncle and aunt shared with my grandmother had a different flavor. We were objects of pity and concern, not just festive visitors.

There was a real question about where we would live. Sydney in the late stages of the 1939–1945 War was a city bursting at the seams. Few houses had been built during the Depression, and none during the war, while the city had become the staging point and recreation center for many thousands of American troops in the South Pacific. Wartime production had brought many from rural towns to the city, so that the resident population had risen by fifteen percent during the war years. There was a black market in housing, with large sums of money changing hands as key money whenever one found a vacant flat or house. Our hospitable relatives were prepared for a long visit, but my mother was characteristically determined to find a flat in the right suburb with the right school which I could immediately begin attending as a day student.

Within a week she had found and rented the upstairs portion of a graceful house in the seaside suburb of Mosman. There was a sizable double bedroom, a bathroom, a vast glassed-in balcony from which one looked across the Harbor to its entrance between North Head and South Head, and a living room which could serve as a bedroom for my brothers when they came home for a weekend away from school. Our meals, prepared in the kitchen below, were eaten looking out at the ocean, enjoying the passing parade of water traffic. In an era of rationing, furniture, carpets, linen, and curtains for the new flat were hard to come by. Brushing aside advice about the difficulty of furnishing a new dwelling, my resourceful mother attended several fire sales and equipped us inexpensively but royally with faded rose and blue Wilton rugs, some passably upholstered easy chairs, and wonderful faded flowery chintz curtains, all from another era. I loved the colors. We never saw such things in the west because the sun and the dust faded them too quickly. Now there was the intoxicating blue of the ocean, the rich designs of the rugs and curtains, and the unfailing wonder of the garden, where everything was always green. The sudden comfort was overwhelming when contrasted with years of fighting the drought. Each garden and house on the street was an object of wonder to be examined and reexamined. Opposite our house was a large, white stucco house with enormous glassed-in verandas, an elegant sweep of velvety green lawn, and spring daffodils in bloom. I could not stop looking and watching for the creatures who lived in such a place.

Although the third term of the school year

had begun, I was enrolled as a day student at Queenwood school, and before another week was past my mother delivered me there on a rainy morning. The gates opened onto a macadam-covered inner yard enclosed on three sides by buildings. On one side was a tennis court and gymnasium, on the second a low, cream brick building housing cloakrooms, and on the third side, a red brick classroom building approached by grey basalt steps. I found the small world inside the school gates alien and intimidating. Having never had a playmate, I did not know how to play. Never having known anyone my own age, I was uncertain about how to begin with thirty or so other eleven-year-olds.

The school yard with its busy ant heap of people skipping rope, throwing basketballs, shouting, and playing hopscotch reduced me to a paralysis of shyness. I had never seen tennis or basketball played, and had not the faintest notion of the rules. I was used to knowing better than most people what needed to be done. Here I was the veriest incompetent, not only in games, but in the classroom, where there were also rules to be learned. It did no good to ask why the rules obtained. Answers were not forthcoming. One ruled the margin in one's book so; one set out mathematical exercises leaving two lines between calculations; one drew maps with a fine-tipped pen and India ink and in no other way. We memorized the provinces of Canada, and recited them starting in the east and traveling westward. I was used to learning very exact details of topography in order to find my way about a countryside with no signs and few landmarks, but when I asked why we listed Canada's provinces from east to west no one understood why I thought directions important.

The routines governing time were also puzzling. One just began studying one subject after everyone had been induced to sit still and be quiet, and suddenly a bell rang, the teacher departed, and we rushed into the gymnasium for an activity called physical exercise. This I could not fathom. I knew how to do hard physical labor, but I was bored by the calisthenics and too clumsy to play the games. The purpose of all the activity was clear to everyone but me, and no explanations were ever given. I could not arrive at the reasons why the first ten minutes of every morning were devoted to something called mental arithmetic. The teacher called out a problem every few seconds, to which we were meant to scribble an answer. Given time, I could arrive at the correct answer, but here speed was important, though no great matter hung on the outcome of the problem solving. I was not used to failing at anything, and resented the exercise both because it seemed foolish to me and because I could not do it well. On the other hand, because I read so much, I could excel at spelling bees. Our parents had taught us to be the best at everything we did, but the things we were supposed to excel in had always before had some practical purpose. Now I was introduced to competition as an end in itself.

When the bell rang for recess or lunch, my heart sank because I knew no one and had no subject of conversation remotely like the cheerful chatter which swirled around about weekend activities. Queenwood was a day school and there were no other girls from the bush there. It was painful when others talked happily about their fathers or boasted about the family fortunes. I couldn't join in either, and became slowly aware that my family and life circumstances were unusual. I was always relieved when it rained and we ate lunch at our desks, for the rain freed me from steeling myself to speak to someone or from making myself walk up to join a group.

Each afternoon I was exhausted, not by the schoolwork, which mostly seemed very easy, but by the stress of coping with so many people and trying to guess what the rules were for each new situation. I came alive on the walk home, a walk which could take forty minutes. The way wound along a pleasant street which skirted the side of a steep cliff for about half a mile. My route then proceeded by three steep flights of stairs zigzagging up the cliff face, to a point at the top where I could see the Harbor and smell the ocean. Then I climbed more gently along pretty suburban streets until I came to Stanton Road, traversed its easy incline to the very top of the hill, where number 42 stood set back in a garden filled with roses and honeysuckle. Most of my schoolmates lived in different directions, so that I relished my walk alone.

Often I came home to a novel situation. My mother might be out, visiting friends, spending time with her eighty-five-year-old mother, conferring with business advisers. With each day that passed in our new way of life, I could see her body relaxing. She was still haunted by grief at the past and by anxiety about the future, but the lines of tension disappeared from her body. She ate well, began to sleep more regularly, and relished the company of our hospitable landlady and her family. Friends came also to take her out to dinner, and I would watch with interest as she set out, the embodiment of elegance in her remaining stylish clothes, leftovers from her holidays in Sydney with my father in the thirties. On most days after I arrived home, we had a leisurely afternoon tea gazing at the Harbor, and then we read for an hour or so before dinner. My mother no longer read to educate herself, but for escape. Now the pile of books beside her chair came from a local lending library; they were the conventional romances and detective stories with which other housewives whiled away the hours. Without ever discussing it, we agreed that my time for children's stories was over. Instead we relished the same detective stories and same spy stories, discovering who could identify the murderer or recognize the villain.

My brothers arrived home regularly for weekends from boarding school. This was a new pleasure for us all. We began to enjoy one another's companionship as children and adolescents rather than as busy workers at the never-ending tasks of Coorain. My brothers and I explored the neighborhood and the surrounding suburbs, orienting ourselves by scrambling around the shoreline from the beach closest to our house. We would return filled with stories about feats of climbing, or of inadvertent trespass on some grand beachfront property, and occasionally the wilder stories would make my mother laugh wholeheartedly.

My brother Bob was usually the story-teller. Then in his last year at school, he was close to six feet tall and handsome in a striking way. His graceful and well-proportioned body radiated energy. His blue eyes blazed with intellect and zest for life, and they lit up a face remarkable for beauty and regularity of feature. His fair tanned skin and thick crop of golden hair made him appear clean and freshly dressed even at the conclusion of a particularly muddy Rugby game. He had grown to young manhood possessing a rare gentleness of spirit, along with fierce integrity, and a readiness to show his love of music and poetry even though the conventional male culture encouraged a laconic and aggressive masculinity. He was unaware of his physical beauty and cheerfully unassuming in his dealings with people. My mother adored him, as did his younger brother and sister.

Like everyone in his generation at school, he had grown up expecting to volunteer at the earliest possible age for the R.A.A.F., as had his friends who left King's a few years ahead of him. The sudden loss of my father, the end of the war in the Pacific, and our move to Sydney left him a little at sea about the immediate next stage in his life. All its expected patterns had been transformed into a new set of questions. For the moment, as we enjoyed the luxury of being together at leisure, he was ready to tease my mother lightheartedly about her old-fashioned ways. He made her listen to American popular music, provoked her by calling her Ma, instead of the hitherto required Mother, and insisted that some of her more Draconian rules for us younger children be relaxed.

My brother Barry, at fifteen, had the same wonderful gentleness of character combined with strength of will and integrity. He had had less high-spirited fun at school than Bob. A mistaken medical opinion rendered early in his school career had convinced my mother that he should not be allowed to play sports. This was a real hardship in a school which revolved around athletics. Worse still, the bush child's susceptibility to infections had really disadvantaged him in class, because of repeated absences and hardness of hearing brought about by neglected infections. He was thus more silent than Bob, and less ebullient in spirit, but as his transition from adolescence began we saw intimations of his later wiry frame, handsome lean features, and great concern for the care of others.

Our life could be relatively carefree because my mother and I were still in transition, and the pressing questions of my brothers' lives were deferred by the moratorium of their school years. My mother's urge to control her offspring was not yet at odds with their development, and so our first months together in Sydney were golden. In the long run, if Coorain continued to produce no income, we could not afford our flat in the lovely house in Mosman, nor would we fit there at the end of the year when Bob finished his last year at boarding school. My mother's careful choice of spacious rooms and wide vistas gave us an interlude of recuperation before facing up to some of the pressing problems presented by the drought and our father's death.

After eight weeks of daily battles with my shyness, I was released by the same bush child's lack of immunity to infection which had plagued my brothers when they came to the city. On the way home from school one mild afternoon, I found myself stopping to rest at the top of each flight of stairs traversing the cliff along my route home. When I reached Stanton Road, our landlady, busy at dividing her Michaelmas daisies in the front garden of number 42, looked up to greet me and exclaimed "You're very flushed. Come here and let me feel your forehead." Testing my fever with an expert hand, she instructed me to go upstairs, lie down till she brought me tea, and then to wait keeping very warm until my mother arrived home. Doing as instructed, I noticed the room waving around and my teeth chattering, although I felt hotter than in the worst heat wave at Coorain.

The doctor, quickly summoned by my mother on her return, announced that I had a streptococcal infection and, golden words, that I must be kept at home until my fever subsided. Subside it did not, and later in the week, straining to hear the lowered voices, I heard him tell my mother that I had pneumonia and pleurisy and must be hospitalized. She announced firmly that no special nurse or hospital staff could give a child better care than she could. My memory of her in the weeks that ensued is clear. She was a wonderful nurse, and a natural healer. She never tired, seemed never to sleep, and her close observation of her patient meant that she knew how I was feeling before I could tell her something hurt.

My recovery was ensured when some of the new, miraculous sulfa drugs developed during the war were procured, and my fever abated as swiftly as it had come. My brothers had taken it in turns to come home from school on weekends to sit by my bed and read to me, and on my first weekend up we had a royal party. I liked being the invalid center of attention, especially as I had been freed from the daily ordeal of school.

Even as she seemed preoccupied with caring for me, my mother was facing up to the realities of our situation. It had not rained at Coorain, and there was no likelihood of income from the place in the coming year. In only a few weeks, Bob would finish his final year at King's, and some less expensive and more spacious quarters must be found to house us all. As soon as I could be left to amuse myself for the day, she set out answering advertisements for rooms in return for housekeeping, or for the care of an elderly or sick person. By the time I was putting in a final two weeks at Queenwood, she had found the opportunity she was seeking —half a house available in return for house-keeping and cooking for an elderly widower in the suburb of Waitara, some thirty minutes' ride by train north of the city center on what we learned to call the North Shore.

Waitara was our first introduction to the delights of Sydney suburbs, where the houses had gardens filled with native Australian plants and shrubs, and the air was permanently filled with the aroma of eucalyptus. We heard our first kookaburras there, learned the varieties of bottlebrush trees and boronias, and saw our first waratah in bloom. We were a tight fit into our half of the house, and it was soon apparent that my mother's standards of housekeeping were too exacting for our landlord. He liked to have his friendly Corgi and Welsh terrier sleep in his room, and his amiable cat was free to roam the house. My mother, convinced that animals carried hazardous germs, was perpetually shooing them from the kitchen and surreptitiously cleaning the landlord's room when he wasn't looking.

Because Christmas recalled our father's death, it was a difficult feast for us. Nevertheless, we had one of my mother's succulent roast turkeys and her ambrosial plum puddings before the boys left to spend the rest of the summer at Coorain. During January, we began to talk seriously about where I would attend school. My mother was daunted by the prospect of more private school fees as our debts grew and our assets dwindled. Did I think I would like the local state school? she asked me. We could see it each time we took a train—it was right beside the railway station, empty at present, surrounded by an acre of unkempt ground. I was startled. I had taken on my parents' values sufficiently to see this proposal as a distinct coming down in the world. Recognizing the worry in my mother's eyes, I said I would.

The first day of school in February was hot, 105 degrees. The school, a brick building with an iron roof, was like a furnace, and its inhabitants, teachers and students, wilted as the day wore on. I hated it from the moment I walked in the door. I was a snob, and I knew the accents of the teachers and most of the students were wrong by the exacting standards we'd had drummed into us at home. Worse still was the unruly behavior of everyone of every age. Boys pulled my hair when I refused to answer questions I took as rude or impudent; girls stuck out their tongues and used bad language. Teachers lost their tempers and caned pupils in front of the class. Few books were opened as the staff waged a losing battle to establish order. Recess and lunchtime were purgatorial. Crowds, or so it seemed to me, of jeering boys and a few girls gathered around to taunt me about my accent. "Stuck up, ain't you," they yelled, as I faced them in stubborn silence.

They were right. Now I was in a more diverse social universe than I had known at Coorain. I had no idea how to behave or what the rules were for managing social boundaries. I had been friends, one could say special friends, with Shorty, or with Ron Kelly, but that was in a simple world where we each knew our respective places. Here, I knew only that the old rules could not possibly apply. Everyone around me spoke broad Australian, a kind of speech my parents' discipline had ruthlessly eliminated. My interrogators could unquestionably be described by that word my mother used as a blanket condemnation of lower-class people, customs, and forms of behavior. They were "common." My encounter was a classic confrontation for the Australia of my generation.

I, the carefully respectable copier of British manners, was being called to raucous and high-spirited account by the more vital and unquestionably authentic Australian popular culture. I was too uncertain to cope. I faced them in silence till the bell rang and we returned to the pandemonium of the unruly classroom.

After school, the same group assembled to escort me home to the accompaniment of catcalls and vivid commentaries on my parentage. I knew these city children could not outlast someone who was used to walking ten or twelve miles a day behind a herd of sheep, so our comic crocodile set out. I, stalking in front in frozen indignation, my attendant chorus gradually wilting as I led them along hot pavements and across streets where the heat had begun to melt the tarmac. After the last one had tired and dropped away, I made my way home where my mother was ostentatiously doing nothing in the front garden, on the watch for my arrival.

We had our afternoon tea in blissful silence. Finally she asked me how the day had gone. "It was all right," I said, determined not to complain. She studied my face thoughtfully. "You don't have to go back," she said. "I made a mistake. That's not the right school for you." Years later, I asked how she guessed what my day had been like. "I didn't have to ask," she said. "You were a child whose face was always alight with curiosity. When you came home that day, your face was closed. I knew you wouldn't learn anything there."

In fact, had I persevered I would have learned a great deal, though little of it from the harassed and overworked teachers in the ill-equipped classrooms. I'd have been obliged to come to terms with the Australian class system, and to see my family's world from the irreverent and often hilarious perspective of the Australian working class. It would have been invaluable knowledge, and my vision of Australia would have been the better for it. It was to take me another fifteen years to see the world from my own Australian perspective, rather than from the British definition taught to my kind of colonial. On the other hand, had I learned that earthy irreverence in my schooldays, it would have ruled out the appreciation of high culture in any form. My mother had no training for that appreciation, but she knew instinctively to seek it for her children. She did not reflect much about the underlying conflicts in Australian culture. She was simply determined that I would be brought up to abhor anything "common," and that, despite her financial worries, I would have the best education available in the Australia she knew.

The next day, my mother acted decisively. By some wizardry peculiarly hers, she persuaded the headmistress of Abbotsleigh, one of the most academically demanding of the private schools for girls in Sydney, to accept me as a pupil in the last year of the Junior School. Although there were long waiting lists for admission to the school, I was to begin at once, as a day girl, and become a boarder the next term.

Before being formally enrolled, I was taken for an interview with Miss Everett, the headmistress. To me she seemed like a benevolent being from another planet. She was over six feet tall, with the carriage and gait of a splendid athlete. Her dress was new to me. She wore a tweed suit of soft colors and battered elegance. She spoke in the plummy tones of a woman educated in England, and her intelligent face beamed with humor and curiosity. When she spoke, the habit of long years of teaching French made her articulate her words clearly and so forcefully that the unwary who stood too close were in danger of being sprayed like the audience too close to the footlights of a vaudeville show. "She looks strapping," she cheerfully commented to my mother, after talking to me for a few minutes alone. "She can begin tomorrow." Thereafter, no matter how I misbehaved, or what events brought me into her presence, I felt real benevolence radiating from Miss Everett.

The sight of her upright figure, forever striding across the school grounds, automatically caused her charges to straighten their backs. Those who slouched were often startled to have her appear suddenly behind them and seize their shoulders to correct their posture. Perhaps because she liked my stiff back we began a friendship that mattered greatly in my future. I never ceased to wonder at her, for Miss Everett was the first really free spirit I had ever met. She was impatient with bourgeois Australian culture, concerned about ideas, restless with the constraints of a Board of Trustees dominated by the low church evangelical Anglican archdiocese of Sydney, and she never bothered to conceal her feelings. She had been a highly successful amateur athlete, and had earned her first degree in French literature at the Sorbonne. After Paris, she had studied modern literature in Germany. To me and to many others, she was a true bearer of European cultural ideals in Australia. She loved learning for itself, and this made her a most unusual schoolteacher. The academic mentality in the Australia of my childhood focused on knowledge as a credential, a body of information one had to use as a mechanic would his tools. With her French training, she saw her academic task as one of conveying to her charges the kinds of disciplines which released the mind for creativity and speculation. This, to many of her peers, was a subversive goal. She was a successful headmistress because she was also an astute politician, bending before the winds of provincial prejudice whenever they blew strongly over issues of discipline and behavior. But it was characteristic of her that she made her mind up about flouting the waiting lists of daughters of old girls because she'd been struck during our ten minutes together by the range of my vocabulary. My mother and I had had a hard few years, she had remarked to get us started. "Yes," I said, "we have lived through a great natural catastrophe." She wanted eleven-year-olds who thought that way in her school and cheerfully ignored the admission rules.

Thereafter, I hurried quickly past the desert of the local state school to the railway station and rode the seven minutes south to Wahroonga, the suburb of my new school. On my path homeward, I only once saw my former attendant chorus ranging restlessly about the local state school grounds. Seeing me, they took flight like a flock of birds, alighting by the fence as I strode past. I was prepared for hostility, but they were remarkably genial. "We don't blame you for leaving this fucking school, Jill," the ringleader shouted cheerfully. "It's no bloody good." I was too young and insecure to wonder what a good school might have made of such high-spirited pupils, and I had as yet no sense of injustice that the difference between our chances for education were as night and day. At Abbotsleigh, even though I was immediately ushered into a classroom of thirty-six total strangers, it seemed as though I had already arrived in paradise. Many students were boarders from distant country areas who had also had to overcome their shyness and become social beings. At breaks between classes they understood my tongue-tied silence. I was placed at a desk next to one of the kindest and most helpful members of the class, and two girls were deputed to see to it that I was not lonely my first day. I could scarcely believe my good fortune. Better still, the teacher, Miss Webb, a woman in her late twenties, knew exactly when to put the class to work, and when to relax and allow high spirits to run relatively free. Our classroom was an orderly and harmonious place where the subjects were taught well and the students encouraged to learn. Even the strange ritual of the gymnasium was less puzzling. The teachers were used to bush children and took the time to explain what the exercises were for, or to tell me that I would soon learn the eye-hand coordination I lacked.

Our curriculum was inherited from Great Britain, and consequently it was utterly untouched by progressive notions in education. We took English grammar, complete with parsing and analysis, we were drilled in spelling and punctuation, we read English poetry and were tested in scansion, we read English fiction, novels, and short stories and analyzed the style. Each year, we studied a Shakespeare play, committing much of it to memory, and performing scenes from it on April 23 in honor of Shakespeare's birthday.

We might have been in Sussex for all the attention we paid to Australian poetry and prose. It did not count. We, for our part, dutifully learned Shakespeare's imagery drawn from the English landscape and from English horticulture. We memorized Keats's "Ode to Autumn" or Shelley on the skylark without ever having seen the progression of seasons and the natural world they referred to. This gave us the impression that great poetry and fiction were written by and about people and places far distant from Australia. Palgrave's *Golden Treasury* or the Oxford collection of romantic poetry we read were so beautiful it didn't seem to matter, though to us poetry was more like incantation than related to the rhythms of our own speech. As for landscape, we learned by implication that ours was ugly, because it deviated totally from the landscape of the Cotswolds and the Lake Country, or the romantic hills and valleys of Constable.

After English (eight classes a week) came history (five times a week). We learned about Roman Britain and memorized a wonderful jumble of Angles, Saxons, Picts, and Boadicea. In geography (three times a week), we studied the great rivers of the world. They were the Ganges, the Indus, the Amazon, the Plate, the Rhine, the Danube, the Nile, the Congo, the St. Lawrence, and the Mississippi. When the question was raised, Australia was defined once again by default. Our vast continent had no great river system; its watercourses flowed inland to Lake Eyre, an anomaly which was quickly dismissed as a distraction from the business at hand. Once a week, we read scripture, sticking to the Old Testament and learning its geography as a distraction from its bloodthirsty tribal battles. Nothing in the instruction suggested that this sacred subject bore any relation to our daily lives, although because we read the Bible, we were supposed to be particularly well behaved during this class.

In mathematics, we studied arithmetic and simple geometry, five times a week. The textbooks were English, and the problems to be solved assumed another natural environment. It was possible to do them all as a form of drill without realizing that the mathematical imagination helped one explore and analyze the continuities and discontinuities of the order which lay within and beneath natural phenomena. We learned to treat language as magical, but not numbers and their relationships. Somehow we knew that mathematics was important, as a form of intellectual discipline. However, our problems to solve had to do with shopping and making change, pumping water from one receptacle to another at constant volumes, or measuring the areas of things. These did not encourage the visualizing of shapes and relationships, let alone hint at the wonders of physics.

Once a week we had choir lessons, lessons in painting and drawing, and in sewing. The sewing was of the nonutilitarian type, embroidery or crewel work. The art concerned lessons in perspective, conveyed with no historical context describing the development of Western ideas about the representation of objects. Choir was group instruction in singing and the reading of music. All these practical subjects assumed some previous background which I did not possess, so that I fiddled away the hour and a half appearing busy enough to escape rebuke, but never really undertaking any project. In choir, I soon learned that I could not carry a tune and that it was better to move my mouth soundlessly and look interested. My imagination might have been fired by reproductions of great painting and sculpture, but we did not look at them. Nor did our classes ever hint at the great body of Australian painting which already existed, or the vitality of the artistic efflorescence taking place in our own city even as we studied. As with our study of art, we were not taught what music *was*. It was enough that a lady knew how to carry a tune and to read music. Those who were talented mastered performance, but the rest of us were left to learn about music and dance as forms of expression on our own.

Although our curriculum ignored our presence in Australia, the school itself demonstrated how the Australian landscape could be enhanced by a discerning eye. Its ample grounds were a far cry from the barren setting of my local state school with its hot dusty building and gritty yard. It stood on twenty or so acres rising up a hillside toward one of the highest points of the gentle hills which made up the terrain between Sydney Harbor and the entrance to the Hawkesbury River, to the north of the Harbor. The school's residential buildings clustered along the main highway running north from Sydney, the Pacific Highway. Behind them, close to the main entrance, two groups of classroom buildings formed a quadrangle with a residence and the administration buildings. Patches of bush had been manicured a little to control steep grades down to two levels of playing fields. Paths led to more dispersed dormitories, and around them were plantings which created places for day students to sit outside at lunch, and for boarders to enjoy during the weekend. Rose gardens, jacarandas, jasmine, honeysuckle, mock-orange, peach, plum, and quince trees perfumed the air in spring, and the planting pulled out the contours of the land without interrupting the sense of the wildness of the pockets of bush skillfully left to separate different grades and functional areas. Tucked away at the northern end were banks of tennis courts and closer to the main buildings were basketball courts and a sunken court with a high cement wall at which budding tennis stars honed their backhand and leapt to smash their forehand drive.

In this setting thronged some three hundred pupils in the Junior School, and another eight hundred or so students in high school grades. Much about our way of life symbolized the colonial mentality. Its signs were visible in the maps on our classroom walls, extended depictions of the globe with much of Africa, all of the Indian subcontinent, parts of Southeast Asia, half of North America, colored the bright red of the British Empire. Our uniforms, copies of those of English schools, indicated that we were only partially at home in our environment. In winter, we wore pine green tunics, cream blouses, green flannel blazers, dark brown cotton stockings, green velour hats, and brown cotton gloves. In summer, we wore starched green linen dresses with cream collars, the same blazer, beige socks, a cream panama hat, and the same brown gloves. Woe betide the student caught shedding the blazer or the gloves in public, even when the thermometer was over 100 degrees. She was letting down the school, behaving unbecomingly, and betraying the code involved in becoming a lady. Ladies, we learned, did not consider comfort more important than propriety in dress or manners. Disciplinary action was taken instantly when it was learned that an Abbotsleigh student had not leapt to her feet in train or bus to offer her seat to an older person, male or female. Speaking loudly, sitting in public in any fashion except bolt upright with a ramrod-straight back, were likewise sorts of behavior which let down the school. When the more rebellious asked why this was so, the answer was clear and unequivocal. We were an elite. We were privileged girls and young women who had an obligation to represent the best standards of behavior to the world at large. The best standards were derived from Great Britain, and should be emulated unquestioningly.

Those were the standards which had led to such a sizable part of the map of the globe being colored red, and we let them slip at our peril. No one paused to think that gloves and blazers had a function in damp English springs which they lacked entirely in our blazing summers.

Speech was another important aspect of deportment. One's voice must be well modulated and purged of all ubiquitous Australian diphthongs. Teachers were tireless in pointing them out and stopping the class until the offender got the word right. Drills of "how now brown cow" might have us all scarlet in the face with choked schoolgirl laughter, but they were serious matters for our instructors, ever on guard against the diphthongs that heralded cultural decline.

The disciplinary system also modeled the British heritage. We were an elite. Ergo we were born to be leaders. However, the precise nature of the leadership was by no means clear. For some of our mentors, excelling meant a fashionable marriage and leadership in philanthropy. For others, it meant intellectual achievement and the aspiration to a university education. Since the great majority of the parents supporting the school favored the first definition, the question of the social values which should inform leadership was carefully glossed over. Eminence in the school's hierarchy could come from being a lively and cheerful volunteer, a leader in athletics, or from intellectual achievement. The head girl was always carefully chosen to offend no particular camp aligned behind the competing definitions. She was always a good-natured all-rounder.

The discipline code and the manner of its administration might well have been designed to prepare us to be subalterns in the Indian army, or district officers in some remote jungle colony. The routine running of the school was managed by class captains and prefects selected by the headmistress. Prefects administered the rules of behavior and imposed penalties without there being any recourse to a higher authority. Cheating or letting down the side were far more serious offenses than failures of sensitivity. Theft was the ultimate sin. It being Australia, prowess at sports excused most breaches of the rules or failures of decorum. Bookishness and dislike for physical activity, on the other hand, aroused dark suspicions and warranted disciplinary action for the slightest infringement of the rules.

Hardiness was deemed more important

than imagination. Indeed, an observer might have believed that the school's founders had been inspired by John Locke and Mistress Masham. Boarders rose at 6:30 A.M. to take cold showers even in midwinter. The aim was to encourage everyone to run at least a mile before breakfast, although slugabeds and poor planners could manage a frantic dash for breakfast without too frequent rebukes.

While this regimen might be seen as a precursor of later obsessions with health and fitness, our diet undid whatever benefits our routine of exercise conferred. We lived on starch, overcooked meat, and endless eggs and bacon. Fruit appeared in one's diet only if parents intervened and arranged for special supplies to be made available outside meal hours. Slabs of bread and butter accompanied every meal, so that the slimmest figures thickened and susceptible complexions became blotchy.

What meals lacked in culinary style they made up for in formality. A mistress or a sixth-form boarder sat at the head of each long rectangular table. The rest of us, bathed and changed into a required green velvet dress for evenings, sat in descending order of age and class until the youngest and most recently arrived sat at the distant foot of the table. Food was served by the teacher or sixth former at the head of the table, and the rules of conduct decreed that one might not ask for more or less, and that one must endure in silence until someone farther up the table noticed that one needed salt, pepper, butter, tea, or whatever seasonings made our tasteless dishes palatable. Foibles in food were not tolerated. If a student refused to eat the main dish and the teacher in charge noticed, it would be served to her again at subsequent meals until it was deemed that a satisfactory amount had been consumed. The youngest were required to wait to be spoken to before starting a conversation, as though those seated higher up the table were royalty. People who made too much noise or displayed unseemly manners were sent from the room and left hungry until the next meal.

All these rules might have made for stilted behavior, but in fact, they barely subdued the roar of conversation in the boarders' dining room, and only modestly curtailed the animal spirits of the younger students intent at one and the same time on getting more than their share of food, and on whatever form of mischief might disconcert the figure of authority seated at the head of the table.

After I became a boarder in my second term, I looked forward to the two hours which followed dinner, hours when the whole boarding population gathered for carefully supervised preparation for the next day's classes. I could usually finish what was required in short order, and then I could relish the quiet. The day of classes and the afternoon of games seemed to my bush consciousness to be too full of voices. I liked to sit and read poetry, to race ahead in the history book and ponder the events described. I also liked occasionally to manage some feat of wickedness in total silence, such as to wriggle undetected from one end of the "prep" room to the other to deliver some innocuous note or message. Ron Kelly's training in hunting had given me the patience required to move silently, and the satisfaction of going about my own business rather than following orders appealed to me deeply.

Much of my time during the first year or so of my schooling at Abbotsleigh was taken up with the pleasure of defying adult authority and systematically flouting the rules. Lights out in the evening was merely a license to begin to roam about the school, to climb out the window and appear as a somewhat dusty apparition in someone else's dormitory. Restrictions on what one could bring back to school in the way of food were an invitation to figure out the multifarious opportunities for concealing forbidden chocolates, sponge cakes, fruit cakes, soft drinks, and other bulky items as one returned to school from weekly trips to the dentist or weekends of freedom at midterm. Locks on the door of the tuck-shop were no barrier to country children used to dismantling doors and reassembling them.

These escapades were natural reactions to regimentation. They were also my first opportunity to rebel without the danger of doing psychological damage to adults of whom I was prematurely the care giver. It was a delicious and heady feeling undimmed even when my mother was told of my misbehavior. She took it that I was keeping bad company, although this was hardly reflected in my academic performance. I knew that I was being perversely carefree and irresponsible for the first time in my life. I could not articulate a criticism of my mother yet, but I could see the pretenses behind many of the school's rules, and I enjoyed being hypercritical of the people who tried to make me sleep and wake to a schedule, always wear clean socks on Sundays, and never forget my gloves when leaving the school.

After one rebellious scrape led to my being gated over the Easter break, my mother called on Miss Everett and began to apologize for my bad conduct. Miss Everett, with an imperious wave of the hand, interrupted her in mid-sentence. "My dear Mrs. Ker, don't fuss. There's nothing to worry about. I've yet to see Jill's mind fully extended, and I look forward to the day when I do. When she's really interested, she'll forget about breaking rules." These comments, duly reported to my brothers, led to much teasing, and examinations of my head to detect signs of stretching, but they also gave me some freedom from my mother's pressure for perfect conduct, freedom which I badly needed.

I was not a popular student. No one could call me pretty. I had ballooned on the school's starchy diet, developed a poor complexion, and I looked the embodiment of adolescent ungainliness. Moreover, my pride prevented me from seizing opportunities to correct my lack of coordination. I could not bear to begin tennis lessons with the seven-year-old beginners, but could not pretend to play like my classmates, who had been coached for years. A month after arriving as a boarder, I purchased a magnifying glass, found a quiet spot in the sun, and burned the carefully inscribed name off my tennis racket. Once I was satisfied with the job, I turned the racket in at the school's lost property office and escaped further lessons by bewailing the loss of my racket. Basketball was different. Everyone was beginning that game more or less as I began. With diligence my height could be turned to advantage and I earned a place on a team. Thereafter, afternoons could be filled with basketball practice, and Saturday mornings with competition. I liked the excitement of the game, although I never learned to treat a game as a game, and not to care about losing.

I was as intellectually precocious as I was socially inept. I never understood the unspoken rule which required that one display false modesty and hang back when there was a task to be done, waiting to be asked to undertake it. I also took a long time to learn the social hierarchies of the place: whose parents were very rich, whose family had titled relatives in England, whose mother dressed in the height of fashion, which families owned the most stylish holiday retreats. My boarder friends were mainly the daughters of the real backcountry, people who were homesick for the bush and their families and accepted the school as a term which must be served uncomplainingly.

I liked getting out from under the pressure of my mother's company, but at the same time, I was burdened by the sense that she had taken on two jobs, a secretarial one by day and a nursing one at night, in order to pay my fees. As soon as she had delivered me to Abbotsleigh as a boarder, my mother moved back to my grandmother's house, settled Bob in a rented room down the road, and began to work in earnest. Once she had satisfied herself that she could earn enough to pay Barry's and my school fees and pay the rent for herself and my older brother, she began to concentrate her energies on the kind of investment which would be needed to make Coorain profitable again. She had no thought of selling it, but planned to revive it as a sheep-raising venture once it rained. She had a sure instinct for the economics of a small business, and long before others in our drought-stricken district began to think about restocking, she had realized that if she waited for the rain to fall before buying sheep, the price would be so high it would be years before she paid off the cost of the purchase. Once the drought had broken in areas two to three hundred miles from Coorain, she began to look for suitable sale sheep to form the basis for rebuilding the Coorain flock. She planned to hire a drover to walk her purchases through the stock routes in country where the rains had come until the drought broke at Coorain. On the day she borrowed sixteen hundred pounds from her woolbroker and signed the papers to purchase twelve hundred Merino ewes, she arrived home to learn that there had been two and a half inches of rain at Coorain. The value of her purchase had doubled within a matter of hours and she was rightly jubilant. Two weeks later, there was another inch and a half of rain and by the time the new sheep were delivered by their drover to Coorain, it was producing luxuriant pasture. From that day on our finances were assured, thanks to her inspired gamble.

None of the new earnings were frittered away on improving our style of life. Instead, every penny went back into building up the property, replacing buried fences, repairing the stockyards, buying new equipment. My mother kept on at one of her jobs, found us an inexpensive house to rent in an unfashionable, lower-middle-class suburb to the west of the city, and gradually began to re-unite the family.

The reunion at the end of my second term as a boarder at Abbotsleigh brought together a group of young people on the edge of major life changes. Bob, at nineteen, was a young man impatient to savor life, and in search of the adventure he had once expected to find in wartime. Barry, at seventeen, was intent on leaving the King's School before completing high school. He had by then been in boarding school for seven years, and he was convinced that he would learn more from work experience and evening study than during an eighth year of routine in the closed world of the school he no longer enjoyed. I, approaching thirteen years old, looked and felt an awkward adolescent. Our mother, now in her forty-ninth year, looked her years, but she had regained some of her old vitality. Release from stress, and the chance to recoup the family fortunes at Coorain, had restored some of her beautiful coloring and brought back a sparkle to her eyes.

Although many men friends, including our favorite, Angus Waugh, tried to per-suade her to marry again, she rebuffed them all. She had loved our father deeply, and she clearly did not want to share the raising of their children with anyone else. She still found herself swept by waves of anger and grief at his loss. Strangers who sat opposite her in the train or the local bus would occasionally be startled by the gaze of hatred she turned on them. She would literally be possessed by rage that other men were alive while her husband was dead.

The intensity of her feelings did not bode well for anyone's peace of mind as we children moved at various paces toward adulthood. She was out of touch with the mood of the postwar world we were entering. She now found it hard to imagine vocations for her sons except the land and the life of a grazier. The boys, understandably, given our recent experiences, did not want to embark on that path. I, for my part, was teetering on the edge of a more mature awareness of the people in my world. I found my brothers entrancing, developed romantic crushes on their friends, and tagged along as often as possible on their diversions.

These were mainly concerned with music, music being the one sociable activity at home my mother approved of and encouraged. Bob began to study the trumpet, Barry the clarinet, while their circle of friends revolved around jazz concerts, listening to recordings of the great jazz musicians, and studying music theory. Our tiny rented house was often crammed with young men participating in or listening to the latest jazz session. When the small living room could not contain the noise of the excited improvisation, I would be dispatched to sit on the curb across the street to listen and report how it really sounded. Doubtless, had we lived in a stuffier neighborhood there would have been complaints about the noise. Our kindly neighbors approved of a widowed mother keeping her sons at home and away from the Australian obsession with pubs and gambling.

My mother's code of thrift, sobriety, and industry had served her well growing up in a simpler Australian society, but it had little appeal for her children, hungry for excitement and experience, and made aware of a more complex society by their urban schooling. Postwar Australia was a society transformed by the economic stimulus of the Second World War. In contrast to the cautious mentality inherited by the generation shaped by the Depression, we were agog with the excitement of prosperity, and the questions raised by Australia's wartime contact with American culture. We went to

American movies, used American slang, and listened to American music.

The boys, reluctant to remain dependent on their widowed mother, seized the best jobs they could find, unaware that it was in their long-term interest to attend university and acquire professional training. In my mother's generation, higher education was a luxury available to a tiny elite. In ours, it would become a necessary doorway to opportunity. The choice of early employment meant that Bob and Barry did not find excitement and challenge in the fairly routine tasks which made up their jobs with woolbrokers. They sought excitement instead in music, and later in the world of fast cars and road racing. By reason of my gender, I was not marked out for a career connected with the land. Moreover, as our finances improved it was possible for my mother to dream that I would fulfill her ambition: attend university and become a doctor. So the stereotypes of gender worked in my favor. Unlike my brothers, I grew up knowing that my life would be lived in peacetime, and that it was an unspoken expectation that I would finish high school and attend the University of Sydney.

In 1948, my fourteenth year, my mother decided that the returns from Coorain were substantial enough to permit buying a proper house for us in Sydney. She chose a wonderful modern house in Pennant Hills, a suburb far from the city to the northwest but close enough to Abbotsleigh for me to become a day student. There was a bedroom for each of us, a wonderful garden, and a vast room to house our piano, a table-tennis table, and as much music as we cared to make. She was confident enough of the future to stop her office work and take up the role of suburban housewife and mother. Thus, rebel that she was, she settled incongruously into the model domesticity that was to be the ideal of the fifties. She dreamed of the perfect house and garden, inhabited by handsome and intelligent children, busy with flocks of friends, the entire group revolving around her powerful maternal figure.

For a little while, we actually lived the dream. Bob's life was taken up with piano lessons, music theory, and a growing interest in classical music. Now six feet four and a half in height, he was so handsome that people turned to stare at him on the street. Women and men alike found him instantly attractive, and he made friends easily with people of all ages. He seemed unconscious of his striking physical beauty, and was likely to take his little sister along to concerts as well as the young lady of the moment. He was unaffectedly happy at his progress as a pianist, tireless in practicing, and always ready to supervise my first efforts at the keyboard when I arrived home from school. Because he thought it important, he went along with me to the youth concerts of the Sydney symphony orchestra to enlarge my musical education and encourage my beginning interest in performance.

Barry, now eighteen, promised to be as tall, though of slighter physique. He and Bob shared an interest in all things mechanical, especially cars, motorcycles, and the finer points of automotive design. The ancient sports cars of their friends were frequently pulled up outside our garage, while clusters of sun-bleached blond heads bent intently over temperamental engines, or while the group gazed silently at some wonder of engineering.

On my fourteenth birthday, the two boys presented me with my first grown-up dress. It represented their recognition of my early maturity, a recognition that startled my mother, who was reluctant to recognize that I was no longer a child. In fact, I was five feet six inches tall, emerging from my schoolgirl pudginess, and by turns precocious and childish. I circled happily around my brothers' world and joined their expeditions, becoming as familiar with the language of sporting car enthusiasts as I already was with jazz.

Because of the attractions of my brothers' company, I did not connect fully with my own generation. My school friends, now a lively and intelligent group of day students, began to discuss their romantic attachments with their counterparts at the neighboring boys' schools, but I was too entranced by my brothers and their friends to share the interest. I was also too shy to strike out on my own and move beyond the world provided for me by family and school. I spent much time at weekends with my mother, and slipped back into the role of her confidante and emotional support. She would pour out her considerable body of worries to me, for as our financial pressures eased, her anxieties were simply redirected. She worried about whether my brothers' friends were suitable, about simple decisions relating to the management of Coorain, and ominously, this most vigorous of women began to worry about her health. Feminist though she was, she did not question the accepted wisdom which defined the menopause as a time of ill health. She counted every hot flash or night of interrupted sleep as a portent of disaster to come, and her confidences led me to see her as in delicate health. I was at a loss to offer relief from her worries, and there was sadly little in our environment to take her mind off them. Had she continued working in the city, friends might have got her to the theater, concerts, and lectures. As it was, she paced her lovely house, worried endlessly, and waited for her children to come home.

As Miss Everett had predicted, I began almost without noticing it to become absorbed in my studies at school, and it was these rather than the entertainments of my school friends which drew me into a world outside the family. Chemistry and biology were not just subjects, they offered the vision of an ordered material and living universe, whose elements and their components were arranged in complex patterns, the principles of which were dazzlingly simple. The wonder of making crystals and understanding the reasons why they formed left me so preoccupied I missed my stop on the afternoon train, and had trouble explaining why I was so late home. History classes now treated the question of causation, leaving the memorization of dates for larger questions of free will and determinism. Our study of Shakespeare was no longer the prettier comedies, but *Henry V*, opening the possibility of seeing history as a glittering pageant of greed, ambition, nobility, courage, and suffering.

I became possessed with the need to understand the world which produced Shakespeare, and began to comb the catalogues of my mother's lending library for books on Tudor England. By accident, I came upon my first of Shakespeare's sonnets, and was launched on reading about the Dark Lady guided by Miss Shell, one of the learned and brilliant literary scholars who taught English to the senior classes at Abbotsleigh.

I began to do very well academically, except in mathematics, an area in which the Abbotsleigh of my day displayed a tragicomic flaw. Much as we all admired Miss Everett, we could not help holding her accountable for her selection of Miss Allen as the vice-principal of the school. Miss Allen, who taught senior mathematics, had the mind for detail and the passion for order which meant that she was more than willing to assume responsibility for working out the yearly class schedule. She flourished at administering stern rebukes to students who had misbehaved, and she throve on intimidating the younger teachers. She liked to be feared, and managed her classrooms by instilling fear in her charges. Her voice, usually sharp, would become soft and liquid as some poor student blundered from error to error in algebra. We all knew that she was savoring the chance to show up stupidity and that she would drag out the ordeal with feigned patience, until she turned with a sickly smile in the last minutes of the class to elicit the correct answer from someone who had known it all along. She was an extremely poor teacher whose temper could flare into hysterics if the students she regarded as gifted mathematically ever failed to get the point. Then her books would be slammed on the teacher's desk, she would utter cries of rage and frustration, and sweep sobbing from the room.

We could not comprehend why such a person was kept in authority, and were too naive to understand that she performed unpleasant tasks for the Head, who was ready to acquiesce in other matters because the tiresome details of school administration were performed tirelessly and effectively. Miss Allen possessed great talents for self-dramatization, so that there were periods of hush around the staff room, as everyone kept quiet so as not to try Miss Allen's nerves while she labored over the next term's schedule. Indeed, much of the school's discipline rested upon the universal agreement of all who came in contact with her that Miss Allen's extremely delicate nerves should not be tested. We would collapse in nervous laughter at the recollection of one of her rages and undignified exits, yet we were careful to modulate our voices whenever she hove in sight. Comic as the emotional storms seemed, we were also aware of real inner suffering in Miss Allen, and consequently the classes in which she lost her balance were a torment even as they were absurd. I dreaded mathematics classes, froze when she entered the room, and made my way through the various levels of senior mathematics by committing the solutions to all the problems in every text to memory, exactly as I would have set out to memorize the telephone book. She instilled an aversion to mathematics in everyone but the most mathematically talented, and convinced us all of the impossibility of ever developing the most modest mathematical skills.

Fortunately there were other, wonderful teachers, who gave us a sense of competence, and encouraged high intellectual aspirations. History and English literature were taught by women who might well have held university positions, yet who had the gift for fitting the level of their teaching to the abilities of their students. Miss Hughesdon and Miss Shell taught extra classes in their own free time for students with special interests in history and English. Our curriculum, set by the state educational authorities, contained no reference to Asia and Asian history, but Miss Hughesdon created extra classes for those curious about Japan, China, and our near neighbor Indonesia. Miss Shell happily read poetry with interested students, and it was in a borrowed volume of hers that I first read T. S. Eliot and discovered modern English poetry.

In 1949, the year my brother Bob turned twenty-one, I was in my third year of high school, transformed from adolescent rebellion to genuine intellectual interests. That year, I refused instruction for confirmation, explaining to a disapproving school chaplain, aptly named Canon Pain, that I had no religious faith. To my own experience of disaster at Coorain, I now added the pictures of Belsen and Dachau, and the chilling photographs of Hiroshima and Nagasaki. While these might well have convinced me of the truth of original sin, they served me at the time as further confirmation of the malign nature of the fates, and reinforced my sense of religious faith as a sentimental illusion.

My mother, normally a stickler for the correct thing in such matters, raised no objection, since she had become interested in the anti-Christian ideas of Theosophy, and in the popular cult of spiritualism. Her interests were expressions of her inability to accept her own personal tragedy and her quest for some certainty on which she could rest a troubled spirit. Here her lack of education was a real handicap, because she had no historical or philosophical perspective from which to analyze her own experience of loss and grief. Because we lived in the cultural wasteland of suburbia, there were no schools or evening classes she might have attended which could offer an intellectually disciplined approach to her quest. Nor were there any churches which might have offered comfort through the beauty of their liturgy. The local Anglican church was evangelical and, like its neighboring Protestant congregations, was more concerned with controlling behavior than with death and salvation. So her quest led her to small sects and groups of bereaved persons like herself who looked for insight from scrambled versions of Eastern wisdom, or sought comfort in contact with the spirits of the dead. She looked for tangible signs of the survival after death of those she loved even as she studied great Oriental texts on surrendering the attachments of this world. My first awareness of her fallibility came from my recognition of the contradiction between these two desires, but the insight which this recognition prompted was indefinitely delayed by the fresh disasters which quickly turned my mother's suburban dream into an uninterrupted nightmare.

The tensions within our household which unfolded around the celebration of Bob's twenty-first birthday indicated the fragility of the illusions on which my mother's dream rested. They were tensions of three kinds, all brought to the surface by the question of celebrating Bob's coming of age. Our ample house would have been ideal for a party on the occasion, but my mother was reluctant because she disapproved of the manners and mores of the boys' friends. Since these were mostly jazz musicians, music students, or sports car enthusiasts, they were a cheerfully iconoclastic lot, not the buttoned-up socially respectable types of whom my mother approved. Then there was an irreconcilable difference of views about what refreshments should be served at such a party. Australian mores dictated champagne, or spirits and beer for such an occasion, and if these were not available, Bob wanted no celebration. My mother, equally intransigent, refused to consider a party for young people which served alcohol. So there was no celebration. Underneath these conflicts was a more profound one. My mother, who could be cheerfully sociable in the known world of the outback supported by her husband's reassuring presence, never wanted to enter into the social world of a large city. She might want her children to make what she thought desirable friends, but she was incapable of creating a social world in which they might meet them. She could manage a sheep station superbly, but managing a social world alone as a hostess was simply beyond her consciousness. This meant that her efforts to control our destinies were mostly negative, and that our youthful quests for peers and lively social relationships took place entirely outside our home. It also meant that she relied more and more on her children for intellectual and emotional companionship, and that there was no constructive outlet for her formidable energies.

Bob's birthday was marked by the gift of a tiny vintage car, antiquated, contrary, and endlessly fascinating to him as he fiddled with its engine, assembled and disassembled its transmission, and fussed with its valves. We had hilarious rides in it, tearing noisily around our neighborhood, pushing it as much as we rode, elated at the pleasure of riding in an open car in the perfume-filled midday sunshine of Sydney's mild winter climate. It was a symbol of release from train and bus schedules, the promise of speed and motion just at the moment when we were all straining to break free of childhood constraints. We were certain that Bob would win many prizes driving it, and that with the three of us to shine it and polish its every nut and bolt it would triumph in tests of its class.

The second weekend after Bob's birthday was a school long weekend for which I invited home a boarder friend, Jocelyn McLean, a beautiful and gentle person I had sat next to in class for several years. We were to enjoy a variety of feasts from my mother's kitchen, plumb the pleasures of a matinée at the local movie house, and take long walks in the beautiful countryside which verged on our pretty suburb. Bob was to be away that weekend competing with a friend in a road rally which would last two days and nights. We saw him off, blue eyes shining, after he had dashed in for his piano practice and collected the maps that were needed to chart the complicated route of the drive. His excitement was infectious. He was part of a two-man team, driving an open sports car, and they were well favored to win their class. Barry went from work to speed them on their way, and join in the lively party of the various clubs which were participating in the rally.

Our evening at home was taken up with the usual occupations of schoolgirls: long confidences about ourselves and our families; laughter about the personal quirks and absurdities of our teachers, tall stories for my mother about pranks of the past. We fell into bed at eleven, full of hot cocoa and cookies, and talked drowsily for a very short time before falling asleep on what turned out to be a very frosty winter night.

I was awakened by a loud knocking at the front door, after what seemed like a night of sleep but was in reality only a few hours. I was accustomed to slipping down to open the door for my brothers, who sometimes forgot a key, or had had too lively a party to open the door with ease. My mother always slept on her good ear and was unwakeable, so banging at the door did not alert her to the hours her sons kept. This night, expecting Barry, I found a young policeman standing nervously in front of me. He asked first for my father, then for my mother. When I said I wouldn't wake her until I knew what was the matter, he took a sheet of paper from his pocket and read in a monotone. "I regret to inform you that at approximately 11:40 P.M., there was an accident to the vehicle in which Robert Ker was a passenger. He was thrown from the vehicle, suffered severe head injuries, and was taken to Penrith Hospital. He died there at 1:53 A.M., having never recovered consciousness. You may learn further details about the accident from the Parramatta police at this number. His body is at Penrith Hospital, and you are asked to make arrangements to remove it as soon as possible in the morning." He handed me the piece of paper, avoided my eyes, and asked if I needed further help. "No," I said, "I think I'll wait a little while before I tell my mother."

After he left, I was overcome by the need to do my grieving privately for a while. I wanted to sit alone and take it in. I also knew it would be a long time before my mother slept peacefully again, and thought she would need her rest for what was awaiting her tomorrow. I sat in the dark in the living room, thinking very clearly. This time I knew no effort at committing a loved face or voice to memory could arrest the passage of time. There would be a time when I couldn't recall his voice and his laugh at will. I might live on a large part of my life without the laughter and the joy he brought into it. As I took in the facts and imagined the battered thatch of golden hair, I felt a sharp physical loss, as though my own body were mutilated. I was literally glad to have time to take in his death alone. It meant that in my incestuous way I could hold on a little longer to something about him which for the moment was mine alone. He had been like the sun in my universe, and most of my aspirations at school and in my daily life had centered on winning his approval. Now there were not just my father's wishes to be carried out in his absence, but Bob's too. I realized I would always be trying to live out his life for him.

As the cold night wore on, I began to gather my wits and worry about Barry. I hadn't heard him come in, and I dreaded the thought of giving this news to my mother alone. Finally, looking at the time, I understood that he must have come in hours ago. I stumbled frantically into his room to waken him and whisper the news. Downstairs, we sat together again, waiting out the night, just as we had waited out the day of our father's death together. As the first light came, it struck me like a blow that the sun would soon rise on a world without Bob. With the light we stirred ourselves and agreed upon a plan. As soon as dawn arrived, Barry would go out to a phone box and call our uncle. He would then borrow a neighbor's car, collect our uncle, and bring him to our house in time to help tell my mother. There need be no waiting then. They could set out at once for the hospital and the police. While Barry went to make his phone call, I crept about the kitchen to make us hot tea. When he returned we drank it, our teeth chattering against the cups from cold and shock. After he left I settled in to wait, watching the sun rise, staring at the new day in frozen sorrow. We had thought there could be no greater grief than the loss of our father, but there was and it was upon us. I knew with foreboding how it would affect our mother.

Barry and our wonderful, reliable uncle arrived almost before it seemed possible that they could be at the door. I gave them hot tea while we talked in low voices, each of us putting off the time when she must be told. Finally he went upstairs. There was a long silence. Then he returned despondently, saying, "I hope I never have to do something so hard again. She'll be down soon. Treat her gently. She's in shock."

Shortly my mother appeared, dressed and ready to leave. She looked like a character in a fairy story on whom a sudden spell had been cast. She said in an incredulous voice to no one in particular, "But he was my *first* baby." We nodded and then they set out.

6

Finding The Southern Cross

After my brother Bob's death, it seemed as though I had lost the capacity for emotional responses. Daily life was in black and white, like a badly made film. My trancelike state excluded music, feeling, color, desire. Although on the surface I was doing well, I was actually going through each day like an automaton. I was vice-captain of my class at school and I mastered intellectual tasks with the same ease as in the past, but they gave little pleasure. I knew that I would win several academic prizes at the end of the year, but they didn't seem to matter very much. I gave up athletic competition because during the practice hours after school I was haunted by the knowledge of my mother, alone at home. I often came in to find her just sitting gazing into space.

I never touched the keys of a piano again, nor could I listen to music. When I heard something Bob had played or that we had listened to together I could not manage the feelings of grief that swept over me. Just as with our departure from Coorain, my consciousness had retreated to a great distance. It was hard to bring it back to earth unless I was concentrating every energy on some difficult intellectual effort. I came to love my hours of homework because when I finally sat down alone in my room with my books, I could get my mind and body together again, and escape the discomfort of watching the world from the other side of some transparent but impenetrable window. At school I laughed when people told jokes and listened to the detailed descriptions offered by my classmates of the dresses to be worn at dances, or tales about the sweetheart of the moment, but I could not really participate. When we went to the theater, I sat physically in the stalls but was emotionally somewhere up with the lighting tracks and girders of the building. Well-meaning family friends tried to jolly me along, but it was no use.

Each weekend my brother and I would feign interest in some expedition or diversion so we could get our mother out of the house, talking to people, seeing scenery, doing anything but sitting alone, or attending the séances which had become her obsessive interest. If we were sad, she was distraught. I often wondered if it would be better to rend one's garments and tear one's hair to express grief. My mother was quiet, but frozen.

My brother and I had to contend with the fact that our anxiety-crazed mother now confidently expected that our lives would also be cut short by accidental death. A missed train or a miscalculation about how long an errand or a weekend trip to the school library would take brought us home to a trembling, white-faced woman who had been steeling herself for the inevitable disaster. We learned to exaggerate how long the simplest journey would take, and ourselves swung between sharing her foreboding and laughing nervously about it to one another. The fates had conspired to bring about the turn of events which brought her urge to control her children into exquisite harmony with her protean anxieties. It took great efforts of will on my brother's part to resist her determination to control his every movement and keep us both close to home. For my part, I was too depressed to resist the demand to account for every moment, and too listless to care whether I was pressured to come home or not. Eventually, I even went compliantly to the meetings of the small society for psychic research which was my mother's only distraction.

The society was a rich blend of eccentrics. The flavor of the two rooms where it held its meetings was as distinctive as the aroma of a strong blend of very smoky tea; it was a blend of intellectual pretension mixed with suppressed longing. All conversations at the society followed a predictable pattern. A seeker for information would address questions to a long-standing initiate. Descriptions of psychic phenomena would follow, table rapping, predictions of the future, extraordinary instances of telepathy. At the conclusion of the conversation, the knowing person would roll his or her eyes expressively, implying that there was more to be learned for those so inclined. Newcomers would cluster earnestly about such figures of authority seeking enlightenment. Meetings would usually number twelve to fifteen people, women predominating. Some showed the hesitancy of the perpetually marginal. Others exuded confidence, wore colorful clothes, and generally behaved as if in the possession of important knowledge they were about to reveal to a waiting world. They modeled themselves on Madame Blavatsky and collected disciples. The few men were usually autodidacts, walking compendiums of unrelated information, opinionated, bossily talkative, and devotees of pseudo-scientific jargon. They talked rapidly of astral phenomena, the third eye, automatic writing, and a strange gadget called a planchette board which figured heavily in communication with the "other" world.

At the back of the room, we always found a group clustered around the medium, usually a person of startling ordinariness, who was treated with a mixture of deference and fervid curiosity. A few of the society's members were genuinely bereft like my mother. For some, the quest to know the world beyond this life was a quest for a deeper reality which lurked below the surface of things. For others, the long catalogues of experiments in mind reading or telepathy offered a sense of power. They *knew* things other people were too foolish to recognize or understand.

Although I went along with my mother whenever she asked for my company, I had acquired habits of skepticism from my schooling and found it difficult not to crawl around looking for the mechanisms which had elevated the table, or to postulate other explanations for the examples of telepathy always volunteered to end the meetings. I did not like the picture of reality which animated the true believers. It was one perfectly calculated to feed the anxieties of the gullible. Beneath and beyond the world of the senses seethed a world of spirit influences, causal factors in human affairs which were capricious, uncontrollable, and unmistakably nonmoral. While people discussed the dangers of malign spiritual influences, they also believed in a foreordained future which could be deciphered by those with "second sight."

The group catered to the worst of my mother's fears. Anyone could see that she was worried about the safety of her remaining children, something she undoubtedly communicated many times to her circle of fellow psychic researchers. After séances she would come home to report dire predictions about the future. There was one frantic occasion when her mentors had told her that we must not travel this weekend for there were bad influences afoot. Barry, imperturbable, set out for his planned weekend in the country with friends, confident that time and repeated proof of error would convince her of the folly of her anxieties. In this he never succeeded. For her, it was easier to muse about some unceasing supernatural war of good and evil than to accept the futility and meaninglessness of the accidental. Because she lived in a moral world of black and white which contained no grey shades of ambiguity or self-doubt, the idea of an unceasing war between good and evil suited her temperament.

Soon I detected troublesome signs that my mother's friends in the society were beginning to call on her for financial help; would she contribute to enable some valued medium to get medical treatment for an ailing child? Would she help a valued expert in telepathy travel in search of a cure for back problems? The fates provided a comic deliverance before I needed to argue with her about these escalating requests. Help came in the form of the errant libido of one of the seedier male members of the society, who, to my fifteen-year-old astonishment, fell to caressing my knee amorously during the darkness of a Saturday afternoon séance. My announcement of this turn of events caused my mother to take a harder look at her new circle of acquaintances. We attended no more meetings and the books on psychic research disappeared from my mother's bedside table. But she ceased seeing other adults and relied more than ever on our company.

Like me, my brother Barry found it hard to develop a sense of purpose after Bob's death. He went faithfully to car rallies, but the smell of racing fuel and the scream of tires didn't have the same savor. He too lost the capacity to enjoy music. His work experience was no corrective. He moved from one job to another in search of something he could not define. The search led from journalism to an agency which dealt in British sports cars, to an automobile service center, where, along with standard maintenance, the owner's cars were "hotted up" for road racing. The quest was evident, but the journey had no clear direction.

Just as we became incapable of really enjoying luxury, our economic fortunes soared. Coorain's sheep flourished during a series of good seasons. Their wool was quickly sold at what seemed astronomical prices to clothe the armies being raised for the Korean War. To cap those high returns, the British government finally repaid Australia's woolgrowers for the wool supplied below cost throughout 1939–1945. We were no longer just comfortable. We were positively prosperous.

We acquired visible signs of our status. The first was a sleek battleship grey Rover sedan, not just a means of transportation, but a wonder of engineering and craftsmanship. Barry, now expansive with his own earnings, acquired a wonderful fire-engine red MG, a British sports car, with racy lines, a feisty performance, and a luxurious smell of new leather emanating from its upholstery. In it we made many companionable journeys exploring the countryside around Sydney, gradually comforting one another simply by being together. We never spoke about Bob, or about our mother's worrisome state. We enjoyed the quiet, unspoken communication of two inarticulate but devoted people.

In August of 1949, my mother was galvanized by the kind of challenge she was best suited to meet. She was needed to nurse a dying friend. Eva McInness had been my mother's partner in her small cottage hospital in Lake Cargelligo, and the witness to her wedding. Eva, in her turn, had married a grazier from the Lake Cargelligo area, and the families had been as close as distance and the restrictions of the Depression and the war would allow. The McInnesses had left their drought-stricken property to be beside my mother at my father's funeral, and their phone calls and visits had helped sustain her in the hard months afterwards. Now we learned that Eva had come to Sydney for surgery for cancer of the uterus. The surgery had revealed cancer in several vital organs, and Eva, just fifty-one, had very little longer to live. The pair of experienced nurses conferred, and decided that she should not be left to die alone in the hospital. She would come home to live with us. My mother would nurse her by day, with special nurses to take over at night. The McInness family were to stay nearby so that her last months could be homelike and companionable.

To be needed in a critical situation called out my mother's best self. No one could organize a sickroom better, comfort a stricken family more tenderly, or talk more sensitively about last things with the dying. She was matter-of-fact about death, sent us regularly to sit with Eva, and when she sensed that the doctor was reluctant to provide the dosage of morphine which would relieve Eva's suffering, she confronted the doctor before us all and secured the needed prescription. I was glad to see her in charge again, but sobered by my first encounter with lingering death. I had thought of life as fragile, wiped out in a moment; watching Eva's agonizingly slow decline, I now realized that to die in an accident while in the prime of life might be a blessing. It was a sobering thought.

One day not long after the confrontation with the doctor, I told my mother after my morning visit that I thought Eva's condition had changed for the worse overnight. Her breath smelled badly, and she was very restless. "That's not bad breath," my mother said practically. "It's the smell of death." My mother gathered the family and sat with her friend all day, talking quietly, keeping everyone on an even keel until toward evening Eva drew her last breath. I was amazed at my mother's strength and energy, her directness and readiness to face hard things. She seemed so unlike the grief-paralyzed woman of a few months ago. Later I found her in her room weeping, and realized that it was her professional self which had been so strong. Whenever it was called upon she could do anything. Without it she was a different person.

Shortly after the household returned to normal following Eva's death, my mother began to worry that we would soon face another hollow celebration of Christmas, another season preoccupied with the awareness of loss, and with our inability to disguise the sadly shrunken size of the family gathering. A woman who knew no half measures, her eye was caught by an advertisement for an eight-week Christmas cruise to Ceylon by P. and O. liner. She quickly calculated that the cruise combined with three weeks of exploration on the island of Ceylon would nicely straddle the Christmas and New Year's holidays, returning us in time for me to prepare for school in early February. Mindful of her promise to Eva to care for her motherless daughter, she added her to the party. Before I knew what was happening, I was being taken on a euphoric shopping spree designed to clothe my unstylish fifteen-year-old form with cruise clothes and evening dresses suitable for dressing for dinner in the first-class P. and O. dining room. Hitherto I had been forbidden to attend my classmates' dances, and I was usually barred from parties where alcohol might be served. Now I was suddenly being prepared for a much more sophisticated adult world. My choices in clothes betrayed my lack of experience and introduced me to the discomforts of whalebone and strapless evening dresses. I was five feet six, overweight, and tormented by blotchy skin. Severe tailoring and careful choice of colors might have helped to camouflage this predicament, but I settled on pink tulle, white piqué and lace, and pale green organdy with rosebuds. The result was predictably awkward, but I knew no better. Barry, happy up to now with a tweed jacket and tie for formal occasions, was dispatched to acquire a dinner jacket and evening shoes. We became possessors of passports along with our fine clothes and began unaccustomed reading about the mysterious East. Suddenly, when I rode across the Harbor Bridge and looked down at the glittering white ocean liners lying at their moorings below, I saw them no longer as unattainable romantic symbols of a glamorous international world, but as a form of transport that I would shortly use.

My mother could not have decided upon any experience better calculated to banish our daily routine and superimpose startling new experiences on the troublesome memories of the year. They began the day our ship, the MV *Strathnaver*, sailed. Before the days of regular air travel, the departures of ocean liners were major events in Australia. Encouraged by postwar prosperity, thousands of Australians flocked aboard the P.

and O. fleet of liners to make their ritual journey "home" to England before settling down in their real homeland. Each vessel was farewelled by an alcoholic crowd, its members cheering and weeping by turns, shouting advice (much of it crude references to the ways of foreigners), remembering last messages, singing sentimental songs, and waiting at the docks until the last paper streamer thrown to friends aboard had broken. The *Strathnaver* was going "through to Tilbury," having picked up almost a full complement of passengers in Sydney. It sailed for eight days around the coast of Australia, stopping at Melbourne, Adelaide, and Fremantle, before setting out for seventeen days across the Indian Ocean to Ceylon.

Many passengers were made seasick by the swell going across the Great Australian Bight, and some were troubled by the pitching of a storm a day or so out from Perth, but we were entranced; exploring the ship, seeing our first flying fish, watching the other passengers. In the beginning, I was intimidated by the first-class dining room. The menus were enormous, remnants of an Edwardian style of dining. I was uncomfortable in my unaccustomed finery, and totally inexperienced in polite dinner table conversation. Gradually I learned the delights of choosing between caviar and smoked salmon for a first course, sampling grouse and other English game, eating my first Stilton cheese, and entering into serious discussions with our steward about what kind of soufflé would be best for dessert. I set to so heartily as a trencherwoman that no amount of pacing the deck could atone for my appetite, and the whalebone supporting the pink tulle began to be very confining indeed.

The evenings lived up to every movie I had seen about ocean voyages. The wake glowed with phosphorescence, the sea breeze blew gently, the band played sedate dance music, and a wonderful array of older people disported themselves on the dance floor. It was fascinating to work out with my mother which couples belonged together, who was having an affair, what widow was setting her cap at what retired major. My mother was as diverted as we were by the change of environment, but she was puzzled by her children's behavior. We were agog to find our place among the other young people on the ship, whereas she, still grieving, wanted to retire early and expected us to accompany her. My determination not to remain dutifully by her side was reinforced by our traveling companion, Eva's daughter, a few years my senior. She was understandably determined to enjoy a shipboard romance, and more than ready to argue about my mother's expectation that we would retire when she did. My mother could not require our presence to avert anxiety about road accidents so, reluctantly, she gave approval for us to retire when we chose. As soon as she went down to her cabin, we broke most of her carefully prescribed rules. I danced clumsily with strangers, Barry sampled more than the beer at the bar, and we began to get to know some of the other passengers.

Besides the usual Australian tourists, the ship carried Indian and Pakistani army and air force officers, families from the former Indian and Ceylonese Civil Service, the children of tea and rubber planters en route home from school and university for the summer holidays, and numerous retired English couples who made the journey out to Australia and back to escape the English winter. Some of the passengers must have been aware that India and Pakistan had just endured two years of murderous racial strife following Independence, and that British rule in Ceylon had ended less than a year ago. But we lived on shipboard as though the great British navy and merchant marine still controlled the globe. I became enamored of the son of one British planter family from Ceylon, and freed from my mother's supervision, I saw in the New Year at a particularly bibulous party in his cabin, where Barry came upon me, cheerfully tipsy at 1:00 A.M. This united us in a happy conspiracy of silence about our secret misdemeanors. My host and his friends seemed unaware that their world was about to collapse. Instead they gave me experienced advice about how to manage "the natives."

Elderly men and women told me romantic stories about the glamorous Northwest Frontier of the old British Raj; Barry and I listened enthralled to the war tales told by colorfully dressed Pakistani Air Force officers; all of us were regularly regaled with lengthy sea chronicles told by the petty officer who looked after passenger entertainment. His most memorable stories were of the wild behavior of the Australian troops the *Strathnaver* had carried to the Middle East in 1940, and brought home again in 1942 to defend their homeland from the threat of Japanese invasion. For me, he was the star of all the characters gathered on our voyage. More than six feet tall, he carried an enormous beer-inflated belly with stately dignity. His talk was always slipping toward profanity, and his language was peppered with vivid imagery. He ran the horse races and bingo games expertly, calling the numbers in rhyming cockney slang with a voice more gravelly than any I had ever heard. His dissipated eyes looked as though they had seen every form of human depravity and his demeanor of barely controlled scorn softened only when he talked about his adored ship. He liked instructing me, and never let fact stand in the way of a striking story. Ceylon, he told me, was an island so beautiful and so laden with spice trees and gardens that the perfume told one to expect landfall many miles out to sea. He had a gift for language. When he described Aden, the next port after Colombo, with its blue-grey mountains ringing the harbor and the sails of the Arab dhows reflecting the sunset, it seemed as though my life would be incomplete without seeing it with him to identify the forts and the British naval vessels lying at anchor in the roadstead. I began to understand the wonders of travel.

Once we disembarked in Ceylon, this understanding changed quickly to ambivalence.

The Australia of my childhood contained only a minuscule population of non-British descent, so that I had never really seen another culture. Reading could carry me in imagination beyond the confines of Coorain or Sydney, but it could never make me experience a non-British world, let alone test the usual British imperial attitudes of superiority toward other peoples. Schooled as I was in all Australia's class sensitivities, I was unprepared for a society of caste. Colombo was a teeming Asian city where begging was a way of life. At the Grand Oriental Hotel, an ancient "punkah boy" slept on a mat outside my bedroom door in case I called for anything in the night. I was troubled by having to beat the beggars away on the street, and by the instruction to ignore the tugging hands of the children who grabbed my skirts crying for money. I felt so disoriented by the extremes of poverty and by my uncertainty about how to behave that I could not relax and enjoy the color, the vitality, and the richness of the new sights and sounds. People told me that the children with stumps for legs, or holes where their eyes had been, were that way because they had been deliberately deformed so as to be more effective beggars. That did not help me sort out how

.to behave to them or what I thought about this new society.

The Grand Oriental Hotel, our base for a week in Colombo, lived up to its name. Its Edwardian splendor was fading in 1949, but its vast white marble lounge, sprinkled with cane tables and chairs, cooled with potted palms and soporific ceiling fans, seemed very grand to me. In the afternoons, there was a thé dansant, when the band played Strauss waltzes and Hungarian gypsy music. This was the hour when the white-clad young men who worked for the British banks or insurance companies came to sip cool drinks and dance away the afternoons with women whose toilette and elegant silk dresses had clearly commanded the attention of skilled servants. One of our shipboard friendships had been with a family traveling to the wedding of their eldest daughter to a young English bank officer, so we were soon introduced to this society. Its members brooded every afternoon over gin and tonic about the decline of the British Empire and the mess the Sinhalese would make of ruling themselves. Such expectations of nonwhite people had been one of the unquestioned verities of my world, but after my first actual encounter with the way a multiracial imperial society worked, I began to be less sure about everything. I could feel the hostility of the street crowds and the ever-present watchfulness of the hotel servants. They made me uneasy.

A new view of history began to shape my perceptions as soon as we left Colombo. The city itself, with its fragrant gardens, white-galleried buildings, and thriving commerce, registered only vaguely through my jumble of emotions about the poverty and the thinly veiled resentment of British-looking people. Our first visits to Buddhist temples and sacred sites gave me what then seemed the astonishing information that this great religious figure had existed nearly six hundred years before Christ. Each great temple contained relics of the Buddha, objects of veneration, just like Christian relics. Why had no one taught me more about this earlier faith so similar to Christianity in so many respects? Moreover, why had I been taught to date everything from the birth of Christ and the emergence of the Christian West, when great capitals like Anuradhapura, among whose white, gold, and grey ruins we climbed, had been thriving three hundred years before Christ's birth? Seeing these remains was an unexpected culture shock which meant that Europe could never again seem "old." After that, ancient remains always conjured up for me the greying rocks of Anuradhapura, the outline of its temples and palaces in perfect scale, clearly visible despite the encroaching jungle. Hitherto I had dated my understanding of political life with the development of the British parliament. As our guide talked about the thriving empire ruled from Anuradhapura and the political conflicts which had flourished there, the picture captured my imagination and made me realize that there were other political traditions about which I knew nothing. Military history also took on a new aspect after the scorching day when Barry and I climbed the hill fortress of Sigirya, dating from the sixteenth century. At the top, surveying the plains below, one could picture the ruling monarch whose armies had ridden elephants and had controlled the exuberant fertility of the irrigated plains below. One entered the pathway to the fortress through the fierce mouth of a lion carved in the mountainside, as large and commanding a monument as an Egyptian pyramid. Away from the massed population of the city, I could take in the beauty of the island and register such vivid new sights as the outline

223

of the Temple of the Tooth in Kandy. Nearby, a patch of rain forest of breathtaking beauty, containing an undreamed-of profusion of exotic vegetation, had been preserved. The avenue of palm trees in the gardens of Kandy along which processions mounted on elephants had once paraded became a symbol for other kinds of grandeur than the photographs of England I had been taught to revere.

Despite the fact that such powerful and enduring subversive perceptions were being etched on my mind, I was not a happy traveler. I had been raised in a household of such precise regularity, governed by such an obsession with cleanliness, that I shared my mother's fears about whether our rooms were really clean, and I joined her in rejecting the unfamiliar-tasting food. Along with this low-level anxiety, I was puzzled about how to understand and organize the daily flood of new images. My first sight of a Hindu wedding procession outside a small village looked like such fun. The bright colors, the flowers, the music, and the energy expressed in the procession as it flowed sinuously along captured my imagination. My mother remarked that the bride was a child, and that village people often sent themselves into bankruptcy for such festivities. I knew this was true, but when I contrasted the scene with my mental picture of the kind of wedding I and my classmates would likely have, I wondered for the first time whether ours might be a little stuffy. It was disturbing to be prompted to such thoughts, and I was not certain I enjoyed it. So much of the culture we were viewing in our journey round the island was the product of religion. This was a Buddhist and Hindu country. I wondered idly what Australia was. Did people in Ceylon believe in karma and a cyclical view of history to explain away the terrible inequities between classes and castes? This set me wondering what beliefs we had at home to justify our inequities. Such ideas were unheard of. I began to look forward to going home and settling into a familiar routine.

As our return voyage drew to its close, it was clear that my mother was also relishing the thought of home. She had set about the journey impulsively and had given us an expensive and luxurious vacation, hoping to ease the sadness of Christmas without Bob. She had managed that wonderfully for Barry and me, and for Eva's daughter, but she had not reckoned with what her actions would mean. She had introduced us to the very world of fashionable luxury she had previously ruled out of bounds. Her action was prompted in part by guilt at the thrift which had prevented her from gratifying some of Bob's much simpler wishes. While she recognized this, she felt, childishly, that we should be more visibly grateful for the largess than we were. Our journey together made clear that she was no longer the center of our world, and that we were poised to search for new adventures on our own. She kept her peace while we were traveling, but on our return her wounded feelings began to show.

On the second weekend after our return, Barry and I, sitting idly with the Sunday morning paper, found ourselves in the midst of a hurricane of disapproval. Why were we lounging around? Couldn't we see that the grass needed cutting, the shrubbery cried out for pruning, and the garden was choked with weeds? Had we been so spoiled by our ten weeks of sea cruising that we were incapable of taking care of the place? Her words and her bearing conveyed the impression of someone vexed by the recognition that she must face the future dragged down by a pair of useless drones. Without exchanging a glance, we leapt to attention and fell to with a vengeance. As I set about attacking the weeds, an inner voice I had not heard before remarked, "So, we are going to have to pay for it." I quickly silenced it as unworthy. Yet it was there, waiting to be attended to. It was a long time before I heeded it seriously, but from this point on, at one level of my consciousness, I knew that my mother's gifts came at a considerable price. They might seem to be freely given, but there would come a time afterwards when they had to be earned.

The general cloud of disapproval vanished on my return to school, with the discovery that I had been chosen as captain of my class. My mother was genuinely delighted when one of her children excelled, and this recognition from the respected Miss Everett counted heavily with her. Barry, however, was not so fortunate. My mother told him sternly that his current life lacked focus, that he was drifting from one kind of work to another, and that this could not be tolerated. She asked him to go back to Coorain to work under the supervision of the manager, Geoff Coghlan, and to prepare himself for the day when he would assume responsibility for running the property.

That my brother's life lacked focus was certainly true. But the remedy betrayed little understanding on my mother's part of herself, her son, or the manager she had chosen to run Coorain for her. Her notion that she would happily release the reins of management of the family enterprise to her son in the not-too-distant future was pure fantasy. She was incapable of such an action. She took her psychic energy from being in charge and could not delegate the smallest decisions to her long-suffering manager, let alone her young son. Barry, at twenty years of age, was dispatched to work as a subordinate on the property my mother herself had found an unbearably lonely place without the companionship of her husband. Just at the time he longed for friends, for laughter, and for lively society, Barry found himself alone, without young companions, without the stimulus of new ideas, without any element in the daily schedule but the hard labor of caring for sheep. Moreover, he was caring for them under the aegis of a crusty and unsympathetic taskmaster. Geoff Coghlan was a good and upright man by his lights, but he was not a saint. Only a man given to self-sacrifice would have trained his replacement and encouraged my brother to feel his powers of command, when Coorain represented to Geoff and his wife the home and the independent life circumstances which the accident of Geoff's age and generation had withheld from them. Instead, Barry, whose self-confidence had withstood a school which did not encourage slow learners, now found himself working daily enduring the burden of regular criticism and encouragement constantly withheld. His time at Coorain was a test of endurance which he survived, but his letters home, while outwardly optimistic, revealed the price he was paying. It was from this time that I dated his taciturnity, his difficulty showing his feelings, and the clouding of a naturally cheerful nature by a stoic view of life.

My mother, intent on establishing her son in the country, tried to persuade several of his friends to join him as workers on Coorain. She filled them with stories about the wonders of the independent life in the bush, the pleasures of seeing direct products from one's work, anything but the truth about the hardships and the inevitably losing battle with the seasons. My brother would write back to her urging restraint and reminding her of the realities of life in the bush: the loneliness, the harsh weather, the grinding routine of heavy labor, "the general deadness of the place," and the difficulty a landless young man would encounter in building a real competence through work for others. He was the twenty-year-old realist, and she the impractical romantic.

In fact, she thought little about the consequences for others of the plans which would serve her objective of the moment. By the time Barry was ready to abandon the bush, recognizing the impossibility of the role in which he had been cast, one of his friends was en route to Coorain, to experience the same disillusionment, and the same postponement of realistic career plans. As it became clear that Barry's experiment was not working, my mother tried the expedient of buying him a small plane and inviting him to Sydney to undertake the necessary training to fly it. Once he had his pilot's license, he could escape the loneliness on weekends, and at least in theory, enjoy the best of both worlds.

It was one of my mother's more endearing characteristics that she thought big about removing the obstacles to her objective of the moment. Thinking in large terms about the problem of reviving Coorain after the drought had stood us all in good stead. However, this tendency to the broadest possible attack on the problem could lead her to offer very large incentives to her children to fall in with her wishes, without much reflection on whether the wishes were really in her child's best interests. Had she succeeded in keeping Barry at Coorain, the future would have been grim for him, working for a woman who could not bear her children to be independent. Fortunately, after eight months of determined effort Barry's good sense triumphed and he announced that he was leaving Coorain for good.

At Abbotsleigh, I had fallen happily into the routine of the lower sixth form. All our efforts were now bent on preparing for the School Leaving Certificate examination which would come at the end of the following year. The school prided itself on the number of women who went on to the University, and on the number of honors earned by its sixth form. There was a general air of seriousness about our classes, increased by the departure of many of our more lighthearted friends for finishing school or country life after the Intermediate Year. We now had the best teachers, the most convenient schedule, and the excitement of a not-too-distant goal.

Better still, the course of study prescribed by the New South Wales Department of Education was intensely interesting. In our Intermediate Year, we had studied Australian history using a textbook of such comic inadequacy that we were reduced to gales of laughter in class by its flat-footed statements. All we were taught of Australian history was the story of the exploration of Australia, mostly a sad tale of headstrong efforts to cross trackless deserts, missed rendezvous, death from thirst or starvation. The matter-of-fact chronicle of disaster touched our sense of the absurd as we were asked to recite the dates of this or that ill-starred expedition, or to explain why Leichhardt or Burke and Wills had perished and where they had met their tragic end. We giggled also because of the sheer nonsense of treating Australian history as the history of exploration while neglecting the history of its settlement, the growth of its cities, the evolution of its constitutional arrangements, its place in the British Commonwealth.

Now in the lower sixth, we began to study modern European history, and the facts and figures we committed to memory helped to raise tantalizing questions about the world of our own day. Would there have been a

Hitler without the Treaty of Versailles? Were the same mistakes being repeated in the peace treaty with Japan, being negotiated as we studied? We argued passionately about this, in class and outside. Our history teacher, Miss Hughesdon, took some of us to the Australian Institute of International Affairs to listen to John Foster Dulles discuss the terms of the treaty with Japan, so that we would gain the sense that we too were part of great historic moments. When I volunteered my views on the need for generosity with Japan at home, they evoked such an angry response that I began keeping what I was learning to myself.

Our French teacher, Mrs. Fisher, long jaded by years of teaching recalcitrant pupils, took the offensive on entering the room. "You, today you're Public Enemy Number One," was her frequent first utterance at the opening of a class. The enemy could be someone lounging listlessly, someone laughing, or someone she correctly suspected of not having mastered her irregular verbs. This approach could convert a French class into a war of nerves, rather than an attack on the opaqueness of language. After three years of desultory attention, I suddenly began to be able to read French and to engage in the pleasures of accurate translation. Language was no longer simply the words to which we gave utterance but a set of structures of miraculous complexity.

Learning another language made me hear English more acutely. For six years I had marched every morning into the school assembly and listened idly to the instructions and sermons of the day. Because we sat on the floor of the gymnasium for these meetings and the teaching staff sat on a raised platform, our eyes were usually directed at the level of the teacher's feet. This meant that I developed careful anthropological classifications of people in terms of their footwear and the shape of their ankles but I retained not a word of the good advice delivered from the platform. Now, as though I had been deaf before, I began to hear Miss Everett's beautiful voice lingering lovingly over the cadences of the King James Bible. I had loved poetry before because of its imagery, but now I heard language as a form of music, and I waited for the succession of readings marking the liturgical year as though I were a traveler looking for familiar places along a well-traveled path. This sense transformed my reading of Shakespeare, which I now began to read aloud to myself, instead of memorizing the blank verse with silent joy. I went with friends to the first postwar Australian performance of the Stratford Shakespeare company and became addicted to Elizabethan theater as though it were a drug. I could never hear and see enough. I could scarcely read a page without self-discovery, for it seemed as though my experience of life and the one expressed in the plays were identical. When Hamlet spoke of the smallness of man washed up "upon this bank and shoal of time . . . creeping between earth and sky," it evoked my sense of smallness before the vastness of the bush. The inexorable swiftness with which the fates closed in upon Macbeth reminded me of my childhood. Henry V's call to English patriotism seemed utterly contemporary. The plays were about great men and great events, larger than life-size human passions, causes to which people committed every ounce of their energy. Beside them, Sydney and its sunny suburbs, or the Australian pastime of sunbathing at the beach, seemed unexciting.

After I discovered Shakespeare's sonnets, I began to bombard my teachers with requests for references to read about the Dark Lady of the Sonnets, and moved on from these to any book I could find about Tudor England. J. B. Black's detailed histories of the Elizabethan Parliaments were just coming out, and I hung upon the appearance of the next volume as though I were reading a popular serial. These brought me to the character of Elizabeth I and my first model for a woman leader. It was a new and comforting idea—greatness in a woman. I had not been conscious of hunger for such an image, but it was immensely satisfying to learn about this woman with "the heart and stomach of a prince." I used my pocket money to buy copies of the plays of Beaumont and Fletcher, Marlowe and Ben Jonson. Their images and characters peopled my imagination far more than anyone in my everyday suburban world.

At the very end of my year in the lower sixth, when we had completed the required syllabus, our English teacher, Miss Shell, appeared with copies of T. S. Eliot's *Murder in the Cathedral* which she distributed to the class, instructing us to read it over the coming weekend in order to perform a proper play the following Monday.

Here was a new and astonishing discovery. Someone in my own day who wrote blank verse and who shared my feeling of distance from the emptiness of modern life. Eliot might have been writing about my feeling of detachment from the surface of things, and my longing for a world of real feeling and passion, instead of the polite proprieties of afternoon tea in the suburbs. I quickly borrowed *The Waste Land* from Miss Shell. It was a revelation. Here was what I took to be an English poet whose attitude to nature was not romantic, who mentioned deserts and whitening bones. It was great poetry about a landscape I *knew*. No one told me Eliot was an American poet, or that his imagination was rooted in a midwestern American landscape. I just knew that it resonated for me in ways English romantic poetry never could. I began to think that when I got to the University of Sydney, I would study English literature.

My final year at Abbotsleigh raced away. I was made a prefect, a status which conveyed many privileges for the ten or twelve senior girls chosen. We had our own study, a large room with a spacious bay window, a large study table, and comfortable shabby furniture. Our presence or absence at class was no longer recorded or questioned and our blazers were emblazoned with a special badge indicating our special role. Our corresponding responsibilities were to administer discipline outside the classroom. We were responsible for the decorum with which people marched to morning assembly, for their bearing during all formal school occasions, and for getting people in and out of classrooms when the school bell rang before and after every break. We could detain the unruly after school, assign punishments, or haul up some unlucky younger student, caught teasing or badgering another student, for a thorough dressing down.

Outside our study, we were models of decorum, but within our sanctuary we were a noisy, irreverent, and lighthearted group. One of our number, a gifted mathematician with shining aquamarine blue eyes and pigtails of unbelievable tidiness, straightened out all our confusions on mathematics homework. My good friend Robin and I, friendly rivals for the school history prize, coached people who were slow to get the point of history questions. Everyone argued vociferously about the interpretation of the English text of the moment, while those who had chosen biology instructed the group about evolution, and the physics and chemistry wing talked portentously about the splitting of the atom.

One of the pleasantest parts of the day came when we made our way to the study at lunchtime, produced sandwiches, tea or coffee, sat in a circle around the window seat, and talked about life. While several of us had been close friends for a number of years, our group, formed by Miss Everett's selection, quickly settled into amiable collaboration, rather like a group of junior officers in wartime. Being Australian, we exchanged no deep confidences. Our talk ranged from current events to our favorite films and music, our parents and their vagaries, to the question of what we would do after finishing school. We were all economic and social conservatives and mirrored our families in rejoicing that the politically conservative Liberal Country party coalition had ousted the Australian Labor Party in 1949, and defeated Labor's plans to nationalize Australia's banks. We were also aesthetic conservatives. Our tastes in music and art were conventional, and although we were living in a period of great artistic achievement in Australian painting and literature, we had registered very little about it. Our favorite films were British, the music we hummed American, and the clothes we wore derived from British and French fashion.

239

As young women, we were in an anomalous position. Our school, whatever its colonial blind spots, existed to maximize the talents of its students, taught them to strive, whether intellectually, in athletics, or in seeking social eminence. Our group of prefects had been singled out as leaders and encouraged to take charge, albeit in minor and symbolic ways. While we lived within the boundaries of the school, being ambitious was rewarded, but as we approached graduation we had to resolve personally the contradictions which were observable within the ranks of our teachers about what should be our goals in life as adults.

Miss Everett's message was crystal clear. We were privileged young women who owed it to society to develop our minds and talents to the limits of our ability. She let us know repeatedly about her hope that we would distinguish the school by the numbers of us who continued our studies at the University of Sydney, then the only full university in our city of close to three million. Other messages were more puzzling. Some girls' parents, planning on their early marriage, did not want them to waste time in university study. Others were encouraged to think about something practical like nursing training, which did not take too long, and provided a limited but reliable professional skill. The message was clear that they would not be doing this kind of work for too long. Then there were clear injunctions from the adult world about what fields of university study were appropriate for a woman. "Not law," we were told, "it's not a good field for a woman. You'll only end up trying divorce cases, and besides no good law firm would take you in." I loved chemistry, but then there was the specter of Miss Allen and my undistinguished record in mathematics. "Don't take science," family friends advised. "There is too much mathematics, and besides, what would a girl like you do in an industrial laboratory?" The things that were "nice for a woman" to study were unintellectual, like nursing, physiotherapy, or occupational therapy, or strictly decorative, like music or a foreign language, subjects which only the strangest parents thought their daughters might pursue professionally.

My mother favored "something practical" like medicine. A woman needed a strong professional training before any thought of marriage, she said. One never knew whether a marriage would last, or when one might be widowed, and a woman's most precious possession was her economic independence. I didn't much like the idea of caring for sick people. My years spent caring for the emotional needs of others made me long for some wonderfully abstract study, elegant, clear, free of messy human demands.

Miss Shell and Miss Hughesdon, my English and history teachers, swung the balance. "It will be a great loss if you don't go on to do further study in history and literature," they told me. "You could do outstanding work." I didn't know what was involved in doing outstanding work, or where the study of English and history might lead, but if they said so, I was ready to follow their advice.

As my time to leave Abbotsleigh approached I suddenly realized how much I had come to love the place. I forgave it its foolishly hot uniforms and its genteel rules of behavior; I even forgave some of its less admirable pretenses. It had given me a secure and orderly environment in which to grow, and adults to admire who took it for granted that women would achieve. Moreover, it had been a haven of sorts from the pressures of home. Each morning when I left there was no challenge about my departure, nor after I became a prefect was there any challenge about the time I came home. It had also given me friends with whom I could grow slowly from childhood to adolescence. In our time there, we had all come to accept one another like comfortable pieces of furniture, and no longer had to earn one another's approval. I had almost forgotten my paralyzing shyness during my seven years as a member of this companionable group. Now I began to wonder how I would manage without them.

I knew I couldn't cope with the world outside my family and school yet. I'd never managed to learn to chatter easily with strangers, partly because my home and family wasn't the kind I could chatter easily about as most young people my age did. The silence in our house was palpable. After her abortive interest in psychic research, my mother had settled back into her solitary ways. There were no laughing parties of young people coming and going, because my mother's sense of what was appropriate for entertaining the young simply didn't fit with the way my classmates lived. Even had I been able to persuade her otherwise, the effort of having company exhausted her, and I knew it was better to leave well enough alone. My party clothes hung unused in the cupboard after our fling on our cruise to Ceylon. There was literally no occasion to wear them. My weekends were spent in reading and gardening, and doing errands for my mother. We lived together like an elderly couple with an iron routine which was never broken. If the preordained order of things was interrupted, my mother became flustered, didn't sleep well, and suffered from headaches. When I went to the houses of friends, I would look hungrily at the fathers and mothers who were quietly amused by their sons' and daughters' scrapes, and wish above all else to have a normal family.

But there was no getting away from the fact that mine wasn't normal, and that I was different from my school friends. So much of my time had been spent with my older brothers and their companions that I didn't really find the high school boys my friends went around with interesting. Outside school I still spent all my time with adults. My obsession with Tudor history and Elizabethan drama did not make me an interesting conversationalist with young men who wanted to talk about last weekend's football game, or the newest hero of the surf club.

My appearance didn't give me many opportunities to be bored by young men. At seventeen there was no getting away from the fact that by the Australian standard of prettiness I did not measure up. Good-looking girls were slender, almost boyish, athletic, always ready for tennis or some outdoor amusement. Their skin tanned easily, and their blond hair curled delectably whether at the beach or on the tennis court. My hair was fair, but fine and wispily straight. No matter what efforts were expended to improve it, it always collapsed dolefully at the beach. My skin, easily irritated by the Australian sun, meant that a day by the sea resulted in scarlet suffering. Our household diet still made me overweight. My friends had slim ankles. Mine puffed and swelled by the end of a hot day. Later I learned that this was the result of a reaction to too much salt in my diet, but as this condition got worse in my last year of school, it meant that fashionable footwear reduced me to hobbling pain by the end of the day. My mother's comments about my appearance were tactless. She wondered out loud how someone whose ankles were as elegantly slim as hers could have produced a daughter with such problems.

If my mother's comments about my swollen ankles were tactless, her comments about some of my other personal defects were downright depressing. When I inveighed against the hopelessness of doing anything with my limp straight hair, she looked at me with genuine puzzlement. Her hair had always been abundant and curly, and she couldn't think what could be done about mine. I should just wait to grow out of my heaviness, she assured me, not realizing that her generous hand with salt in cooking was part of my problem. "Puppy fat" always disappeared in one's twenties, she said, and too much concern with dieting was foolish. Meanwhile, I watched my school friends become willowy and graceful, and felt more than ever an ugly duckling.

There was more than my appearance to worry about. My family and school friends agreed that I was "brainy." This was a bad thing to be in Australia. People distrusted intellectuals. Australians mocked anyone with "big ideas" and found them specially laughable in a woman. My mother herself was divided on the subject. One moment she would be congratulating me on my performance at school, and the next contradicting her approval by urging me not to become too interested in my studies. If I did, I would become a "bluestocking," a comically dull and unfeminine person. The more I heard these predictions, the more I struggled to become just like all my classmates. This was not easy to do because the aspiration brought me into conflict with my mother over what was appropriate in dress for a seventeen-year-old. I wanted to dress in grown-up clothes, and to buy expensive and stylishly tailored dresses. My mother, mindful of my derelictions on the trip to Ceylon, gave me only enough pocket money to pay for my train fares and a few weekend jaunts to films or the theater. I didn't go as often as I might have because she kept on buying me girlish flowered dresses which made me look and feel "all wrong" when I went out with school friends.

There was a lot to build my ego at home despite my insecurity about my appearance. With adults I overcame my shyness. My mother made clear her reliance on me, and her gratitude that I was such a steadfast source of company. "Jill's a great companion," I heard her tell our neighbors. "She's a wonderfully sensible person. Not flighty like most girls her age." She had long since persuaded me to apologize for neglecting her to run off with a group of young people on our voyage to Ceylon, and my character was once again cause for congratulation. She now discussed every detail of the management of Coorain with me and told me, even though Barry was himself working hard toward that goal, that she expected that one day I might run the place. When we went together to see our wool on display before the annual sales, she boasted about me to her woolbrokers. "Jill's her father's daughter. She's a fine judge of wool and she knows as much as I do about raising sheep." "I don't know what your mother would do without you," my uncle and aunt frequently told me during their weekly visits. They were the only visitors my mother genuinely loved to see, and their arrival on a Saturday or a Sunday afternoon presaged a leisurely stroll in the garden, and an island of talk in a silent week. I swelled with pride at discharging my responsibility to care for her so well and at the approval given my conduct and sagacity. I might not be pretty, and I was certainly dangerously bookish, but it was clear that I won lots of approval from the adult world. That was no help when I thought about leaving school and finding my way among the teeming thousands of young people at the University of Sydney. I knew I loved to study, but just what I would do there was unclear.

What would I become after three years of higher education? Try as I might I couldn't conjure up a single image to fill in the blank prospect of the future. I knew it would involve the responsibility for the care of my mother and Coorain, but my picture of myself as an adult was as empty as the western plains. I tried hard to develop the right aspirations, but I had no map of the future to guide me. Fretting about this just before the end of my final school year, I remembered my father's advice about what to do if one were ever to become lost in the bush. "Don't panic and rush about," he said. "Stay in the shade, and wait for the night sky. You'll be able to see the Southern Cross, and you can navigate by that." I wished there were pointers for life's journeys like the planets and constellations which could help pilot us along the surface of the earth. I needed some pointers for the future because I dreaded being stranded at home, the only companion of an increasingly dependent mother, even as I took my sense of self-worth from doing the job well.

The actual day of my departure from Abbotsleigh was an anticlimax. I was tired and a little overwrought for the ceremony which we called Speech Day. The afternoon before,

I had returned from the rehearsal for Speech Day to find that my mother had fallen in the garden, a fall that resulted in a compound fracture of her right wrist. Barry, returning earlier in the afternoon, found her where she had fallen walking along a path edged with sharp rocks. Her wrist had hit against one jagged edge as she went down, and had borne the full weight of her body. The result was a compound fracture which she was gazing at in puzzlement as he picked her up. He took her to the emergency room of the district hospital where an inexperienced young intern set the fracture. As they came in the door she was complaining about the tightness of the cast, the swelling, and the pain. We had a wakeful night, caring for her, so that I felt unusually detached as I made my way alone to the ceremony which marked the end of my schooldays.

I looked at the happy families, fathers, mothers, younger brothers and sisters, clustered around my classmates, and indulged in a brief fantasy. What might it have been like to have my smiling father and Bob there, alongside Barry, and a healthy smiling mother? Inwardly I told them the achievement we would shortly celebrate was for them, to compensate for the shadows that had fallen over the family. No matter how many times I told myself this was so, I found my lion's share of the prizes accompanied by an emptiness of the heart. I looked at the growing pile of prize books, engraved with the school crest, which mounted beside my chair. Why hadn't I realized how empty success was? I had fooled myself by thinking that covering myself with honors would be some sort of surrogate fulfillment for the promise of my dead father and brother. It was not, nor, I realized sadly, was it ever likely to be. The real satisfactions of my schooling had been the friends I had made. Panic set in briefly as I surveyed them and recognized that we would separate within a matter of hours.

I concentrated firmly on the platform and the daughter of the Governor of New South Wales, who was handing out the prizes and would shortly address us. She was the embodiment of vice-regal propriety, white gloves, navy suit, well-polished shoes, carefully composed features and smile. I noticed that when she shook hands as she presented our prizes she did it with the smooth practice of one accustomed to official parties and reception lines. When the time came for her to speak, she told us to remember our responsibility to society and to those less fortunate, and to uphold the standards of the school and the Church of England when we in our time established families, and had children of our own to educate. These unexceptionable sentiments pleased the assembled parents, but for me they slid smoothly past the immediate question of why we had been educated and what we were supposed to do with the next stage of our lives. My anxiety made my stomach hollow. Did helping the less fortunate mean that I was really meant to live my entire life caring for my mother, filling the emotional void left by my father and Bob? I took myself to task for the uncharitable way I asked this question. She was such a *good* mother. "Yes," the thought popped into my mind, recalling Hamlet's unhinged comments about the Queen, "Good mother is bad mother unto me." My mother's devotion to me, the self-denial which had sent her to work to educate me properly, her frequent references to the fact that I was her consolation for her past tragedies, weighed on me like the Ancient Mariner's albatross. I knew how well she meant but that same devotion was also a curse, a burden of guilt for ever wanting to do other things and be like other young people. I set these thoughts aside as unworthy, rising absentmindedly with the crowd to sing "God Save the King." Then the ceremony was over, my favorite teachers and the parents of friends clustered round with congratulations and good-byes, and shortly I was walking out the gate toward the train station for the last time.

At home, my mother was upstairs in bed, furious. Below, Barry was in consultation with the family physician. Why had she fallen, and what could be done about the badly swollen wrist? The doctor, a blunt speaker, said her dizziness might be attributable to high blood pressure, or then again, it might be the result of the tranquilizers she had become accustomed to since Bob's death. He gave us a prescription for painkillers and sleeping pills, told us to take her back to the hospital for more X-rays in the morning, and went his noncommittal way.

As I came into her room my mother looked up and said bitterly, "Bloody doctors! Look at that swelling. Why can't he do something about it? I think I'll cut this plaster off." Barry and I spent the rest of the evening trying to soothe her and convince her that it would be better to wait to change the plaster until someone was at hand to supply another.

253

It was difficult to do because she was angry about the smallest things. I didn't make the gravy for dinner quite right, I was clumsy in helping her change her nightgown. I was forcing her to endure more pain by urging her to keep her cast on. Her anger shook me. How could she think my motives so base? I noticed that her face looked a little mad, and then guiltily told myself I was dreaming.

The next day, we took her back to the hospital to receive a new cast, the process this time supervised by a more experienced doctor. But nothing could disperse the storm of anger which emanated from her. This wasn't the stoic woman of my childhood whom I remembered pacing the house with a bag of heated salt held to her infected ear while I stoked the fire to keep a fresh supply heated. She hadn't murmured when the eardrum burst, but now her complaints were never-ending. She needed to be dressed every day, her food cut up, helped upstairs, undressed at night. I slept close to her room, ears alert for her calls, afraid her sleeping pills and painkillers would produce another fall. It was plain that her recovery would take a long time. And it was equally plain who would take care of her. The date for Barry's departure for Coorain was already set for late January. I would be alone with her again after that. I braced myself for the responsibility, proud that I could cope, but at the same time dreading assuming the role I now saw being laid out for me. Thoughts of escape were unrealistic. Daughters in Australia were supposed to be the prop and stay of their parents. Would I ever get away? Was it wrong to want to? How on earth could I set about doing it? How could I tell this woman who lived for me that I did not want to live for her? I began to have trouble sleeping, telling myself the insomnia came from listening in case my mother called for something in the night. I often watched the Southern Cross in the night sky, but it was not just a compass bearing I needed now, it was a judgment about what would be the moral path to choose.

7

The Nardoo Stones

In the 1950s, one's first vision of the University of Sydney from its main gates was of a graceful sweep of lawn curving up a gentle incline to the point on the brow of the hill where the nineteenth-century Gothic quadrangle and Great Hall commanded the surroundings. Though the shape of the buildings recalled the misty light and the grey stones of the Oxford and Cambridge colleges so lovingly evoked by the founders of the institution, the tranquil golden stone quadrangle reflected the Australian sunlight and, in the late afternoons, its leaded windows glowed pink with the declining sun. Its planners were visionaries who dreamed, in the 1830s, of a great university for the Colony of New South Wales which would educate an elite of learning and cultivation. The founders gave the University an architectural form which proclaimed their reliance on the traditions of Oxbridge and paid no heed to the local environment. The University was to be an institution which transcended Australia's geography, a bearer of the cultural standards of "home."

One saw the grand view of the University only if one entered its main gates by car. The traveler by public transport traveled east or west along the bustling main Sydney thoroughfare of Parramatta Road, and climbed a flight of steps up from the road to enter the University's main east-west path of traffic. From this entry one crossed a small courtyard to enter the quadrangle on its northern side, emerging from the heat of the day and bright sunlight to the inner view of the Quad, its cloisters providing cool paths of shade, and its warm balustrades and arches framing pools of light against dark shadow. Clusters of talkative students lounged along the balustrades. They leaned against arches, laid out full-length upon the stone embrasures, or sat cross-legged in the sun—perpetually in animated conversation. At certain times of day the griffins and other heraldic beasts which decorated the inner facade threw strong black shadows on the four inner rectangles of immaculate lawn, but the thick stone walls and paving blocks hollowed by the passage of generations of feet kept the classrooms and offices arrayed along the Quad's four sides cool. The high ceilings and narrow mullioned windows allowed for ample ventilation, so that a style of architecture developed for another climate seemed admirably adapted to the Antipodes. The rest of the campus might be an undistinguished aggregation of brick and stucco reflecting the styles of the thirties, the permanent "temporary" buildings of wartime, and the hurried constructions of the immediate postwar period, but the Quad, which housed the Fisher Library and the offices and classrooms of the Faculty of Arts, was an architectural statement about a heritage from Europe which was totally satisfying.

In the late summer of 1952, arriving by taxi to consult the Adviser to Women Students, I felt a thrill of excitement at seeing this architectural expression of the European tradition of learning. Because I was too shy to ask people for directions, I got lost twice before I found the Adviser to Women tucked away in a small inner quadrangle adjacent to the Quad. The Adviser was the sole counselor to the entire enrollment of women students, and could not spend time learning about each of the several thousand entering women freshmen. The University of Sydney had expanded when returning service men and women enrolled in large numbers in the late 1940s. It was thus already crowded when the national government established a scholarship program in the early 1950s to expand access for regular age students.

Lacking funds for facilities or faculty expansion, the University authorities admitted all who qualified, but expected more than a third to fail or drop out during the freshman year. I was one of the seven hundred young people entering the Faculty of Arts in 1952, more than half of them women and a good percentage, myself included, holders of Commonwealth Scholarships. Given our numbers, the Adviser to Women could be forgiven for averting the worst academic blunders and waiting to see who was left to advise in the following year. She and I settled briskly on my first-year program. French, philosophy, history, and English (a full course load), with elementary German as a subject I could audit to see if my real bent proved to be for modern languages. Like most freshmen, I had no idea of how much time each course might take, or what emphasis each department placed on what aspects of the discipline in question. I thought philosophy would be about wisdom, that

French would enable me to read more of a literature I found enchanting, and that history and English would be more of the subjects I had loved at school.

The week of Freshman Orientation was sunny and hot. When we began to crowd into the University's largest lecture hall at the beginning of Orientation week, the crowd was vast and intimidating. Outside it seemed as though throngs of young people occupied every square inch of the campus. They all seemed at ease and clear about what they were doing, whereas I was in a constant state of anxiety. It began with my morning at home. Would I get everything done in the house before setting out for the thirty-minute walk to the train station? "Everything" involved seeing that my mother had what she needed for the day, that she was downstairs safely, and that the house was in apple-pie order. If it was not, she would begin trying to clean and polish things with her left hand, and be in a mood of angry frustration by the time I arrived home in the late afternoon. Once I made the train there was another cause for worry. Would it be on time? The train system was notoriously unpunctual, and I might be late. Lateness was purgatorial, because that meant going into a lecture room after the class began. Most of the time my nerve failed me and I couldn't do it. I could not endure all those eyes turned toward me as, dry-mouthed, I climbed up to the back row. When I was on time there was the problem of where to sit, and how to summon up easy conversation with total strangers. I wished the earth would swallow me up immediately I uttered some inanity.

I sometimes made dates to eat with my friends from Abbotsleigh, but on most days their courses and schedules were different from mine so I had to solve the problem of lunch by myself. The Women's Union was close to the Quadrangle, but to enter it was to face a sea of tables filled with eagerly talking groups. I went through the line to find a sandwich and coffee, but then where to sit? With whom? I didn't feel entitled just to occupy space by myself.

The causes of my extreme shyness were complex. I didn't look right and couldn't blend with the crowd. I worried constantly about my responsibilities at home. At a deeper level I felt I had no right to exist unless serving the family in some tangible way. At the University, the reassurance of playing that role was not possible. I knew that a young woman's existence could be justified by being attached to the appropriate young man, but I radiated too much nervousness and anxiety to make any new friends, let alone to find male company.

When I rushed to the afternoon train, I should have settled down to working at my books during the journey home. However, my Abbotsleigh training was immutable, so on the crowded commuting trains I usually stood up for much of the fifty-minute journey. I was hot and tired when I arrived home and began to cajole my mother into a good mood. While we had a cup of tea, I listened to a diatribe against the physiotherapist who came daily to massage her wrist, now free of its cast. Then there was dinner to prepare. If my mother ate after 6:30 P.M. she couldn't sleep for dyspepsia, so the meal must be promptly on the table and prepared without deviation from my mother's exacting standards.

At school sitting down to my books in the evening had been the happy occupation which capped the day, but now I was too weary to enjoy the work. I might have been lifted out of it by the interest of my work, but I was finding most of it dull or disappointing or both.

The French Department insisted that one

speak with a near-Parisian accent before settling down to studying French literature. I
had no mimetic faculty, could not make the
required sounds, and the two-thirds of my
week's French classes which were conversation exercises were a constant humiliation.
No amount of drilling could convert what I
had taken in from Mrs. Fisher's Belgian accent into Parisian sounds. In philosophy, I
could do the logic exercises, but I didn't
really care whether an argument contained
a syllogism with an undistributed middle
clause or not. The meaning of what I read
or heard was perfectly clear to me, but this
painstaking analysis of language seemed
dull. I had looked forward to reading Plato
and studying Greek philosophy, but the
hours spent on the *Euthyphro* were not spent
dealing with what it meant and how that
fitted into the Greek view of life, but on
analysis of every word, comma, and phrase.
In English we read Chaucer and studied phonetics. I wasn't interested in Middle English.
I was champing at the bit to read T. S. Eliot
and to study Shakespeare's tragedies, but
these were nowhere in sight. Only history
lived up to my expectation, but one didn't
do anything in first-year history but attend
lectures of two or three hundred students

until toward the end of the term when the term's essay was assigned. I raced through the assigned books, many of which I had read before, loving every moment of them, but there was not enough history to make up for the boredom of those hours trying to make French *r* sounds, fussing over the punctuation of the translation of the *Euthyphro*, or converting Chaucer to phonetic script. German, being at 9:00 A.M., quickly fell by the wayside. To get to the University in time for the classes, I would have had to rise at five o'clock to finish my household tasks and make the train journey in time.

I lasted to the middle of the year before using my mother's increasing ill health as an excuse to escape from the daily ordeal of having no friends and no place where I felt I belonged. I told my mother truthfully that I was bored with most of the academic work and couldn't imagine how I would ever use what I was learning. I knew she agreed with this. Once I began to attend the University, her attitude to my studies became more ambiguous. She had a romantic picture of what university study would be like. All her frustration at not having completed high school was loaded into her questions. Each day she asked me hungrily what I was learning, hoping to live out her own thwarted longing for education through me. When all I could tell her was an account of classes in logic or phonetics, she would make some derisive comment and remind herself and me that at my age she had already been working and supporting herself for many years. If ever I mentioned needing more pocket money than train fares and change for lunch, she would raise her eyebrows, remind me of the same information, and change the subject.

I came to the decision to drop out of the University just as Barry announced that he was leaving Coorain for good. He was not going to make the land his calling in life. Coorain was too lonely. Instead, he would use his spanking-new Auster aircraft as the basis for launching a country air charter service. He settled on the pleasant country town of Narromine in the central western part of New South Wales for his base, and opened his business, combining his charter services with teaching flying at the local flying club. He was happy from the moment he began. He was more than a competent bush pilot. He was an inspired one. He throve on landing in out-of-the-way places to whisk sick people away to the hospital. His physical endurance and courage earned him admiration and considerable réclame during a season of dangerous floods when he was always ahead of the flood waters saving households or carrying needed medical supplies. Every country town and its outlying regions needed such services desperately. Barry delivered them with courage and daring combined with quiet and efficient concern for the safety of others. Other bush pilots might be lackadaisical about their aircraft and its maintenance, but Barry reminded me of my father in the way his plane and everything associated with it was lovingly cared for. He had made his own place in life, was sought after for skills everyone valued, and his circle of friends grew with the passage of each week.

My mother, nonplussed at this turn of events, oscillated between admiration of Barry for defying her and complaint that he was using her gift for purposes other than hers. To me she complained of her worries about who would take care of Coorain for her in the future. It was a sacred trust, she said, our last link to my father and our once happy family life there. I embraced this responsibility energetically, seeing it as a comfort to my ailing mother, whose complaints were now numerous. She had an inflamed gallbladder and gallstones. She developed high blood pressure. Her thyroid gland became enlarged and she was diagnosed as being slightly hyperthyroid. These conditions were susceptible to medical management had she been content to accept a consistent pattern of medical care. However, she went from one doctor to another, in search of one whose manner she liked, only to rage against the follies of the medical profession, and to abandon one program of medication after another. High blood pressure and a hyperthyroid condition, she decided, required a totally predictable life with no distractions, no deviations from her schedule, and no emotional pressures of any kind. This meant that any attempt to oppose her will produced dramatic results. A disagreement raised her blood pressure, bothered her thyroid condition, or triggered a gallbladder attack. No matter the hour of the affront, it left her sleepless. She would emerge white-faced from her room the next morning, every line in her body an accusation for causing her such discomfort.

When I went out to Coorain to be on hand for the shearing that year, I relished my chance to be alone on the journey. It was comfortable to be working there, once again tracing familiar patterns over the contours of the land. After my unsatisfactory studies, the practicality of simple physical labor delighted me. I could see for myself why Barry had left. The house at Coorain, always simple, now lacked my mother's touch. It wasn't polished like a new pin. The garden was gone. A lot of the machinery was wearing out. Because my mother was oblivious to the passage of time, and too thrifty to invest in much comfort for her employees, it had been a negotiation worthy of the Congress of Vienna to get her to agree to replace the 1940 Ford utility with a new one.

Working for Geoff was a constant test of whether my life in the city had made me soft. I kept up the pace he set, but when I got back to Sydney I was eight pounds lighter. I presented no threat of replacement to the Coghlans, and received their warm hospitality and affection, but I could see that Coorain would be a heartbreakingly lonely place for any young person to work.

On the train journey back I came to my decision. I would not go on being financially dependent on my mother, listening to her undertone of contempt for people who didn't earn their own living. I would find a job, save some money, and gain some independence. Finding a job in the expanding Australian economy of the 1950s was simply a matter of reading the newspapers. The daily Help Wanted or Positions Vacant advertisements (segregated by sex) were many pages long. They read "Help Wanted—Men" or "Help Wanted—Women," regularly listing lower wage rates for the same job when the employee was a woman. To me the difference was part of life, like the weather. The week I returned to Sydney I scanned the women's column of Positions Vacant in the morning paper and decided to claim, falsely, that I could type, so that I could apply for a job as a receptionist for a medical practice in the nearby suburb of Castle Hill. I was accepted, and began to work the next week for two partners who shared a sprawling medical practice in a group of suburbs on the northwestern fringe of the city of Sydney.

During the next eighteen months a series of heavy burdens slid from my shoulders. The work was undemanding in its routines, but endlessly interesting in its human details. I learned that once a person dressed in a white starched coat, however unqualified, chances among those seeking medical advice, the mantle of authority descends, and his or her advice is sought about all manner of human predicaments. I had scarcely sat down at my desk in the outer office of the surgery than the first talkative patients arrived and began to volunteer all sorts of startling information about their intimate lives. My shyness was irrelevant to people who needed to talk about themselves and their problems. Listening and making soothing sounds, I saw the uncertainties and worries behind people's appearances, and realized that my troubles in life were modest in relation to the human predicaments which people paraded before me daily. I was an all-purpose medical records clerk, receptionist, appointments secretary, and occasional practical nurse when a child needed stitching up, or emergency procedures were necessary for someone brought in with injuries needing immediate attention. The complexity of the human drama each day was gripping. When times were quiet I read my way swiftly through my employers' medical texts. When the office was busy I received a more concentrated education. It was not simply about the ailments which brought each patient to the doctor's office, but about the social context surrounding each patient and his or her family. I saw the usual range of neurotic suffering which wanders through the door of a general practitioner's office. Seeing the terminally ill coming regularly for their visits to the surgery, their courage and laughter carried me past my fear of the dying. I began to be able to distinguish the telephone voice of the alcoholic complainer from the quiet dismissive voice of the man or woman who was disguising fear of illness with false heartiness. I came to know and like the young mothers, stuck at home, trying to cope with the newest baby and the five-year-old who had just fallen out of a tree. My employers were good physicians who showed humor and sensitivity in their dealings with their patients. I liked seeing them at work, and enjoyed laughing with them over the follies of the day or the sheer lunacy of some of the daily life situations we learned about. It was like being thrust inside the mind of a gifted novelist. Thenceforth I looked at people, myself included, with more compassion and more distance.

My mother's respect for the fact that I was earning my own living was palpable. A year after her injury some strength returned to her broken right wrist. She became more active, her moods improved, and patches of sunshine broke through our stormy domestic

271

scene. She was almost childishly delighted when I bought tickets for the ballet or the theater and took her out for an evening's entertainment. Besides planning diversions for my mother, I spent my early earnings on attending an evening school where one could learn how to make the best of one's appearance. The school sent me to a hairdresser who knew how to cut my kind of hair, a task completed with transforming effect. Armed with new knowledge about diet I steadfastly refused to eat much of my mother's daily fare of meat and potatoes. More pounds joined those run off in hard labor at Coorain and a new shape emerged to accompany my well-coiffed head. Able to ignore my mother's critical oversight, I bought the kind of clothes I thought suitable, and won grudging approval from her even as she exclaimed over my spendthrift ways. I didn't care. I knew my appearance was beginning to approximate the glossy fashion magazines I studied so assiduously. I was painstakingly constructing an acceptable public self.

This was easier to do as my mother's refrain of criticism diminished. Our happiest times came on the weekends when we ranged far and wide about the city and its environs, looking for rare plants, nurseries with desirable strong stock, books about the prop-agation of plants. We shared a genuine obsession with growing things, and could spend hours happily pondering whether a yellow or a pale orange rose would complete the color composition we were planning for some corner of the garden. In springtime the results were breathtaking. Yellow daffodils and deep blue iris marked the meandering edge of the front garden. Behind them were pink and white azaleas backed by white and yellow jasmine, white mock orange, and graceful blue buddleia. In a sheltered corner were seven different species of scented daphne, their perfumes competing with the heady onslaught of port wine magnolia and ginger plant. One could hear the hum of the bees on sunny spring afternoons as they drowsed homewards through the air fragrant with the pungent smell of lemon-scented gums and the heavier perfumes of daphne, magnolia, and ginger.

My evenings were no longer spent exclu-sively at home. One of my older brother's friends, for whom I had nurtured hopeless romantic feelings since my early teens, sud-denly reappeared in our life and began to squire me around. He was handsome, happy-go-lucky, and good-natured, a combination ideally suited to provide for relatively painless first love. It suited my pride that he was older than most of my Abbotsleigh friends' companions. I felt that at last I was traveling at a heady speed toward adulthood, dressed to kill and ready for adventure. My mother observed my comings and goings warily, but I was too elated to notice her watchful and guarded behavior.

Within twelve months the routine of the medical practice had begun to pall. My bank account contained what looked to me like large resources, and provided she stayed within her iron routine, my mother's health was robust. Her most recent arguments with the manager of Coorain had been resolved, and there was adequate help on the place. As my mind began to turn to finding more stimulating work, I regretted my foolishness in giving up my scholarship and dropping out of the University. My mother surprised me by urging me to return. She could easily afford to pay my fees. Furthermore, she acknowledged that she'd been giving me a miserably small allowance in my first student year. We worked out what would be a comfortable allowance for food, clothes, books, and travel. I could scarcely believe this happy state of affairs, nor my good luck when a kindly official in the Department of Education reinstated my scholarship for my readmission to the University of Sydney in the late summer of 1954.

This time I took a leisurely three subjects: a comfortable nine hours of lectures in history, English, and psychology. I knew my way around, and now accustomed to talking to strangers, I could chatter easily with whomever I sat next to in lectures. Within a matter of weeks, coming brazenly late to a class I met Toni, a young woman of striking beauty and elfin charm, a latecomer also seated in the back row in a history lecture. We took to one another, and began one of the intense undergraduate friendships through which young people learn about themselves by discovering the inner life and feelings of friends. Toni was dark-haired with dazzling cornflower blue eyes. Her cultivated voice and her talent for self-mockery fascinated me. She seemed to take nothing seriously, to laugh at life, and to look upon her parents' generation as denizens of a world to be tolerated but not taken seriously. She and her brother, who studied economics, became regular companions. They came from a country family, had attended schools like mine, and shared my questions about whether I belonged to Australia's bush culture or to its urban professional classes. They were cheerful hedonists who took it for granted that one should enjoy one's university life, paying only the modicum of attention to studying which was necessary to "get through" each year's annual examinations. Once approached in this fashion, university life could indeed be wonderfully leisurely. There was only one annual examination at the end of the year, attendance at lectures was not compulsory, and the written assignments for each term were not onerous.

Before I knew it I was skipping lectures on fine days to walk in Centennial Park, dashing off to the one remaining vaudeville theater in Sydney for the afternoon matinée to learn the music hall songs of the thirties, setting out for the zoo on the whim of the moment for a ride on the elephants, or simply spending long afternoons talking, talking, talking. Our conversations were not intellectual, but focused on our parents, our families, our uncertainties and insecurities, our feelings about being Australian, our puzzlement about what to do in life. Toni was in the midst of romantic turmoil, hopelessly in love with a suitor disapproved of by her family. We talked the year away, our conversations interrupted only by vacations. I began to emulate Toni's bon mots, her talent for telling funny stories, and her casual but stylish dress.

It was perfectly easy for me to keep up with my courses by reading at home in the evenings or on weekends. My essay assignments were occasionally daunting, such as the required essay in first-year English language on the origins of the fused participle, but these too could be crammed into systematic work on weekends without affecting the pleasures of the week. From Toni and her brother I learned the art of enjoying life, of stopping to savor the joys of the moment, and of letting the cares of tomorrow wait. In my mother's eyes, I was staggering under a burden of academic work, since I fell to with a vengeance when at home and scarcely lifted my head from my books. She was unaware of how I spent my daytime hours, and impressed by the longer and longer hours I seemed to need to put in at the Library.

My new way of life might have gone undetected for years, but at the end of my first year, during the annual examination study period, I fell into the classic undergraduate scrape. My mother had chosen the weeks of November and early December to visit Coorain, taking with her a woman friend her own age. Her friend was widowed, with a daughter close in age to me, so it was arranged that the two daughters would live together in our house while the two mothers made their trip to the bush. My mother was scarcely out the front door before I invited Toni to join me so that we could study together. Various and sundry other friends came for meals, overnight stays, parties, conviviality. I quickly became too engaged in cooking, cleaning, and the general duties of a hostess to notice that my new arrangements were grating on the nerves of my authorized guest, who departed after a week to stay with other friends. News of her new arrangements filtered through to Coorain, so that the day before my first history examination I learned that my mother was returning early to investigate. The comic scene of the mice playing while the cat traveled was interrupted, requiring feverish cleaning and tidying on my part to erase all signs of visitors before meeting my mother's train which arrived at 6:30 A.M. the following morning. I went to meet her feeling like a political prisoner, conscious of no real wrongdoing, but nonetheless headed for the gallows. The storm would descend and I could do nothing to avert it.

My mother surveyed the house tight-lipped. It was spotless. The sole focus of disapproval was therefore my behavior. She told me she was deeply disappointed in me, but that we would reserve the discussion of my multiple sins until after the examinations were concluded. For the remainder of the day a deep calm descended upon me as I turned to reviewing the fragmentary notes of the few lectures I had actually attended and glanced over the books assigned for the year. I was up and away the next morning before my mother appeared so that I could be at the University an hour at least before I had to begin the examination in the Great Hall. Despite a sleepless night, my sense of calm and detachment remained, so that when I took up the paper and began to write my head was clear. I was long past having examination nerves.

The examination was on Tudor and Stuart history, a subject about which I had been reading extensively since my early teens. My attitudes to study were still those of a high school student, so I didn't realize that I was very well prepared for the examination. Being "prepared" in my book then meant having committed to memory everything the instructor said, all the notes of lectures, and key sections of the textbooks. Having failed to undertake this counterproductive labor, I was obliged to rely on my years of reading. It was astonishing how easily quotations came to mind to illustrate my points, and how broad I discovered was the spectrum of interpretations of Tudor and Stuart constitutional history I had read and could discuss. The map of Elizabethan London was in my head. I knew exactly the peregrinations of Cromwell's Parliaments, and R. H. Tawney's resounding prose from *Religion and the Rise of Capitalism* echoed in my mind as soon as I turned to discuss the dissolution of the monasteries and the Puritan Revolution. The resulting examination was more thoughtful and reflective than any I might otherwise have written. I hoped it would suffice and turned determinedly to tackling the obstacle course of three-hour examinations which came in rapid sequence during the next few days.

By the time the examinations were concluded, my mother's lecture on my conduct was delivered more in sorrow than in anger. It was clear, she said, that I had frittered the year away through my foolish predilection for inappropriate company. Mine was a weak character too easily swayed by the influence of others, and I had doubtless wasted my year through my folly in spending my examination preparation time in partying when work and adherence to my mother's plan was what was called for. Privately I thought I had scraped through in all my courses, but I listened to the rebukes and recognized the wisdom of agreeing not to err in this fashion in future. Toni's cheerful attitude to the older generation had given me sufficient distance to listen dutifully, but pay no inner heed to the injunctions.

When the annual examination results were published just before Christmas, my mother and I were in Queensland for a Christmas holiday. For the first time in our lives we were alone at Christmas that year. Barry had taken the profits from his air charter business and used them to finance a journey of exploration to Europe. When his *Wanderjahr* was over he planned to buy a light aircraft and fly it home, exploring the Middle East and Southeast Asia along the way. For diversion my mother and I were spending the holidays at the small, unspoiled coastal resort of Surfer's Paradise, about forty minutes' drive south of Brisbane. We loved the slow pace of the town with its cluster of simple beach houses. A few unpretentious blocks of flats, and one modest hotel, hard by the miles of quiet, uncrowded beach. No Sydney papers reached such a sleepy little town, so we were startled when telegrams of congratulation were delivered from my uncle and aunt, and half a dozen other Sydney friends. My mother, who had been expecting to discuss my failure and lay down the terms on which she was prepared to support my studies in future, was taken aback. We agreed that I should drive up to Brisbane, find a Sydney paper, and return with the news. Finding a paper at Brisbane Airport, I scanned the list of passes for each subject and saw with horror that my name was not there. Then I saw it in the list of honors and prizes, and gradually it dawned on me that I had done very well. I drove back down the coast in a trance. My vindication was complete. I had come first in history, earned high distinction in English, and had ranked high in the class in psychology.

I had scored a smashing psychological victory. It was hard to see how such results might have been improved on, and since success was what counted for my mother, the basis for future strictures about my conduct had suddenly been completely undermined. Better still was my inner feeling that I had found something I could do well, and my new awareness that university study was about learning and reflection, not the cramming of texts and information. Now I had a purpose in life. I would take an honors degree, rank high in the class, and set about choosing between the variety of promising career opportunities which went with such achievement. Some of the inner tension went out of me because I saw a solution to the dilemma I could discuss with no one. If I were to become a success academically and chose a career which would take me away from Sydney, it would finesse the whole question of leaving home. My mother would never stand in the way of success. Moreover, if it were public enough, its sweetness might cushion the blow of my departure. I could remain true to my obligations to the family by covering the family name with honors. For the moment, the path ahead was clear. I could settle down to my studies for the next three years, and let the future take care of itself.

My mother's apology for her mistaken assessment of my firstyear performance was handsome. One morning shortly after we returned home, I found a jeweler's box beside my breakfast plate. It contained a diamond and sapphire pin and a graceful note expressing pride in my achievements and an apology for her unwarranted disapproval. As I exclaimed with delight and pinned it on, I forgot my earlier insights about my mother's lavish gifts. I was too excited by the future I painted in my mind to practice the most elementary caution.

The beginning of my second year at the University of Sydney was a heady time. People knew who I was. Faculty, hitherto superior beings clad in black gowns, now nodded as they passed me in the Quadrangle. Everyone taking history or English honors in the years above me began taking an interest in what I was doing. I started out taking a double honors program in history and English, enjoying the special status that this ambitious program brought. The pass course was taught by lecture to classes of hundreds of students whose relationships with faculty were of necessity limited. Each department prided itself on its honors program, however, which was based on very detailed seminar work with small groups of students, whom faculty came to know very well indeed. I loved literary studies as much as I did history, but there was no comparison between the level of intellectual challenge offered by the first year of the history honors program compared with that of the English Department.

In history we took seminars on modern European and British history, and on historiography. We plunged into reading Vico, Marx, Hegel, Burckhardt, Acton, Mannheim, Max Weber, and modern philosophers of history like Collingwood, without pausing to consider whether we had the background to analyze them critically. In seminars, our discussions were about the 1848 revolutions in Europe, the character of industrial society, the concept of alienation, the rise of fascism and anti-Semitism, the modern trend toward authoritarian mass societies, the differences between realpolitik and romantic notions of democratic liberal or socialist world order. Our instructors were the liveliest and most challenging minds among the history faculty: Alan Shaw, Oxford-trained, witty, urbane, and an inspired teacher; Ernst Bramstedt, a German Jewish scholar, of formidable intellect, exiled from Germany by the Nazis, an early collaborator with the great Karl Mannheim; Marjorie Jacobs, the one woman on the history faculty, learned, intellectually incisive, the first person I met who did not automatically see Australia and the world from a conventional European point of view. We spent six hours a week in the company of these fascinating minds, discussing the most central ideas and problems involved in understanding the twentieth century. The seminars never really ended because some segment of the student part of them moved off for coffee and more talk. Milton Osborne, son of an academic family, brilliant, whippet-thin, radiating intellectual energy and insatiable curiosity, possessed the most interesting and rigorous mind of my fellow history honors students. Ken Hosking, a more reflective and more aesthetically concerned person, was the needed counterpoint in an argument. Rob Laurie, intent on a career of public service, provided a spirited defense of traditional conservative points of view. I found myself intoxicated by the pleasure of abstract ideas, by the company of others who shared my interests, and by the notion that one could get beneath the appearances of events to understand the property and class relationships which constituted the stuff of politics and culture. Milton and I, whose families were near neighbors, spent endless hours arguing about historiography, politics, life.

Marx and Engels opened my eyes to another way of seeing my parents and the enterprise of Coorain. Was it true that we were monopolizers of land, that Shorty and all my other shearer friends were expropriated laborers? Were the family values of thrift and industry simply signs that we were bourgeois? Who were the rightful owners and users of the land I had always thought to belong to us? I began to wonder about the aboriginal ovens I had played with as a child, and the nardoo stones we had so heedlessly trodden upon as we entered and left the house. What had happened to the tribes which once used to hunt over our land? For that matter, where had those huge, pink, delicately hollowed stones been carried from to end up on Coorain? Why had they been discarded?

I read *The Origin of the Family, Private Property and the State*, treating its subject as though it were about some distant and different race rather than my own sex. Certainly it reminded me of my mother's outraged complaints at her investments and the product of her labor being subsumed in my father's estate, but I had unthinkingly taken on the identity of the male writer and intellect present in all that I was reading, and did not take in emotionally that the subordination Engels wrote about applied to me. Obtusely, I did not pay heed to the fact that I was the only woman taking history honors that year, or how unusual I seemed to all my friends because I was aspiring to excel academically.

I was excited to find myself arguing about Marx and Engels with two intellectually able young union organizers, friends of Milton's, who were history honors students in the year ahead of me. They were tolerant in the kindest way about my "best girl's boarding school" appearance. They sent me off to collect one of the free sets of the works of Marx and Engels handed out by the Communist Book Shop in downtown Sydney. "Go on, Jill, why pay for them? The Party members won't eat you," they urged me as I teetered on the brink of paying good money for these necessary texts. "You'd better park that fancy grey Rover up the street so they don't see what a bloody plutocrat you are." I did as I was told, sidling anxiously through the door, and emerging half an hour later with my arms full of books and Party tracts.

When I reported the mission accomplished the next day, I produced shouts of laughter, and was escorted off to a real working-class pub for a beer and congratulations. For the first time, I glimpsed what a choice had been made when my mother took on her extra job to send me to Abbotsleigh. I liked the loud conviviality of my left-wing friends and the union "mates" they introduced me to. They were amused at the sight of someone like me in my proper North Shore uniform of cashmere sweater, grey flannel skirt, and English walking shoes, genuinely puzzling about Marx, but we were denizens of different worlds. Inwardly, although I had adopted the uniform of well-brought-up young women of my generation, I was curious about the other Australia I had fled so precipitously as an eleven-year-old. The shearers and station hands I'd known as a little girl were important figures from my childhood, as were the values I'd picked up at smoko time listening to the shearing team talk about life.

Whenever I went off to work on Coorain, I was conscious that academic Australia was made up entirely of urban social types, people totally different from the tough, hard-bitten men and women of the western plains. In the winter of 1955, when I made my first visit to my brother, now operating a flourishing air charter service in the western Queensland town of Charleville, where he had settled on his return from Europe, I had the same experience. Charleville was a town poised on the edge of real wilderness, with the uncharted land beyond the Cooper and the Diamantina rivers to the west, and the vast, isolated cattle stations of western Queensland and the Northern Territory in its hinterland. Here I saw another authentic outback world. Nothing could have been in greater contrast to the sedentary life of the urban scholar. Barry was up at four, the plane ready at sunrise, and we were off across trackless barren country until we landed at a lonely station or beside the drovers and a herd of cattle making their slow passage to the railhead three or four hundred miles away. On the return flight, having carried out the mission of the day and dropped our passengers, we were free to dive down to see some beautiful waterhole filled with wildfowl hundreds of miles from anywhere or to watch the herds of wild Arab horses which bred up in the isolation of the land across the Cooper, spread out galloping, manes flying, symbols of Edenic freedom. Juxtaposed in my mind when I returned to the city would be the image of some wiry Queen-slander, body burnt brown above tattered khaki shorts, heaving around petrol drums at a backcountry airport, or the faces of the aboriginal stockmen who came into Charleville on their days off. I could make a class and race analysis of this world according to the categories I was learning in my history seminars, but I was also groping for a way to describe it which recognized its difference from the industrial working class in England or the jacquerie of the French Revolution. I was already reading the standard left versions of Australian history, but they didn't satisfy me either. They had been written by sedentary people who had never lived in the bush and had no notion what settling it was like.

By contrast with history, the first year of English honors was heavy going. We learned Anglo-Saxon and read *Piers Plowman*, intellectual tasks which required lots of *sitzfleisch*, but didn't offer much excitement. My fellow students were mostly headed toward master's degrees and high school teaching. I could learn languages easily enough, but found it hard to care about them, except as they opened new literatures and new experiences to me. The literary part of the English honors program came in the second year, but by that time I had decided to concentrate my efforts in history and take the pass course in English.

There was more than enough excitement for me in the pass English course where we studied the modern novel, romantic poetry, and Shakespeare's comedies. It didn't matter that there were no seminars and discussion groups because the lectures were superb, balancing critical insight with historical context and attention to technique. I had taken to jotting down in the margin of my notebook all the references made to major critical works, and simply read them on my own early in the term before time was needed for essay writing. There were often long afternoons when I became so entranced by reading John Livingston Lowes on Coleridge, or Keats's letters to his brothers and sister, that I noticed the passage of time only when the slanting afternoon sunlight disappeared and the lights came on in the Fisher Library.

I made many earthshaking discoveries in the Fisher Reading Room, as I sat at one of the long heavy mahogany tables, semioblivious to the rustling of other students' papers and the counterpoint of whispered conversations. I was thunderstruck by reading

Samuel Butler's *The Way of All Flesh* for our course in the modern novel. Toni's sardonic view of her family had shown me someone who looked clear-eyed at family relationships, but Butler's full-fledged satirical treatment of the Pontifex family and its shameless exploitation of the young, exploitation justified by parental authority and through the mouthing of empty pieties, left me feeling that I had been struck by lightning. I heard for the first time the self-deception in my mother's often-repeated "Of course I want my children to be free to do what they want, travel where they choose, and not be tied to me." "Jill's very dependent on me," she often told people, neglecting to mention that most of my trips away had to be canceled because she began to have dizzy spells. "I can't stand parents who think they own their children," she would announce, not mentioning her ferocious attacks on the character and motives of any friends I was incautious enough to bring home. From that afternoon in the Fisher Library on, I listened to her complacent voice differently. I still saw her as a moral agent, the heroic figure whose courage and industry had rescued us from disaster and sheltered me from my childhood insecurities, but these images were now paired with less favorable ones.

The afternoon I finished reading Joyce's *Portrait of the Artist as a Young Man*, for the same course, I sat for a long time gazing out the window of the library. In Stephen Daedalus's argument with his student companion about *claritas*, I saw my ideal of intellectual life perfectly articulated. That was it. Like Stephen, I was seeking "wholeness, harmony and passion," the *claritas* which was the equivalent of the Christian vision of God. Somewhere, somehow it must be possible to reconcile the conflicts of the emotions, the pains of life, the sense of beauty, in one unifying understanding. This was what I was doing here, what these stone walls had been built for, and why these books had been painstakingly accumulated. Joyce's Dublin and the indictment of his Catholic education were merely a backdrop for me for this sudden vision of what the young were seeking from a university.

Another thunderbolt struck one afternoon when I turned idly to look at the shelves behind me, my preparation for the upcoming lecture in psychology finished, and fifteen minutes remaining till the class began. I lifted from the shelves a volume of Jung's

Collected Works. Flipping through the pages, I began to read an essay entitled "The Positive and Negative Aspects of the Mother Archetype." It was astounding. There I was, described to a T. There was my mother sitting on the page before me, as though Jung had known her every mood. I never went to the lecture on abnormal psychology, but instead read like one possessed. I needed no convincing that we were Demeter and Persephone, and that my mother would indeed turn the world about her into a desert of grief if she were to lose me. It was a comfort to see my life situation so well described, but it was also alarming to realize that it was even more elemental than I had supposed. The next time I was at a bookstore, I bought the *Collected Works* of Jung and set it on my bookshelves to go back to again and again. My psychology course was strictly behavioral in approach, and psychiatry in the Sydney of my day was the recourse of weaklings and emotional cripples. Yet there was no getting away from the fact that my mother's emotional need for me went far beyond normal limits. Whenever my mind went down this path, I braced myself, gritted my teeth, and told myself not to complain. She had suffered a great deal and her care was my responsibility.

My afternoons in the Fisher Library were solitary after the first term because early in the year Toni was dispatched on the standard Australian trip to Europe, a family stratagem to divert her from unacceptable romantic attachments. It was sad to see her walking, bright-eyed and elegant, out to the Qantas Constellation, shortly to depart in a flurry of propellers for Singapore, Karachi, and farther points en route for London. I knew I would miss her merry and intelligent laughter, and her sense of life as an unending human comedy. She had been wonderful company during my year of playful discovery of the University, and her good example had taught me that I need not be as compulsive about working as was my natural disposition.

Not long after Toni's departure, coming early to a lecture in Romantic poetry, I sat down beside a fair-haired young woman who, like me, always sat close to the front of the class. She stood out in the group for the melodiousness of her voice and her silvery peal of laughter, heard whenever the lecturer said something witty. We fell to chatting about the subject of the day's lecture, and progressed quickly to introducing ourselves. Nina Morris was a few years my junior, and also in her second year at the University. Our paths had not crossed before because she had been educated at Catholic convent schools, whereas Abbotsleigh was Anglican. So great was the social chasm dividing Catholics and non-Catholics in Australian culture that schools did not compete in athletics across denominational lines, and the two groups kept pretty much to themselves during the first year of University. After the lecture, in which the instructor had inspired us all by describing Keats's sense of the creative imagination as the capacity to pass through the house of life, never resting before a closed door, but instead opening the doors to one new experience after another through the power of empathy, we wandered off for coffee to prolong the excitement created by the skillful lecture and its wonderful subject.

Nina became a daily companion. I was fascinated by her zest for life, her inexhaustible sociability, her curiosity about people, her religious sensibility. She was the first well-educated Catholic I had met, and her interest in sacred music, in contemporary painting and modern theater, opened a range of aesthetic interests to me which had not entered my life before. She was also the center of a lively group of friends who quickly also became mine. Cam McKinney, the child of an American father and Australian mother, looked at our world from the perspective of someone whose high school education had been in the United States. His vibrant, musical voice was never silent, and was regularly to be heard expounding on matters of taste and modern aesthetics with unconscious but well-informed authority. His quizzical gaze took in one's appearance at a glance, and we all became accustomed to receiving his exacting grades for stodginess or style in our appearance. He was critical of the Australian female tendency to flowery emulation of the Royal Family, and mocked us into awareness of New York and Paris as the source of style and elegance. He studied anthropology and was forever explaining the social symbolism of our comings and goings, or of significant events in Australian life. His creative energy was so infectious it was impossible to be dull in his company.

Vanessa Schneider, the most dazzling beauty of the group, shared Nina's religious concerns; Patty O'Connel, vivacious, redhaired, bubbling with Irish wit, had the same talent for wicked social commentary that was so amusing in Cam McKinney; Ken Hosking and Hugh Gore, good-humored and hospitable neighbors in residence at St. Paul's, the Anglican men's college, shared Nina's love of music and theater. All congregated in a circle held together by Nina's zest for life and gift for entertainment. She was the hostess whose parties in her parents' spacious flat in Mosman kept us all in lively contact. It was she who organized the delectable picnics we took to the beach at Newport or Palm Beach to celebrate the end of the examinations and the arrival of summer. A beach picnic under Nina's supervision involved the provision of plentiful beach umbrellas for the morning to avoid sunburn for people with skin like mine; at least three courses of magically cooled food, eaten in the early afternoon on some treeshaded rock above the beach where ants and flies never appeared; and an evening party at someone's nearby house where we could shed the day's sand, cool our sunburn, eat ravenously again, and talk late under the stars.

I always enjoyed wandering into the dining room at the Women's Union on days when Nina was about because I knew I would find her at the center of a lively group, eager to introduce me to interesting new people she had met, to tell the newest story, or offer a knowledgeable commentary on the orchestra's performance at last night's symphony concert.

One afternoon, in the second term of our second year, I came in to find her with several newcomers in the group, including a newcomer I took for an Englishman because of his accent and manners. The general conversation was about Australian theater, and a new play which treated the experience of cane cutters in northern Queensland as though they were the stuff of Greek epic. My curiosity was piqued by our new companion's comments. It was clear that he knew the London stage well, but little about Australia's new and vibrant theatrical world. I was excited by the play and immediately dived into the conversation to defend it. It was the first I'd seen to treat real Australian types, and to make their experience universal. Seeing the world that way on the stage helped to undo a lifetime of lessons in geography. On our way to our three o'clock English class, Nina told me her friend was the heir to one of Australia's great mining fortunes, but had been educated since early childhood in England and Europe. He was

300

back in Australia to get to know his native country and to sample its culture for a year or two of university education.

Peter Stone quickly became a member of our group, and soon my frequent escort. I liked hearing his downright views about Australian society announced with the self-confidence of an old Harrovian. They were a mixture of love for the natural world and its scenery, and impatience with Sydney's provinciality. To my astonishment and delight he liked clever women and didn't seem to think my reputation for learning detracted from my attractiveness. I was used to concealing how well I did academically when in male company, and to feigning interest in explications of subjects about which I knew a great deal more than the speaker. This was required conduct for women in Australia. It didn't do to question male superiority in anything. One learned early not to correct mistakes in a male companion's logic, and to accept the most patent misinformation as received truth. Peter would start to tell me something, watch my face assume the required expression of rapt interest, and burst out laughing. "But why am I telling you something you know all about anyway?" It was intoxicating not to have to set a watch on my tongue, to be actually found more interesting because of my mind. In his company I enjoyed the experience an intellectual woman needs most if she has lived in a world set on undermining female intelligence: I was loved for what I was rather than the lesser mind I pretended to be. Our deep attraction for one another was mutual. He needed the affection of someone with a sense of purpose in life. I was totally unlike any debutante of the season, and bored by trendy small talk. I scarcely comprehended the international world in which he had been reared and on which he needed to gain perspective. Our lives and our interests were bound to diverge, because I was, without really knowing it, a genuine intellectual. He was intent on a career in business or government, something in my current phase of life I did not value. While we both teetered on the brink of adulthood, we were one another's ideal companion, providing exactly the emotional energy needed to meet life and rise to its challenges.

Peter's mother and her friends were a window on another world. She had made several fashionable marriages and it seemed to me that she clearly intended to make another. Her friends were world-weary international travelers who talked about money and political scandals and told risqué jokes. They were amused by our intense affair and ever ready with worldly advice. "Why are you wasting time on Peter," one remarked to me as the ladies took coffee apart from the gentlemen after a dinner party. "Why don't you go off to London for a season. With your brains and your looks you could make a *really* splendid marriage." It was comforting to be accorded such impressive sexual powers, and endlessly amusing to see how the world looked to such people, even as I was encouraging Peter to set course for a more purposeful and creative life. The thought of an imaginary London season could always divert and reassure me when I felt my afternoons working painstakingly in the library at my history research papers were unexciting.

By forming my first deep attachment with Peter, I had complicated my life enormously. At home I made no secret of the depth of my attraction. Immediately I had to juggle a new set of conflicts. My mother waged undeclared war on the relationship, using every weapon in a formidable arsenal, and showing a brilliant tactical sense. If Peter's Harrovian ways could be made to look foolish or superficial, she found the way to do it. If I could be embarrassed in front of him, she managed it with artistry worthy of Mrs. Siddons. Never an inspired cook, she contrived the most numbing combinations of backcountry food to give him "a taste of Australia." Yet in another dimension of herself, she enjoyed watching me come into my own. Her lingering sense of adventure made her favor exploring new worlds. It reminded her of her own youth, and some of my stories made her recall her own growing up laughingly. It was when I spoke of forming a permanent attachment that her mood darkened and she insisted that I must finish my degree before I could consider any such commitment. After some painful discussions I learned not to raise the subject, because I encountered her in a new persona, a sardonic woman who mocked my emotional life as though it were the stupidest farce. I was startled and troubled by the destructiveness she revealed and tried to explain it away as the result of ill health.

Peter's lively sense of the absurd made him more than equal to tests of his digestion or mockery of his manners, but he was less tolerant of the time I needed for my work. I hadn't experienced this conflict before, and dealt with it badly. I let tomorrow take care of itself, spent long golden afternoons wandering in rapt conversation through Sydney's beautiful parks or along its shining white beaches, and let the hours needed for everything but the term's required written work slide by. Then, when the last possible moment came for preparation for examinations, I simply disappeared to study and refused all invitations. This incomprehensible conduct produced many storms which left me feeling guilty about studying, a new and startling experience. Doing one's best work was sacred in my family, and pressing though my mother's demands for my company had been, she always yielded to my claim that I needed to be alone to study. When presented with the conflict, there was no question on which side I would finally come down. Studying history was more important to me than the strongest infatuation. I knew this was not the way women were supposed to be, but I couldn't change my deepest motivations. I wondered what it would be like to be loved for one's working self. In the Sydney of my day that didn't happen to a woman.

As my third year unfolded, my work became daily more intensely interesting. The third year was devoted to the study of the development of European imperialism, the history of the British Empire and Commonwealth, the history of the United States, and the emergence of the modern Dominions—Canada, South Africa, Australia, New Zealand, and India. As we studied European imperialism the French, British, and Dutch empires were collapsing: the French army facing defeat at Dien Bien Phu; client states like Chiang Kai-shek's China yielding to Mao Tse-tung's Communist Chinese army; the new state of Indonesia, literally next door to Australia, was consolidating under an authoritarian regime following bitter ethnic and ideological strife; Australian troops fought beside the British in the campaign to suppress the Communist uprising in Malaya. It was logical to ask, Could Australia remain a white island in the South Pacific? In the postcolonial era, should it even try? To ask was to question the White Australia Policy, a racist article of faith which united every spectrum of political opinion in Australia, except the Communist Party.

The study of imperialism could lead to comfortable identification with the metropolitan society and its values, something which had happened for many of my teachers, who were products of graduate study at Oxford or Cambridge, people who took Oxbridge to be the intellectual center of the globe and eagerly awaited their return there on sabbatical leave. Or it could open up profoundly subversive questions, even about contemporary Australia. If one looked at the baneful effects of cultural imperialism in India, what were they in Australia? My schooling had been supposed to be training an elite for leadership, but it had really been training me to imitate the ways and manners of the English upper class. To talk of Australian elites was to realize that the people I and my brothers had known in school were working not on Australia's social and political problems, but on gaining recognition from an external British world. My male peers at the University of Sydney strove for a Rhodes scholarship, not so they could come back to tackle Australia's problems, but to settle down happily to the life of an Oxford or Cambridge don, and forget about Australian culture as soon as possible. My friends on the left were no different. They were hostages to the worldview of the British working class, and the history of the nineteenth-century industrial revolution. Australia was different. Its class conflicts were real but they needed analysis on their own terms, not automatic redefinition in terms of received British Labour views. Study of the American Revolution raised the question of why Australia remained under the British monarchy, especially as Australia's defense was now guaranteed not by Great Britain, but by the ANZUS Pact. Why did the crowds go into such an undignified frenzy whenever George III's hardworking but intellectually undistinguished descendants paid a ceremonial visit to Australia? What was wrong with us? My generation knew it was the United States which had rescued Australia from occupation by the Japanese in the 1939–1945 War. Moreover, talk of the establishment of a postwar European Economic Community made us aware that Australia's economic links with Great Britain were eroding. It was time to give up the pretenses of the old British Empire, recognize that we were a Southern Pacific nation, and begin to study and understand the peoples and countries of our part of the globe. I read Southeast Asian history and began to learn as much as I could about the politics and geography of the part of the world where I really lived.

This change of worldview made for difficult relations with the older generation, and even with one's peers who were not students of history and politics. When I told my mother that the White Australia Policy was wrong, a racist heritage from British colonialism, she burst into tears, claiming that she never expected to hear such heresy from a child of hers. From my new perspective, the ANZAC Day we celebrated with such respect, remembering the courage of Australian troops at Gallipoli, had a different symbolic meaning. Colonial troops had been sent on an ill-conceived and bungled mission by a callous British government, which could afford to run the risk with troops whose parents, wives, and children were not voters at home. I saw Australia's proud military history differently: the troops raised for the expedition to the Sudan, for the Boer War, for 1914–1918, for 1939–1945, were cherished for their valor and military prowess, but they could also be sent on the most dangerous and foolhardy expeditions (like the Canadians sent to certain death at Dieppe) without too serious political repercussions in Britain.

As these political perceptions shattered most of the ideas I'd been brought up to take as the bedrock of moral and political values, my course in English literature had an equally profound impact. It was an extraordinary year. In English poetry, we studied Yeats, Eliot, and Pound, but Professor Wilkes, one of the most brilliant intellects of the Faculty of Arts, concluded the course with the poetry of Christopher Brennan, an Australian-Irish poet of great power. We had in our instructor someone who took Eliot's conversion seriously, and whose own learning made it seem easy to comprehend the range of symbolism in Eliot's poetry. He read poetry beautifully, so that one could hear people lay down their pens to listen to him recite "Ash Wednesday" or "Little Gidding." I had never thought it possible to entertain religious belief, accepting, before I knew how to state it, Marx's view of religion as the opiate of the masses. Now I listened while the intellectual and spiritual progression of one of the twentieth century's great poetic geniuses was analyzed with great sensitivity. The verse became as much a part of the inner landscape of my mind as Shakespeare's sonnets, and its language made it possible for me to examine my own religious feelings. To do so was unfashionable in the extreme. Australia's academic culture was one of conformity to shallow rationalism and positivism. To think about taking Catholicism seriously was to begin to enter my father's religious experience, and also to challenge my mother's fierce belief that Catholicism was Popish nonsense aimed at the suppression of women. Nonetheless, I started reading other Catholic writers, Hopkins, Waugh, Graham Greene.

I was so intent on the lectures about Christopher Brennan, my first encounter with serious Australian poetry, I might have been turned to stone at my seat. We traced our way through Brennan's life, the inspiration of his muse, his theories of language, his reaction to the Australian natural world. It was a new experience to hear verse in which the landscape and imagery were drawn from my familiar Sydney, its trams and ferries, the very buildings and classrooms of the University of Sydney I now inhabited. That year, I bought Australian verse and read the literary heritage that up to now had been obscured by an exclusive focus on English poetry. It was hard to contain my excitement.

I found the study of Australian history an exercise in frustration. Its focus was almost exclusively political, and of necessity this meant seeing the colony and its population through the eyes of the British army and naval officers who were its administrators.

The documents we studied were the memoranda and letters of Englishmen in Australia to the Secretary of State for Colonies. The constitutional crises were the battles over the relationship of the executive to the colonial legislature, and the efforts of both to expand their powers at the expense of the other. The tradition of left-wing writing about Australian history was equally unsatisfying. It required the romanticizing of the population transported to the colonies, and the exaggeration of the wickedness of the hardworking but unimaginative colonial governors. I could not see what process but capitalism would have converted Australia from a penal colony to a free society, and in any event I was more interested in what Australian history *meant* than whether some past historian had misread the correspondence of Governor Bligh to Lord Bathurst, or whether Governor King had made land grants to all his political cronies. I wanted to know what difference the environment had made to the people who settled it. What new kind of society had emerged here, seen not as derivative from Great Britain, but on its own terms?

Knowing the bush, I wanted to know the things most urban writers left out. How did people learn to find their way around, to find water, to know where to start looking for gold? Much of the nineteenth-century history of Australia revolved around the economic results of the grazing of sheep, yet every account of the breeding of the flocks I read was patently absurd. Sheep which had been hair-bearing were supposed to have sprouted fabulous coats of wool on being exposed to the Australian climate. How had it really happened? When had they learned how to breed for wool and how many generations had it taken to produce those elegant merino flocks? What did it feel like to be one of those early squatters, lord of all he surveyed, out beyond the limits of settlement, looking toward the vast interior, planning sheep runs on a scale beyond anyone's dreams of avarice? When had they and their sheepherders first come to love the landscape and feel at home in it? What did its colors mean to the first settlers? Were they ever afraid of the space and emptiness as I had been as a child? Were they different from Europeans as a result of conquering such fears? How different were they? What was our poetry and painting about if not that same existential awareness of the continent? None of this was in the history texts and at first I thought no one but me noticed its absence.

Late in the year, Professor Manning Clark, of the newly founded Canberra University College, came to deliver a series of lectures in our Australian history course, lectures which dealt with Australian culture and its contradictions. He pointed out the contradiction between the average Australian urban experience and the Australian imagination formed by vicarious awareness of the empty continent. We saw ourselves too much as though we were bush settlers, he thought, and so we failed to notice our cities, churches, artists, and writers. He was obsessed by what the Australian experience had all added up to since the days the first Asian predecessors of the aboriginals had landed on Australian shores. An essay he published that year chastised the Australian historical profession and Australian universities for standing in the way of a real flowering of Australian culture. In Clark's view, Australian academics saw Australia as something less than Europe and by conveying these attitudes to their students taught them to see Australia as derivative. The important questions for Australian intellectuals, Clark said, were about what being Australian meant without reference to any external standards, except those which had made Western culture historically minded: the search for the meaning of mankind's journey in time. I agreed with him passionately, although his essay ruffled many feathers among my teachers.

I took out my frustrations by writing a term paper on the process by which Australia's merino flocks were bred, correcting, as I laid out the story, the errors and omissions of many generations of Australian historians. It was fun to get away from the bureaucratic prose and read some real accounts of the settlement. I could imagine what it was like to be the first person to ride out onto the plains beyond the coastal range of New South Wales, and could catch the tone of excitement in the diaries and letters I read describing the experience. It never occurred to me to think of the story from the aboriginal point of view. This was a new country and a new society, I thought, and there was a history about it I wanted to write.

My aspirations to write history were real, but unfocused, and at odds with the other purpose which was forming in my mind. I wanted to be part of the exploration of Australia's relationships with its Asian and Southern Pacific neighbors, to play what I saw as a practical role in the general reorientation of the country's culture and external relations. Along with Milton Osborne and Rob Laurie, my two closest friends in the history honors program, I decided to apply as a candidate for admission into the junior ranks of the Australian Department of External Affairs. Since the three of us ranked at the top of our class, our selection seemed reasonably certain, lending to our discussions after classes a new theme on the subject of Australian international affairs. This objective would, I hoped, finesse nicely the question of when and why I would leave home. My mother would not oppose so prestigious a career. I would be posted abroad, and with the Department of External Affairs as an unwitting but cooperative deus ex machina, I would be released from my predicament at home. This objective in turn flew in the face of my attachment to Peter, and fueled the tensions between us about my commitment to my work. Caught as I was between my mother's hostility and skillful war of nerves over my ties to Peter, and his anger that he did not take precedence over my work and my family, I began to feel trapped. My response was to speed up the pace of life, make more contradictory promises to everyone demanding my attention, and to ease my taut nerves with stiffer and stiffer doses of Scotch. I was headed for a traumatic confrontation between ambition, love, and duty. It was a contradiction Australians were taught to resolve through stoic adherence to duty. I knew that turning one's back on one's duty was dishonorable. So far as my ambitions were concerned I knew they were deviant. Women were supposed to be governed by love. Yet, though he had been dead more than a decade, I still heard my father's voice saying, "Do something, Jill. Don't just put in time on this earth." In this hierarchy of values, romantic attachments were a poor third. Intellectually, I might criticize Australian values and the elders who imparted them, but in a crisis I fell into line. When the inevitable confrontation came I chose duty and ambition, motivations I still thought compatible, and abandoned romantic love.

This denial exacted its toll. I very nearly didn't make it through the last examination in the series that year. I took my seat and picked up the questions feeling disembodied and very strange. The examination was on historiography and I had been looking forward to it. Now feeling uncannily detached, I began. I would use the question on Hegel to define history; make the answer to the question on Marx and *The German Ideology* a means of elaborating my theme; and conclude with a discussion of Collingwood and *The Idea of History* which would round out my picture of the way the discipline had evolved since Hegel's extreme claims for the philosophy of history. The whole paper would then read like an extended essay on a single theme. I became so engrossed, I forgot my immediate predicament and kept writing until the end of the three hours.

By all the received romantic scripts of a woman's life, the next year, my twenty-third, should have been an unhappy one. Instead it was golden. Our major task in our fourth year was to carry out a major piece of historical research, and write it up as a dissertation. All the requirements for our honors degree were finished except for a series of history seminars, and it was possible to live the life of a scholar, rather than that of a student. Milton, Rob, and I had all chosen dissertation projects which required us to carry out our research in the manuscript room of the Mitchell Library, a handsome public library and state archive which looked out across the Sydney Botanical Gardens to Government House and Sydney Harbor. Our days of scanning documents could be broken by walks in one of the world's most beautiful gardens, and occasionally we could treat ourselves to an elaborate lunch in one of the bistros selling fine Australian wine and simple, elegant food which were beginning to appear in Sydney's downtown.

Sometimes I would meet Nina, now graduated and working for the Australian Broadcasting Commission, for a drink after work. Often, a group of us congregated for pasta in an Italian restaurant, ready to catch up on the gossip of our now scattered circle. Whenever Barry paid a visit to Sydney, he and I met at one of the city's best restaurants, and he treated me to a long, leisurely luncheon. This was when we brought one another up to date, talked about our plans for the future, recalled the past, and deepened our understanding of one another as adults.

The most enjoyable part of the year was unquestionably the chance to become a real professional historian, to undertake the labors necessary to reconstruct some piece of the past, and to extract its meaning. I chose to write the history of the early settlement of New South Wales, and to trace the evolution of its pastoral industry in the context of the distant European markets for wool and their transformation through new technologies. Australian social history was undeveloped at the time, the history of its merchant families and bankers little understood, and many of the collections of documents of important colonial families had only just become part of the state archives. I never tired of reading colonial newspapers, or of sorting out the crabbed, crossed handwriting of nineteenth-century family letters. Observing the evolution of a merchant family through three or four generations gave one the feel of the society, its silences and pretenses, its deepest emotions and its formulae for expressing them. It was fascinating to discover which Australian entrepreneurs, many thousands of miles distant from the British cloth industry, understood the potential of new technologies for combing and spinning wool, and raised the capital from distant bankers to benefit from the opportunity. How was one to account for their mentality, as compared with their compatriots who simply aped English country life and paid only a modicum of attention to the breeding of animals and the development of bloodlines? I tried to understand how some new arrivals could *see* the land and its potential, and others lived out their lives complaining how different it was from England.

The very best part of the year was the actual writing of a monograph, balancing accuracy and style, footnotes and the full panoply of scholarly reports, with a smooth-flowing and compelling narrative. My characters spoke for themselves through the rhetoric of eighteenth- and nineteenth-century letter writers, and I believed that by telling their story I was also tracing the way their prose changed from the conventions of early romanticism to a crisper, clearer sense of Australia as a place not just to be conquered and made to yield wealth, but a piece of the earth where one sinks one's roots and learns to live as a native rather than an exile.

The last test of the year was our journey to Canberra, as part of the group of aspiring trainees seeking to enter the Department of External Affairs. We were full of youthful idealism, our heads crammed with information about the various issues facing Australia in her relationships with the rest of the world, walking compendiums of statistics about trade, the possibility of economic recovery for Japan, power relationships in Southeast Asia. Our interviews aped many aspects of the fabled British Foreign Office weekend, where recruits were put through their intellectual paces and tested for their social graces and their general sangfroid.

The beginning of the first day was not auspicious. We were ushered into an elevator at the Department of External Affairs, along with several senior officers. They wore striped trousers, carried furled umbrellas, and as they entered the elevator removed bowler hats from perspiring heads. I could not believe my eyes. It was 103 degrees outside and these men were dressed as though they were in Whitehall. I was careful not to meet Milton's eyes lest we be caught in irreverent laughter.

Keeping the proper expression of gravity was not hard for the rest of the day, as we were taken through our paces in discussions of Australia's regional interests, and her proper stance in all the trouble spots of the world. I was used to arguing forcefully for my point of view in our history seminars and insisted on having my say by means of interruption, if necessary, in this all-male group. Our evening dinner was bland, and before nine we were released to our government boardinghouse and the blankness of a Canberra suburb. Our next morning was a further series of discussions, followed by personal interviews about our career aspirations and motivations for wishing to join the Department of External Affairs.

When the results of the selection were announced, Milton and Rob received invitations to join the Department of External Affairs, but I received a blandly courteous letter thanking me for my interest. I was dumbfounded. Milton and I had ranked first in our class and were to be awarded the University Medal jointly for our academic achievements. I could scarcely believe that my refusal was because I was a woman. Inquiries made by faculty friends and friends with connections in Canberra confirmed that this was the case. "Too good-looking" was one report. "She'd be married within a year." "Too intellectually aggressive" was another assessment. "She'd never do for diplomacy." I knew I was no more and no less intellectually aggressive than Milton and Rob. That left my sex and my appearance. I could not credit that merit could not win me a place in an endeavor I wanted to undertake, that decisions about my eligibility were made on the mere fact of my being female instead of on my talents. It should have made me angry, but instead I was profoundly depressed. What was I going to do with my life? Where could I put my talents to some useful work? How was I now going to extricate myself from my dilemma at home? If there was no justice in such things, I could never expect to earn a place in life through merit. People were taking what I'd justly earned from me. It was all prejudice, blind prejudice. For the first time, I felt kinship with black people. I could never remember the image of my parents resting in the evening, sitting on the front veranda step at Coorain, quite the same way again. In one dimension, it was a golden image from childhood. In another, I saw that their feet resting heedlessly on the nardoo stone step were resting on the tribal treasures of black people, things our ancestors had felt free to possess because of the aborigines' blackness. They and I were participants in the process by which those black people's land and rights had been taken away from them.

Now I understood directly and personally what injustice rooted in assumptions of biological superiority meant, I could see with sudden clarity what our use of the nardoo stones signified. As it came home to me that my sex rendered my merits invisible, I thought differently about the way we had taken over the aborigines' land. It chilled me to realize that there was no way to earn my freedom through merit. It was an appalling prospect.

8

Recharting The Globe

Although I didn't see it that way at the time, the Department of External Affairs did me a great favor by refusing my application for a traineeship. I would have been unhappy working in one of the stuffiest parts of the Australian civil service. The glamorous history of the British Foreign Service haunted the imagination of the department's senior officers, and the colonial mentality with which I was so impatient dominated its culture. I needed a few hard knocks to foster a little humility and shatter the complacency which comes with being bright in a small society where there are few real competitors. Above all I needed to be made to think about what it meant that I was a woman, instead of acting unreflectingly as though I were a man, bound to live out the script of a man's life. This one blow of fate made me identify with other women and prompted me, long before it was politically fashionable to do so, to try to understand their lives.

In the short run, the consequences of my first brush with outright discrimination were painful and sometimes paralyzing. I lived for the satisfaction of working hard at important tasks, and my initial response to my rejection was to worry desperately about what I was going to do with myself. What could I do? Where would what I could contribute to the world around me be welcome? My last years at the University of Sydney had been filled with systematic, disciplined intellectual effort and I dreaded having to stop. I made perfunctory efforts to article as a law clerk, but the two firms I contacted were discouraging. One rejected the idea of taking on a woman out of hand; the other agreed on the understanding that I would never expect to work on anything but divorce and family law. Earlier in my life I might have jumped into the study of law confident that my merits would convince people not to treat me like other women. Now I was wiser. I was furious with myself for having been so blind and stupid as to expect that I could, by some special merit, leap over the barriers society placed in the way of serious professional work for women. How could I have studied the newspapers every day where jobs were advertised in segregated lists, or listened to people's disparaging remarks about women doctors or their jokes about bluestockings, and not realized they were about me? I used to dismiss Dr. Johnson's often quoted remark about a woman talking in public being like a performing animal as a sign of the benighted attitudes of the eighteenth century, but they were around me every day in my fellow students' comments about the tiny number of women faculty.

I was angry with myself for being so upset by receiving the treatment I ought to have expected anyway. I took myself to task for my feelings of sadness that there seemed nothing intellectually challenging that I could usefully do. I was a privileged young woman in a privileged society, and my small injuries were nothing beside the whole weight of human misery that weighed down the twentieth century. Beside the Holocaust or the genocide taking place at that very moment in Indonesia, where millions of men, women, and children, members of ethnic minorities, were being killed, my affronts were trivial. They were nothing beside the handicaps my aboriginal friend Ron, who had been such a loyal worker at Coorain, faced every day. Yet try as I might, I couldn't choke back a sense of grief for my lost self.

My new ability to empathize with other women made me see my mother differently. My perceptions were so painful I could hardly bear them. As I sat listening to her railing against life, her language growing more extreme as she progressed through several of the brandy and sodas she liked in the evening, I would place beside her in my mind's eye the young competent woman, proud, courageous, and generous, I'd known as a child. I was living with a tragic deterioration brought about because there was now no creative expression for this woman's talents. Lacking a power for good, she sought power through manipulating her children. The mind that once was engaged in reading every major writer of the day now settled for cheap romances, murder mysteries, and a comfortable fuzz of tranquilizers and brandy at the end of the day. No one had directly willed her decline. It was the outcome of many impersonal forces, which had combined to emphasize her vulnerabilities. The medical fashion of the day decreed that troubled middle-aged women be given tranquilizers and sedatives. She, once a rebel, had acquiesced in settling down to live the life of an affluent woman. Society encouraged a woman to think her life finished after her husband's death and encouraged a woman's emotional dependence on her children. I forgave her neurotic illnesses and her long, angry tirades against the doctor of the moment. I heard them now as expressions of her own frustrations at having no chance at professional training in medicine. She, who would have been a great healer, was now busily contriving her own ill health. I often needed several very stiff Scotches to get myself through an evening with this inner monologue proceeding while I feigned attention to the subject of the moment.

I found it hard to go through all the celebrations of graduation that marked the end of our college years. After several stiff drinks I could genuinely congratulate my men friends on their plans for careers in the professions or public service, and listen affably to my women friends' plans for marriage. I didn't plan to attend my own graduation or to be present to receive my University Medal. It would have been a bizarre charade to me then, for I thought I had learned all too quickly what its real value was. Instead, I agreed to accompany my mother on her long-dreamed-about journey to England and Europe. I was too depressed to care whether we managed the journey in harmony, and whether her obsessive need to eat and sleep at exactly the same moment each day would become unbearable. I knew that my education had been made possible by her efforts, and that I owed her the travel she would be too shy and too dependent to undertake alone. What I would do after that I didn't know. I couldn't see myself settling down to become a professional scholar. The year of my graduation was notable for a series of petty wrangles between Australian historians on subjects of only minor antiquarian interest. I feared becoming similarly pedantic, and at a deeper level I feared choosing a career that was universally seen as unfeminine. I feared the only sensible choice for me, the life of a scholar, because I was too uncertain of my identity as a woman to risk the cultural dissonance the choice involved. My moods swung all around the compass. Sometimes I thought I should just settle down, marry, and get on with the expected pattern of an Australian woman's life. Sometimes I thought I might simply stay in England after my mother's journey of discovery was over. Despite my criticisms of Oxbridge and my impatience with Australian deference to England, my view of academic life outside Australia was still conventionally colonial. Study abroad meant study in England. Just before we left on our travels, I met a brilliant young medical researcher, recently returned from doctoral work in the United States. His attitudes to life were just what I needed to hear. He wasn't troubled by the restrictions of Australian academic life, he told me. One could be a scholar with an international group of colleagues anywhere in the world. One didn't necessarily have to accept the Australian definition of the role. He set me thinking about the future less parochially, and encouraged me to think about creating new styles of scholarly life if I didn't find the current ones congenial. He was an inspiration at a low point in my life, a new model of a professional scholar, very much to my liking.

Traveling in England and Europe with my mother proved as trying as I had expected it to be, but it was filled with sudden wonderful moments of illumination, and with recognitions of things hitherto only half-understood. When we sailed on the P. and O. liner *Orsova,* in early January 1958, I thought I knew my sixty-year-old mother well. After we'd unpacked and settled into our comfortable flat off the King's Road in Chelsea, I discovered a new person.

My mother's reactions to new sights and new mores were strong and spontaneous. On our first necessary pilgrimage to Stratford-on-Avon, she announced that she didn't care for the English cottage gardens she'd always admired when seen on chocolate boxes in Australia. "Too flowery and fussy," she said definitively. But when I took her to Syon House, for a Sunday afternoon expedition from London, she was as excited as a child by the flawless Inigo Jones facade and the Adam interiors. Capability Brown's garden at Syon House barely rated comment. No matter how I expounded on the notion of garden merging imperceptibly into landscape she was unimpressed. It was untidy. Her obsessions with regularity in time took on a new meaning for me, and I wondered whether she could have been relaxed and spontaneous in a world of eighteenth-century balance.

After we had made all the routine tourist visits to the sights of London, she asked to go back to St. Paul's. Thinking her interest related to its symbolism for the distant Empire during the war, I suggested that we take the time to study Wren's plans, climb to the galleries, and look out over the city to imagine the way Wren had planned the relation of his great monument to the eighteenth-century city. We had the luck to come upon a pleasant and well-informed guide, so that even though the climb was agonizingly slow because of my mother's worries about her blood pressure and her rheumatism, we eventually made the 627 steps up to the golden gallery; we lingered there while the guide described Wren's plans for the great square and colonnades surrounding the cathedral, and pointed out the eighteenth-century buildings which could help one imagine London as he saw it. When we descended hours later and made our way to our car parked in Paternoster Square, my mother suddenly dissolved into tears. Thinking her exhausted after hours of climbing and gazing at great heights, I began to make soothing noises and to hurry her home to our comfortable Chelsea flat. "You fool," she finally got out through clenched teeth, "I'm only crying because it is so beautiful. Why have they destroyed it now with all this clutter of buildings?" From then on I knew the day would be a success if it included a great eighteenth-century building, or a manicured garden in the classical style.

For me, schooled as I was in English literature, my mental habits formed by the relationship to nature expressed in Renaissance and Romantic poetry, actually seeing the landscape was a disappointment. The light was too misty, the air too filled with water. The Cotswold hills, the deer grazing in the park at Knole, even the great heath that inspired Hardy's Egdon Heath in *Tess of the D'Urbervilles* seemed on the wrong scale. I had imagined it on a larger scale, and kept wanting to get a longer perspective on things. It took a visit to England for me to understand how the Australian landscape actually formed the ground of my consciousness, shaped what I saw, and influenced the way a scene was organized in my mental imagery. I could teach myself through literature and painting to enjoy this landscape in England, but it would be the schooled response of the connoisseur, not the passionate response one has for the earth where one is born. My landscape was sparer, more brilliant in color, stronger in its contrasts, majestic in its scale, and bathed in shimmering light.

The powerful visual images which took hold of my imagination were architectural. Medieval history was not taught in my university because the library collections were inadequate for serious research. Although the cities of my childhood Australia were vast, they were modern creations of the railway and automobile, without the spaces and buildings which expressed a coherent urban community and culture. The conventional tourist visit to Bath, made early in our stay, was unforgettable. Here was the Roman city clearly preserved; growing organically within it was the great medieval town which had supported the building of Bath Abbey, with its spare graceful windows and entrancing facade, decorated with a sprightly Jacob's ladder of angels going to and fro from heaven, an image commemorating a dream of its founder, Bishop Oliver King; flourishing beside it was the great eighteenth-century city, yet another coherent urban expression, each of the three more powerful on its own terms than anything I'd seen before. Thereafter, I planned an itinerary which wound through the great cathedral cities, the sites of Roman remains, and the shattered reminders of the dissolution of the monasteries. We made the obligatory visit to the Lake Country to inspect the landscape which had inspired the Romantic movement, but it remained picture-postcard-ish in my memory, whereas Ely Cathedral, first seen at sunset and then viewed through the deepening dusk while the rooks wheeled to settle on its facade, stayed detailed and three-dimensional.

Hungry for sun after a misty English spring, we set out in early April for southern France, Spain, and Portugal. New facets of my mother's character emerged as soon as she encountered Latin culture. She loved to sit sipping tea in an open-air café, watching the life of the square, getting into conversation with strangers by means of signs, broken English, and her few words of French or Spanish. I marveled at the sight of this woman, totally solitary at home, in animated conversation with strangers. Hitherto an adherent of the meat-and-three-vegetable school of English cooking, she cast caution to the winds and ate whatever was the dish of the region. She was less curious about seeing buildings and museums than she was about people. I could leave her happily ensconced at some bar or café, and wander through the buildings she thought too cold and damp for her rheumatic joints.

When we arrived at Santiago de Compostela I left her, promising to be gone only an hour or so, to see the cathedral. I knew it was one of the three most important places of pilgrimage in the Middle Ages, but was unprepared for my first encounter with one of Europe's great holy cities. On the way in, I stopped to study the map showing the routes followed by the pilgrims, often as many as two million a year, traveling down a series of old Roman roads through France and across northern Spain, to make their prayers where their faith taught that the bones of St. James rested. The cathedral literally took my breath away. The vastness of its scale, the beauty of the proportions, the stone carving so powerful one felt one was meeting the whole kaleidoscope of a society etched in the walls, adorning the arches, shown in every pose of walking, striving, and reaching up to heaven. Hours later I wandered out into the great square, was stunned by the scale of the palaces and university buildings which lined it, and then noticing the sun, guiltily returned to my abandoned mother, who reminded me with some asperity that my tardiness would make her late for her next meal. I was glad of her frosty silence as we drove to our evening's resting place. I had more time to reflect on the marvel of the day's startling discovery. Was it true, I wondered, as the guide had told me, that St. Francis of Assisi had made the pilgrimage and himself founded the monastery, not far from the great plaza, which bore his name? I ran through the list of famous pilgrims, imagined the sights and smells of the city they had found as the ninth-century shrine took shape. It was clear that I had to learn more about medieval Christianity because it had produced a world more beautiful than any I had ever seen.

My mother was blind to this beauty, so blind that there was a comic divergence between our states of mind whenever we went together to a great monument of Catholic culture. When we arrived in Seville, the Spanish city she found most entrancing of any on our travels, I told her that the cathedral, where it was claimed that Columbus lay buried, was one of Europe's great monuments, and that the square surrounding it, vast in scale, fragrant with the blossoms of its hundreds of orange trees, was something she should see. We happened to reach it on Friday afternoon, in the season before Easter, when it was the custom for the people from the surrounding countryside to fall to their knees on entering the square and progress across it kneeling while reciting the innumerable rosaries it took to traverse the vast space and progress up the steps of the cathedral's grand entrance. I was struck by the faces of the penitents, their dignity and austere beauty, but my mother's tirade about the exploitation of the peasantry by the Church was an obbligato to my exploration of the building which, more than any other, expressed the high point of Spanish culture after the discovery of the New World.

We could each enjoy standing on the spot on the banks of the Guadalquivir River from which Columbus set out to discover the Indies, and we were each entranced by the gardens which were Spain's heritage from the Moors. In this dry, hot climate, the Moorish influence shaped the use of water and dictated the pattern of walled courtyards where cascades of greenery and the ever-present sound of water banished all sense of heat. "If only I had seen this when I was making my garden at Coorain, I could have made us all feel much cooler," my mother remarked. "I was trying to copy English gardens when this should have been the model." For each of us, in our separate ways, the journey involved the redefinition of our relationship to the past and reconfiguring our sense of geography. Just as we know ourselves in relation to others, so I knew how beautiful Australia was only after encountering the real rather than the imagined landscape of England and Europe. So also, I could not comprehend the blank spaces in Australian urban culture except by seeing the physical expressions of other notions of urban community. The square, the cathedral, the university, and the palace, all grouped around a public space made for theater and processions, yet all on a human scale, made me aware that the heart of our cities was deader than any arid part of the continent, and that our civic and community life was starved of ritual.

In the late 1950s, the Spanish Mediterranean coast north of Barcelona was yet to be discovered by organized tourism. English visitors had been coming there in high summer since before the Spanish civil war, but they stayed in one or two small resort towns, leaving the small fishing villages which dotted the rugged and beautiful coast untouched. If one did not mind rutted roads, negotiating one's car across the fords which were the only ways of crossing many shallow streams, it was possible to find one's way into small fishing communities where, because of Spain's poverty, the way of life of Catalonia was relatively untouched. Every

English person is supposed to shed inhibitions when exposed to Latin culture, and my mother was surely the archetypal one. She didn't make her customary complaints about the plumbing of the simple inn in the small village where we stayed, and she never tired of walking the beach to see the colorful boats of the sardine fleet drawn up after the catch was brought in. The smell of the pines in the hot afternoons, or the shade of the cork woods which alternated with vineyards during our walks along the high jagged coastline, conveyed a strong, definitive sense of place, juxtaposed as they were with one dazzling view of the dark blue ocean after another. At night when the village was filled with the sound of guitars and people could be found dancing the sardana in every small bistro, she abandoned her iron rule about her hour of retiring and stayed happily watching for hours, entranced by a kind of spontaneity and grace she had never seen before. When I told her that legend claimed that the Holy Grail was housed at the monastery of Montserrat, high in the jagged mountains behind the coast, she did not give her usual snort of derision, but said that perhaps we had better make an expedition to Montserrat because she could believe anything possible here. She liked the simple economy of the region, based on harvesting sardines from the sea, wine from the sweet grapes produced along the sunny coast, and cork from the forests. "You may stay in England, or wherever you like," she said, "but I think I may sell Coorain and settle down here, in one of these stone cottages with geraniums tumbling out the window."

Our days in Catalonia were the most relaxed and pleasure-filled of any in our months of traveling together. We had no news from Australia for months, and it seemed foolish here in this world of long siestas and moonlit dancing for me to be fretting about the future. Our visit to Montserrat, laughingly undertaken, proved another moment of cultural revelation. I had been taught about the romantic notion of the sublime, the sense of the grandeur and terror of nature, in contrast to the more domestic and social quality of beauty. Two sites in Europe, Montserrat and the Grande Chartreuse, appeared and reappeared in discussions of the power of nature so revered in romanticism. So it was with my mind filled with Edmund Burke's phrases on the sublime and the beautiful, and Wagner's imagery in *Parsifal* that I drove up the steep and narrow road to the monastery. It was true that from this high point in the mountains one could see the ocean and the expanse of the eastern range of the Pyrenees. It was a grand extended view on a scale I was used to, but I felt nothing here akin to the mystical sense of oneness with nature I felt alone on the plains of New South Wales. On the other hand, when we went into the chapel at Montserrat and heard the boys' choir singing at the end of mass, the same chants such a choir had been singing for seven hundred years, I was transported by the beauty of the first Gregorian chant I had ever heard. I realized that the English romanticism I had taken for a universal was a cultural category in which I did not participate. Nothing made it clearer to me that I was from another world and would have to arrive at my cultural values for myself. Sacred music and ecclesiastical architecture expressed real universals which spoke to me wherever I met them. I hadn't expected to be moved by the imagery and sounds of Catholic Europe, but I was.

After we left Spain, my mother's good spirits vanished. Reading the mail that caught up with us in Toulouse changed her mood. It seemed clear from the bulky packet of letters that my brother was close to marrying the sweetheart of the moment and that the manager of Coorain was taking advantage of my mother's absence to undertake many much-needed maintenance projects and replacements of equipment. With these events in the forefront of her mind, she scarcely noticed where she was. Our travels took us from Toulouse to Geneva, along the route across which Hannibal had marched his elephants to mount his campaign in Italy. As the scenery of Provence unfolded, and we began our climb through fertile valleys overlooked by hill villages of great antiquity, every one looking like the background of some early Renaissance painting, she began to rehearse her memories of her life at Coorain obsessively. Each day as the sun made its passage through the sky, lighting our way through towns and villages which recalled layer after layer of Roman and medieval history, she sat beside me asking whether I thought this new fence necessary, or whether that piece of farm equipment would have lasted longer if properly maintained. The sound of her voice was like a broken record and no matter what my response, it was refuted angrily. Her change of mood was accompanied by her customary concerns. The food was too rich, it was not rich enough; the tea too weak, too strong; the beds too lumpy; the rooms too noisy. By the time we reached Geneva, I was wondering sardonically why I was spending time traveling with someone so impermeable to the stimulus of other cultures.

After Geneva, we turned eastward following a meandering course toward Paris, which was to be our home while we explored northern France. We found Paris on the verge of yet another political revolution, the newspaper placards along its leafy boulevards announcing the rebellion of the French paratroop regiments in Algeria as we drove into the city. De Gaulle's solitary decision to accede to Algerian demands for independence and to bring to a close the colonial wars which had sapped France's energy since 1945 was being proclaimed as we unpacked our bags. It was surreal to hear the ebb and flow of my mother's stream of consciousness about Coorain at such a moment. No matter how she complained I left her alone in our luxe small hotel on the Right Bank and set out for the Assembly, arriving in time to join the crowd awaiting the modest car from Colombey which carried General de Gaulle to one of the great moments in modern French history. Although I was aware that the placards of the newsstands carried nothing but foot-high letters announcing the arrival of the paratroop regiments, I scarcely heeded them in my delight at seeing the beauty of Paris. It was an unaccustomedly empty city, drained of the people who had left in anticipation of a military occupation, and this made it easier to see the Place de la Concorde or to stroll along the Seine, free of the roar of unceasing traffic. Strolling along the Left Bank, alternately browsing at the booksellers' kiosks and stopping to gaze at Notre Dame, I heard on the radio from a nearby wine shop de Gaulle's voice begin *"Françaises et Français, aidez-moi"* and proceed to announce his decision that it was the moral choice for France to withdraw from Algeria. It was a riveting speech, all the more remarkable to me for being heard in the company of the French workmen and casual passersby who had gathered to listen. The group was divided and deep in political argument seconds after the speech concluded. I was entranced. Here were the French left and right obligingly acting out their roles in real life, verifying everything I'd read about French history. As we made our way home after dinner that evening, my mother's flood of conversation was arrested by the sight of tanks parked at street corners and uniformed soldiers carrying submachine guns. The city was preparing seriously for battle, a battle anticipated for dawn the next morning. Suddenly focusing on the present, her response was characteristically British. "I want to leave at once," she said. "These French quarrels have nothing to do with me."

By the late summer, we had spent more than six months in England. I had walked my way through the collection of cities which joined to make the center of London. There was scarcely a trace of Elizabethan London I had not found, nor a section of the city and its museums we had not explored. Our excursions to the countryside were planned to explore a region and its country houses, gardens, churches, and museums, and our overnight stays introduced us to every variety of country inn and great house turned hotel. We made friends in London, visited English acquaintances made on our voyage over from Australia, and made many new friends in the large Australian expatriate community in England.

I delighted in transacting the details of daily life along the King's Road near our

Chelsea flat. The variety of accents, the shops crammed with produce from every part of Europe, the neverending fascination of antique shops filled with furniture and porcelain, the parading Chelsea matrons with their dogs, and the nannies with perambulators were an unfailing source of amusement. Our flat was minutes from the Chelsea Pensioners Hospital, and after I had sat in the garden enough times I made friends with several pensioners, and could count on them to regale me with tales of 1914–1918 or of Second World War campaigns.

I liked the cheerful butchers and grocers, and the superior being who discussed wine with me in a hushed voice at Harrods' wine department. When we made weekend visits to the country, I was less certain about our English hosts, hospitable though they were. They could not have been kinder, but I resented their air of superiority toward Australians. I wasn't used to being patronized by people less well read than I, nor to having the history I knew so well explained to me as though I could not possibly know anything about it. I came to wait for the ultimate compliment which could be counted on by Sunday breakfast. I knew the confidential smile and the inclination of the head would be followed by "You know, my dear, one would hardly know you were not English." I couldn't control the irritation produced by such accolades, and would usually begin to tell preposterous stories about life in the outback to emphasize how different I was.

Australia's class system seemed harmless enough when one observed British snobbery and class consciousness at work. I chuckled at overhearing one friend my mother made on shipboard tell her proudly about the dinner party at which she and her husband had been guests the night before. "My dear, we were sixteen sitting down to dinner, and Freddy and I were the only ones without a title." But it was not so funny to see the very intelligent child of the caretaker of our flat taken from school at fifteen and sent to work, so that he wouldn't get ideas above his place.

It was startling to meet the men who ran the fabled head office of the land and finance company which sold our wool and invested in Australian land. Throughout my childhood, this company hierarchy had been represented as the ultimate in economic wisdom. Now, on meeting its members, I saw not men of financial genius but comfortable bureaucrats who throve on borrowing money at one rate in the London financial markets and then lending it to gullible colonials at a three or four percent higher rate. Australia's predictable droughts could be counted on to send many clients into bankruptcy, and thus the land and finance company had acquired its vast Australian landholdings with little risk and less economic enterprise. This was not the way the men in question saw themselves. They saw themselves as financial wizards, performing important services for the development of Australia. Certainly, the managing director could count on a knighthood after enough years of presiding over this enterprise and contributing regularly to the Tory Party.

Wandering around Westminster Abbey, through some of the churches which were regular places of worship for Guards regiments, or the smaller churches which were home to a county regiment, one could not help wondering whether the Anglican Church of Elizabeth I, a compromise I admired, had become by stages more concerned with the worship of the British Empire than with matters of salvation and damnation. Plaque after plaque commemorated bloody battles—Lucknow, Omdurman, Mafeking, the first and second Opium

Wars—all occasions at which some luckless colonial people had been obliged by superior force to accept the benefits of British rule. I had known in theory that the church and the army had been the pillars of traditional European society, but it took seeing the sacramentalizing of empire embodied in the walls of Anglican churches for me to comprehend what the mystical blending of church and state meant. I stood in the dampness of the Abbey, and thought at one and the same time of the coronation of Edward the Confessor, and the perspiring Sunday congregations praying in some far-flung outpost of the Empire for the reigning British monarch. I couldn't get the two images into any harmonious relationship in my mind. I respected the unbroken monarchical tradition reaching back to the eleventh century and the British capacity for compromise which had enabled the parliamentary tradition to flourish alongside the monarchy. But I couldn't stomach the selfsatisfied exploitation of colonial peoples which was clothed in comfortable rhetoric in peacetime and exposed as cold calculation in time of war. That was the problem with my attitudes to this beautiful and perplexing country. I loved its medieval and early modern history and detested its imperial complacency. One thing was clear. I was not at home here and never could be. I could perhaps learn to speak idiomatic French and settle in Paris or Provence with no psychic difficulty, but in England these contradictions would always irritate me like a hair shirt worn under fashionable outer garments.

It was tiresome to have such contradictory reactions. To see St. Paul's or to hear Big Ben was to be reminded, with a tug at the heart, of London in the Blitz. All through my childhood we had clustered around the crackling radio to hear the sound of Big Ben striking, and then the impeccable BBC accent announcing "This is London" in tones that conveyed British determination to resist the evil of Nazism to the end. Yet, when I was in a fashionable West End restaurant, I would find myself gazing around at the other patrons, wondering which pink and well-fed face belonged to someone who had been all too ready to collaborate, too proGerman to believe any of those ridiculous fabrications about the persecution of the Jews.

I loved the fashionable Mayfair world. Its discreet shops dispensing impeccable tailoring, its perfumes and leathers, its jewelers, its quietly authoritative opulence. For a few months, I dabbled at the customary occupation of tall, willowy Australian girls and worked as a model for a Mayfair couturier. Still smarting from rejection of my intellectual talents, I took the job when offered, just to see whether people would actually pay me for what I looked like. This childish gesture contributed to my education in many unintended ways. It required only modest powers of observation to see that most of the designers and fashion photographers didn't like women, enjoyed seeing them looking ever more foolish in some outlandish getup, and treated the models like so much horse-flesh. From the inside, promoting fashion and beauty was a business like any other, intent on stimulating demand and creating obsolescence. Once I knew how those stunning fashion photographs were posed, I stopped buying fashion magazines, began to wear comfortable shoes, and started to dress as I liked rather than slavishly following the dictates of the season. If one looked at the subculture of designers and dressmakers as an anthropologist would, they assumed their place in the long continuum going back to painting the body and putting bones through one's nose. I was determined that my particular form of nose bones would be comfortable from now on.

These discoveries offered distraction for a season, but as the promised year abroad accompanying my mother wore on, boredom set in. I knew now what I was going to do. I was going home to study history. It was no use pretending that I wasn't a scholar. I could certainly make myself an idle life in London being another expatriate Australian enjoying the cultural riches of the city, but that was to live perpetually by the standards of a culture I now saw as alien. I didn't want to take another degree at an Oxford or Cambridge college either, for that would involve going more deeply into the contradictions of being a colonial in the metropolitan society. I'd made one or two excursions to senior common rooms as the guest of fellow Australians. I found I wasn't interested in the rituals of scholarly one-upmanship which seemed to delight my hosts. Several times, I was outraged by the unmistakable undertones of studied rudeness to women. I wasn't interested in becoming less womanly to avoid that hostility, and I certainly wasn't interested in becoming more English and less Australian. I was going back to Australia to test my new sense of the world and my new perspective on Australian society. So far as my mother was concerned, I told myself I would see her established in Sydney once again, and then break the news that I would not be living with her.

I thought, as we made the long journey home by air, that it might even be an easy transition to make. Just before we set out for home, the news came that Barry had married the pretty young nurse I had met on my last visit to him in Charleville. Soon, I thought, there will be grandchildren to fill my mother's life with interest and affection. A lot had changed about her from the days of our childhood, but though she was often paranoid with adults, she blossomed when with small children.

I heard the broad Australian accents of the Qantas stewards and hostesses with new appreciation, as we listened to the flight announcements before our departure from London Airport for the two and a half days in the air required to reach Sydney by the shortest route home from London across the United States. Once I'd thought those voices a tiresome sign of deviation from standard English speech. Now they were an accent like any other, an inheritance of history and dialect. The flight was long and tiring, but always made amusing by the slangy good humor of the crew, and the friendliness of the other passengers.

After Shannon, Gander, and Sydney, Nova Scotia, came New York. I was asleep when a fellow passenger shook me awake and pointed below. There was New York, glittering in the light of an early autumn morning. There was the island of Manhattan, the Statue of Liberty, the outline of the Chrysler Building. I hadn't expected to be curious about America (the name all Australians inaccurately gave the United States) but at seeing the skyline made familiar by countless photographic images, I suddenly wished I were stopping for long enough to explore.

Two days later, I was gazing down at the coastline north of Sydney, waiting for the first sight of the Harbor to appear. I'd always thought Sydney beautiful, but now I planned to look at it on its own terms. It was a great seaport city, lying on the rim of an arid continent, Mediterranean in light and vegetation, its greys and scarlets and lemon scents unique to its native eucalyptus. It looked out across the vast expanse of the Pacific, not to Europe but to Japan and continental Asia. To arrive where we started and know the place for the first time, I thought, as Sydney's golden beaches appeared, strung out like a necklace around the grey-green city, dancing in the morning sunlight. I promised myself I would never speak about the Far East again. It was absurd that it had taken me until I was twenty-three years old to get oriented on the globe, but I was glad that I finally knew where I was.

9

The Right Country

Although I'd promised myself I would make the break with my mother as soon as she was settled after our return to Sydney, I kept backsliding. For one thing, it took a long time to get her settled. No house seemed to suit her exactly. We were no sooner home than she needed treatment for gallstones, and the prospect of surgery loomed in the future. The house and garden she finally liked wasn't available for another six months.

At Coorain, a much-needed new breeding strategy required introduction. Our flocks had been developed to produce long, fine combing wool for the British market. Now the bulk of Australian wool was sold to Japan, where new technologies made it possible to comb and spin high-quality woolen thread from a shorter-stapled fleece. It was a touchy business convincing my mother that higher earnings would come from breeding larger-bodied sheep with denser, shorter fleeces, but she eventually seemed persuaded. She agreed to the expensive purchase of a new line of rams and the culling of the existing flock for sale, provided I would supervise the operation. Telling myself that I would get her through one set of changes at a time, I temporized about my departure. It would be foolish to bring on the possible break in our relationship before I'd got the economic future of Coorain on a solid base.

Within weeks of our return I made the first step toward the eventual break by taking a teaching assistantship in the History Department at the University of Sydney and enrolling as a student for an M.A. in Australian history. The teaching assignments which secured my economic independence were simple and enjoyable. I gave tutorials in European and British history to groups of ten to twelve students, gave occasional lectures in the Australian history course, and graded large piles of essays and examinations. There was no course work for the M.A. degree at the University of Sydney. One simply found one's own thesis topic, persuaded someone to direct one's research, and wrote the dissertation. I wasn't sure there was anyone in the Department of History who would want to direct the kind of study I wanted to write, but to get myself started I signed up with John Ward, the head of the department and the occupant of its only chair. Before I embarked on more research it seemed sensible to turn my undergraduate honors thesis into a series of articles for publication, an exercise which kept me happily at work for the first three or four months after my return. On publication, the essays were well received. They cast new light on the early phases of colonial economic development, and earned me a reputation as a likely future contributor to Australian history.

My occupation introduced me at once to a new society. The people who had previously taught me now became colleagues. It was the custom of the department to ignore generational differences on all social occasions, and different as our places were in the academic hierarchy, we all sat round the same lunch table, or gossiped together over coffee as though we were more or less contemporaries. It was a heady experience to shift gears and begin to call Alan Shaw, my former instructor in British history, whose wit and learning I relished, by his first name. Ernst Bramstedt, the *echt* German scholar who had taught me European history, now consulted with me about the course and pressed offprints of articles in German on me. Duncan MacCallum, the impossible but lovable eccentric who taught Australian history and had trouble moving the class beyond the mid-nineteenth century in the course of an entire year, was suddenly eating his vegetarian diet of raisins and carrots at my side, and offering bizarre but often brilliant comments about Australian politics. Bruce Mansfield, the warm and gentle humanist, who persevered in believing one could study Erasmus in Sydney even though no library resources were available, gave me a new sense of what it meant to be a scholar. Marjorie Jacobs, already a friend, delighted me by her capacity to cut laughingly through the petty detail of her colleagues' discussions and get the conversation to the point in minutes. They were a wonderful group of friends, encouraging about my teaching, interested in my career. My one problem was that they had very little interest in intellectual and cultural history. I couldn't make them understand the kinds of events I thought interesting. Our department was strong on techniques of research, but no one could understand the kinds of cultural documents I wanted to study. They weren't in archives, but in people's minds and imaginations. Marjorie Jacobs, the most sensitive observer, noticed my frustration, and kept urging me to go abroad to study. "If you don't like England, go to the Sorbonne. Go somewhere where you can see things from another perspective. Whatever you do, don't just stay here." I knew she was right. The question was where.

The pretense of equality masked the fact that the academic structure of Australian universities was inordinately hierarchical, with a single professorial position dominating each discipline, and more junior readers, senior lecturers, and lecturers filling out the ranks of the faculty. Whoever held the chaired position dominated appointments and could virtually build the junior ranks as he pleased. I was fortunate that John Ward had liked my honors dissertation, and was an encouraging friend and mentor. Through my appointment I acquired at least a portion of a room of my own. I was assigned to share a spacious second-floor office, looking out on the tranquil green Quadrangle, with a young Englishwoman who worked in medieval history. She was in Sydney because of the posting of her naval officer husband on an assignment to the Australian navy, and was an intelligent and cultivated observer of Australian society and academic life. I hadn't known many intellectual women before, let alone one close in age to me, so that my friendship with Ruth Chavasse was important.

Early in the 1959 academic year, I was taken aback to be called into John Ward's office and asked if I would pinch-hit for him by giving the lectures in the American history survey course for the next term, since he'd been advised to have medical treatment requiring a term's absence. As my face registered astonishment he said, sensibly and practically, "Come now, Jill, you know much more about this field than the students, and just about what I did when I first began to teach it, so I'm sure you will do it very well, and without too much difficulty." John was Cambridge-trained, but an innovator in his day for his insistence that an educated Australian must know the broad outlines of the history of the United States. I gulped and agreed to give the lectures. It was one thing to give a few lectures on my own particular area of knowledge in Australian history, but quite another to be asked to get up a course at short notice, and do all the lecturing myself. When I asked if there was a syllabus I should follow, John Ward said airily, "Why don't you make up your own. It's always more effective teaching about what interests you. You're interested in the West and the settlement of Australia. Teach them Turner and his critics. It will help you think about your own work."

Suddenly I was as busy as I liked to be. In Sydney some part of each day went into reading nineteenth- and twentieth-century American history. On many weekends, I drove the five hundred-odd miles to Coorain to review the expenditures planned for the next year's maintenance, the sheep sales which went with redirecting the flock to produce the new type of wool favored by Japanese buyers. The two new demands on my time were mutually stimulating. John Ward had given me a nudge in the direction of reading American history, just at a time when I was spending long hours traveling back and forth to the bush, free to speculate about the differences between Australian and American society. My reading about Frederick Jackson Turner's frontier thesis, Oscar Handlin's studies of immigration as a factor in shaping American society, and Perry Miller's analysis of the way the physical environment of North America began to shape the mind and imagination of American colonists introduced major themes for reflection as I made my regular car journeys through several climate zones out to the western plains.

On those journeys I liked to leave Sydney about 4:30 or 5:00 A.M. so that I was away from the heavy traffic on the main routes over the coastal mountains by breakfast time, and ready to settle down to maintain a steady eighty miles an hour west and southwest along the straight dirt roads of the bush, until after about ten hours' driving I arrived in a cloud of red dust by the front gate of Coorain.

In springtime the road west to Bathurst across the mountains was a wonderful passage of extended views across valleys and early morning mist. On the western side the mountains' gentler hills sloped down to rolling countryside; valleys covered with rich black soil sheltered streams winding westward. The gentle slopes rising from each watercourse were crowned with orchards in blossom, while below the contoured patterns of spring crops burst in brilliant green from the dark earth. I liked looking at this scenery with the dew still on it, well before the heat of the day. I always brought breakfast with me: strong tea, brown bread and butter, hard-boiled eggs, and fruit. These I ate at favorite spots: in the middle of a deserted pear orchard alive with bees, or on the roadside at the brow of a hill where the patterns of agriculture—green, brown, gold, and red—could be looked at with half-closed eyes to produce an instant impressionist painting.

Here where the farming was intensive, each curve of the land had its plume of smoke rising from a homestead, nestling beside its accompanying silos and dairy barns. My new interest in American history prompted reflection on how this land had been settled, and on the political heritage of the nineteenth-century battles to wrest it from the hands of the squatter pastoralists, to make it available for small family farms.

Several hours later, one hundred and fifty miles or so beyond the eastern slopes of the mountains, I entered what we called the scrub country. Its bright scarlet earth nourished stunted mallee trees, four to five feet high, twisted by wind and drought, supported by huge gnarled roots. Much of it had been cleared, the roots painfully grubbed and burned, to make way for dry wheat farms, which throve in good seasons and produced relentless, red, dusty heartbreak when the rains did not come. These farmhouses were poorer, the outbuildings shabbier, and the children and dogs playing about skinnier than one saw closer to the coast. The red earth, the blazing sun, and the broken hearts of these settlers were the recurring subjects of great Australian painting. It had never occurred to me before to wonder why we didn't celebrate the plenty and lyrical beauty of the fertile slopes beyond the mountains. Now I occupied hours musing about why it was that this experience of the marginal wheat farmers shaped Australian imagery about landscape, as did the figure of the drover and the drover's wife silhouetted against the emptiness of the western plains my journey would bring me to about one or two in the afternoon, when the sun dominated the sky, and the mirages were shimmering on the horizon.

Why was my mind full of images of exhausted, marginal people, or outlaws like Ned Kelly, rather than triumphant frontier figures like Daniel Boone or Buffalo Bill? I knew that somehow it had to do with our relationship to nature, and with the way in which the first settlers' encounter with this environment had formed the inner landscape of the mind, the unspoken, unanalyzed relationship to the order of creation which governs our psyches at the deepest level. Australians saw that relationship as cruel and harsh, and focused the mind's eye on the recurring droughts rather than the images of plenty I could recall from the rich seasons at Coorain. It startled me to realize that although I was now running the enterprise at Coorain to produce an income that was handsome by any but the most plutocratic standards, my emotional life was dominated by images of the great drought. I wished there were a clear way to understand the process by which a people's dominant myths and mental imagery took shape. Now I had seen England and Europe, these myths seemed more important to me than any study of the politics of Federation, or of the precise details of nineteenth-century land policy. I could see that there were models for thinking about such questions in the writing of American history. There was so much to learn I could barely fall asleep at night because my mind raced on at fever pitch about a set of questions I felt no one else understood, or even cared about much.

The actual experience of delivering my

first course of lectures was daunting. I had surmounted my shyness in most social settings, but standing up before several hundred people and talking connectedly for fifty minutes was a grueling test. Because university education was virtually free, many students were just putting in time in university study, and lacking motivation, could be raucous.

The morning of each lecturing day, I woke up with a hollow feeling in the pit of my stomach and set out for the University like a prisoner headed for the guillotine. I was beset by a sudden new set of worries about my appearance. I didn't want to hide my anomalous female self under the conventional black academic gown. People must accept or reject me for what I really am, I thought. I'm a woman standing here teaching, not some apologetic, sexually neutral person. I didn't have the powers of analysis to understand that my tenseness and anxiety came from crossing social boundaries, but I did have a visceral sense that if I gave in and muted my female appearance I was lost. At night I had nightmares of standing naked before laughing audiences, or of losing my notes and standing on the platform in terrified silence. In the mornings I taught the day students, all a year or so younger than I. In the evenings I lectured to an older, more thoughtful and diverse group of evening students. They were from every walk of life: taxi drivers, schoolteachers, civil servants, construction laborers. Slowly, cured by exhaustion and frequent exposure, I began to be able to walk toward the lecture hall without my knees knocking together, or becoming sick to my stomach with nervous anxiety. My students mostly listened attentively, and some of the older ones even became friends. I began trying out some of my ideas on the parallels and differences between Australian and American culture on them. People began to ask questions. I started to enjoy teaching.

Outside the University, my new role set me apart from most of my own generation. On the round of Sydney cocktail parties I learned not to volunteer what I did for a living. If I did, most men my age looked at me in astonishment and turned to talk to someone less formidable. Most women were puzzled and didn't know what to talk to me about, assuming, mistakenly, that I wouldn't be interested in talking about the usual women's subjects: clothes, parties, the latest films. Someone doing what I was doing was a real anomaly in the Sydney of the

1950s, and no one in my generation knew what to make of me. In strange company I often told people I was a secretary, just to see how they would react to me if they were not perceiving me through the stereotype of a professional woman. It was hard to drum up much interest in the usual round of Sydney charity parties. My London model days had cured me of wanting to cut a swath as an exponent of fashion, and my daily occupation did make it hard to manage standard party small talk.

It wasn't any more satisfactory to spend time in real intellectual circles. The history department at the University of Sydney was the model of solid respectability, and not noted for its intellectual daring. The most interesting circle at the University revolved around the philosophy and political science departments, and a small coterie of gifted faculty and students who were iconoclasts, cultural rebels, and radical critics of Australian society. I liked their ideas, and enjoyed the fact that their circle also contained journalists and serious writers about Australian politics. The trouble was that their intellectual originality went along with a stultifying conformity to what were considered "advanced" sexual mores. Everyone regarded marriage and monogamy as bourgeois conventions, and it was more or less de rigueur to join in the sexual couplings of the group to share its intellectual life. At their parties, the men dressed colorfully, were lively talkers, and laughed a lot. The women, having rejected bourgeois fashion, often seemed rather drab. They talked intensely about ideas, but their eyes were watchful because it required close attention to sort out the shifting amatory relationships of the group. When I rejected the inevitable sexual advances, I was looked at with pained tolerance, told to overcome my father fixation, and urged to become less bourgeois. It was a bore to have to spend my time with this group rebuffing people's sexual propositions when what I really wanted to do was to explore new ideas and to clarify my thoughts by explaining them to others. I didn't know then that I was encountering the standard Australian left view of women, but I could see that the so-called sexual liberation had asymmetrical results. The women of the group, often brilliant, worked as librarians or journalists, and came home to care for the children in the evening, while their men friends retired to the study. I needed their irreverence about Australian academic life and their clear-eyed analysis of the Australian universities as guardians of a colonial establishment. But in time I came to see that their position of isolation from the mainstream of Australian society was an unhappy and paralyzing one. There *was* no social group on which cultural radicals could base a program of action in Australia. Nothing could be more straitlaced and conservative than the traditional Australian Labor Party. People who were radical and avant-garde in the arts could not have been more comfortably wedded to middle-class mores in other respects. That left my friends living the life of the mind with no audience to whom they could communicate. We might spend all the time we liked discussing McCarthyism in the United States and the antidemocratic tendencies of Catholic Action in Australia, but there was no one waiting for our pronouncements on either subject. My radical friends were isolated and alienated, more like a religious sect within an uncaring secular society than their models, the European intelligentsia who labored intellectually in a world where ideas *mattered*.

The place I was most at home in was the bush. The older I grew the more I liked backcountry people. I enjoyed the slow and stylized way conversations with strangers developed—the weather, the state of the roads, where the kangaroos were swarming this year, whose yearling had run well at the picnic races. It was as easy as wearing old clothes to arrive at the ram sales, lean on a fence, gaze attentively at the pen of animals, and argue with Geoff Coghlan about which ones would be best for the Coorain flocks.

On my weekends at Coorain I sometimes took an extra day and drove over to spend the night at Clare. I loved Angus Waugh just as much now as I had as a child. It was just plain comfortable to sit by the fire in the evening at Clare, beneath the paintings of highland cattle, and listen to Angus tell stories. His tales were full of close observation of people, psychological insight, and a wonderful sense of the absurd. He would tease me for being "a bloody intellectual," but underneath the laughter was an old-fashioned Scottish respect for learning. When he came to Sydney for the annual agricultural show, we always made a date to spend the day there, looking at sheep and cattle, agricultural equipment and sheepdog trials, and talking about the wool business. We stayed away from the subject of my mother, because the Australian code didn't permit complaining about life's difficulties, but there was an unspoken understanding between us about why I was spending so much time at Coorain, and about how difficult she had become. After the ceremonial dinner in Sydney's best hotel dining room which finished the day, I always left him smiling to myself over his unique and pungent personality. He never failed solemnly to tip the headwaiter sixpence, out of a combination of tightfistedness and the desire to watch the pained expression on the man's face. "Doesn't he ever give you a hard time getting a table?" I asked once after observing this transaction. "No, the poor bugger can't do that," Angus replied. "He knows I've been staying here for forty years, and my father before me."

I sometimes toyed with the idea of settling on Coorain myself, but much as I loved it, I knew I would become a hermitlike female eccentric if I settled into that isolation alone, with no company but the odd stockman and a few sheepdogs. Most backcountry boys never finished high school, or, if they did finish, quickly set about forgetting the book learning they'd been forced to acquire. So if I chose the bush, I would be choosing life alone, and that I didn't want. Moreover, I had a nagging sense that slipping too easily back into the bush code might be my undoing. These ambiguities came into focus for me on one of my drives out to Coorain, in hot November weather. I'd promised to be out by a set day to help with crutching, only to find the night before I was to leave that two dangerously violent prisoners had broken out of jail near Sydney and were reported to be traveling west to Booligal, the next town to Hillston, on my route. I thought briefly about putting things off for a day, but knew that I would never hear the last of "that time you were late coming out because those two jailbirds were on the road." In the backcountry only cowards were cautious. Deciding that any backcountry felon would be too bush-wise to be caught by the police on the main road, I set out, not made any more relaxed by the news that two people had been killed by the escapees, at points along the route I was to follow.

My journey was routine in blistering summer heat until on an isolated stretch of road between West Wyalong and Rankins Springs I felt a rear tire blow out. I was out of the car almost before it had stopped and underneath it fixing the jack to the rear axle when a car drove up from the opposite direction, and from my prone position I could see two solid pairs of working boots approaching. Shortly two upside-down but genial faces hove into view as the new arrivals bent down to look under my car, inquiring whether I needed a hand. I slithered out and said, "Yes. I need to change a wheel fast. I'm trying to get to the other side of Hillston by dusk." My helpers were both familiar types. The elder, wrinkled and burned deep brown by the sun, wore the usual broad-brimmed backcountry felt hat and spoke in a characteristically laconic bush fashion. The younger man was a Scot, clearly recently arrived, his face burned scarlet, his gingery eyebrows seeming blond question marks on a sea of crimson. "Where're you headed beyond Hillston?" the elder asked. "I'm going to Coorain, Mossgiel way," I replied. "Coorain? You're not Bill Ker's daughter, are you?" the elder questioned. I nodded. "I was with your father on the Menin Road, a long time ago now," he said. "I always remember what a great horseman he was. Now I look at you, I think you look a bit like him." The Scot, meanwhile, had changed the back wheel and, kneeling to screw on the bolts, looked up to me to say, "Lassie, you're crazy. Don't you know there's a pair of murderers on this road?" Before I could speak

378

my father's old A.I.F. friend answered for me. "She was born in the right country, Jock. She doesn't stop home for any bugger." Jock was unimpressed. "You need air in this tire. Make sure you stop in Rankins Springs and get the other tire mended. You've got a long way to go before you're home tonight." Thanking them for their help, I thought privately, Jock's right. It is silly, what I'm doing. Only someone not part of this culture would have the sense to point it out. It wouldn't do to slide too comfortably back into this world.

I was puzzling about my future and what world I really belonged in when, in early 1959, I went to spend a week with my brother and sister-in-law after the birth of their first child, a strapping son, to be named David, whose godmother I was to be. They seemed so happy in their tiny house in Charleville that my own life seemed rather empty. Its fulfillments all seemed to lie in the direction of work, because there was no one in any of the variety of circles in which I moved who could participate with me in all the various worlds I liked to inhabit.

The first night of my stay we went to dinner with a visiting American, Alec Merton, whose company was one of the best clients of my brother's air charter business. I remembered that, during his bachelor days, Barry had introduced me to a lively and amusing new American friend who was the mobilizer of venture capital for what then seemed a hopeless search for uranium in western Queensland and the Northern Territory. Now, several years later, the search had been vindicated, and the geological team hired by the American speculators had located exploitable deposits in what we had grown up learning was a barren, resource-poor desert. The dinner was by way of celebration of the discovery, and of the birth of Barry and Roslyn's two-week-old son.

In the Charleville heat our host looked mildly incongruous, dressed as he was in an American seersucker suit and bow tie, while everyone else was in shirtsleeves. In all other respects it was plain to see that this mid-thirtyish, mild-mannered man was at home in this world of cattle ranchers and back-country types. I learned that he was from Arizona, had been educated in the East, had learned his financial skills in New York, but now worked from Phoenix on financing mineral exploration around the world. I was amused that he was able to tell tall tales that were equal to any of the Queensland variety told by the other guests with great gusto and attention to elaborate detail as the party warmed up. It also emerged that when he had first arrived in town he had quickly established his credentials with most of the heavy hitters in the local bar who had planned a cheerful hazing for the visiting Yank. Invited on a bibulous hunting trip which involved heavy rum consumption in the early hours of the morning, while waiting for the dawn and the first flight of ducks, he had acquitted himself with considerable style. While his hosts showed signs of wear and tear and missed many of their shots, each one of his knocked a bird from the air. He had made a point of ostentatiously delivering his lion's share of the plump wild ducks to the wives of each of his hosts, to drive home just who was the best shot, and who had been sober.

It wasn't until one of the cattle-rancher guests suggested a game of poker that our host openly took charge of the evening. Poker was out of the question. He wanted to learn two-up, so that he'd be ready for his future visits to Australian mining camps. A suitable place was found, pennies were produced, and a team of hardy gamblers gathered in a circle. Alec Merton produced a wad of notes and set them in front of me. "Here, Jill, honey. You play for me as well." The game was fast and furious, the stakes high, and his pithy commentary on this Australian game, only half as good as craps, was uproariously funny. By the time Barry and Roslyn left to relieve their baby-sitter I was one of the half-dozen people left playing, now as hooked as any of the compulsive gamblers at my side. Around midnight I began to have a winning streak. After the third win I started to pick up some of the winnings. "Don't stop now, for God's sake, hang in there," my backer, who was losing heavily, said in my ear. I did as instructed and cleaned out the remaining players after the spinner did his job three more times. "This bloody game's no good," one of the losers said cheerfully. "Good Lord, Barry's sister's beat the pants off us all. Come on, Jill, you're the winner. You've got to shout for everyone." Shouting involved sending for more bottles of Scotch from the bar, the closing of which at 1:00 A.M. was never more than a surface legal formality in Charleville. It was 2:00 A.M. when Alec Merton drove me back to my brother's house during one of the sudden thunderstorms of the Queensland interior. Although I was a little tipsy and still flushed with my winnings, my driver seemed perfectly sober. The high-spirited gambler was gone now and in his place was a man with a startling command of the English language and a more profound view of life than I would have imagined from seeing him egging the game on a few hours before. He talked about the uncertainty of human affairs and the emptiness of success, recited some lines from the Old Testament apropos the setting forth in life of Barry's child, said he'd long remember watching my eyes fixed on the spinning pennies, kissed me soundly good-night, and was gone.

Alec later said he was attracted to me by my reckless gambling, my looks, and my brains. Every intellectual woman wants to be loved for her whole self, to be found attractive for mind as well as body, and I fell deeply in love with Alec in return. I hadn't realized I was looking for an educated male companion who understood my university world, yet was at home in the outback I loved so profoundly. When he came to Sydney to visit me I was astonished to discover that he respected my work and didn't want his presence to detract from it. When I began hesitantly to explain that I would be teaching an evening class the following night and would not be available till after 10:30, he stopped me in mid-sentence. "Why, Jill, you are a busy professional woman, and must turn in your best performance without worrying about me. I'll be waiting for you, when you can get to me." I couldn't believe it; I'd found a man who respected my work and shared my exacting standards about it.

Like all people whose business involves speculative risk, Alec had a talent for living completely in the moment and letting tomorrow's worries wait. He made no secret of his intention to marry within his faith. I made no secret of my plans for an independent career. Meanwhile we took the time to be happy, to savor the pleasure we took in one another's company. In many respects he was the first really sane, thoughtful, and mature person I'd known, and as a result he began to set me straight about many of my approaches to life. When I asked him to meet me in a rundown old bush hotel on the route back from Coorain to Sydney, he came, cheerfully uncomplaining about the battered bedrooms and the marginal plumbing. He was curious about what I was doing out there. "Just why are you fussing about this mother of yours, and spending time running a ranch when you ought to be writing history?" he asked. When I mentioned duty and responsibility to the family, he just shook his head. "Your duty's to your talents," he said. "Never forget it. You can pay someone to run that ranch almost as well as you'll do it. But no one else can develop your gifts."

He had no patience with Australian stoicism. "You mean you weren't allowed to cry when your father died?" he exclaimed, when I tried to explain my lack of emotional expressiveness. "Well, cry right now. I'll sit here and cry with you. It's a tragic story, and you shouldn't try to behave as if it hadn't happened." I found that once I gave in to tears there was no stopping them, and that I was suddenly sobbing about past sorrows I'd scarcely allowed myself to think about. My upbringing had been based on the rule that one didn't intrude one's feelings on anyone else. That was selfishness. Certainly, showing one's feelings was the worst possible breach of taste. Alec was interested in all of my feelings, whether they were sad or happy, and ready to share intensely in them. I hadn't known it was possible to be so happy, or so certain that I was loved in every dimension of my being. This knowledge gave me new kinds of courage. The next time I was in Hillston, I didn't drive right by the cemetery. It was a dry season, the topsoil lifting in a persistent red cloud as I stopped and began my search. It took me a long time to find my father's grave in a lonely, unkempt corner of the graveyard. I pulled the dry weeds away, dusted off the headstone, polished by fifteen years of blowing sand, and wept over it for a long time.

Alec didn't approve of my saturnine worldview and my belief that what was important was to manage one's comportment in life well in the face of inevitable tragedy. "You should read a little less economics and try some theology," he said. "We were created to be happy on this earth." I told him I thought the pursuit of happiness not a very noble purpose for the creation. He said there wasn't a better one, and that I should try to cultivate faith in a benevolent creator.

Whether serious or playful, we were euphorically happy. Alec's business brought him to Australia for a month at a time four or five times a year. We came to know our special places in Sydney and its surrounding countryside in every season of the year. Our favorite spot was a small restaurant, set in a tiny garden, perched high on a cliff above one of Sydney's loveliest beaches. It was a remote, out-of-the-way place, surrounded by eucalyptus forest so untouched that, sitting in the garden, one could sometimes find oneself overlooked by a solitary koala bear, solemnly munching gum tips. On sunny days, the sound of the sea, the smell of ocean mingled with eucalyptus, and the brilliant colors of the garden were intoxicating before one ever sampled the host's well-chosen cellar. On stormy days, it was just as pleasant to sit inside by the fire, look out at the raging ocean, and eat platefuls of sweet Sydney oysters. Sometimes I would look up from daydreaming, gazing into the fire, to find Alec shaking with laughter. "A professor," he would repeat unbelievingly. "I'm having an affair with a history professor." We often lazed away a whole afternoon in the garden, leaving reluctantly as the dusk thickened and the lights of yachts began to twinkle on the ocean.

By the time of our second winter it was clear that we two highly emotional people were in danger of losing control of the situation. We each came to our sickeningly final and sensible judgment at about the same time. It was time to part before our feelings for one another became too deep. We had started out playfully enough but had gotten into something more powerful than we'd bargained for.

When I saw him off for the last time, we were both distraught, speechless with suppressed emotion. We stood by the Pan American departure gate in Sydney Airport in floods of tears. "And you're the woman who didn't know how to cry," he finally got out lovingly before embracing me and then walking very slowly out to the plane, stopping to look back just once.

We were both much stronger people for the beautiful sixteen months. It seemed as though I had been loved enough for a lifetime, and as a result, I was less needy, more able to see and hear others, more confident about my own feelings. Alec, for his part, had been a little jaded by wealth and success when he met me. Like most men and women who are successful at a relatively young age, he needed a new purpose and a surer grasp on the important commitments of his life.

Without the new emotional strength and confidence Alec had given me I might have dealt differently with the challenges which erupted in my life at home. Life with my mother was increasingly stormy. About a year after our return from England she sank into a deeper state of paranoia. The change in her behavior came on so slowly that at first I thought I must be imagining it. The seriousness of the problem hit home after I found her white-faced and quivering, clutching one of the quarterly statements from our land and finance agent. The statement showed the price paid to purchase new rams for breeding the Coorain sheep. We had discussed the change endlessly, repetitively, and she had finally sat down reluctantly to write the necessary authorizations. Six months after the fact, she had no recollection of agreeing, and accused me of plotting to make the changes behind her back. "I'll cancel all this at once," she shouted. "Your father would be turning in his grave." When I explained that it was too late to reverse the plan because the new rams had been delivered and already bred, she simmered angrily for weeks, but did no more than call her bankers to complain about my behavior and to insist that in future only she, in person, could authorize expenditures. There were other terrible explosions, which I became inured to, intent on completing the assignments I'd given myself before moving on.

I hoped the excitement of Roslyn's first visit with my mother's first grandson would focus her mind on more positive things. David was a handsome, healthy baby, and his pretty young mother was justly proud of him. I didn't see too much of the daily interaction between my mother, her daughter-in-law, and her new grandson, because the visit coincided with my busiest time of year at the University. My dealings with David consisted of giving him his late-night formula and dandling him on my knee while I worked feverishly at lectures. When Barry joined his wife and child, I thought sentimentally about how splendid it was that our now enlarged family was all under one roof. I should have warned my brother and his wife about my mother's sudden terrible, irrational outbursts, but it was the kind of subject Australians don't discuss, especially when the family was supposed to be putting its best foot forward to welcome a recent bride and a brand-new mother.

Just as Barry and Roslyn were packing at the end of the visit I heard my mother, upstairs, shouting at Roslyn, in the high, excited voice which went with her wildest accusations. I knew she was launched on one of her irrational, angry outbursts, but to my brother and his wife the unprovoked scene was monstrous. My brother and sister-in-law were told to leave the house instantly, my mother, in her madness, claiming that Roslyn had damaged some insignificant piece of furniture. I hurried to tell them to pay no heed to this craziness, that she was often like this these days, that I had endured many worse tongue-lashings—but the damage was done. The outrage was too great. It was heartbreaking to see them depart, shocked, wounded, literally reeling from the unjust and unwarranted attack. The incident and its aftermath would do them both incalculable harm, and I was powerless to do anything about it.

After their departure my mother was in a high state of excitement. She kept on and on like a fugue demanding that I agree with her that her actions had been warranted. When I told her they weren't, that she had behaved unforgivably, the whole cycle was repeated again and again. It was after midnight before I could retreat to my study and assess the events of the day. Because the explosion had not been directed at me, I could see it more clearly for what it was. My mother was now an angry and vindictive woman, her rages out of all proportion to any real or imagined slight. She was most destructive toward her own children, especially where she had the power to damage their relationships with others.

In a moment of weary illumination I saw that she was as impregnably entrenched in her quest for self-immolation as if she occupied the fortified heights of Gallipoli. I'd made many forays to breach those defenses in recent years, incurring some not insignificant wounds in the process. Now I realized, in what amounted to a conversion experience, that I was going to violate the code of my forefathers. I wouldn't tell myself anymore I was tough enough for any hazard, could endure anything because, as my father's old friend had said, "she was born in the right country." I wasn't nearly tough enough to stay around in an emotional climate more desolate than any drought I'd ever seen. I wasn't going to fight anymore. I was going to admit defeat; turn tail; run for cover. My parents, each in his or her own way, had spent the good things in their lives prodigally and had not been careful about harvesting and cherishing the experiences that nourish hope. I was going to be different. I was going to be life-affirming from now on, grateful to have been born, not profligate in risking my life for the sake of the panache of it, not all-too-ready to embrace a hostile fate.

I had set things in good order at Coorain, but that was the last thing I would do for my mother. The woman I knew now was a far cry from the one my father had made me promise to care for. I'd postponed facing what she was really like in the present, but now there was no escaping it. She jeered at psychiatry and mocked the clergy, so there was no way to seek healing for her sick spirit, and hers was very sick. Perhaps, if I got far enough away, I'd be able to see the causes of her undoing. I knew I wasn't without fault in her decline, and that there were parts I was going to have to atone for.

It was dawn when I went to bed, but I wasn't tired. The light was coming up on the day I began my departure. I wasn't exactly elated about it. I felt more like an early Christian convert who has died to the old ways and lives under a new law. Mine was going to be a law of affirming life regardless of past training. It was true I could not look at paintings like Sidney Nolan's Ned Kelly series without total identification with the view of the human predicament they expressed. I resonated totally to Nolan's Kelly, the outlaw, facing corrupt and hostile authority, triumphing existentially even as he is destroyed. When presented with a challenge or a chance to serve a lost cause my spine straightened and my psychic jaw stuck out ready for defiance. But I could use my reason to live by another set of rules. As a historian I knew how few free choices ever face us in life, but this choice of mine now was unquestionably one.

On my way to my first class in the morning, I stopped by the Registrar's Office to pick up the address of the Harvard History Department and the Radcliffe College Graduate School. By the time I went to my evening class, I'd already mailed my request for the necessary application forms. Once I'd surrendered adherence to lost causes I realized that my plans to write a new kind of Australian history couldn't be fulfilled at the University of Sydney. There really was no graduate program in the humanities at Sydney, and I needed professional training and a group of intellectual peers to progress much beyond my current level of historical understanding. I didn't want to join my radical friends in railing against a heedless society. I didn't want to write old-style institutional history of the British Empire and Commonwealth. I wanted to study in the

Harvard History Department, where most of the American historians I admired were on the faculty. They seemed to know how to explain the development of a new culture, and I was ready to learn from them. It helped clinch the decision that Boston and Cambridge were about as far away from Sydney as one can get on this planet, and that I'd be totally safe from family visits.

When the forms arrived I was amused to discover that the applicant was asked to write a short biographical essay describing for the Admissions Committee the reasons why he or she had chosen to study history at Harvard. What would the hapless committee chairman do if I wrote the truth, I wondered? That I had come to an intellectual dead end in Australia; that I had rejected the cultural values of the country, and wanted an escape while there was still emotional life in me; that I needed to be somewhere where one could look at the history of empires truthfully; that life had been so trying recently that I had taken to drinking far too much, and hoped that life on a modest graduate student's stipend would help sober me up; that Cambridge was halfway round the world from Sydney, and that was a comfortable distance; that I was looking for a more congenial emotional environment, where ideas and feelings completed rather than denied one another.

Chuckling about the plight of the Admissions Committee if I and the other applicants told the truth, I wrote dutifully, to the Renaissance scholar who chaired the committee, "Dear Professor Gilmore, For the last eighteen months I have been teaching Australian history at the University of Sydney, and reading American history as best I can here. I want to enroll in the doctoral program in American history at Harvard, for the 1960–1961 academic year, so that I can develop a deeper understanding of American history and explore the parallels and differences between the Australian and American experiences."

When the acceptance came, my mood changed, though not my resolve. I was haunted by my knowledge of the silence that would enfold the house when I left. I could see my mother, already aged beyond her years, becoming more stooped and skeletal as she forgot to eat and lapsed into greater eccentricity. I had to avert my eyes from the emaciated and frail older women I saw on the street, or in the train, portents of what was to come. I told her my plans just before the arrival of guests, so that she could think of the news as something to boast about. We had lived in a state of armed truce since Barry and Roslyn's unhappy visit, so that the communication was a little like a communiqué between nation-states. She didn't falter. By telling her my decision as I did I established that we were going to act out these events by the script she followed in public, the one in which she was the strong woman urging her children to range far and wide. She knew our relationship had changed and that my resolve was firm. But it never entered her mind that I was not coming back, and I never told her. I dreaded the parting but after some rough moments I learned that time manages the most painful partings for us. One has only to set the date, buy the ticket, and let the earth, sun, and moon make their passages through the sky, until inexorable time carries us with it to the moment of parting.

The hardest leave-taking by far was with Coorain. I made a last visit there, in early September, just a week before I was to leave. I hoped it would be drought-stricken and barren, but there had been good winter rains, and the plains were ablaze with wild flowers, the air heavy with pollen. There was a spring lambing in process, with enough short new shoots of grass to make the lambs feisty, ready for the wild swoops and dashes that young lambs make on a mild sunny day when comfortable and well fed. The house at Coorain was shabbier than ever, and the only trace left of my mother's garden was the citrus grove in fragrant bloom. I looked at it all hungrily. "People will grow old and die; the house will decay, but the desert peas and saltbush will always renew themselves. That's the way to remember it. Even if I never see it again, I'll know just how they look, and the places where they grow."

On my last Sunday, we went over to Clare for lunch. Angus, spry and cheerful, was playing host to a large group of red-haired Waugh nieces and nephews. Much of the lunch was taken up with laughing stories of the early days of Coorain, my parents when young, my brothers and me as children. When it came time to leave, Angus gave us all a small shot of straight Scotch to drink my health. "Take a good look at her," he said. "She's leaving for America tomorrow, and you may not see her again for a long time." As we were downing our toast I wondered whether he knew I wasn't coming back. The question must have passed across my face because as I caught his eye across the room he winked at me, the exaggerated stage wink he'd always given me as a child, when we had a secret we weren't going to tell my parents. It was a benediction.

Having already sold my car in preparation for leaving, I'd made my way out to Coorain by flying to an airport one hundred miles south of Mossgiel. Since I was making farewells I arranged to go back to Sydney by train, to make the familiar journey one last time. As the Diesel gathered speed away from the Ivanhoe station, I remembered my forty-seven-year-old mother and my eleven-year-old self setting out fifteen years ago. That had been an expulsion from Eden and a release from hell. The journey I was about to take didn't fit so neatly into any literary categories I knew. It was certainly no romantic quest. I had had my great romantic experience and sought no other. And there was no way to see it as an odyssey, for I wasn't setting out to conquer anything and there would be no triumphant return. I was leaving because I didn't fit in, never had, and wasn't likely to. I didn't belong for many reasons. I was a woman who wanted to do serious work and have it make a difference. I wanted to think about Australia in a way that made everyone else uncomfortable. I loved my native earth passionately and was going into emotional exile, but there was no turn of political or military fortune which could bring me back in triumph. I was going to another country, to begin all over again. I searched my mind for narratives that dealt with such thorough and all-encompassing defeats, but could come up with none. Then calling on my newly acquired sense of allowing time and events to carry me along, I settled down at the window to watch the familiar scenes go racing by.

That night as the Forbes Mail labored up the western side of the Blue Mountains I lay awake in my sleeping car berth, reminded by the familiar red plush compartment of my parents as an energetic young couple shepherding us children to Sydney for a seaside holiday. I wanted to follow the Old Testament injunction to honor them, but it had become impossible. I understood, after much self-examination, that I'd been a willing participant in the process of my mother's addiction to alcohol and tranquilizers. I'd wanted a calm, gentle woman for a mother, like the other smiling parents I met at the houses of school friends. I should have left her to her rage, fought her harder, not picked up the prescription at the drugstore, not helped pour the brandy. But it was too late now. It was hard to think of so strong-willed a woman as a victim. So much of her deterioration seemed self-imposed. Yet in another sense she was the victim of lack of education, of suburbia, of affluent meaning-lessness. Her rage at fate was justified, it was just not tempered by any moral sense or any ability to compare her own lot with the pre-dicaments of others. It was sad that the form her anger took was something I couldn't cope with any longer. I had certainly tried to rescue her, stimulate her interests, get her involved in charities, anything to harness her energies creatively, but I had to admit that I'd been a dismal failure. The only way I could pay her respect now would be through some sublimated expression of my guilt, generalized toward caring for all frustrated and angry older women. To begin with, I'd have to understand the history of women's situation in modern society better. It was too simple just to blame men for it, as my mother did, in a primitive and nonmoral way. I wasn't sure what set of individual or collective wills to blame for the injustice that deprived most women and many men of education, of a creative use for their energies, of a chance to keep on growing and learning as adults. Of one thing I was sure, one couldn't ascribe all the free will to men and all the determined life experience to women. That might be true of slavery, but not of the relationships between women and men. I wasn't sure how to go about studying those relationships and their evolution over time, but clearly I was going to find out. It wasn't exactly the way I'd expected to find a vocation, out of guilt transmuted into an intellectual calling, but perhaps it was as good as any. I had a talent for history, and the fates were prodding me toward putting it to use.

I knew I could manage my departure gracefully if no one came to see me off. Then there would be a predictable succession of events, all helpfully practical. A farewell to my mother at the house, loading the luggage in the car of the friend who dropped me at the airport. A quick farewell at the curb. It was only if I had to be falsely jolly to a crowd of well-wishers that I might flub this rite of passage which was both a sentence and a release. I was so vehement in my requests to be left alone that all my friends stayed away, except for Nina, who must have waited hidden in the crowd, for she appeared, as if by magic, just as my flight was called, to thrust a tiny package and an envelope in my hand. She hugged me, uttering fervent wishes for a happy journey, and then she disappeared as quickly as she came.

As I walked out to the plane in the balmy air of a Sydney September night, my mind flew back to the dusty cemetery where my father was buried. Where, I wondered, would my bones come to rest? It pained me to think of them not fertilizing Australian soil. Then I comforted myself with the notion that wherever on the earth was my final resting place, my body would return to the restless red dust of the western plains. I could see how it would blow about and get in people's eyes, and I was content with that.

P9-CDF-995

The Root of Thought

The Root of Thought

*Unlocking Glia—The Brain Cell That Will Help
Us Sharpen Our Wits, Heal Injury,
and Treat Brain Disease*

Andrew Koob

Vice President, Publisher: Tim Moore
Associate Publisher and Director of Marketing. Amy Neidlinger
Editorial Assistant: Pamela Boland
Operations Manager: Gina Kanouse
Digital Marketing Manager: Julie Phifer
Publicity Manager: Laura Czaja
Assistant Marketing Manager: Megan Colvin
Cover Designer: Stauber Design Studio
Managing Editor: Kristy Hart
Project Editor: Jovana San Nicolas-Shirley
Copy Editor: Deadline Driven Publishing
Proofreader: Water Crest Publishing
Indexer: Erika Millen
Compositor: Nonie Ratcliff
Manufacturing Buyer: Dan Uhrig

© 2009 by Pearson Education, Inc.
Publishing as FT Press
Upper Saddle River, New Jersey 07458

FT Press offers excellent discounts on this book when ordered in quantity for bulk purchases or special sales. For more information, please contact U.S. Corporate and Government Sales, 1-800-382-3419, corpsales@pearsontechgroup.com. For sales outside the U.S., please contact International Sales at international@pearson.com.

Printed in the United States of America

First Printing June 2009

ISBN-10: 0-13-715171-3
ISBN-13: 978-0-13-715171-4

Pearson Education LTD.
Pearson Education Australia PTY, Limited.
Pearson Education Singapore, Pte. Ltd.
Pearson Education North Asia, Ltd.
Pearson Education Canada, Ltd.
Pearson Educación de Mexico, S.A. de C.V.
Pearson Education—Japan
Pearson Education Malaysia, Pte. Ltd.

Library of Congress Cataloging-in-Publication Data

Koob, Andrew, 1976-
  The root of thought : unlocking gila— the brain cell that will help us sharpen our wits, heal injury, and treat brain disease / Andrew Koob.
     p. cm.
  ISBN 978-0-13-715171-4 (hardback : alk. paper) 1. Neuroglia—Popular works. I. Title.
QP363.2.K66 2009
612.8'2—dc22

                           2008055452

Contents

1

Cities and highways

Back in the 1960s, it was discovered that glial cells are 90 percent of the brain. Neurons make up 10 percent. One would think that as a result of this revelation, the conclusion reached would have been that glial cells function as a main component of the nervous system. But it wasn't. The conclusion was that we use only 10 percent of our brain.

From an early age, we are taught that the major cell in the brain is the neuron. We are also taught that neurons hold all the information in the brain. Even through graduate-level studies, the central tenant of neuronal importance is the basis of the study of neuroscience. But the Neuron Doctrine has become more religion than scientific truth, explaining away even the most blatant facts with assertions such as, "We use only 10 percent of our brain."

However, no sustainable argument or discovery has been made to give insight to where our thoughts come from, where our imagination resides, our dreams ignite, and how creativity burgeons. These are mysteries that have been explained with ideas such as "random neuronal firing" or "interconnectibility." But the truth is that the neuron is the least likely cell in the brain for the root of thought.

Until recently, glia have been considered the structural elements to the active neurons, like void space with no purpose except to hold the brain together—the nuts, bolts, and the frame of the engine of our minds.

The importance of the neuron is being aggressively challenged in the field. The recovery from brain injury, the cause of degenerative diseases of the brain, the treatments for psychiatric disorders, and an understanding of human intelligence can be fully realized only through the study of glia.

The surge in glial interest is due to three main reasons. First, glia signal to each other in a manner conducive to storage of information. Second, glia have long been known to be the cellular makeup of most brain tumors. Third, researchers now know glia are the adult stem cells in the brain.

It was once thought that our brains develop in the womb and during early childhood, and then remained in this state until we died. It is now known that we regenerate cells throughout adulthood. The stem cells of the brain are glia, which can reproduce themselves and neurons if needed.

Glia can also regenerate locally in order to store more information. One of the most fascinating studies in the last 30 years was the analysis of Albert Einstein's brain. When markers for different types of cells were analyzed, Einstein's brain was discovered to contain significantly more glia than normal brains in the left angular gyrus, an area thought to be responsible for mathematical processing and language.

If glia are the libraries for information storage in the brain, and assuming humans have the highest intelligence, then lower life forms should have less glia. One of the most striking research events has been the discovery of a single glial cell for every 30 neurons in the leech. This single glial cell receives neuronal sensory input and controls neuronal firing to the body. As we move up the evolutionary ladder, in a widely researched worm, *Caenorhabditis elegans*, glia are 16 percent of the nervous system. The fruit fly's brain has about 20 percent glia. In rodents such as mice and rats, glia make up 60 percent of the nervous system. The nervous system of the chimpanzee has 80 percent glia, with the human at 90 percent. The ratio of glia to neurons increases with our definition of intelligence.

Not only does the ratio of glia to neurons increase through evolution, but so does the size of the glia. Astroglial cells in the human have a volume 27 times greater than the same cells in the mouse's brain.

The folded cortex of humans is not noticed in other animals until you reach higher-level species such as cats, dolphins, and other primates. Humans have 35 percent more glia in its cortex than the chimpanzee.

This excess glia in our brains might explain the fact that humans are more susceptible than other animals to develop degenerative diseases of the brain such as Alzheimer's and Parkinson's, which disrupt thought. In

fact, in all degenerative diseases of the brain, loss of sense of smell is the first sign before the onset of symptoms. The olfactory bulb is known to have the highest turnover of cells in the brain because of the nature of smell. It is ever changing, and our olfactory bulb has to adjust as such. Glia are the stem cells necessary for this turnover.

The study of degenerative diseases of the brain in most labs today focuses on proteins that aggregate in neurons, the byproduct of the disease. This is like thinking a pothole is the reason a road is falling apart.

When a mechanism for glial proliferation is overactive, glia turn cancerous. Almost all tumors of the brain are gliomas, which are comprised of glia. Is it possible that glial regeneration is a normal process of the brain that needs to remain at a constant level depending on the amount of information learned and integrated? Is it possible that when it is lacking, degenerative disease occurs, and when it is aggressive, a tumor grows?

Our brains were also always thought to lose neurons as we grow older. Upon further review, it has been shown that neuronal numbers remain the same, whereas increases and disruptions are seen in glia. And just recently, it has been revealed that glia communicate to themselves in electrical waves through extensive nets involving calcium ion influx. These influxes of calcium can spread locally through glial networks. It has also been shown that glia express the receptors necessary to receive basic input from neurons, as well as signal to neurons themselves.

Neurons communicate down long processes called axons. Neurons either fire or they don't. This is called the "all-or-nothing" phenomenon. Glia are much more complex. Their wavelike communication may be more conducive to fluid information processing.

What are neurons if glia process and store information? Since researchers know that glia signal to neurons, it would seem neurons are simply static cells that fire at the beck and call of glia to other glial areas, which need to be ignited to produce related thoughts.

For instance, if you, like the author, think about pizza, and then you think about mozzarella, which leads you to think about Italy, you are igniting three glial centers in your brain. To get from one center to the next, if they are a significant distance, you must connect through a neuron. When the glial center for mozzarella receives strong neural firing from the center for pizza, then it ignites and thinks about everything related to mozzarella in that glial center.

For a century, scientists have barely questioned the idea of the dominance of the neuron. Even today, it's not a stretch to say that 99 percent of the laboratories studying the brain around the world focus on neuronal research.

But, as will be seen, this is the equivalent of aliens landing on earth in southern California and arriving at the conclusion that the freeway between San Diego and Los Angeles is more important to explore than the cities themselves.

References

Diamond, M.C., A.B. Scheibel, G.M. Murphy, and T. Harvey. "On the Brain of a Scientist: Albert Einstein." *Experimental Neurology*, 88: 198–204, 1985.

Hatton, G.I. and V. Parpura. *Glial—Neuronal Signaling*. Boston, MA: Kluwer Academic Publishers, 2004.

Kettenmann, H. and B.R. Ransom. *Neuroglia*, Second Edition. New York: Oxford University Press, 2005.

Laming, P.R., E. Syková, A. Reichenbach, G.I. Hatton, and H. Bauer. *Glial Cells: Their Role in Behavior*. New York: Cambridge University Press, 1998.

Murphy, S. *Astrocytes: Pharmacology and Function*. San Diego, CA: Academic Press, Inc., 1993.

Verkhratsky, A. and A. Butt. *Glial Neurobiology*. Chichester, West Sussex: John Wiley & Sons Ltd., 2007.

Volterra, A., P. Magistretti, and P. Haydon, *The Tripartite Synapse: Glia in Synaptic Transmission*. New York: Oxford University Press, 2002.

2

Dust settles on the battlefield

Until recently, our imagination and thoughts were believed to reside entirely in neurons. Glia, the most abundant cells in the brain, were considered inactive—a buffer to the electrical neuronal firing of our secrets and dreams. The contrived creation of neuronal supremacy appeared somewhere at the turn of the twentieth century after the widespread use of the microscope. At this time, the neuron was considered the crowning achievement of brain research throughout human history. What glial cells did, or how they functioned, was undermined and barely considered, with only slight hesitation, when the preeminent brain scientist at the time adopted his brother's idea that they were insignificant. Looking far back into the reaches of brain science can reveal why.

The earliest notions for the seat of our thoughts, imaginations, creations, and dreams were recorded in ancient Greece and Egypt. The ancients believed the heart was responsible for thought. The butterflies you experience and the anger you feel creates visceral responses in your abdomen. When looking at dissected humans after death, the prominence of the heart, with its connections to the major fluid in the body, the blood, led the ancients to the conclusion that the heart was responsible for our creativity, intellect, language, and emotion.

But Hippocrates, who lived from 460–379 BC, challenged this view. To Hippocrates, the evidence of traumatic injury to the head and the resulting deficits in language and emotion were because the brain was the seat of intelligence. Trepanation—the drilling of a hole in the head to release pressure and a technique still employed by brain surgeons today to alleviate some symptoms of injury—was also evidence for his theory.

Hippocrates wrote, "Men ought to know that from nothing else but the brain come joys, delights, laughter and sports, and sorrows, grief,

despondency, and lamentations. And by this, in an especial manner, we acquire wisdom and knowledge, and see and hear and know what are foul and what are fair, what are bad and what are good, what are sweet and what are unsavory…in these ways, I am of the opinion that the brain exercises the greatest power in man."

He would also conclude that we suffer when the brain is hot, cold, moist, or dry. He thought madness occurred when the brain was moist and that only when the brain is "still" could a man think properly. These last sentiments might not be entirely true, but they were to inspire Aristotle (384–322 BC). Aristotle tried to include Hippocrates' studies with those in the heart camp. He still believed the heart was the seat of higher thinking, but that the brain cooled the heart when it overheated with emotion. Rational humans were those with better brain-cooling capacity.

In Roman times, the physician to the gladiators, Galen (AD 130–200), was and still is most prominent. He sided with Hippocrates' view. He spent careful time dissecting animals, such as sheep, and looking at gladiators who suffered traumatic injury. His conclusions definitively set the seat of intelligence in the brain.

Cavities called ventricles in the center of our brains and the spinal cord contain cerebrospinal fluid. At this time, there was a perception of the existence of four vital fluids to the body: blood, phlegm, black bile, and yellow bile. To Galen, the ventricles contained yellow bile. To control thought and movement, the brain somehow sloshed the yellow bile throughout the nerves that extended into the body. His view lasted for 1500 years until Descartes (1596–1650).

Descartes didn't necessarily create a different view, but sought an anatomical idea of the human based on the perceived undeniable truths of religion. He thought the brain worked as a center for the spirits of the soul. The spirits were the fluids, and like Galen, Descartes believed they controlled our thoughts and then flowed through the body to cause movement.

But Descartes believed Galen's explanation for humans as similar to sheep could not be reconciled with the notion that humans were created in God's image. He thought the mind stood separate from the physical body as a wisp in the ether that could act on the body. The pituitary gland was a pump through which the mind controlled the spirits. As modern technical inventions have influenced how we understand the workings of

the brain, the invention of hydraulics at this time in France solidified Descartes' idea. The pumping of the pituitary by the mind created fluid to reach the muscles and cause them to contract, much like a hydraulic instrument when pumped.

With the advent of the microscope in the seventeenth century, scientists were enthralled by the prospect of seeing for the first time a view of the nerves through which spirits flowed. If they could see what was responsible for the soul, they could become closer to God. When the nervous system was first analyzed with the microscope in the late seventeenth and early eighteenth century by Dutch scientist Anton von Leeuwenhoek (1632–1723), parts of the tissue were mashed between two glass slides like squashed mud. In the peripheral nerves, he saw what looked like cylindrical tunnels. Descartes' tubes for the transfer of spirits were confirmed.

This belief stood for a century and a half until the microscope became more reliable at the beginning of the nineteenth century and the term "cell" was in use to describe the functional unit of other organs and lower life forms such as the single-cell amoeba. It became obvious the brain was comprised of cells as well. Then Hermann von Helmholtz (1821–1894) discovered that when the brain was placed in wine alcohol, it wouldn't decompose and would extract water from the tissue, leaving behind the cells for analysis. Whatever thought led Helmholtz to toss someone else's decaying brain into his wine is certainly evidence for the limitlessness of human original thought and creativity,

Descartes' notion of spirits was challenged when religion took a back burner to science. Before alcohol fixation (and formaldehyde at the turn of the twentieth century) when the brain was removed initially after death, it looked like a gob of sticky grey goo, which was connected by long white fibers. The fibers were attributed the most importance—the avenues for Descartes' spirits and the housing for the method of thought.

Glia are everything else outside the fibers. The term glia comes from ancient Greek meaning something slimy or sticky in appearance. In modern Greek, and perhaps fittingly for those that believe in the predominance of neurons, the root glia remains in a word that means a filthy and morally debased person. Of course, this can be a badge of pride for glia proponents. In Herodotus, the word means "gum" and in the plays of Aristophanes, it means "sticky" or "knavish." The man who took this word from Greek and applied it to the brain was Rudolf Virchow

(1821–1902). In 1858, while looking at glia cells, he thought they were "nerve putty." These ubiquitous cells throughout the brain didn't seem to be the root of the fibers going out to the body, the important containers of the yellow bile, the spirits. And now it was believed the white fibers were obviously conducting electricity, but where did they come from?

Finally, with Darwin's theory of evolution in 1859, the cell as the functional unit and from which all life has evolved was common scientific belief.

Scientists were now on the brink of discovering the cellular unit in the brain that was responsible for thought—the same cells Darwin used to invent his theory. Because the fibers were perceived as the connections driving thought, researchers wanted to definitively know what they were. One of Virchow's students, Otto Deiters (1834–1863), and Albreicht von Kolliker (1817–1905) began to make the first accurate drawings of nerve cells, which had tails on the ends of them. The sperm-like structures were intriguing, but it was not definitive that the tails were the fibers. The discovery of Robert Remak (1815–1865), who examined the nervous system of the ox, that the cell body in the spinal cord was attached to the fiber began to convince scientists that the fiber was part of a cell, and the tail-like structure reaching out was the fiber.

The idea that cells in the brain had tails on them (called processes) that emanated out into the body as fibers meant that these cells must hold all the information in the brain. They were subsequently called neurons. And everyone had jump to conclusions a tad early.

Two men stood at the forefront as advocates for the neuron. One was by all accounts a pompous self-promoter. His coiffure was well-groomed. His mustache rivaled Teddy Roosevelt's. He was a dashing Italian who loved women, cigars, alcohol, and himself. He discovered one of the most important cell illuminating pigment stains in the history of science. His name was Camillo Golgi (1843–1926), and working in a small town in northern Italy, he discovered the silver nitrate staining method. Using silver nitrate on preserved tissue—an idea he got from early photography methods for staining film—Golgi could visualize the individual cells in the brain, and more importantly, he could visualize the tail-like processes extending from the cell bodies that make brain cells unique. He became a professor of histology and pathology at the University of Pavia, and the stain is now called the Golgi stain.

The other man was the grimacing, menacing Spanish histologist at the University of Madrid, Santiago Ramón y Cajal (1852–1934) (see Figure 2.1). Cajal was described as quiet and diligent. He was like a grumpy bear in the woods catching fish. He wrote volumes of clear and concise books on what he saw under the microscope using Golgi's staining method and his own advancements using gold chromide. Determined, meticulous, and over-confident—three qualities valued in science—Cajal gained the utmost respect from his peers. One of the most important talents for a researcher during this time period was artistic ability. In order to represent what was seen in the microscope, a researcher had to draw it. Golgi's artistic ability was unmatched, but Cajal detested the liberties Golgi took with his representations. Although Cajal couldn't draw as well as Golgi, he believed he was more accurate. He peppered his books with his drawings of brain anatomy and writing about what he understood to be happening in the brain.

FIGURE 2.1 Santiago Ramón y Cajal, the dour curmudgeon

It wasn't until Golgi (see Figure 2.2) developed his famous staining technique that researchers could definitively follow the tail-like process

(now called an axon) throughout the brain, understand the fibers extending from a cell body, and confirm Remak's findings. Based on the previous ideas from Galen, through Descartes to the present, this cell body was believed to be the important storage of the information and thoughts in the brain. Axons traversing from one side of the brain to the other and to the muscles were the long-distance communication of the information storage.

FIGURE 2.2   Golgi, the visionary

Golgi's stain also visualized glial cells; they looked like little spiders throughout the brain surrounding the large cell bodies of neurons and axons.

Golgi believed the brain worked like a syncytium, or a net. He thought that all the cells were connected and not discernibly separated. They worked in the manner of a reticulum; in other words, he thought the cells in the brain responsible for thought functioned together fluidly and not incrementally. He believed the main function of glia was to feed neurons. This was because the glial processes seemed to connect with blood vessels and neurons.

Cajal and Golgi disliked each other immensely. Golgi rubbed Cajal's meticulous manner the wrong way. Perhaps it was petty jealousy or simply blind rage, but Cajal completely discounted any idea Golgi formed. To Cajal, any blundering scientist could see from the staining method

that the brain was comprised of incremental cells like the rest of the body. These increments were divided into two main cell components: neurons and glia. Neurons were most important because the cells extended longer distances. The cell body was in the middle, and the processes reaching for information looked like the branches of the tree. Although it was clear information was transmitted down a long trunk called an axon, Cajal wasn't sure what to think of glia.

A brilliant student of Virchow's, Carl Ludwig Schleich (1859–1922) (see Figure 2.3), went against his mentor and was the first to propose that glia and neurons were able to signal to each other. This revolutionary idea completely abolished the "fiber-central" view passed down from the time of Galen and was a major leap of innovation in brain research. He thought the gaps between neurons signaling to each other made it possible for glial cells to modulate the connection. Glia must help inhibit neuronal signaling, he postulated.

Of course, these ideas were placed at the end of a paper in 1894 on the introduction of local anesthesia, Schleich's main contribution to medicine. In the same year of Schleich's publication, Sigmund Exner (1846–1926) published a neuron-only view of cell communication in the brain.

FIGURE 2.3   Carl Ludwig Schleich lounging

Three years earlier, Wilhelm Gottfried von Waldeyer (1836–1921) coined the term neurone to describe specific cells with long processes. Looking at these cells, Exner was the first to specifically claim how they were the most important cells for information storage in the brain. With crude drawings of grids and a pared down view of the seat of intelligence, Exner elucidated the method of neuron transmission. Cajal took the theory as his own, and then expounded and improved upon it. Each cell was separate and not connected as Golgi thought.

Schleich's idea of glial signaling was lost in the shadows of the luminous idolatry of Exner and Cajal. The importance of the neuron was given the term the Neuron Doctrine. And like any doctrine, it was built on faith.

The priests of the Neuron Doctrine set about trying to reconcile how they could account for this abundant glial cell without knocking the neuron off its pedestal. Carl Weigert (1845-1904) proposed a popular theory based on Virchow's original idea in 1858 that glia were simply structural elements or glue. Now that it was known that the long, sinewy tendrils extending from the brain into the spinal cord and out to the muscle were the processes of neurons, could it be that glial cells were just structural elements that filled space unoccupied by neurons—the neural putty everyone originally thought it was? Cajal wasn't sold. But then his brother Pedro adopted the idea and put forth that glia were simply insulators that prevented the undesirable spread of neuronal impulses. Cajal agreed and glia were pushed to the back burner. This idea is still taught today.

Maybe as a cruel joke, the Nobel Prize committee decided to give Golgi and Cajal the Nobel Prize in Medicine jointly in 1906. It was time for a showdown. Golgi was allowed to talk the day before Cajal, because without the Golgi stain, Cajal's research would not exist. The speeches were tense, with Golgi titling his talk, "The Neuron Doctrine: Theory and Facts." After introducing the theory, he went on to say, "While I admire the brilliancy of the (neuron) doctrine, which is a worthy product of the high intellect of my illustrious Spanish colleague, I cannot agree with him on some points of an anatomical nature, which are, for the theory, of fundamental importance…" Golgi firmly believed in a nervous organ working as a reticulum, with cells physically connected and comprised of glia as a neuronal booster through its access to the blood stream.

Knowing Golgi had for some time gone out of favor among scientists and knowing Golgi was now an Italian senator and less inclined to keep up with modern science, Cajal simply stuck to his guns in his speech the next day. Cajal defended his theory by citing Waldeyer, Exner, Deiters, and Kolliker, staying above Golgi's potshots and stating the facts as he saw them. Neurons were all separate cells and not physically connected. He didn't mention glia. Later, he wrote he was furious at Golgi for his "display of pride and self-worship." He said Golgi's ego was "hermetically sealed... and impermeable to the incessant changes taking place in the intellectual environment."

Although Golgi also believed in a secondary importance for glia, he perceived a more active role than Cajal. But after the dust settled, neurons had won and glia were forever obscured to oblivion, the byproduct of the brain child of Santiago Ramón y Cajal's brother Pedro. This was not the equivalent of Billy Carter being asked by Jimmy what he thought of the Iran hostage situation. Pedro was a satisfactory scientist in his own right, but it was still strange for Cajal to toss aside a cell he had helped illuminate through his meticulous studies. Not to mention the most abundant cells in the brain. The Neuron Doctrine fit together nicely, the way he liked it, and the neuron was contrary to Golgi, which was also the way Cajal liked it.

The modern study of neuroscience was born, and Santiago Ramón y Cajal became the father of the field. Cajal made sure to let everyone know what was right and what was wrong. And Golgi's skewering by Cajal at the Nobel Prize ceremony did not encourage detractors. Glia went unstudied for six decades.

References

Azmitia, E.C., J. Defelipe, E.G. Jones, P. Rakic, and C.E. Ribak. *Progress in Brain Research: Changing Views of Cajal's Neuron.* Elsevier, New York: Elsevier Science, 2002.

Clarke, E. and L.S. Jacyna. *Nineteenth-Century Origins of Neuroscientific Concepts.* Los Angeles, CA: University of California Press, 1987.

De Vellis, J. *Neuroglia in the Aging Brain.* Totowa, NJ: Humana Press, 2002.

Finger, S. *Origins of Neuroscience: A History of Explorations into Brain Function*. New York: Oxford University Press, 1994.

Kettenmann, H. and B.R. Ransom. *Neuroglia*, Second Edition. New York: Oxford University Press, 2005.

Ramón y Cajal, S. *The Neuron and the Glial Cell*. Springfield, IL: Charles C. Thomas Publisher Ltd., 1984.

Shepherd, G.M. *Foundations of the Neuron Doctrine*. New York: Oxford University Press, 1991.

Verkhratsky, A. and A. Butt. *Glial Neurobiology*. Chichester, West Sussex: John Wiley & Sons Ltd., 2007.

3 ———————————

I sing the body electric

Romans in ancient times were probably wise to avoid the doctor if they had a headache. If you traveled through time to ancient Rome, and the trip gave you a headache, you might want to just grin and bear it. If you went to the doctor, he would go to his saltwater tank and delicately scoop up an electric fish (not with his hands) and touch your forehead with it, shocking the headache out of you. Although not entirely understood, the human species has known about the existence of electricity since the first evolved human saw a lightning storm. Smashing some rocks together produced sparks, and after metallurgy, so did the metallic crashing of swords. Of course, electric rays and fish were pondered as far back as the ancient Greeks. Why Romans thought applying the shock of a fish to the head would cure a headache instead of exacerbate it is beyond the scope of this book.

When glia were discovered after the advent of cellular stains, and immediately discounted, it was the direct result of the characterization of electricity in the eighteenth and nineteenth centuries. Ramón y Cajal's Neuron Doctrine and acceptance of Pedro's glial theory that followed were based on the view of the supreme importance of electrical signaling in neurons. It is now known that all cells have an electrical potential and gradient.

In the eighteenth century, electricity was the rage in science. It was the equivalent of quantum physics today. Everyone in the scientific field had a theory or insight into the origins of electricity and the applications of it. It was a mysterious phenomenon that could be the wrath of God, the golden tendrils of angel's tears, or the teetering spark of universal destruction. Now we believe electricity is essentially a normal byproduct of living in an atomic world, and harnessing it might have been the most important advance in human history.

In the biological field, the first experiments attempted to describe how physical beings are able to conduct electricity were on electric eels and electric rays. The anatomy of the electric ray was described by John Hunter (1728–1793) in 1773, around the same time that scientist John Walsh (1726–1795) described the electrical properties of the torpedo fish, or ray.

Walsh equated the electrical activity of the fish to the Leyden jar, a device used to condense electrical potential. Developed by Pieter Van Musschenbroek (1692–1761) in the late 1740s and named after the Dutch city where he created it, the Leyden jar used wires to conduct frictional electricity into a flask of fluid. The fluid would build up electrical potential and a shock could be administered through a wire coming out of the jar. Walsh believed the fish was able to take outside electrical fluid and concentrate it within its body and shock other fish for it to devour. Hunter thought the fish was able to "will" the electrical power.

Knowing the Leyden jar could shock a person, scientists naturally took the idea to cadavers. There's nothing like shocking a dead guy on a sunny Saturday afternoon. Using the Leyden jar, scientists noticed muscular contractions in the cadavers. The convulsions of the dead when shocked electrically led to many speculations of the nature of electrical conductance in man. But knowing our bodies contain fluid, the idea needed to be investigated more thoroughly because our bodies might act like the fluid at the bottom of the Leyden jar, passively conducting it through rigid muscles.

The Leyden jar was used for entertainment as well. In the court of Louis XIV in Versailles, 180 French soldiers were lined up holding hands with metallic disks in the palms. When a soldier on the end touched the Leyden jar output, it was conducted through the entire train of people to the other end. One poor soul was shocked by touching the last man with his bare hand. This was replicated by 700 monks at a Parisian abbey to demonstrate the power of conductance through our bodies.

However, inherent electricity in a life form was still reserved as an aberration of the electric fish. People weren't going around shocking each other like Emperor Palpatine in *Star Wars*. But a cat's hair standing on end in the presence of a hand or a finger shock caused thoughts of the possibility. Mostly, evidence pointed to the fact that we are wet bodies unable to summon electricity, only to passively conduct it through our presence.

Much of the excitement over electrical phenomena resulted from the research of Benjamin Franklin (1706–1790) in 1751. His portly, rotund physique and stately demeanor, with glasses on the end of his nose, affecting a glance at you, deterred his gaze at important work. Yet, behind those wizened eyes, Franklin could express love and castigation paradoxically at the same time. In a quick glance from him was the ultimate human representation of provocative thought. He's an odd person to contemplate when you lay down a hundred dollar bill on a blackjack table. Without electricity, there would likely be no United States because lightning gave Franklin the credibility to be a voice for a revolution.

Franklin demonstrated the equal and opposing electrical action and coined the terms "positive" and "negative" electricity. The inside of the Leyden jar was positive and the outside was negative to Franklin. Franklin wouldn't have any trouble "jumping" his car. He used his ideas to develop a metal plate to conduct electricity. The plate became known as the Franklin square.

After Franklin's work, and the convulsions of dead bodies when electrically stimulated, scientists had the necessary tools to research electricity as the nature of animal movement. Electricity seemed to be a candidate that could finally explain and justify Galen's humors (the yellow bile) and Descartes' spirits. Even Newton had a similar idea. He claimed the ether in our nerves pervades every aspect of life and that humans can control it in our nervous fibers. Electricity fit the bill for the Newtonian vision as well.

By 1780, Franklin's theories and descriptions of the Leyden jar were generally accepted and widely read throughout Europe. Like Thomas Edison in the late nineteenth century, Luigi Galvani (1737–1798) took Franklin's knowledge and revolutionized the meaning of electricity. Galvani, a reclusive scientist working at the University of Pavia, the same university where Golgi would discover his stain 100 years later, applied Franklin's theories to dissected frogs to see if animals have an intrinsic electricity, and more specifically, if this intrinsic electricity could be the conductor that causes physical action.

Galvani dissected the frog's spinal cord, leaving the legs and leg muscles intact. His drawings of the experiments look like the legs were torn off Kermit the Frog's body by a maniacal mass murdering puppeteer (see Figure 3.1). Legend has it that he prepared the frog legs for his sick wife's dinner and got the idea while abstractedly bending them up and down. Hopefully, she got something else to eat that night.

FIGURE 3.1 Doc Galvani's fried frog legs

Jan Swammerdam (1637-1680), a Dutch biologist with an awesome name, was the first to dissect the frog muscle and nerve. Galvani was the first to shock them. Using the Leyden jar or the Franklin square (Galvani called it the magic square), a current was conducted through the tinfoil-wrapped spinal cord with the legs contracted. Galvani also hooked the legs to a wire on an iron rail in his garden in order to observe atmospheric electrical influences on the legs. However, bored with waiting because storms in Italy didn't arrive on command, he began to introduce different metals to the lightning rod and observed leg contractions. He realized that an inherent potential existed in the animal based on these experiments.

A curious development began as an offshoot of Galvani's theories. Controlling physicist Alessandro Volta (1745–1827) didn't believe Galvani understood all the current research in electricity over the 40 years since Franklin published his original work. An original Galvani supporter, Volta now believed that the reason for leg contractions was similar to the reasons that electric shock was produced in bodies when presented with an electric current, and this might not be due to inherent animal electricity at all. He thought the two opposing metals created the

current, and the body simply acted as a fluid through which it was conducted, as previously explained by the convulsions of a cadaver and the
French Legion with the Leyden jar.

To demonstrate his ideas, he stacked two opposing metals and created an electric potential. He showed that brass and iron can create an
electrical potential like the Leyden jar. There is an electrical gradient
between the metals that generates energy. And by applying this to an animal, convulsions would be expected. The stacked metal became known as
the voltaic pile, the precursor to the modern battery. In his rash fervor to
discount the quiet reclusive Galvani's theories, Volta inadvertently
invented the battery. Sadly, it is true, sometimes invention and creativity is
the result of someone trying to tear down their fellow man. This discovery
resulted in his name being forever associated with electrical potential.

In his experiments, Volta began introducing an electrical current to
his own body by his tongue. He produced sensations of taste. By covering his eye in tinfoil and introducing a current, he produced the sensation of seeing flashes of light. Volta interpreted this to mean that his body
was simply a fluid that conducted current and it did not have an intrinsic
charged fluid. He told anyone who would listen to him. It's wise to listen
to a guy who'll go so far as to cover his own eyes with tinfoil.

Galvani remained publicly quiet throughout Volta's challenges during the seven years before he died after his original publication in 1791.
The first shot across Volta's bow was published anonymously in 1794.
The nerve of a frog was cut and then applied to the nerve of an intact
frog. The releasing electrical current caused the intact frog's legs to contract vigorously. The experiment definitively proved Galvani correct.
Most researchers didn't notice the article because of the anonymity
attached to its publication, and people were too busy paying attention to
Volta's rants and raves. It is now known that Galvani published the
anonymous report.

The controversial theory raged for a few decades. Although Galvani
eschewed the fight, Giovanni Aldini (1762–1834), Galvani's nephew,
took up the cause.

Aldini was an ardent supporter of his uncle and believed Volta conclusively wrong. In fact, Aldini went so far as to conduct experiments on
newly acquired heads off the guillotine during the Napoleonic Wars. As
soon as the head was chopped off, Aldini would take it to make sure it was
fresh and apply currents through the ears and mouth. The decapitated

heads contracted into different facial expressions: smiling, grimacing, and coy expressions.

Aldini also presaged electroshock therapy by applying the Voltaic pile to his head and shocking himself at arbitrary strengths. He reported it as unpleasant and causing insomnia for a week. It's probably better to stick to electric fish to the head. The contractions were of interest for those treating the mentally insane because of evidence that camphor-induced seizures were therapeutic for the clinically depressed. Shocking the hell out of you will surely get you out of a funk.

Scientists weren't the only ones interested in animal electricity. The public and governments of researchers ardently consumed any new experiment. The public's fascination with the subject peaked in the early nineteenth century with the publication of *Frankenstein*. Taking the frightening and grotesque scientific literature produced by Volta and Aldini, which induced hysteria similar to cloning and stem cells today, Mary Shelley, in Switzerland with her husband and poet Percy Bysshe Shelley and friend, poet George Gordon, Lord Byron, brought back the dead while telling ghost stories late at night.

With Volta still on his soapbox denouncing Galvani's work, after *Frankenstein*, people were relieved that animal electricity might not be true. However, in Italy, Galvani's homeland, animal electricity was still avidly pursued, with the next notable discoveries by the physicist Leopold Nobili (1784–1835) and his student Carlo Matteucci (1811–1868) in the 1830s. Using only saline after decapitating a frog, they placed the trunk in one jar and the legs in another and connected them with a cotton thread soaked in salt solution. Contractions occurred without Volta's iron and brass metallic arc.

Many of the cellular ideas of the brain at the time were solidified in the same lab by students who all graduated around the same time from the University of Berlin. These students included German scientist Johannes Müller (1801-1858), who advised several prominent experimenters; Robert Remack (1815-1865), who determined the nerve fiber hooked up with the cell body; Hermann von Helmholtz (1821-1894), who developed the theory for the conservation of energy; Rudolph Virchow (1821-1902), who was one of the first to discover the glial cell; and finally, the one with the most forceful personality, Emile du Bois-Reymond (1818–1896), who was the father of the action potential.

Emile du Bois-Reymond came to Müller excitedly with a copy of Matteucci's work and proclaimed his interest in pursuing animal electricity. Müller knew Matteucci had recently become frustrated with his experiments and completely denounced animal electricity—going so far as to claim that he shared Volta's view that the nerves were filled with a non electric fluid or Newton's ether, a belief also shared by Müller. But he decided to give his student the project to further study the earlier phenomena Nobili's lab discovered. Du Bois-Reymond ran with the work and first developed more sensitive galvanometers to understand whether electrical potential existed.

If Volta was persuasive in his condemnation of Galvani, du Bois-Reymond was just as influential in his trumpeting of Galvani's virtues. He replicated many of Matteucci's experiments. But, after stimulation, he measured electrical conductance moving along the nerve to the muscle. He then was able to determine the speed of the conductance after causing contractions in the frog nerve. He determined that from stimulation to contraction, the speed was 30–40 meters per second. This is similar to what is reported today. But a problem then was that it was much slower than the electrical conduction that occurred through a wire.

Many other Descartes' vitalists who believed that the functions of a living organism are due to the hydraulic pumping of fluids still searched for the essential element and sided with Volta claims and Matteucci's flip-flop as evidence for electrical falsity. But du Bois-Reymond portrayed their thinking as moronic. He called vitalism pernicious and went so far as to say, "In one word, the so-called vitalism, of the type as it is currently presumed to be present in all points of the living body, is nonsense." He had no place in his heart for detractors and mercilessly lambasted Matteucci, the man whose research got him his start, to a side note in nervous-system history.

This problem of slower electrical conduction was not resolved until chemists understood that electrolyte solutions conducted electricity at slower rates. The electrical potential in nerves is now understood to be a difference between potassium and sodium ions. Sodium ions outside the cell and potassium ions inside create an electrical potential based on ionic charge difference.

As du Bois-Reymond perpetuated the idea of electrical conductance in the fiber, Remak's studies showed the neuron is where the fiber originates. Finally, to open the way for the electrical neuron to gain its level of

importance in the notion of our thoughts, and continuing with the belief that thoughts originate in the cerebral cortex of our brains, in 1870, the first demonstration of cortical function was achieved by Gustav Fritsch (1837–1927) and Eduard Hitzig (1838–1907). Dog cortices stimulated by electricity showed that motor control originated from the grey matter. They removed the skull and applied an electrical current through flat electrodes that would not damage the cortex. They noticed that movement occurred on the opposite side of the body from where they stimulated the cortex. They also showed that different parts of the cortex were responsible for different types of body movements. If they stimulated in one area, the dog would extend its leg; stimulation in another area resulted in the dog contracting its leg.

The backlash to their published work was immediate. Every eminent physiologist of the day called the experiments false and fabricated because they contradicted the prevailing edict that deep brain centers initiated movement. However, just as Galvani's experiments were replicated easily by other experimenters, so were Fritsch and Hitzig's. Cortical control of movement was soon noticed in the monkey as well.

Five years later, Richard Caton (1842–1926) came along and discovered changes in electrical activity while recording different areas of the cortex after stimulating the eyes and rotating the heads of monkeys and rabbits. Sensory nerves carried electrical impulses in the same manner as the motor nerves that cause muscular contractions.

Then Ramón y Cajal combined everyone's work and developed his palpable Neuron Doctrine. All our experiences, imagination, creativity, and memory reside in these beautiful cells, with their dendritic trees sticking out the top like poofs of scraggly hair, their triangular-shaped cell bodies as uniform as a doll's face, with their elegant transmitting axons each extending electrically out like the torso of a lover.

The tricky little problem was the glial cell. Cajal's acceptance of Pedro's theory that glia exist to buffer the electrical firing in neuronal communication came before it was understood that almost all cells have an electrical potential and gradient.

The electrical revolution ended 100 years after Galvani's work. The foundation was set for studies on the root of thought. As Walt Whitman asked, "And if the body were not the Soul, what is the Soul?"

But Fritsch and Hitzig's studies showed only a simple movement, and all electrical stimulation studies of neurons since have focused on reflexes

and stimulation of base desires. Ablation studies and examining the consequences of injuries allowed researchers to understand what cortical area was responsible for speech (left temporal cortex), hearing (temporal), and vision (occipital). What about the cells in the cortex—an area dominated by glia?

The assumption from electrical and cellular studies presented until the twentienth century was that the neural cell body was responsible for everything. Its axon was shown to extend from the brain to the body. And now that it was known to be electrical, all the thoughts in our brain were believed to stem from this electrical pulse in the peripheral nerves demonstrated by Galvani.

In the twentieth century, by placing neurons in a vacuum tube with sensitive electrodes with such small points they could stab into a small bundle of axons, scientists were able to accurately judge the electrical conductance in an axon. Britain's Charles Scott Sherrington (1857–1952) developed ways to scientifically study reflexes. He coined the understanding of the synapse as the interstitial space between neurons the year Golgi and Cajal received the Nobel Prize and would win the Nobel Prize himself in 1932. The incremental notion of separate cellular structure by Sherrington and Cajal eliminated Golgi's concept of the syncytium.

At the end of an axon, the synapse is the breach between communicating to the next neuron. The first molecule discovered to transmit across the synapse was acetylcholine at the muscles (the chemical compound that activates muscles and is a major neurotransmitter in the autonomic nervous system). Subsequently, nicotine was known to mimic acetylcholine. Scientists looking at the action of drugs discovered many of the other currently known transmitters. Cocaine led to the discovery of dopamine, morphine/heroin led to the discovery of serotonin, marijuana led to the discovery of cannabinoids, and nitrous oxide led to the discovery of nitrous oxide. These molecules are important transmitters between cells.

The eventual accurate "in-depth" reporting inside an axon was accomplished with a giant squid axon. British scientists Alan Hodgkin (1914–1998) and Andrew Huxley (1917–) and half brother of famous writer Aldous Huxley) inserted an electrode through a single axon and determined the resting potential as –60 or –70 millivolts in 1939. In 1908, Walther Nernst (1864–1941) published an equation that predicted electrical potential based on electrolyte distribution. When measuring

extracellular and intracellular space, nerves would have –85 to –90 based on the equation. This was eventually reported by Australian scientist John Eccles (1903–1997) in the 1960s. All of these men would win the Nobel Prize.

How a Neuron Transmits

When the nerve is stimulated, sodium ions enter inside the cell through exclusive channels that are opened only when firing is primed by an active cell upstream. The resting electrical potential of the neuron is –70 millivolts. When enough sodium enters the cell and the electrical potential changes enough that it crosses a threshold, it shoots to +50 millivolts as the floodgates open and sodium rushes in causing potassium to rush out. Afterwards, a resulting undershoot below resting potential occurs. During this "refractory period," the neuron is unable to fire until it returns back to the normal resting potential of –70 again.

But all of this groundwork was been done in long peripheral axons extending to the body. It has been done on simplistic relexes. Not at the cellular level in the brain. The studies have revealed a lot about the neuron, but have only been able to infer how we think on a cellular level.

It is commonly believed that neurons transmit to each other constantly and that our senses solidify some connections while reducing the influence of others. They either fire or don't. This "all-or-nothing" firing is believed by some to control thought through a binary code. This constant firing is how our thoughts happen. However, the seat of imagination and the provocateurs of neural action would be best served in a different type of cell, a cell that controls the reflexive action of axonal conductance. This cell is not firing long distance electrical sparks, but is a cell capable of activating like Golgi's syncytium and capable of storing information through attached processes, like billions of octopi that fuse their arms to each other. It is an autonomous cell that creates, imagines, and influences the activity of its active neuronal highways.

This cell likely resides in the cortex. Although Pierre Flourens (1794–1867) and others had difficulty pinpointing areas of the cortex that corresponded to thought it was known that by removing the frontal

lobe in monkeys, they became more docile according to the work of Scottish scientist David Ferrier (1843–1924). Ferrier claimed the monkeys had no discernible post-operation deficits other than tranquility. The frontal lobotomy to treat violent patients came directly out of his descriptions of a tame monkey.

American surgeon Walter Freeman (1895–1972) performed the lobotomies throughout the United States from the 1930s to the 1950s. The van that he traveled in was called the lobotomobile. Mental patients who were difficult to deal with were given the procedure. Freeman was educated at Yale and Penn and was not an amateur. He firmly believed in the benefits of the surgery with many notable patients including Rosemary Kennedy. The results of these tragic surgeries were the understanding that much of higher-level thinking resides in the cortex. With the advent of pharmaceutical treatments for psychiatric disease, his lobotomies thankfully went out of vogue.

But it was the work of American-born Canadian surgeon Wilder Penfield in the 1950s that showed areas of the cortex might be responsible for different functions of thought. Penfield learned under Sherrington and became a master of electrophysiology.

In the 1940s, it was shown that by cutting axons traversing from the right to left hemisphere, seizures could be reduced. While the surgery was being performed, the human patients were put under only local anesthesia applied in the scalp. Touching the brain is not painful because no sensory nerve endings reside there. The patients could talk to the experimenter and he could talk to them. The surgeon stuck electrodes into different areas of the brain as mapped by ablation and previous electrical studies and asked patients to perform functions. Ironically, by stimulating areas electrically, the surgeon could block them from doing certain things such as saying words or moving an arm. Patients could think about a function, but they were unable to perform it. Although this was the opposite of what they expected—hoping to induce action through electrical stimulation, it did reveal that areas of the cortex were important for many levels of thought.

Further work into the idea of localization of thought was performed by Roger Sperry (1913–1994) in the 1960s. Using epileptic patients who had their hemispheres separated by the surgery, he covered one eye and had patients perform tasks that would not be noticed by the hemisphere of the brain opposite the eye. He was able to determine that each brain

hemisphere has a different consciousness. This is where we get the terms on whether we are a right-brained person or a left-brained person, as the right brain was more associated with emotion and abstract thought, whereas the left brain had more concrete mapping of linguistic properties. Although it is not true that each brain area is responsible for only one aspect of the duality of personality, Sperry would win the Nobel Prize for his work.

The cell-based root of thought has eluded us. We might know certain elements about how we think, but nothing has validated the Neuron Doctrine's notion that the neuron is the seat of our intelligence and thought. Thought is intertwined with the ability to imagine and create. The illuminating studies on neurons for their understanding of its electrical properties remain unsatisfactory in their explanation of how we think.

As pre-electrical Swiss scientist Albrecht von Haller (1708–1777) stated a decade before the time of Franklin's experiments in his *Dissertation on the Sensible and Irritable Parts of Animals*, "the nervous fluid must have 6 essential properties. 1) That it be highly moveable. 2) That not only must it be moveable, but that it must be capable of being set in motion only by the will and force of the soul and not by the help of the heart. 3) That it must be a fluid element, and very rapid in movement. 4) That it must be very subtle, so as not to be seen by a microscope. 5) That it must have a particular affinity for the nerves. 6) That it be colorless, odorless, tasteless, and without perceptible heat."

Haller was elucidating principles on which the agent of nervous action could be defined, and specifically, motor nerve action. Looking back, all these criteria fit nicely with electricity except number 2. The neuron undoubtedly conducts electricity, but what spurs it to action— other neurons in a billion-cell complex circuit? Neural conductance is rapid, can travel long distances, can cause muscular contractions and animal action, and it communicates sensory input to the brain. All cells have an electrical potential, but neural structure allows the current to travel long distances in an "all-or-nothing" manner. However, glial cells in the brain exhibit activity in more subtle and elegant mechanisms than neural electrical depolarization. Cajal did not have techniques available to understand glial function, and the Neuron Doctrine prevented glial research with new techniques only until recently. These cells have properties that are more likely to be initiators and masseuses of nervous action, the will of controllable ability.

References

Abrams, R. *Electroconvulsive Therapy*, Fourth Edition. New York: Oxford University Press, 2002.

Aminoff, M.J. *Electrodiagnosis in Clinical Neurology*, Fifth Edition. Philadelphia, PA: Elsevier, 2005.

Andreassi, J. *Psychophysiology: Human Behavior and Physiological Response*, Third Edition. Hillsdale, NJ: Lawrence Erlbaum, 1995.

Brazier, M.A.B. *A History of Neurophysiology in the Nineteenth Century*. New York: Raven Press, 1988.

Galvani, L. *Commentary on the Effects of Electricity on Muscular Motion,* Introduction by Cohen, I.B. Norwalk, CT: Burndy Library, 1953.

Müller, J. *Handbook of Human Physiology*. London: Baylor and Walton, 1842.

Ochs, S. *A History of Nerve Functions: From Animal Spirits to Molecular Mechanisms*. New York: Cambridge University Press, 2004.

Valenstein, E. *The War of the Soups and the Sparks*. New York: Columbia University Press, 2005.

4

Meet the astrocyte

If you look at a tulip, you wouldn't think it was an armadillo. Similarly, looking at a neuron, you wouldn't think it was glia. But you might look at a whale and think it's a fish, until you look at it closely and realize it has no gills and breathes through lungs. Then, you have a problem. Through genetic testing and excavations by paleontologists, we now know it likely originated as a land animal that took back to the sea and is related to hoofed animals like the horse. But before genetic testing and evolutionary biology, classification was based on appearance. This remains true for cellular classification.

Glial cells include Schwann cells, Müller cells, epithelial cells, ependymal cells, oligodendricytes, tanycytes, microglia, and astrocytes—all function as differently from each other as they do from neurons.

Students of scientific fields always claim that learning new terms in the field is like learning a new language. Just as the meaning of an English word can change over time (such as plane, buck, mouse, and gay), the meaning of a scientific label can change after its function is understood.

As functions of cells are understood, the labels have remained. Glia are capable of signaling and communicating, but they will always be referred to as glia (glue). Virchow's "glue" label sticks because it was originally believed that a neuron was the only cell able to signal and communicate. As we can see by the confusing nature of the "planet" Pluto, it is difficult to unclassify the classified. Neuron comes from the Greek for sinew or tendon, and synapse is Greek for clasp, although they all sound like they were coined by an extraterrestrial techno group. The word tomato's origins come from the Aztec dialect of Nahautl in central Mexico, but almost everybody, including the author, doesn't know whether it should be called a fruit or a vegetable.

Of course, things change over time, and that is why the terms "glia" and "neuron" are preferable to some uniform naming procedure that modern biology and astronomy try to force upon us. And really, who knows glia means "glue" anyway? Our brains like to create.

In evolutionary biology, it is not completely understood why life started. It is believed that carbon excluded sodium in the ocean at some point, thus creating a cell. Energy was then required to maintain the electrical gradient created by electrolyte exclusion. Eventually cells aggregated with other cells and worked together for energy. Then plants and animals split, with animals evolving so some of the cells were sensory units that knew where to find the food. Then, more defined motor cellular units developed to help the animal move more efficiently to attain the food.

Neurons are the cells that developed for sensory and motor function and have their roots in the evolutionary reflex to procreate and get food. The higher-level thoughts of imagination and creation could have evolved separately and maybe even before the neuron.

The classical neuron, as described by Cajal, is actually best represented by the cell located in the cerebellum first discovered by Jan Purkinje (1787–1869). The Purkinje cells of this area located in the posterior base of the brain have amazing aesthetic structure. The dendrites look like an elaborate magnolia tree. The cell body is a perfect bulb like a teardrop. And the axons are so long, they extend out of the cerebellum into the pons, a structure next to the medulla at the base of the brain.

However, many other types of neurons exist with different characteristics. Functionally, they are mainly classified based on what connections they make: sensory neurons, motor neurons, and interneurons. In the patellar reflex or "knee jerk" reflex described by Sherrington in the early twentieth century, the tap of the patellar tendon of the knee causes sensory firing to the spinal cord, and the connection of motor neurons there creates contractions in your quadriceps, which causes the leg to jerk. No one who was tapped on the knee would argue that they controlled the reflex with their thoughts.

Because of this reflex, people who rashly respond to something without thinking are derogatorily told not to have a "knee-jerk" reaction and to think before they talk. Someone who punches another person in the face for being called a "sheep lover" is likely not thinking before acting and having a "knee-jerk" reaction. Similarly, if someone's father says he

hates the St. Louis Cardinals, and then his child says he hates the St. Louis Cardinals, too, the kid is probably not thinking about why he hates the St. Louis Cardinals (although this may be a reasonable sentiment) and just copying an authority figure. This is another "knee-jerk" reaction. These reactions are completely neuronal and an occurrence by which nothing happens between the sensory stimulus and motor output.

Sensory neurons are stimulated by the receptors that correspond to our five senses. For instance, the sensory neurons in our tongue respond to different molecules and pH levels in food to tell us whether we taste something sweet, sour, salty, bitter, or one recently discovered by Japanese researchers in the last five years, umami, which is a savory, meat-like flavor.

In our ears, minute hair cell receptors at the end of our cochlea respond to sound vibrations. In our eyes, rods and cones are stimulated by photons and converted into electrical neural signals. Our skin has receptors for temperature and vibration. Our ever-changing nose is constantly turning over neurons and glia in response to the ever-changing nature of smell. The nose is especially interesting because in lower-life forms, the olfactory bulb is more prominent in size ratio to the rest of the brain.

Motor neurons stimulate muscular action. But what is between? When someone tells you to use your noodle, what do you use?

Although the term glia and its first drawings were likely contributed by Rudolph Virchow in 1846, Heinrich Müller (1820–1864)—no relation to Johannes, the great advisor—was the first to describe a retinal glia cell in 1851. The cells are known to modulate signaling in the retina. They can signal to themselves as well. Not knowing what to call them because they seem to be a completely different functional unit than neuronal ganglion cells extending out from the eye into the brain, researchers have classified them as glia and they are called Müller cells.

Müller is often overlooked in favor of Virchow, although Virchow's publication of his 1846 work didn't happen until 1853, two years after Müller's. And Müller's drawings and description were much more intricate. In fact, Virchow got the best of Müller around this time professionally as well. Virchow sided with the revolutionaries in Berlin from 1848 to 1849, eventually losing his chair at the university due to his politics. The University of Würzburg pounced on the opportunity to have Virchow chair its department and chose him over the likely candidate Müller. Müller spent half a year in a sanitarium because of the slight.

The next major glial cell was discovered in the peripheral nervous system by Theodore Schwann. Schwann was also a student of Johannes Müller. If neurons are the highways, then Schwann cells are the construction workers in the peripheral nervous system. The function of these cells is so different from Müller cells that it is amazing they are both called glia. They are about as related as Henrich and Johannes Müller. Schwann had no clue about the function of the cells, only that they were associated with axons in the periphery.

The myelin on axons was not understood until the advent of the high-powered electron microscope in the mid-twentieth century. The electron microscope allowed researchers to see subcellular structures clearly for the first time. It was then that the wrapping twists of myelinating Schwann cells could be seen and the notion of axons secreting the myelin themselves debunked. Schwann cells myelinate the axons which extend out to the muscles so they are able quickly conduct electrical impulses. Schwann cells release the fatty myelin from their cell body and swirl it around a group of axons like a butcher wrapping up some sausages. Umami-flavored sausages.

In the central nervous system, the construction workers that myelinate the axons are called the oligodendricytes. Cajal's Argentine student Pío del Río Hortega first described this cell. Smaller than Schwann cells, oligodendrocytes abundantly reside in the white matter of the brain and wrap myelin around fibers.

Other glial cells that line structures such as the ventricles and blood vesicles in the brain are called ependymal cells, endothelial cells, and tanycytes. These cells are the military defense of the brain. Ependymal cells seem to help cerebral spinal fluid flow with extending filipodia and lining the walls. Epithelial cells line blood vesicles and the retina. Epithelial cells have the important task of not allowing any contaminant from the blood to invade the brain. Tanycytes also separate the CSF and the blood with tight junctions.

Throughout the brain, microglia (the smallest of all the glial cells) respond to injury and infection like the T cells and B cells in the blood. These cells look like ice cream sprinkles when they migrate toward an area of infection. They can be considered the Red Cross of the brain.

However, the cell that has provided such startling discoveries recently is the astrocyte (see Figure 4.1). The astrocytes are the cities to the neuronal highways. This cell is different functionally from the other

glial cells. The astrocyte is the most abundant cell in the human cortex and was first described by Otto Deiters (1834–1863) in an unfinished manuscript in the 1850s. Deiters died at the age of 29, and it was another former student of Johannes Müller—Max Schulte (1825–1874)—who published it for him. Deiters supported Virchow's view that the cells were simply connective tissue. He described the flat star-shaped cells with many processes in the white and grey matter.

FIGURE 4.1   On the left are drawings of neurons in the cortex by Cajal. On the right is a closer view of astrocytes (dark, spidery cells) hanging out next to neuron cell bodies (pale cells with axons extending up).

Jakob Henle (1809–1885), who was also a student of Müller's, believed that the cells were active, functional units in the brain. In 1856, Virchow wrote that Henle was blocking his concept of glia as connective tissue simply to serve "his own interests." In 1869, Henle published his first drawing of these cells.

Later, Golgi conducted studies with his stain where he claimed glia contact with the blood vessels and neurons. Golgi's discovery of the astrocyte's contact with the blood vessels would be the beginning of his idea that the function of astrocytes is to provide nourishment for neurons.

Cajal was quick to discount Golgi, but he had no idea about the nature of astrocytes himself. In his struggles with glia, he once wrote, "What is the function of these glial cells in neural centers? The answer is still not known and the problem is even more serious because it might remain unsolved for many years to come until physiologists find direct methods to attack it."

The word astrocyte sounds like an intergalactic parade, and it was used to demonstrate the star-shaped cells. Michael von Lenhossek (1863–1937) came up with the term in 1891 to describe the "neuroglia." Neuroglia was a vogue term in the nineteenth century as the neuron was being put on the pedestal. Neuroglia meant everything except for neurons. However, they mainly referred to astrocytes as they were abundant, and oligodendricytes had not been discovered yet. Astrocytes were also previously called "spider cells." German pathologist Edgar von Gierke (1877–1945) called the term inadequate because "nobody has seen a spider with as many feet as these cells have processes." Lenhossek thought all glia should be termed spongicytes and divided into subsets, one of which would be astrocytes.

Some cells believed to be related to astrocytes are Bergmann glia in the cerebellum. Their processes are found in the synaptic layer and their cell bodies sit next to neural ganglion cell bodies. Also in the cerebellum and olfactory bulb are velate astrocytes, which ensheath tightly packed neuronal cell bodies like a veil. Fibrous astrocytes are found in the white matter around axons and adjacent to oligodendrocytes. These cells might be different functionally, but currently because of their appearance, we know they are astrocytes. It might be possible that they communicate with each other, but this has not been determined.

Astrocytes of the cortex, mainly astrocytes referred to as "interlaminar" and "protoplasmic," are currently studied in relation to neuronal signaling. They look like octopi or stars. The extending feet that reach out to blood vessels comprise about 80 percent of the cell. No neural surface is left unexplored.

When looking at animals up the evolutionary ladder—the oldest fossil being about 600 million years old—we can see the difference in the behavior related to glial cells.

In the jellyfish, which has virtually all neurons, the basic behavior of the animal is the moving up and down in the water. The jellyfish also has a few reflex responses when something invades its space. The jellyfish is

so simple, it is basically a parachute in the water (and hunted for sport in *Spongebob Squarepants*).

In the flatworm, some glial cells can surround neurons. Flatworms essentially react to their environment with a series of basic behaviors such as righting themselves when they are turned over and twisting their bodies. They are also able to get used to a stimulus. If something non-threatening continues to disturb them, they eventually disregard the stimulus. Glial cells might play a role in some of their more complex behaviors.

The leech is more developed than the flatworm, with one glial cell for every 30 neurons, and the glial cells occupying 51 percent of the nervous system space. Some of their glial cells are stellate like astrocytes. Packets of glia are associated with groups of neurons and are known to regulate the environment and likely signal to the neurons. Glial cells compartmentalize each neuronal area around them. Some species of annelid, such as the palolo worm of the Pacific, aggregate prior to spawning, inducing molecular secretion they use to communicate with each other, which changes their behavior. Earthworms use their neurons to provide reflexive behavior while moving their segmented bodies, the glial cells contributing coordination. If you cut off their head, they survive and will regrow another one on the headless side. The headless side can still copulate, but with less coordination. They also become conditioned by stimuli, but behavior is much more complex, which might be due to more glial compartmentalization of neurons. The species of annelid with the most complex brain has developed the most aggressive predatory behavior.

In insects, glial cells also compartmentalize areas of the brain. In the bee, glia make up 57 percent of the retina. The integration of visual stimulation requires a significant amount of glia in these species. Insects have developed spatial memory. They are territorial and can manipulate their environment. Bees and ants develop complex nests for food storage and offspring rearing. They can communicate to each other via a variety of stimuli to describe where and what type of food is near. The complex social behavior of some insects can be seen as one body separated into individual animals. If our head was the queen and our arm and legs were separate from our body, they could retrieve things for us without our head going with them. It should be said that they don't exhibit individual intelligence. It should be also said that the female preying mantis rips off

the head of its male mate so that copulatory action is uninhibited by the male's brain function.

The invertebrate with the most complex central nervous system are the cephalopods, which include squids and octopi. Cells resembling astrocytes are prominent in their large brains. They have been shown to contemplate stimulus, something that is associated with pigment change on their skin. They have complex courtship behavior and express emotive behavior during decision making as to whether they should run or fight. They can make intelligent decisions based on touch and vision.

In invertebrates, complex behavior increases with compartmentalization of neurons with glial cells. They don't seem to sleep, and little activity occurs when there is no stimulus.

However, it is difficult to speculate on the inner workings of a brain in a species with which we can't communicate. This difficulty is compounded by the fact that aquatic animals must have completely different views on the nature of their existence than we do on dry land.

Vertebrates are distinct because of their myelinated axons. The myelin contributes insulation around the nerve, like plastic around an electrical wire to increase its conduction. Sleep makes its first appearance in fish. Their behavior might seem similar to squid and octopi, but fish respond to stimuli with less variation of behavior and less glia.

Amphibians are not as behaviorally complex as some of the more exceptional fish, but they do learn spatially and have developed specific prey-catching capabilities. They have more astrocytes than most fish and can process information with glial cells. They also exhibit a form of sleep.

More impressive is when we move on to reptiles and birds. Birds are able to process extreme spatial knowledge. They also learn new songs based on what they hear from other birds. A bird raised in isolation develops less elaborate songs. Individual birds can develop unique songs recognized by other birds. Differentiation in birds is almost like mammals. Some birds have been shown to use tools such as sticks and rocks.

Mammals, in general have the most highly developed sequestering of neurons by glial cells. As mammals become more complex, with humans being the most complex (the dolphin and whale might have an argument with that statement), glial:neuron ratio and astrocyte prevalence and contact increases. Glial cells compose 60 percent of the rodent brain and 90 percent of the human brain.

The ratio of cell number of astrocytes in the cortex increases as the intellect of the animal increases. The mouse has about .3 astrocytes for every 1 neuron. In the human, 1.65 astrocytes to 1 neuron are in the cortex. In fact, the increasing number of astrocytes correlates with the considered intellect of the species.

Has the glial cell evolved as some sort of motivation generator for neural activity? In humans, the increased number of glia has always been explained as more support is required to keep the high-powered neurons working in order. However, the electricity in the neuron is not particularly special or unique other than it travels down an axon. It might be conceivable that the increased astrocyte ratio is able to compensate for the required increasing ability for imagination and creativity required for human existence.

As the studies of Wilder Penfield show us, the cerebral cortex—which resembles a crumpled-up sweaty T-shirt—is likely the center of higher thought. Neurons of the cerebral cortex are mainly comprised of pyramidal cells that typically extend long axons to other far reaches of the cortex or axons to other brain centers. These cells are known to have motor function in the prefrontal gyrus of the cortex, as discovered by Gustav Fritsch and Eduard Hitzig. Other candidates are the shorter interneurons throughout the cortex; their classification based on their appearance and protein expression. Interneurons signal through an action potential in the same manner as motor and sensory neurons. Finally, because of the billions of cells in the brain, they create an infinite amount of connections that can be solidified or weakened based on use. This might be the case, but how they get solidified is another debate.

In 1949, Donald Hebb published *The Organization of Behavior: A Neuropsychological Theory*. In this book, Hebb describes synaptic strength as the determinant of how we remember and act. Research on long-term potentiation evolved from Hebb's ideas. Long-term potentiation refers to how synapses might gain strength. We have memories based on experience and the more times we think about that experience, the stronger the synaptic connections are in these neurons. The strong connections are the learning that influences our behavior.

The idea is still controversial 60 years later, and research evidence is under scrutiny. However, if the theory holds to be true, it could be due to the signaling of abundant astrocytes (the characteristically star-shaped

glial cells) at the synapse. If the skeptics are correct, then the astrocyte might prove to be responsible at the learning level. It doesn't matter how many lanes or exits are on a highway.

Hebbian psychologists and behavioralists talk about the "black box" of our thoughts—the area between sensory processing and motor output. Astrocytes are the black box.

When looking at the brains of injured patients, Paul Broca (1824–1880) discovered that the left temporal cortex was responsible for speech. When Penfield electrically stimulated the brains of patients undergoing surgery, he confirmed the function of speech was in the left temporal lobe. We know that the motor cortex lies at the front of the brain in a strip along the midline. Sensory processing from the skin lies just to the back of the midline. The back of the brain is the visual cortex. The parietal cortex between the sensory and visual cortex stores motor memories for playing instruments and sports; however, human verbal communication on the left side of the brain can also be visualized through blood flow.

Positron Emission Tomography—a test that uses a special type of camera and a special test medicine (radioactive tracer) to look at organs—has shown that increased blood flow goes to regions that correspond to areas that Penfield and others described as areas responsible for processing in humans. When someone is told to speak, the area of the left temporal cortex is flushed with blood. Knowing that astrocytes, not neurons, have their end feet on the blood vessels, it is possible that astrocytes signal to neurons to fire to move the tongue in specific manner for speaking while also controlling blood flow to oxygenate themselves and neurons in the area. As sodium goes in the cell, neurons need oxygen in their mitochondria in order to produce the energy they need to pump out the sodium.

Practitioners of the Neuron Doctrine claim that the trillions of connections are sufficient for the construction of thought. However, a cellular breach between sensory and motor function is plausible. It would seem the sensory input to the brain might be processed by astrocytes and astrocytes then influence motor action based on the sensory input attained, whether the motor action is speaking, lifting your arm, making love, or something else. Simple reflexes to frightening or exciting stimuli

bypass the astrocyte. It can be seen as a balancing fulcrum, where one side is a sensory-dominated animal soaking in its environment like a sloth barraging an indifferent astrocyte, an obese dog on a porch in the sun watching the cars go by, or a motor-dominated animal, running about like a chicken with its head cut off. An astrocyte expending energy without thoroughly considering its environment is like a yippy dog chasing its own tail. In the middle are balanced motor and sensory stimuli with astrocytes receiving input, signaling to each other and controlling motor output.

An astrocyte is a self-sufficient, self-replicating cell signaling to itself contentedly. Neurons have no reason to exist except to support astrocytes. Mature neurons cannot function alone, whereas mature astrocytes have no difficulty existing without neurons. When placing mature neurons in a Petri dish, they are unable to survive without astrocytes. Astrocytes are perfectly content without neurons.

Cajal's contributions to the foundations of neuroscience are undeniable. However, the fact that the field is called "neuroscience" illuminates his overpowering influence and the knee-jerk studies of some subsequent researchers. Cajal's intuition told him that glia were likely more prominent than believed, as betrayed by the way he scoffed at Carl Weigert's suggestions that they were merely space fillers with no function at all. With the techniques available to Cajal at the time, he didn't believe he was able to study the astrocyte. However, his powerful conviction of neuronal prominence set back studies on the most abundant cell of the brain area responsible for higher thought.

The Neuron Doctrine explored throughout the twentieth century is the basis for how we understand our brain, but it completely negated for nearly a century what might be the most important cell in the brain. As with any doctrine or regime, any detractors were summarily discounted or laughed at. You certainly did not tell Joseph McCarthy communism "isn't such a bad thing" in the 1950s. You didn't tell the inquisition that Martin Luther "was a decent dude." And you definitely did not tell a brain scientist in the twentieth century that the astrocyte was more important than the neuron. However, the mounting evidence is too glaring to overlook, and the astrocyte might prove to be the reason for neural existence.

References

Fedoroff, S. and A. Vernadakis. *Astrocytes: Cell Biology and Pathology of Astrocytes*, Volume 3. San Diego, CA: Academic Press, 1986.

Gerhart, J. and M. Kirschner. *Cells, Embryos, and Evolution*. Malden, MA: Blackwell Science, 1997.

Hebb, D.O. *The Organization of Behavior: A Neuropsychological Theory*. New York: John Wiley & Sons Ltd., 1949.

Kettenmann, H. and B.R. Ransom. *Neuroglia*, Second Edition. New York: Oxford University Press, 2005.

Laming, P.R., E. Syková, A. Reichenbach, G.I. Hatton, and H. Bauer. *Glial Cells: Their Role in Behavior*. New York: Cambridge University Press, 1998.

Murphy, S. *Astrocytes: Pharmacology and Function*. San Diego, CA: Academic Press, 1993.

Papper, S. *Sodium: Its Biological Significance*. Boca Raton, FL: CRC Press, 1982.

Ramón y Cajal, S. *The Neuron and the Glia Cell*. Springfield, IL: Charles C. Thomas Publisher Ltd., 1984.

5

Riding the calcium wave

Evergreen-shaped neurons, processing information with electrical sparks flying about and crackling our skulls is the current popular held belief of our brain activity. This militaristic science of the brain, with neurons firing like guns and bombarding our brain in the form of thoughts, has been under review for a couple decades. Since the 1980s, scientists discovered the smooth flow of calcium oscillations or waves. Some might think this is the advent of surfing as a popular sport, the unregimented flow of riding waves displacing the arms war of football, and the heaters thrown by pitchers in baseball. If you've been in the military and you've surfed, it's much more likely that your brain works in the manner of the waves. They are even rough in the winter, like the mood of a man, and the flow of waves in surfing might have a subversive effect on neuroscience research. When the movie *Gidget* came out in 1960, surfing became the rage, and soon afterwards, Steven W. Kuffler's lab was the first to take a serious experimental approach to the glial cell.

If astrocytes are the mediators between sensory experiences and motor action—the black box where imagination and creation occur—they must be able to communicate among themselves. Weigart's concept of a static, dull astrocyte contributing nothing to brain function except as a space-filler, like the feng shui placement of a seldom-used dining room table is now defunct. And Pedro's notion of glia as simply a buffer zone for excess electrical neuronal electricity is being turned on its head.

There is no need to put a pointless aesthetic table in the middle of a spacious house, with no functional purpose—just as there is little possibility that the most abundant cell in the brain sits there doing nothing. Only elitist scientists at the turn of the century would think of this crackpot idea for a brain cell, possibly with so many unused tables in their own

homes. Glia are not glue or inconsequential space; it is now turning out to be the exact opposite. Rodin's thinker was certainly using his astrocytes, and Myron's discus thrower was using his neurons.

For the astrocyte to be the root of thought, it must be able to process sensory information coming from neurons. It must also be able to communicate to motor neurons to stimulate action. In the peripheral nerves, electrical impulses rapidly fire through sodium and potassium exchange to the muscles to cause contraction, electrical impulses we know as "action potentials." Action potentials also carry information pertaining to sensory input from the body to the brain.

As the physiological techniques developed to study electrical communication in nerves, scientists began to use these techniques on glial cells in the late 1950s and early 1960s. As scientists stuck electrodes into the cells, they initially believed glia had no electrical potential. They were just sitting there like a piece of wood—something to knock on for good luck. However, these studies were performed inaccurately and were more designed as a confirmation of Cajal's conclusion—the platitudes of yes-men trying to please their revered ancestors.

In 1955, Paul Glees (1909–1999) broke from the neuron religion—and was the first to suspect a noninsulating role for astrocytes. Glees wrote a book titled *Neuroglia: Morphology and Function* and stated, "Apart from a protective, insulating and supporting function, could neuroglia have a metabolic activity exceeding its own requirements, which would influence directly neuronal metabolism or synaptic activity? Until this dynamic concept has been proved, neuroglia will remain largely a domain of morphology and the artistic delight of neurohistologists."

The first studies of the physiology of glial cells in vertebrates were performed on the frog and mud puppy and published in 1966 out of Steven W. Kuffler's (1913–1980) lab at Harvard. Ironically, in the same year, he founded the Harvard neurobiology department. The name of the department demonstrates the influence of the neuron doctrine through the twentieth century. If he were more democratic and more aware of his research, he would have called it the "Brain Biology Department." Of course, this doesn't sound as fancy. Kuffler's groundbreaking studies were also performed with the intent to provide evidence for Pedro's theory, but he inadvertently discovered an electrical potential in astrocytes along the way. At the time, it might have been more appropriate for him to call the department "The Neuro and Check Out This

Random Interesting Stuff We Found Out About This Previously Thought to Be Functionless Cell Department."

He starts the mud puppy paper with the line, "Little is known about the physiological properties of glial cells in the vertebrate central nervous system." In fact, in 1966, absolutely nothing was known about glial cells, the most abundant cell in the brain by a large magnitude.

The studies that Kuffler and his students Nicholls and Orkand performed on the leech encouraged the idea that glia were functioning cells. In science, however, since humans are vertebrates and not octopi, a paper on a leech matters less than one on a vertebrate. In the frog, as in the leech, they found astrocytes exhibited an electrical potential that could be changed dramatically in the presence of potassium. Kuffler was interested in potassium as it flows out of neurons during an electrical potential. He wanted to test (or confirm) the theory that glia absorbs neuronal electrical firing, and the idea that astrocytes respond to potassium might lead credence to the theory.

The finding that astrocytes respond to an ion had long-range implications and inspired scientists to consider them more closely. Electrical stimulation of astrocytes was unable to create an action potential, however, and because this was believed to be the only worthy brain cell communication (the preferred method of the neuron) scientists could not yet grasp the importance of glia.

In an adjoining paper, when Kuffler and colleagues stimulated neurons, they found that glia also depolarized. They assumed that potassium influx in glial cells was the main constituent of this depolarization. However, scientists now know that many factors contribute, with calcium taking the most prominent role.

In 1986, Sean Murphy and colleagues at the Open University discovered that transmitters released from neurons stimulate astrocytes in the neocortex of rats and cause calcium influx. The known behavior of calcium as a cell regulator of communication gave pause to researchers. The year after Kuffler's research on glia, calcium was shown as necessary at the synapse in neurons to release transmitters.

Like sodium and potassium, calcium is also a prevalent oceanic ion and likely had an active role in the original formation of life. Although it was shown that extracellular sodium and intracellular potassium conduct an electrical pulse down a nerve, calcium wasn't believed to be biologically relevant until 1883. Like most research in the eighteenth and

nineteenth centuries (and Kuffler's lab), the story centers on the poor torture of frogs. Sydney Ringer (1836–1910) discovered that a dissected frog heart suspended in sodium would stop beating. When suspended in a blood mixture, the heart would continue to beat. But after removing the blood and then adding a saline solution, it would stop, first growing weaker and then halting after 20 minutes. After this time period, the heart would also not respond to strong shocks.

Adding potassium chloride or bicarbonate of soda to the saline solution would not help the heart to beat. However, when adding calcium, Ringer found the heartbeat could be maintained for four hours. Like most major biological leaps, his discovery occurred completely by accident. Ringer had his student prepare the mixture and instead of using distilled water, the student mistakenly used tap water. When Ringer discovered the calcium element in London tap water was equivalent to the amount of calcium circulating in our blood, he was able to perform the famous experiment.

The emphasis on sodium until that point was largely for obvious reasons. When we go to a lake and take a swim, we taste the cool fresh water that sometimes stimulates our thirst, but if you take a person from the middle of the United States, and put him on a beach in California, he might get the urge to go swimming in the ocean. If you don't tell him what will happen when he tastes the water, he will come up spitting and gagging because of the massive salt content. However, we don't taste calcium. In fact, we are incapable of tasting calcium. Sodium is the ion that is transmitted on our taste buds, and it was believed to be the most important ion because of its domination of the oceans. But sodium is tame compared to calcium.

Calcium highly reacts with the elements nitrogen and oxygen and the water molecule, which are prevalent in nature. It is speculated that the control of this abundant highly reactive molecule is integral to life. In the environment, calcium is mainly combined with chloride and carbon or other anions (negatively charged ions, which have more *electrons* in their *electron shells* than they have *protons* in their *nuclei*) in the form of a salt. Like a game of Tetris, the volatile calcium ions are stacked together to create organism structure. In bones and teeth, it is deposited as calcium phosphate. Seashells are mainly calcium carbonate.

Life apparently started on this planet about four billion years ago. As multicellular organisms evolved, calcium signaling and communication is

believed to be the way cells were able to control other cells and themselves. The evidence for the role of calcium in the organism was left as footprints in the form of fossilized bones.

All beings today use calcium as a cellular regulator in all bodily organs. Calcium is extremely important in development. When an egg is fertilized, a calcium wave through the ovum initiates conception. Cellular development and division are calcium-dependent processes. Without calcium, an embryo will not develop properly and die. High concentrations of calcium are in a mother's milk (among many other things).

In plants, calcium activity contributes in a similar manner. Root growth is stunted and useless if calcium is not present. In animals and plants, cell interaction and adhesion to each other, for an organism to actually be "multicellular," requires calcium. A calcium signal tells flowers to bloom (see Figure 5.1).

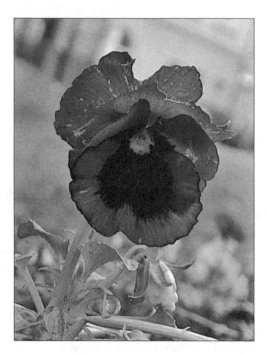

FIGURE 5.1 Calcium in action

In the field of biology, the removal of tissue cells from animals and subsequently culturing them in a Petri dish is a common practice. Cells adhere to each other like in tissue when they are placed in a culture dish.

Just as human beings are social creatures who need other human beings, so cells need other cells, a process that relies entirely on calcium. Without calcium, the cells are unable to grow as quickly and their structures change. They isolate themselves and eliminate cell interaction.

Extracellular calcium is 20,000 times higher than intracellular calcium. However, the cell has internal complexes that also store calcium at 10–50 times the rate of the surrounding intracellular space. The wide disparity of calcium concentrations inside and outside the cell is due to the interactivity of calcium when it is not controlled. Most calcium inside the cell is attached to proteins and sequestered in internal cell complexes. On the planet earth, calcium cannot exist freely without interacting with something. Like the most respected member of a family, all important matters in the cell involve calcium.

Further calcium experiments were performed on muscle after Ringer's famous experiments. Extracellular calcium can stop muscle contraction. When it drops below a certain level, muscles twitch uncontrollably. Calcium is also stored in neurons at the synapse. When the electrical signal reaches the end of the axon, calcium floods the synapse from the extracellular space like people into a store for a 50 percent off sale. The calcium "flux" causes a release of calcium from sequestered stores inside the cell and is required for transmitter release. Because the understanding of calcium in the cell came about later than Hodgkin and Huxley's squid giant axon experiments, the belief is that calcium contributes to the electrical gradient more than previously expected.

In astrocytes, the main signaling comes from complexes inside the cell called "internal calcium stores." Neurons require the electrical axon impulse for calcium influx from the extracellular space to enter at the synapse and affect transmitter release. External calcium influencing transmitter release has been shown to come from astrocytes.

In the short paper published by Murphy and colleagues, which showed that transmitters can institute a calcium increase in astrocytes, they were concerned with a single cell and did not understand the extent of astrocyte reception of neuronal communication. A neuron signaling to an astrocyte could carry information from our senses. If neurons are the only cell involved in mental processing, why would astrocytes respond to the sensory stimulus of neurons? At the point of their discovery, Murphy and his colleagues did not understand that astrocytes might also be able to signal to other astrocytes and to neurons themselves.

A couple papers from Yale, the first by Ann H. Cornell-Bell and colleagues in 1990, demonstrated that calcium waves occur in astrocytes when they are stimulated. After a transmitter acts on an astrocyte or a researcher mechanically stimulates the cell with an electrode—a long plastic tip about 1/200th of a millimeter wide—the calcium wave spreads from one astrocyte to the next. The spread is similar to what Golgi described—through physical connections between the star-like cells long arms—similar to billions of octopi holding hands.

The understanding of how the cells held hands began in 1969. Researchers at the National Institutes of Health, Milton Brightman and Thomas S. Reese, laid the foundation for what would be known as the gap junction. Looking at pictures taken with the electron microscope, they demonstrated that astrocytes—with the ends of their processes probing blood vessels and neuronal surfaces—also come into contact with other astrocytes. It is now known that the end feet of different astrocytes wrap around each other and form a junction through which receptors bind the two cells.

Gap junctions are present in other types of organs as well, such as the liver and the heart. Gap junctions are fused together by intracellular channels. Imagine a lock and a dam. The water level on one side is higher than another, but a free exchange of barges and boats occurs in the lock where water levels can be raised or lowered to the other side's level. The regulated lock and dam of the astrocyte gap junction determines what can pass from cell to cell.

About 230 gap junctions connect a pair of astrocytes in the cortex. If a dye is injected into one astrocyte, 50–100 neighboring astrocytes will be stained with the dye. In different brain regions, the degree of astrocyte cell-to-cell connection differs. Almost all cortical astrocytes are physically connected, as Golgi suspected for a cell responsible for thought.

Oligodendrocytes, the cells that wrap insulation around axons to better help neurons conduct electricity, also form gap junctions with astrocytes. Although they are not as efficient as astrocytes when conducting to each other, astrocyte gap junctions with oligodendroctyes might be a way to control myelination to increase conductance in neurons. This analogy can be better explained if one considers the oligodendrocytes as construction workers that work on the neural road. Astrocytes send an order

to fix the road because cars aren't moving as fast as they'd like down the freeway.

In fact, in development of neurons, gap junctions can exist between astrocytes and neurons. These gap junctions can be understood as the building of a new road between astrocyte centers in the cortex—the architect and city planner building new infrastructure.

The main internal complexes where astrocytes store calcium are called the endoplasmic reticulum, mitochondria, and Golgi complex (named after the same Golgi, who noticed the structure in his stained cells in the late nineteenth century). These compartments are surrounded by membranes and have their own electrical gradient between the rest of the intracellular space of the cell. Because these compartments also exist in the intracellular space, the intracellular space outside these compartments is confusingly referred to as the cytosol.

The other paper from Yale, by Steven Finkbeiner in 1992, explained a series of experiments where they loaded dye into the astrocytes that attach to calcium. The visualized movement of calcium waves from one cell to the next occurs in a curvilinear pattern. One cell stimulates the next like a series of dominoes in patterns similar to the Milky Way.

Finkbeiner's research blocked inositol triphosphate and was able to stop the flow of the calcium wave from one cell to the next.

It should be said here that inositol triphosphate is a painful and boring name concocted by chemists accoding to their naming system. It is not a protein or gene, but a molecule. For what it's worth, inositol means it has 6 carbon atoms, 12 hydrogen atoms, and 6 oxygen atoms. The triphosphate means that three phosphate groups are attached. Some of the worst names in the history of science have come about as we enter the era of biology concerned with genes and proteins. We are subjected to the uniform naming of these poor structures, an idea that usually backfires as researchers realize the protein doesn't do what they originally thought it did. A special place is in everyone's heart for the guys that discovered a protein in the early 1990s and named it Sonic Hedge Hog after the Sega video game they were playing at the time. Even better is that it turned out to be incredibly important in embryonic development. There's nothing more enjoyable than taking a class in biology taught by a difficult professor who is forced to say Sonic Hedge Hog 30 times in 15 minutes.

As it became known that calcium could signal from astrocyte to astrocyte, the implication of known calcium signal attributes became clearer. Calcium can also act on the genes in the astrocyte, affecting long-term changes in the cell's reaction to calcium stimulus. Also, the endoplasmic reticulum, with calcium concentrations from 10–50 times higher than the other intracellular space (cytosol) is separated by its own membrane. Proteins are not sensitive to calcium binding in the endoplasmic reticulum as they are in the rest of the intracellular space because of the high concentration of calcium they are saturated with. In fact, binding of proteins to calcium is 1,000 times higher in the cytosol. This allows astrocytes to contain a ball of reactive calcium in their cells to be unleashed when stimulated. However, it's hard to contain calcium.

For a forest that hasn't seen a fire in a long time, striking a match will send it up in flames. However, the flooded endoplasmic reticulum is like the fire itself; proteins are unable to light if they are lighted already. The extremely high concentration of calcium in the endoplasmic reticulum and the sensitivity of proteins in lower levels of calcium cause constant pressure for the calcium to enter the cytosol. When it does, all hell breaks loose and binding occurs left and right. This short-term protein functioning can also develop into a long-term process, as calcium binding to proteins can change their long-term functions. The action of the actual wave in astrocytes is even more striking. The two types of receptors allow for calcium to leave internal storage sites. One receptor continually recruits more storage sites; the other is the inositol triphosphate receptor. It can be activated by calcium itself. So, as calcium moves in waves from cell to cell, it can continually recruit more calcium (see Figure 5.2).

Blocking inositol triphosphate stops the wave. Inositol triphosphate receptor activation by calcium can desensitize the receptors. Inositol triphosphate is more sensitive to their receptors, but it is also less reactive than calcium and can act over many areas of the cell. Calcium and inositol triphosphate act like a hand on a faucet when they bind their receptors on the endoplasmic reticulum. After turning on the faucet, calcium flows out. The release of calcium from internal endoplasmic reticulum through these receptors results in sparks or puffs before it is sequestered back into the endoplasmic reticulum. These sparks or puffs can be amplified by neighboring endoplasmic reticulum as calcium itself releases more calcium stores.

FIGURE 5.2   A calcium wave starting from a single astrocyte in the middle of the frame (upper left) spreads outward to other astrocytes in the vicinity over the course of the next few seconds.

To get calcium back into the endoplasmic reticulum, energy must be used. ATP (Adenosine-5-triphosphate) is produced by the mitochondria, the power plants of the cell, by using energy from the blood. ATP consumption in the cell is similar to world oil consumption. It is the voracious creation of energy and power. Believe it or not, the ion that stimulates ATP production in the mitochondria is none other than calcium.

When we eat and drink, our body breaks down our foods into energy. This energy is required for the mitochondria to produce ATP. Fats and sugars are broken down into units that are eventually utilized by the mitochondria transport system. When there is not enough energy available, calcium is unable to pump back into the endoplasmic reticulum and calcium diffusion can cause cell death. However, too much energy is stored in our body as fat.

During development, calcium channels on the outside of glial cells are expressed when the cells are growing and differentiating. When the cells reach maturity, the outside channels are removed, like training wheels on a bike. The astrocyte can now control calcium itself and "ride the bike with no hands." The main way of astrocyte signaling in mature cells is from calcium release of internal endoplasmic reticulum stores. Activation of extracellular astrocyte receptors by transmitters released

from neurons creates the formation of inositol triphosphate in the cytosol that causes rapid endoplasmic reticulum calcium release.

When transmitters act on astrocytes, they create a series of calcium "puffs"—sparks that cause a calcium wave that diffuses the astrocyte, recruiting more endoplasmic reticulum and mitochondria through the cell, spreading through gap junctions to other astrocytes in a wave that can spread half a millimeter to all cells in its vicinity. Then more endoplasmic reticulum recruitment, calcium, and inositol triphosphate passage through gap junctions continue to create this incredible event from astrocyte to astrocyte.

The reason for our existence might be the control of calcium, and the abundant astrocytes in the human brain and ability for human communication might be the best expression of this control on the planet. Calcium can affect short changes in astrocyte signaling on the order of milliseconds. It can also change the makeup of the cell to respond to stimuli in a manner that lasts for months or years by binding on genes and proteins and changing their functions.

Calcium waves in astrocytes spread much slower than neuronal communication and is a wonderful way to integrate and process information. It does not take a leap of faith to think astrocytes receive information from fast-acting sensory neurons to store the information for long-term use. In turn, they communicate to neurons when we need to create muscular action or send information to astrocytes in other parts of the brain.

Calcium is hard to sequester because its reactivity with other molecules is so volitale. The spontaneous release of calcium waves from internal stores in astrocytes are intermittent and fluid—like raindrops falling on a lake. These calcium puffs, if strong and persistent enough, can also ignite calcium waves through the astrocytes. If calcium waves in astrocytes influenced by neuronal communication from the senses is us pondering our environment, spontaneous calcium puffs become waves in our moments of inspiration, creativity, and imagination.

Golgi imagined a similar way that we think. Although he imagined neurons, it is becoming clear his ideas are real in astrocytes. Astrocytes are a physically intertwined net with cells in their surrounding environment recruiting more astrocytes and storing information via the calcium wave and changes in calcium signaling. When neurons are introduced, the waves synchronize. Our ability to retrieve information in our brain is likely the grasping of astrocytes by sensory neurons.

Poor Cajal had no idea; although he had his doubts about the notion that glia are unimportant, he clung to his legacy and perceived brilliance by marginalizing the role of astrocytes to support. He was blameless because he hung it all on his poor brother Pedro.

With arms on blood vessels that can increase flow to areas of thought, the astrocytes are activated, illuminating information in the depths of our existence primed to be retrieved for years, months, or minutes. If it seems necessary to act on this information based on the sensory stimulus in our presence, well, send it down the neurons.

The spontaneous activity of calcium in astrocytes might be the nature of our creative and imaginative existence as human beings. Never-heard-before thoughts arising for the first time out of the infinite possibilities. And a wave can flow over, releasing stored information of astrocytes able to solidify those thoughts. The progression of human existence could rely on the calcium, if the original thought is something worth learning by the other astrocytic populations. As the wave flashes through gap junctions, it recruits other astrocytes based on how their calcium release responds as a result of previous calcium signaling.

Surfers know waves are finicky things; some days, waves come in large and forceful in sets of three or four interspersed with lulls, and other days bombarding the beach in sporadic swells. Some days, when the wind is high, they are impossible to navigate because of the choppiness. Calcium waves in the living human brain are something researchers are unable to study directly, but that day is coming. It is known that they can likely be synchronized, like the nice sets surfers lust after. It is thought that they can be more sporadic and unpredictable when they are sitting idly. No matter how astrocytes are influenced—chemically or through changes in blood flow—our imaginations are fueled by such subtleties.

References

Berridge, M.J. "Inositol Triphosphate and Calcium Signaling." *Nature*, 361: 315–325, 1993.

Brightman, M.W. and T.S. Reese. "Junctions Between Intimately Apposed Cell Membranes in the Vertebrate Brain." *Journal of Cell Biology*, 40: 648–677, 1969.

Campbell, A.K. *Intracellular Calcium: Its Universal Role as Regulator.* New York: John Wiley & Sons Ltd., 1983.

Cornell-Bell, A.H., S.M. Finkbeiner, M.S. Cooper, and S.J. Smith. "Glutamate Induces Calcium Waves in Cultured Astrocytes: Long-Range Glial Signaling." *Science*, 247: 470–473, 1990.

Finkbeiner, S.M. "Calcium Waves in Astrocytes—Filling the Gaps." *Neuron*, 8: 1101–1108, 1992.

Glees, P. *Neuroglia: Morphology and Function.* Springfield, IL: Blackwell, 1955.

Hatton, G.I. and V. Parpura. *Glial—Neuronal Signaling.* Boston: Kluwer Academic Publishers, 2004.

Krebs, J. and M. Michalak. *Calcium: A Matter of Life or Death.* San Diego: Elsevier, 2007.

Kuffler, S.W., J.G. Nicholls, and R.K. Orkand. "Physiological Properties of Glial Cells in the Central Nervous System of Amphibia." *Journal of Neurophysiology*, 29: 768–787, 1966.

Orkand, R.K., J.G. Nicholls, and S.W. Kuffler. "Effect of Nerve Impulses on Membrane Potential of Glial Cells in Central Nervous System of Amphibia." *Journal of Neurophysiology*, 29: 788–806, 1966.

Pearce, B., J. Albrecht, C. Morrow, and S. Murphy. "Astrocyte Glutamate Receptor Activation Promotes Inositol Phospholipid Turnover and Calcium Flux." *Neuroscience Letters*, 72: 335–340, 1986.

Verkhratsky, A. and H. Kettenmann. "Calcium Signaling in Glial Cells." *Trends in Neurosciences*, 19: 346–352, 1996.

Verkhratsky, A. and E. Toescu. *Integrative Aspects of Calcium Signaling.* New York: Plenum Press, 1998.

Verkhratsky, A. and A. Butt. *Glial Neurobiology.* Chichester, West Sussex: John Wiley & Sons, Ltd, 2007.

Volterra, A., P. Magistretti, and P. Haydon, *The Tripartite Synapse: Glia in Synaptic Transmission.* New York: Oxford University Press, 2002.

6

Hey neuron, it's me, glia

Draped in astrocytes, neurons witness the calcium waves flowing throughout the cortex. However, they are not innocent bystanders. As the calcium wave breaks and spreads to other astrocytes, it is returned and sequestered back to the internal stores in the cell. But we are not in *A Clockwork Orange*—sitting in chairs with our eyelids peeled open as subjects of experimental aversion therapy. We act on what we experience. Astrocytes process the information coming from our sensory neurons, and in some cases, after communicating with each other, astrocytes might decide to act on our motor neurons, unless we are embroiled in a DVD marathon of course.

Astrocytes are the root of our cognitive function, and therefore, are intertwined in our notions of survival. Maybe their processes, called "endfeet," extend out attaching to our blood vessels and tell us we are thirsty. Astrocytes might decide to pick up a glass of water.

We know calcium is released from internal stores in astrocytes. After it is released, it moves in a wavelike fashion to other astrocytes through gap junctions that enable astrocytes to communicate. This process might be how humans store and retrieve information, create new ideas, imagine, and make decisions.

We also know astrocytes express receptors for every type of transmitter released from neurons. Transmitter action on astrocytes can cause calcium waves to occur. And now we know that an astrocyte can tell a neuron to fire.

In his paper with Stephen W. Kuffler (1913-1980) on the nature of neuron-to-glia communication, Richard K. Orkand states, "The magnitude of the potential fields and their influence on neighboring neurons created by the glial potentials is not known. Available experiments do not support the idea that currents in glial cells influence neurons because the

clefts greatly attenuate current spread between the two cell types." However, in 1990, Harold Kimelberg from Albany Medical College, in an attempt to understand the swelling of astrocytes in brain injury, cultured cells in a Petri dish and added factors that caused them to become impregnated with fluid. This swelling resulted in transmitter release from astrocytes.

Then, in 1994, two papers came out independently of each other and almost simultaneously, in the journals *Science* and *Nature*, that showed for the first time astrocytes communicating to neurons.

Philip G. Haydon's lab at Iowa State University and Maiken Nedergaard at Cornell University studied the calcium action of astrocytes in relation to neurons. In culture, Nedergaard stimulated a single astrocyte and watched the calcium waves emanate to other astrocytes in its vicinity. However, she also noticed that calcium increased in the cell body of the neuron next door—a phenomenon that causes transmitter release.

Haydon's paper, by Vladimir Parpura and colleagues, took it one step further and studied the action of glutamate. Glutamate is an excitatory transmitter prevalent in the cortex and previously thought to be only released by neurons. They show that glutamate could be released from astrocytes and cause signaling in neurons. The implication of glutamate release from astrocytes to act on neurons was revolutionary in the mid-1990s. This was as outrageous as hearing that the Pope faced Mecca on his knees every day. The first notion that glutamate had anything to do with astrocytes at all was in the mid-1980s.

In 1984, Helmet Kettenmann and colleagues at the University of Heidelberg showed that the transmitters glutamate, aspartate, and GABA cause electrical potential changes in astrocytes. Changes in electrical potential in astrocytes without action potential had been known since Kuffler. However, no one believed that a transmitter could act on astrocytes. They were called "neurotransmitters" after all. Then, when Murphy and colleagues threw some glutamate on astrocytes in the mid-1980s, the subsequent understanding that a transmitter released from neurons could produce a calcium wave in astrocytes blew everyone's mind.

The revelation that glutamate can act on astrocytes led to the discovery of glutamate receptors on the astrocyte membrane. The state of the importance of the neuron and the Neuron Doctrine was so influential

that glial cells were the last cells in the body that were discovered to have receptors. Researchers exhibited that human trait of overlooking thought to submit to the will of the more powerful and accepted Cajal for fear of losing their livelihoods or being brandished as crackpots. This detestable assumption of glia being insignificant at the submission of Cajal's intellect led to the most abundant cell in the brain being the *last* cell looked at for receptors. Receptor signaling is ubiquitous throughout the body in all cells. However, in the brain it was thought to only be the domain of neurons. Thinking about the cells of thought was repressed!

The electron microscope pictures from the 1950s onward show the close proximity of astrocytes to neuronal synapses. Researchers were unsure what to make of the junction between these highly electrical firing cells being probed by worthless astrocytes. Sherrington and Cajal would have rolled over in their graves. The silver stains produced by Golgi and Cajal showed a different astroycte, set apart from neurons, in beautiful glory. However, the silver stain doesn't stain all cells, just a few. Microscopes weren't powerful enough to consider the level of cell-to-cell snuggling. Outside the axon, to bear the brunt of an electrical pulse made sense for astrocytes; however, probing like a nosey neighbor into the domain of the neurotransmitter did not make sense. This synaptic contact and subsequent discovery of glutamate-induced calcium waves in astrocytes indicated that astrocytes might process information at the synapse.

When Phillip G. Haydon, Vladimir Parpura, and colleagues found that astrocytes had the capability of releasing glutamate into the extracellular space in a similar manner to neurons—and then subsequent separate studies showed that astrocytes could cause an actual action potential in neurons—the neuron, in all its glory, was being told what to do.

One could look at this as "neurons also tell glia what to do" because of astrocyte expression of transmitter receptors. This is true. However, the nature of neuronal firing ties it to sensory or motor function, signaling from the senses and transmitting to the muscles. The astrocyte has no such attachment. The astrocyte processes neuronal signaling and instigates the rapid action of neurons to muscles and the viscera. This idea can be better understood by thinking of a photograph or video. When a director films a movie, the image she points the camera at is imprinted on the film. The film can be played back to recreate the image. However, you wouldn't say the film is the director. In Figure 6.1, astrocytes are the

processesors of sensory information and the instigators of motor action using neurons as tools. As will be seen in later chapters, astrocyte growth can be achieved through more attention and concentration or focus by the human mind.

FIGURE 6.1   The astrocyte processes and retains information from the senses, and it tells neurons to fire for action.

Haydon described the neuron-astrocyte-neuron action as the "tripartite synapse." According to this theory, the neuron arrives with information to signal to the next neuron, similar to a waiter who delivers a meal to a customer, and the astrocyte adds salt and pepper to the dish. However, the tripartite theory does not take into account the ability of the astrocyte to signal to a neuron spontaneously, without responding to a neuronal stimulus. The astrocyte doesn't just add salt and pepper; instead, it is the cook that prepares the meal.

Let's say you want to punch someone in the face. Maybe the person told you to go to hell. Maybe he insulted your mother. Or, maybe you're a firm believer that the Smurfs were better than the Snorks, and this joker is taking the side of the Snorks. Anyway, you are receiving some sensory stimulus that enters your brain. It reaches the cortex, and your astrocytes produce calcium waves in respond to such a strong stimulus as you process the stimulus of Snork dominance. Previous experience that has been solidified by the calcium astrocyte signaling reminds you that the Snorks suck. The frequency of the waves tell neurons to fire, which respond with you drawing back your arm and punching the poor dude right smack between his Snork-loving eyes.

This response can be so rapid that it acts as a reflex, bypassing astrocytes altogether. Astrocytes have been shown to shrink their cell body to let neurons fire to each other uninhibitedly. Their end feet relax and pull up, like a child on a big wheel going down a hill. The neurons are allowed

to fire rapidly without interruption or influence to create a reflex without the inhibition of thinking.

The processing of astrocytic calcium waves takes much longer than neurons. They might be primed at the synapse for a Smurf-Snork debate because you have thoroughly thought about this subject. Astrocytes at the synapse when you hear "Snorks are better than Smurfs" simply redirect this to your motor cortex for the arm movement of a punch.

In fact, pondering anything intensely, such as cartoons over many sittings through the course of many Saturday mornings, can lead to the point that you drown out all sensory stimuli while considering the question. This original thought might be entirely astrocyte-driven through calcium waves.

Where do original thoughts and ponderings come from? Where does a revelation come from? If the astrocytes are placed with neurons in culture, spontaneous calcium signaling in astrocytes can not only cause calcium waves, but these calcium waves can also cause neuronal signaling to occur. This can explain how we can vocalize our imagination. Where did George Lucas come up with the idea to clothe Darth Vader in a black plastic helmet of that design? Did the apple that hit Newton's head coincidentally spur an astrocyte calcium signal from a puff to a wave? One could say Proust's *Remembrance of Things Past* is one long calcium wave flowing through his cortex. Let's not even get started on where Jim Henson's creations spawned from. Spontaneous calcium signaling and the subsequent neuronal firing could be the act of creation. Spontaneous calcium waves would also flood over astrocytes that store information based on our previous experiences, thereby influencing our creation.

When neuronal firing is blocked, calcium signaling continues in astrocytes. These splashes of calcium waves without neuronal influence might be considered the wild imaginings and dreamlike state of a person in a sensory deprivation tank or the random dreams integrated by calcium flow during neural shutdown.

It has also been discovered that all transmitters not only act on astrocytes, but when they are released by neurons, they can also be transported into astrocytes, where they are broken down and resynthesized. This has been shown to be the case for all transmitters: glutamate, dopamine, serotonin, and so on. However, what happens to these transmitters when they are formed again in the astrocyte was not known until a decade ago.

It was discovered that glutamate released from astrocytes might be the same glutamate that is taken up from the extracellular space when released by neurons (or astrocytes). Glutamate is then released in the same manner from astrocytes that they are in neurons.

Glutamate exists in astrocytes at a concentration between 10–10,000 fold higher than the extracellular space. As is the case with ions, this incredible difference can cause a gradient, where if one room is cold and the neighboring room is hot, when you open the door, the hot air will rush in and the temperature between the two rooms will even out. After a calcium wave enters an astrocyte, the trigger sends glutamate in small membrane balls to the cell membrane, where the balls fuse and glutamate is released into the extracellular space.

To transport glutamate into an astrocyte, two or three sodium ions and one hydrogen ion come in as well, with outward movement of one potassium ion. Glutamate transporters that shuttle the transmitter into the cell during this ion exchange are highly expressed in astrocytes. The stockpiling of glutamate continues until the floodgates are opened.

Other than glutamate, astrocytes have also been shown to release almost every other kind of transmitter. Astrocyte receptors at the synapse correspond to the type of neurons they are near. If the astrocyte is in the cortex, it will likely have glutamate receptors. If it is in the basal ganglia, which is damaged in Parkinson's disease, the astrocytes will respond to dopamine.

There is evidence that channels at the gap junctions (places where astrocytes connect to one another) release glutamate and transmitters from astrocytes as well. When the wave enters the gap junction, glutamate can drip out. However, the function of this channel release is not known.

Release of transmitters from astrocytes is different from neurons in some aspects. Researchers have examined this by using toxins. Toxins, such as tetanus toxin, which can completely stop transmitters from neurons at the synapse by blocking fusion of the small membrane balls within minutes, can block only about 70 percent release of transmitters from astrocytes after 20 hours. This is likely because the astrocyte has many other avenues of transmitter release than neurons. However, botulinum neurotoxin A (Botox) can block astrocytic release of transmitters more efficiently. The lesson is: Don't inject Botox into your brain; you might have trouble thinking.

In the cortex, a single astrocyte lords over the environment surrounding it. Astrocytes control nourishment from the blood. Astrocytes release transmitters at the synapse to control neuronal firing. They not only receive information from neurons, but also imbibe the transmitters released by the neuron. An astrocyte can even dictate the type of signaling it wants a neuron to perform. Neurons have the capability to fire at different frequencies. Studies have shown that short signaling can increase, whereas longer ones are suppressed when a particular astrocyte signals at the synapse.

In the hippocampus, which is the area of the brain responsible for forming new memories, about 80 percent of large synaptic contacts are surrounded by astrocytes. As information comes in from the senses through neurons, calcium waves responding to neuronal firing in the hippocampus move at frequencies comparable to the firing of the neuron. The waves also do not spread unless the strength of the neural firing is sufficient. It was formerly believed that memory formation in the hippocampus resides strictly in neurons. However, calcium waves become more frequent and are more easily initiated if the neuron in the area had previously fired strongly. Strong firing at a synapse indicates that a strong stimulus comes from the senses. Strong firing increases the capability of this axon to fire the next time it is stimulated. However, in astrocytes, a strong stimulus from neurons also increases the frequency of calcium waves, which spread to all adjacent astrocytes. Formation of memories is in the hippocampus, but information resides throughout the cortex. This is the domain of the astrocyte. The stimulus from the senses creates a better road to travel through, a freeway, in the form of a neuron. But the information is processed and resides in the astrocyte.

If someone tries to remember something through repetition, the sensory stimulus of the person repeatedly saying what he needs to remember is fired into the hippocampus. For instance, you are out at a bar and meet a girl named Jenny. You are having a good time with her, but she has to leave, so you try to get her number. The only problem is no one has a pen to write it down. So you repeat the numbers several times—867-5309, 867-5309, 867-5309—to solidify the memory. When you get home, you try to remember—what was Jenny's number? The neural signal fires into your brain as you repeatedly say the number, stimulating astrocytic calcium waves, which increase in frequency because of the repetition of the earlier neuronal firing. Or, you could just put the number in your cell phone.

In calcium wave firing, as each wave rises, a shot of glutamate is released from the astrocyte. An increase in calcium waves results in an increase of glutamate release. This transmitter signaling to neurons doesn't occur strictly at the synapse. Astrocytes can influence the neuron at any point along its beautiful long body. As waves spread to other astrocytes via gap junctions, the other astrocytes will release glutamate and stimulate more neurons in their area. One astrocyte also contacts dozens of cells, releasing glutamate and spreading calcium to all of them.

Not only are astrocytes the cells where thoughts and memory reside, but they can also contribute to our body's hormonal levels. Astrocytes produce proteins in areas of the brain concerned with water homeostasis and microcirculation through the brain. These proteins are called vasoactive intestinal peptide, atrial natriuretic peptide, and brain angiotensinogen—three names you won't see on a law office. They influence neurons that release hormones into the blood. The hypothalamus has neurons that can secrete hormones into the blood as well.

Hormone secretion is influenced by glial cells in the area of whole body fluid balance. Glial action on neurons causes the release of vasopressin and oxytocin in the blood, hormones directly responsible for regulating whole body fluid.

Astrocytes can also change the synapse's appearance. Acting like water to plants, the astrocyte rains on the neurons and helps them grow. Without astrocytes, the neurons are stunted and produce few connections. Similar to dried-out crops during the desert wasteland of the dustbowl, neurons sit brittle and pathetic in their Petri dish, forlorn and sad entities. They are probably crying. Your heart goes out to them.

However, throw down some astrocytes beside them and everything blooms, as though ET has pointed at them. The amazing transformation is due to the capability of astrocytes to influence axon outgrowth. Astrocytes can also cause neurons to form many more synapses. Neurons in culture by themselves form few synapses and are immature. Astrocytes build roads for their long-distance information transfer.

Mauch and colleagues in Frank W. Pfrieger's lab in Strasbourg, France in 2001 were able to isolate the molecule responsible for the increase in synaptogensis. They were not anticipating they would find this all-important molecule to be cholesterol. Astrocytes have the capability to synthesize cholesterol and release it from their cell bodies.

Astrocytes maintain a synapse simply by their presence, which strengthens the connection through signaling of transmitters and growth factors. It has also been shown that glia have the capability to eliminate synapses. Apparently, when a synapse has fallen out of favor, it is torn out like a railroad track no longer in use.

If neurons require this much maintenance from astrocytes, how can they be behind our motivations and thoughts? As human beings, an animal on this planet searching for food and procreation, we have sprouted evolutionarily out of some control of the elements of our surroundings. The volatile calcium ion, which is the integral element in cell-to-cell signaling in all organisms, might just be the haphazard chance fount from which organic life exploded. And calcium flowing in waves is the main signaling mechanism behind glia, the cell that is the most abundant in the brain and the cell whose ratio increases up the evolutionary ladder, taking a special place in the brain of human beings in the form of the astrocyte.

As scientists slowly come to the realization of the folly of 100 years of naming everything in the field after the neuron, they do it with their astrocytes.

References

Hatton, G.I. and V. Parpura. *Glial—Neuronal Signaling*. Boston: Kluwer Academic Publishers, 2004.

Innocenti, B., V. Parpura, and P.G. Haydon. "Imaging Extracellular Waves of Glutamate During Calcium Signaling in Cultured Astrocytes." *Journal of Neuroscience*, 20: 1800–1808, 2000.

Kettenmann H., K.H. Backus, and M. Schachner. "Aspartate, Glutamate and Gamma-Aminobutyric Acid Depolarize Cultured Astroyctes." *Neuroscience Letters*, 52: 25–29, 1984.

Kimelberg, H.K., S.K. Goderie, S. Higman, S. Pang, and R.A. Waniewski. "Swelling-Induced Release of Glutamate, Aspartate, and Taurine from Astrocyte Cultures." *The Journal of Neuroscience*, 10: 1583–1591, 1990.

Mauch, D.H., K. Nagler, S. Schumacher, C. Goritz, E.C. Muller, A. Otto, and F.W. Pfrieger. "CNS Synaptogenesis Promoted by Glia-Derived Cholesterol." *Science*, 294: 1354–1357, 2001.

Nedergaard, M. "Direct Signaling from Astrocytes to Neurons in Cultures of Mammalian Brain Cells." *Science*, 263: 1768–1771, 1994.

Parpura, V., T.A. Basarsky, F. Liu, K. Jeftinija, S. Jeftinija, and P.G. Haydon. "Glutamate-Mediated Astrocyte-Neuron Signaling." *Nature*, 369: 745–747, 1994.

Verkhratsky, A. and A. Butt. *Glial Neurobiology*. Chichester, West Sussex: Wiley, 2007.

Volterra, A., P. Magistretti, and P. Haydon, *The Tripartite Synapse: Glia in Synaptic Transmission*. New York: Oxford University Press, 2002.

7

Developing relationships

Imagine the earth slips through a rift in space and time and comes out the other end into a completely different universe. Imagine this experience coincides with all the blueberry bushes in the world growing 1,000 percent more blueberries. However, the blueberries look different; they have sprouted arms stretching over and around the bush and they are controlling the branches. Then the blueberry bushes get up, walk around, and talk, creating blueberry bush societies. Now, imagine you are a botanist who specializes in blueberry bushes and you want to kill one to find out how the blueberry bushes suddenly became so smart. Where would you study first—the branches or the numerous odd-shaped blueberries that suddenly grew and are now reaching around and controlling all the branches?

Before we are born, a neuronal framework like the branches of the blueberry bush is established. Then astrocyte growth snowballs at birth. Unfortunately, neuronal studies have dominated.

We can gather some evidence from neuronal-focused research into how astrocytes grow and develop in the womb at birth and early childhood. With neuronal tendrils sinewing out of the grey glial goo, transmitting rapid signals at the beck of our pondering, contemplating and understanding astrocytes, the pre- and post-natal development of the primate brain are established when we are born. Neurons are used by beings to acquire rapid information about their environment through their limited senses. Only with our regulatory muscle—our astrocytes—can we reach beyond our limitations by considering the sensory information. Only through our glia can we reach a higher understanding of our existence.

The cortex is where higher thought is processed in our astrocytes. Although most research has been neuronally focused, in the last 30–40 years, a better understanding of the nature of our cortical development has been taking shape. One of the first scientists to tackle the method of cortical development was none other than our old friend Cajal. Cajal speculated as to the nature of connectivity in the cortex while, as usual, assuming the neuron held the greatest importance.

When the brain develops before birth, cells called radial glial stretch out from the ventricular fluid. The ventricles sit inside our brain like a pond in spring and summer. All growth and activity surrounds the pond. Like the growth of tadpoles becoming frogs, ventricular pools of fluid influence cell division. Cells divide next to the pools and expand out to form the brain in an inside-out manner. Cells dividing from radial glia can become any cell type in the brain. Neurons are formed first and set down like the streets of a housing development.

Much of our wealth of knowledge into brain cell development comes from Pasko Rakic and his wife Patricia Goldman (1937–2003), both developmental neurobiologists at Yale University. Rakic started his career in the former Yugoslavia in the Soviet eastern bloc. Injecting monkeys with radioactive material in the 1960s, Rakic was able to follow cell morphology and lineage in the primate brain during development.

Prenatally, radial glial cells extend long distances from the center of the brain to the outside surface. If you think of the ventricle pools as the body of a porcupine, the radial glia are its quills. Radial glial cells appear around gestation week seven as the part of the embryo's brain sprouts and grows. Shortly after radial glia appear, they begin dividing at the ventricle. The cycle of cell division starts with the radial glial cell body migrating up its long and thin processes that stick up from the ventricle; the porcupine quill reach up like a blind man's cane to test its environment. This phenomena is demonstrated in Figure 7.1. As the cell decides to divide, it begins to replicate its DNA as it migrates down the porcupine quill back to the ventricle. It then becomes two cells, one of which migrates back up its long radial glial cell mother and becomes a neuron.

The radial glial cell is also a mother in the sense that it guides its progeny to their places in the world. In this case, the world is our brain. After each new cell migrates up the radial glia to its new position in space, it morphs into a neuron. When mapping the cortex in the late nineteenth century, Cajal did so based on connections neurons make

when bringing information from the sensory and sending to the motor environments. Based on neuronal connectivity, the cortical layers are numbered 1–6. Layer 1 is closer to the outside surface of the brain; layer 6 is deeper inside the brain.

Reprinted from Brain Research Reviews, Vol. 55, Issue 2, Rakic, P., "The Radial Edifice of Cortical Architecture: from Neuronal Silhouettes to Genetic Engineering," p. 208, Copyright (2007) with permission from Elsevier.

FIGURE 7.1   A neuron climbing like a squirrel up its radial glia mother tree

Layer 6 forms first in development. Radial glial extend short processes near the ventricle, and bulbs of cells are laid down like seeds. At this point, as the fetus is bathed in embryonic fluid, the ventricular fluid takes up almost the entire space of the peanut-sized brain.

For the next 100 days, radial glia extend further out of the brain. They push through already established layers, through its continual neuronal offspring to what will be the outside of the brain. After the last layer is formed (layer 1, which is at the extreme outside of the brain), the neuronal support infrastructure of the cortex has been laid down like a map. In the second month of pregnancy, at the peak of proliferation, it is estimated that 200,000 neurons bud every minute.

The explosion of cell proliferation in primates compared to other animals is believed to be the reason for our unique folds of the cortical surface when we observe a brain removed from its skull. In a rat, the cortex has no folds and is simply an outer sheath covering the basal areas of the brain. However, in humans, the cortex folds and refolds to fit all the cell bodies in the cortex. It can be compared to shoving a crumpled blanket in a box that is too small. It won't fit if you lay it flat, but if you fold it up or mash it in the box, it fits nicely. Because of our unique brain structure, the massive amount of cells in the cortex is one of the reasons the cortex is believed to be where higher thought is processed.

The cortex of the human is only about twice as thick as the rodent. Most mammal brains have long white tracks of axons from neurons extending out of or in to the cortex from our sensory and motor functions. However, if you flattened out all the folds and spread out the cortex like a cookie sheet, the human cortex would take up about 400–500 times more area than a rodent cortex. Of course, this isn't as impressive when one considers the size of an elephant brain. Complex cortical folds exist in whales, elephants, and dolphins. For all we know, an elephant might have finally solved many of the problems of quantum theory. Although the cortical area from an elephant brain would probably take up more area, the human brain has a significantly higher glia-neuron ratio in the cortex.

After the neurons are put in their proper places, the last trimester of pregnancy is spent making neuronal connections in the brain. When the neuron reaches its niche after climbing like a caterpillar up the radial glial tree, it extends out growth cones. Like the head of a snake, the growth cone explores its environment for the best place to make a connection. Usually this is when it encounters another neuronal process. Both the axons and dendrites of neurons extend through growth cones. They have little hair-like structures on the end that help them move through the environment. The shaft of their extensions from the neuronal cell body extend incrementally as they reach out.

When they contact the next neuron, they form a connection and begin laying out the groundwork for the transmitters and receptors they use to communicate with one another.

The initial transmitter expression in the womb is a calcium-dependent process. Early in the embryonic stage, spontaneous calcium-dependent

electrical changes in neurons cause the transmitter to be expressed that will be used in the future by the neuron. If the calcium levels are tweaked, different types of transmitters can be expressed in the cells. This curious regulatory control by a calcium pulse draws parallels to the calcium wave of astrocytes as the control of information processing in the cortex.

While this occurs, areas near the ventricles begin dividing inter-neurons and oligodendrocytes. These cells provide functions to maintain the previously developed neuron—the interneurons inhibit other neurons and oligodenrocytes wrap fatty tissue around axons so they can better conduct electricity.

At this stage, deep brain structures nominally understood to be the seat of unconscious activity are formed. The limbic system and the basal ganglia become solidified. The basal ganglia are responsible for motor neuronal efficiency and are disrupted in Parkinson's disease. The limbic system deals with our basic subconscious desires such as food and sex. Both are covered by the cortex, like a baby in a folded blanket.

After the neuronal framework is established, avenues and highways traversing the bulb behind our eyes, mouth, nose, and between our ears, extending to our limbs through our tail-like spine, are ready to be populated with our mind. Astrocytes begin to grow and fill niches near their support neurons, in places where they have easy access to sensory information to influence their calcium wave, places to experience the beauty of life, think about it, and transmit ideas into action through long-distance, quick communication down neuronal lines. Astrocytes are our mind. As they are about to peak, we slip out into the world, fully equipped to experience life as a human being.

Astrocyte proliferation coincides with birth. In rodents, which have a gestation period of three weeks, the peak of neuronal formation occurs at two weeks during the embryonic stage. Then astrocytes peak at birth or two days postnatally. A second wave of oligodendrocytes peak after birth. In humans, the timeframe follows the same course. As we are born, astrocytes become the houses next to the neuronal roads.

After the astrocyte explosion at birth, radial glia also stop dividing and turn into astrocytes themselves. Their long processes, now extending to the outer regions of a fully layered cortex, shrink back to the ventricles and assume an astrocytic morphology, like a man on stilts coming down

to the ground and taking off his clown makeup. There astrocytes reside next to the ventricles as we enter adulthood. They are able to divide and create new cells throughout our lifespan.

Astrocytes are the basis for life in the brain. They self-replicate, are promiscuous, spit out progeny, and give us the ability to attempt to make sense of our world.

After the astrocytes have been placed next to their neuronal roads, synaptogenesis occurs. Synaptic connections have already been made. However, for proper communication, the strengthening of synapses through bulbs sprouting off the axons and dendrites, like flower buds, need to be formed. Neuronal connections are meaningless without astrocytes there to tell them what to do. This astrocyte influence over synaptogenesis sadly has not been adequately studied. However, the obvious implications that it does not occur until astrocytes are present means that astrocytes communicate this effect. Interestingly, evidence in the last 15 years has pointed to a reduction in synaptogenesis in Down's syndrome. However, the role of astrocytes in reduced synaptogenesis in this disorder has never been studied.

The extreme growth of the brain around birth and immediately afterward is when the skull enlarges. The weight of the human brain more than doubles in size from birth to age 1. Much of this is due to astrocyte proliferation.

Apoptosis is a prevalent phenomenon involved in development—it is the term to describe the killing of useless cells. Excessive neurons are created during development. As the brain grows after birth, an incredible amount of synaptic connections are also made. However, in a twisted mass genocide, other cells send signals that eliminate the excessive cells to make room for their own. The cells are ultimately scavenged away. How the elimination of synapses occurs is largely unknown. However, it might be possible that astrocytes cause the extensive generation of the synapses and then decide which ones are necessary and which ones are expendable, like a medieval king choosing his harem.

From gestation week 29 until birth, our brain grows by 160 percent. When we are born, our brain is 25 percent of the adult volume. By the time we are 6 years old, our brain reaches 90 percent of the size it will be when we are an adult.

The long neuronal axons, which constitute the white matter regions of the brain, increase in volume systematically after birth. After

oligodenrocyte differentiation, throughout childhood, they begin to actively wrap fatty tissue around neurons. The graded increase in brain size is likely due to white matter size increases and fatty tissue around axons. It is known that astrocytes can communicate to oligodendrocytes, and some aspects of the intense insulation of axons might be controlled by astrocytes.

Although the brain increases in size overall throughout our childhood development, more interestingly is how the cortex increases and decreases in size. After birth, development of the cortex increases until about age eight. At this time, the brain begins to become systematically streamlined. The volume of the cortex is much smaller in adults than in eight year olds. At about age four, we begin to experience memories and dreams, after glia arrive and establish themselves postnatally. If neurons were responsible, wouldn't we have memories of the third trimester?

Interestingly, different areas of the cortex have different ages for the peak in their volumes. It was shown that from preschool until ages six to nine, a 13 percent increase in the volume of the cortical grey matter occurs. This then declines by 5 percent into adulthood. Frontal lobe areas reach their peak volumes at age 12. Parietal lobes reach their peak volume at about 11 years of age. Temporal regions reach their peak volumes at about 16 years. Occipital regions where visual integration occurs show a continuing linear increase into adulthood.

The thinning of the cortex into adulthood is thought to occur through the apoptotic genocide of excess synaptic contacts. The thinning of the cortex was also associated with higher IQs in children at the ages around 7–11. This makes one wonder if the loss of childhood—to develop the focus that is required for an IQ test—is a good thing. To not care to focus on a test and to think in the most wild and creative ways only a child can are eliminated to prepare us for the tasks in adulthood.

Studies on the cortex and maturity have been conducted only through imaging techniques and not studied on a cellular level. It would be interesting to see the role of astrocytes in the cortical thinning process. Although it seems to be a synaptic solidifying event, it might be possible that children have more astrocytes than adults and the imagination and creativity that arise from increased astrocyte amounts cannot yet be controlled and are therefore sacrificed. However, because we know astrocytes can continue to grow into adulthood, we might be able to increase genesis through more learning and experiences. More astrocyte

cities would need to grow to house newly learned information and experiences. The more astrocyte cities, the more places for spontaneous calcium puffs—the spontaneous release of calcium in the cortex that can ignite a wave. This can be the root of human imagination and creativity. As the wave spreads to astrocytes already representing information, new thoughts emerge in our mind—thoughts not thought by any human before.

As we know, children have more accessible imaginations, but adults have better control of their thoughts. This neuronal firing of simply taking in information and then acting on it instead of spending more time using astrocytes in the form of thoughts can eliminate or surpass the ability to imagine and create.

This model provides a way for adults to increase their intelligence. After the synaptic connections are better streamlined for neuronal action, astrocytes can regenerate and create a pattern necessary for calcium wave communication to effectively influence their neuronal support networks.

One thing is known for certain in development: It seems that when rats are given more enriched environments, they are able to learn mazes faster. This is supposed to translate into a higher intelligence for kids who have access to many "enriched" activities. The theory is that increased synaptogenesis occurs in the brains thereby increasing intelligence. However, because it is obvious that synaptogenesis and neural connections diminish from childhood to adulthood in the cortex, increased synaptogenesis might not be the seat of intelligence and learning.

We do know that astrocytes grow throughout our lifespan. The growth is intense when we are younger. Increased growth and the pairing down of neuronal connections might be how we think deeper, tipping the balance for astrocyte communication over the base reflexive neuronal communication.

Nobel Prize winners David Hubel and Torsten Wiesel tried to understand the question of whether our environment can change neuronal wiring. In the visual cortex, columns through the grey matter correspond to different points on our field of vision. Looking specifically at this area of the brain, Hubel and Wiesel were able to determine what effect experience has on neuronal wiring.

Using monkeys and cats, they sutured their eyes shut when they were born. With some animals, they sutured both eyes shut, and with

others, they sutured only one eye. They injected a dye to look at the neurons in the animal brains after four weeks. With both eyes sutured shut, when the researchers looked at different time points after opening their eyes, there was a gradual decline in the ability to see properly.

However, in the animals with one eye sutured shut, the cells in the cortical column of the shut eye didn't develop properly and many were eliminated. Smaller cell bodies were seen in the ones remaining, and the synaptic connections were weak. In contrast, the column in the cortex corresponding to the good eye was much more robust than it should be.

These experiments have been interpreted as evidence for the Hebbian philosophy (Donald Hebb) of neuronal plasticity—that more elaborate neuronal connections are the result of active learning. However, glia were not studied at all in these experiments. Glial cells explode at the time of birth and are more numerous than neurons in the areas explored. The stunted glial growth most likely contributes to the lack of synaptogenesis and neuronal death.

However, at the time of the experiments, glia were not considered important and were not known to communicate to each other and to neurons. It is conceivable that when glia were growing in the area at the time of birth, they did not notice any sensible firing from the neurons in this area from the sensory experience of the eye. Glia develop where they can get sensory input.

In humans who are born deaf, MRI studies confirm they use areas of the cortex normally reserved for hearing when they are performing visual tasks. The belief is that because the area is not used by auditory sensation, the brain has decided to access this area when interpreting other senses such as vision.

Children with brain injuries also are able to "rewire" and sometimes acquire the back aspects of language they have lost by activating other brain areas and repairing the area that has been damaged. The ability for the brain to use unconventional areas to perform tasks happens more often in children than adults. Children's brains also have a surprising ability to repair damaged brain areas.

What is believed to be neuronal plasticity is likely the phenomenon of glial growth. More astrocyte growth and activity in brain areas, which can assume control from nonfunctioning or damaged areas and actually repair these areas, might explain the ability of children to be able to retain behavior of what was previously lost.

The growing astrocytes, in swirls of activity, pop like popcorn in areas of neuronal support frameworks. They continue to grow as neurons send and receive information between glial processing centers. The glial cell creates neurons to use for its purpose and divides only after the neurons have been able to sense the environment for them. Glial cells are the wedge between neuronal feeling and doing and explode into activity as we enter the world.

References

Goldman, P.S. "Functional Development of the Prefrontal Cortex in Early Life and the Problem with Neuronal Plasticity." *Experimental Neurology*, 32: 366–387, 1971.

Hubel, D.H. and T.N. Wiesel. "Ferrier Lecture: Functional Architecture of Macaque Monkey Visual Cortex." *Proceedings of the Royal Society of London*, 198: 1–9, 1977.

Hubel, D.H., T.N. Wiesel, and S. LeVay. "Plasticity of Ocular Dominance Columns in Monkey Striate Cortex." *Philosophical Transactions of the Royal Society of London, Biological Sciences*, 278: 377–409, 1977.

Klyachko, V.A. and C.F. Stevens. "Connectivity Optimization and the Positioning of Cortical Areas." *Proceedings of the National Academy of Sciences*, 100: 7937–7941, 2003.

Levi, G. *Differentiation and Functions of Glial Cells*. New York, NY: Wiley-Liss, 1990.

Rakic, P. "A Small Step for the Cell, a Giant Leap for Mankind: A Hypothesis of Neocortical Expansion During Evolution." *Trends in Neurosciences*, 18: 383–388, 1995.

Rakic, P. "Elusive Radial Glial Cells: Historical and Evolutionary Perspective." *Glia*, 43: 19–32, 2003.

Rakic, P. "Mode of Cell Migration to the Superficial Layers of Fetal Monkey Neocortex." *Journal of Comparative Neurology*, 145: 61–83, 1972.

Cajal, Ramon y, trans. Lloyd Guth. *Studies on Vertebrate Neurogenesis.* Springfield, IL: Charles C. Thomas Publisher Ltd., 1960.

Stiles, J. *The Fundamentals of Brain Development: Integrating Nature and Nurture.* Cambridge, MA: Harvard University Press, 2008.

Verkhratsky, A. and A. Butt. *Glial Neurobiology.* Chichester, West Sussex: Wiley, 2007.

8

The time machine

Not all animals are flawless. Toads are clumsy. They flop around the grass like offensive linemen playing hopscotch. When mowing the lawn in Iowa for the first time in 10 years, the smells of grass and pollen pound my brain like a 10-ton weight. A few toads scramble frantically away from the mower, desperately avoiding the rumbling vibrations, like soldiers in a war movie flailing away from a tank. The way they trip and fall reminds me of another experience I had with clumsiness—walking through a gully between two bluffs by a creek in the crisp air the day after Thanksgiving, a sand crane floated through the air. He noticed me out of the corner of his eye, ahead of his quiet flopping wings. The gully was silent; all the clamoring loud aggressive birds had traveled south. The squirrels were sitting in the trees eating nuts; only the sand crane and I were out in the cold. He was as surprised to see me as I was to see him. I couldn't stop watching his breathless flight, and he watched me probably because he simply didn't trust me. As he flew past, still watching me, now less threatened and showing off his capabilities, he didn't see a tree branch in front of him and flew smack into it. Branches broke off and cracked, and he tumbled down, landing hard on a lower branch and gathering himself. I started laughing. My cackle echoed up and down the creek, bouncing off rocks. The poor bird sat hunched, embarrassed, and slightly peeved. He didn't think it was funny at all.

As I pondered this, I mowed over some mushrooms, and remembered my fake plastic toadstool on three feet of string that I used as bait to try and catch toads in the back yard, the hay field, the wooded bluff, and the cornfield. I wasn't successful; I believed that toads sat on mushrooms and had an inherent desire to seek out mushrooms like addicts. They wanted to sit on mushrooms. They needed to sit on mushrooms,

and I was going to catch a pet toad on my fake plastic mushroom. It never worked, obviously, but I did find a toad in the yard.

The intertwining nature of smell and memory forces everything back to me, from the scent of fabricated plastic while playing wiffle ball so often that a natural, musky, dirt baseball diamond formed in the yard, to swinging on the tangy, perfumed limbs of a willow tree. The plastic leads to thoughts of playing with Legos in that dirt—making towns and high-ways with lumber yards, gas stations, tool-and-dye operations, factories, farms, tractors, and cars. The towns would expand from, second base to home plate through the pitcher's mound. If the ball cleared the neigh-bor's clothesline, it was gone. And the path I took to mow the lawn every week came back to me; the trees in the yard are much bigger now (wiffle ball would be impossible), plus there are strategically placed new trees to mess with my mowing path.

After mowing, I have to run some errands and so many sights, sounds, and smells cause memories to flood back to me: mud suckers in an ancillary creek and three kids playing red light/green light on a side hill by the river.

Memory is an entirely personal experience. Some things are known about universal memory, but I can know only my own memory. I can know only how I feel and how I seem, and sometimes I can selectively forget what I want to forget and embellish what I want to seem more poignant. There's a reason that stories passed down become distorted. When we store something, we add our own touches to it. It's our link to the past, but if Marty McFly drove the Delorian into his brain, the sur-real nature of the past he'd see would be incomplete, filled with holes, delusions, incongruities all meshed together in a pile to make sense out of a past experience to better understand how to get through life now.

We all have unique floods of feelings from our childhood; I've barely considered how to play red light/green light in 15–20 years until I saw the kids playing the other day. It's a game for that wonderful period of life between third and sixth grade; when we are just old enough to carry on a conversation on the wonders of life and not old enough for every conversation to carry the weight of life. This is about when our cortex is the largest, when growth is peaking, and time is slower and our brain begins to pair down some unnecessary cells. Brain scientists have attempted to track down the biological basis of our memory for a long time. Modern terminology begins with William James (the brother of

novelist Henry James), who coined the term "plasticity" in the 1890s. Plasticity is the phenomenon where there is a bend but not break aspect to our learning and memory abilities; we can learn enough to change our memory, but not enough to break memories from the past.

Humans have known for some time how to improve memory. The study of mnemonics from ancient Greek and Roman times is a way to improve memory through repetition and putting things into context to make them easier to remember; for instance, the classic acronym method of remembering lists is one we use. All musicians know "every good boy does fine" and my cousins from Minnesota remember how to spell Iowa with the (in the author's opinion) witless phrase "idiots out walking around."

The biological basis of memory has lagged other aspects of brain science because of the difficulty in grasping an ever-changing elusive process. The first experiments on memory were psychological in nature. Hermann Ebbinghaus, a German professor of philosophy in Berlin who had received a medical degree, painstakingly made a list of 2,500 nonsense words, such as REN and KUR, and tried to memorize them. In 1885, in a book titled *Memory: A Contribution to Experimental Psychology*, Ebbinghaus published several numerical graphs describing how he was able to acquire a memory, such things as "rate of forgetting" and how many repetitions solidifies a memory. Ebbinghaus discovered that some things were remembered only briefly before forgetting, whereas others were remembered for a long period of time. He provided the first evidence for the difference between long- and short-term memories.

Long- and short-term memory was expounded upon by James and Ebbinghaus, a philosophy professor who had obtained a medical degree. In his books written in 1890, the first psychology textbooks, James cites Ebbinghaus. Short-term memory happens at the moment, like remembering Jenny's phone number immediately after she says it or a bartender remembering a drink order until he makes it. Long-term memory is strong and meaningful enough to last in some form for your whole lifetime.

The rule 7 +/– 2 has become a major track in psychological studies. It represents that people can immediately repeat back a series of seven (give or take two) objects in the short term before forgetting them. Psychological research has settled on this number. Also, grouping objects together can add more to the 7 +/– 2 phenomenon. For instance, you can

probably remember the nine letters NTUAGBOSP if you have good short-term memory. However, if you can't remember nine and have the capability to remember only seven, it would be best to categorize them into groups that you already understand as GUN, PAT, and SOB. This way, you only have to remember three things, which gives you room for four more, so you can remember many more letters.

Memory has been considered since the written language. It was always thought that we possess the ability for short- and long-term memory: one being our constant acknowledgement of our present situation and another being our ability to reach into time and acquire the past.

As the psychological ideas of memory were being categorized with modern scientific terms, the biological seat of memory eluded researches through the nineteenth century and into the twentieth. It was always believed to lie in the cortex after the discoveries set down by French anatomist Pierre Fluorens and later in the work of Germans Gustav Fritz and Eduard Hitzig, which determined that higher thought and information storage occurs in the cortex. Researchers also noticed that our capacity for memory and information storage surpassed other animals (as we understand it) and our cortex is much larger and complex than other animals.

In the 1920s, while looking for a locus of memory in the cortex, Karl Lashley (1890–1958), a psychologist at Harvard, trained rats to run a maze and then removed parts of their cortices. He found that it didn't matter where he removed parts of the cortex; they learned the same. However, if he removed a substantial amount, they would have trouble. Trying to understand where memory was, he became frustrated and wrote with, tongue in cheek that "reviewing the evidence...learning is just not possible" and "in spite of the evidence against it, learning sometimes does occur." This ability for information storage to be elusive in the cortex points to the pliable nature of calcium wave communication.

At the same time, Ivan Pavlov (1849–1936) in Russia was showing memory in action with his dog. As everyone with a dog knows, it salivates when presented with food. Pavlov rang a bell every time he gave his dog food and soon the dog salivated only when the bell rung. This type of learning by association held widespread implications for human manipulation and psychologists. This reflexive learning likely resides in the domain of neurons—surpassing astrocyte processing and causing an

unconscious motor reflex. However, to Lashley's chagrin, this tells us nothing about the seat of memory biologically.

Later, in the 1950s, using the knowledge acquired by Wilder Penfield on the electrical impulses in the brain among awake patients, members of the McGill University staff tried to eliminate epilepsy by removing parts of the brain. They were eventually successful with the removal of tracks of neurons called the corpus callosum that join the right and left hemispheres. However, one of their failures proved to be scientifically useful, if not terrible for the patient. The patient has always been referred to as HM in the scientific literature. They removed the base and part of the sides of his brain, at about the area of the temple and curving under deep into the brain. This area of the brain is called the hippocampus.

The hippocampus is a gateway between the subcoritcal and cortical structures. Hippocampus is Greek for seahorse, and in sections (see Figure 8.1), it kind of does look like a seahorse. It curls up like the side of a fist. Inputs come in from basal parts of the brain and go out to the cortex.

FIGURE 8.1 **A section through the hippocampus as seen and drawn by Golgi (left) and Cajal (right).**

The removal of the hippocampus and the adjacent part of the cortex, referred to as the entorhinal cortex for its similarities to a rhino horn, completely eliminated learning in HM. He was unable to remember anything from one moment to the next. He could not learn beyond a couple minutes before everything he learned was lost. His experience was eerily similar to Alzheimer's patients without dementia. He was able to recall with long-term memory everything before the surgery, but couldn't remember anything afterwards because nothing would stick. If information was a light particle, his brain was a black hole.

Oddly, HM could learn and improve from day to day how to draw a picture or play the piano. HM's physical memory was not impaired. And his intelligence was not affected by losing his hippocampus. He just couldn't learn any new facts about his existence.

Sherrington, the man who discovered and coined the synapse, first described learning and memory on a cellular level. He confirmed Cajal's notion that neurons in the brain were separated from each other and referred to the learning and memory in the brain as the enchanted loom, which is like a spinning web of string that can remove, replace, and add new strings at will. He imagined it being spun passively by the workings of our neurons, our environment determining the strength and choice of the strings.

Of course, while studying the Neuron Doctrine in the church of Ramón y Cajal, one can learn that he was the first to propose that synapses become strengthened when learning occurs. This philosophical idea sprung from the knowledge that less synapses could be seen as a person ages. Like many of Cajal's exquisite ideas, researchers have spent most of the twentieth century until the present ardently attempting to determine its truth.

This idea, combined with Donald Hebb's notion of "synaptogenesis," led to two opposing biological tenants regarding learning and memory. These ideas completely disregard the possibility for a role in glia in one of the most important processes in human thought, with wide-ranging implications from intelligence to cures for dementias for the aging.

Donald Hebb's idea of synapses sprouting extra arms when learning occurs has long been considered true along with Ramón y Cajal's theory. They have now been combined to indicate that synaptogenesis is how synaptic strength occurs. Eric Kandel and colleagues, using the inert

ocean animal, the aplysia (a type of large sea slug), tested this theory. The aplysia sits on the bottom of the ocean and reacts to incoming stimulus through a series of sensory nerves. Kandel's experiments were comprehensive and focused strictly on the action of neurons in the simple animal. They found that when stimulating a sensory neuron, the synaptic strength lessened as the animal became habituated.

This analogy can be best understood if one considers the *Blues Brothers*. Jake sees Elwood's place for the first time since he's been out of jail. It's in Chicago right next to the El. Every time the train goes by, the entire apartment rattles as though they are shaken in a box. Jake looks around and asks, "How often does the train go by?" "So often you don't even notice," says Elwood.

Elwood's statement defines habituation. The decrease of transmitter release from neurons as they are repeatedly (habitually) told to fire. If one thinks about this in terms of glia, the excess transmitter release is taken up into the surrounding astrocytes. The astrocytes will then perform calcium waves throughout the area. However, the trigger of becoming habituated might be a signal from the astrocytes back to the neuron to decrease firing.

Another form of learning on the cellular level described by Kandel is called sensitization; this is the result of combining a normal stimulus with a noxious stimulus, creating a stronger synapse. For instance, if as you are reading this and you get kicked in the shins out of the blue, you might get sick to your stomach the next time you read this paragraph.

Learning through sensitization in humans can also be regarded when one thinks of the instant of Kennedy being shot, the Challenger disaster, or the terrorist attacks in 2001. People distinctly remember where they were when these events occurred. The increase in synaptic strength from sensitization is also the result of increased neurotransmitter release.

Glial function during the phenomenon of habituation and sensitization has not been studied. Synaptogenesis, as described by Hebb, is glial dependent. Increased or lack of transmitter at the synapse could also be the result of glial function. After the glial process the excess transmitter (the sensory input from getting "kicked in the shins"), the glia will not allow the neurons to become habituated. Instead, the glial cells let the nerouns continue to fire extreme amounts of transmitters in the advent it

might happen again and you will be reflexively prepared. All associated stimulus will also be primed. The glial cell centers know processing is not needed and open the neuronal floodgates.

However, studies spearheaded by the work of Joseph Altman in the late 1960s at Purdue University started a new line of research pertaining to memory in the area of "adult neurogenesis." In relation to learning, Cajal firmly believed that after development, cell growth is halted, and the brain remains in its state until we die. His notion of increased synaptic strength fit into his neuronal dominated theory for thought and gave room for the possibility of slight changes to incorporate the obvious phenomenon of learning and memory.

Altman's idea abolished one of the facts most researchers took for granted without examining closely. Obviously, his studies met with staunch resistance. His experiments were completely overlooked. No one wanted to consider an experiment that claimed new cells divided in adult rats, much less that learning could increase cell division.

Altman took rats and had them perform learning tasks while injecting them with radioactive thymidine. Thymidine can insert itself into the DNA of cells in the process of dividing. When the brain is removed and sliced up, then stained for thymidine, the researcher can see where the cells were dividing. After periods of intense learning, Altman discovered cell division in the hippocampus increases and that some of these cells form neurons.

Now it is known that the cells that initially divide through adulthood in the hippocampus are astrocytes.

Altman's studies were buried by the discovery of long-term potentiation (LTP) in 1973 by Tim Bliss and Terje Lømo in England. LTP is the fancy way of saying synaptic strength increase shown electrically. They took out the hippocampus of rats after they performed maze learning. They were able to determine electrophysiologically that neurons required fewer stimuli to fire in the hippocampus of rats that had learned. Through learning, the neurons had been primed and sensitized. Thee threshold had been lowered for the firing to occur, as if one could barely breathe on a gun trigger to get it to fire.

LTP is still being worked on extensively, but the idea is simply an electrical confirmation of the synaptic strength theory proposed by Cajal, Sherrington, and Hebb, and confirmed molecularly by Kandel. The notion of LTP receiving so much attention is similar to if someone saying

a wheel is round made front-page news. LTP has yet to be confirmed in humans.

Altman's studies were forgotten for 20 years until Arturo Alvarez-Buylla and Fernando Nottebohm ignited the field by confirming cellular genesis in adult songbirds learning new songs. Now we know that humans also regenerate new cells throughout their life and all newly regenerating cells in adults are astrocytes. Alvarez-Buylla and colleagues have shown conclusively that the regenerating cell is not a neuron. They have characteristics of astrocytes, turning over to produce more astrocytes and only occasionally producing a neuron. The implication that astrocytes are the seat of information through cell growth during learning and memory processes is just gaining steam.

Astrocytes constantly divide in our brain throughout adulthood. When we learn, they divide more rapidly. In the hippocampus, they occasionally become neurons. Similar to when a city grows to the outskirts and the town commission decides to build a new highway, astrocytes decide to lay down a new neuron.

In the 1990s, Fred Gage and colleagues at the Salk Institute in San Diego confirmed that cell division occurs in the human hippocampus; other labs have shown that the cells dividing in humans are astrocytes.

When discussing thought, it must be noted that learning is not intelligence; education improves intelligence as judged by standardized tests, but most would agree that intelligence is not education-dependent. Someone who only made it through the third grade can think on a higher level than someone with a graduate degree. It's a matter of using your brain and learning many things to draw from, whether it is facts about human anatomy or nuances of human body language. Astrocyte cell growth is essential to this process.

The nature of the glia communicatory fashion indicates that they might contribute to memory in the cortex. Hebb suggested that assemblies of cells, distributed over large areas of cortex, work together to represent information. This idea, which Hebb believed occurred with neurons, can now be explained as the domain of glia. A glial center can access neurons to travel long distances, and astrocytes control all compartments of the cortex. The only way to abolish cortical memory is to block glutamate reuptake—a function that is dominated by astrocytes.

The strengthening of synapses, LTP, and synaptogenesis can be astrocyte-dependent as well. It would make sense for the hippocampus

to create new neurons to lay down short-term memory into long-term memory. Without successful cell division and the laying down of neuronal highways, information cannot travel into the cortex to be stored in astrocytes. If someone needs to travel from Iowa to Boston and there is no way to get there, that person stays in Iowa.

Your nose, ears, and eyes all transmit information to the cortex and hippocampus. These quick pathways are vehicles for astrocytes to understand their environment. The hippocampus is the generator. Similar to the guard at a desk who decides whether you can enter a building, the stimulus must have the proper ID or it remains in the short term and is lost, such as what occurs in HM or Alzheimer's patients whose hippocampuses are destroyed. In this case, the building is locked and nothing can get in. More studies on astrocytes will reveal why.

One interesting side note to Ebbinghaus's experiments on memory—he noticed that he remembered more of his nonsense words than normal after he slept. Something learned right before sleep is better retained than something learned and attempted to recall shortly afterward with no sleep. He thought it didn't mean anything, that he hadn't used random enough nonsense words and discarded any notion that going to sleep would help his memory. Now exhaustive research has shown that sleep does in fact help memory retention. It is possible that glia are more active and regenerative while we sleep, such as fingernails and hair grow more when we are sleeping. Information storage might likely reside in cortical astrocytes. The information gets into the cortex through long-distance neuronal communication combined with glial calcium waves.

A classic story from the Roman essayist Cicero on memory concerns the ancient Greek poet Simonides. Respected for his memory, Simonides was asked to a banquet to recite a poem for the wealthy host. At the time, poets usually included a long homage to the twin gods, Castor and Pollux, who were thought to make up the constellation Gemini. The host, upset that Simonides didn't devote the poem to him, paid him only half of what he was owed and told him he could pay the other half to Castor and Pollux. A little while later, Simonides received a message that two men wanted to see him outside; he went out, and while he was gone, the banquet hall collapsed and everyone inside was crushed beyond recognition. The two men were Castor and Pollux, and by removing Simonides to safety, they paid him what he was owed and then some. When the

families of the deceased wanted to know who was who, Simonides was able to accurately remember where everyone was sitting by using the method of association with other structures that were in the room.

Simonides was able to use his hippocampus more efficiently to lay down new memories normally in the short-term domain and store information into his cortex. Yet researchers still have not been able to understand how the cortex is able to contain information. This knowledge is on the horizon as research on astrocytes progresses.

We now know astrocytes divide and regenerate in the hippocampus. If needed, they can become neurons. As will be seen, astrocytes, not neurons, are capable of dividing and growing in the cortex, providing an interesting method for the possibility of storing new information—the way Simonides was able to store the seating map at the banquet.

References

Bliss, T. and T. Lømo. "Long-Lasting Potentiation of Synaptic Transmission in the Dentate Area of the Anaesthetized Rabbit Following Stimulation of the Perforant Path." *Journal of Physiology* (London), 232: 331–356, 1973.

Bliss, T.V.P., G.L. Collingridge, and R.G.M. Morris. *Long-Term Potentiation: Enhancing Neuroscience for 30 Years*. New York, NY: Oxford University Press, 2003.

Bourtchouladze, R. *Memories Are Made of This: The Biological Building Blocks of Memory*. London: Weidenfeld and Nicolson, 2002.

Graf, P. and N. Ohta. *Lifespan Development of Human Memory*. Cambridge, MA: The MIT Press, 2002.

Maquet, P., C. Smith, and R. Stickgold. *Sleep and Brain Plasticity*. New York, NY: Oxford University Press, 2003.

Martinez, J.L. and R.P. Kesner. *Neurobiology of Learning and Memory*. San Diego, CA: Academic Press, 1998.

Pavlov, I.P. *Conditioned Reflexes: An Investigation of the Physiological Activity of the Cerebral Cortex*. New York, NY: Oxford University Press, 1927.

Seifert, W. *Neurobiology of the Hippocampus*. London: Academic Press, 1983.

Squire, L.R. and E.R. Kandel. *Memory: From Mind to Molecules*. New York: Scientific American Library, 1999.

9

Sing a new song

The growth of our brain when we're born—as flush and full as an Amazonian jungle until we reach young adulthood—was thought to be followed by a period of constant death. As if the rainfall has stopped, global warming has set in, the wind has increased, the jungle is subjected to the elements, and then tragically declines into a desert wasteland and petrified forest. This original belief after Cajal approved the Neuron Doctrine occurred for obvious reasons. Our brain does get smaller as we age, particularly our cortex, and the complete jungle was considered to have enough room for a lifetime of experience.

However, new glial research has shown the brain is more like a living jungle throughout our lifetime than originally thought—with dead trees replaced by new ones and constant spawn and spreading of seeds to spaces suitable for new vegetation. Ground space is limited but growth is constant. One of the largest mistakes of the twentieth century was the notion that after childhood brain development, our brain just remained in the same state until we died. Our neurons were constructed, made connections, and those connections were permanent, similar to a statue constructed to honor our memory, sitting there chipped away by the wind and rain until it crumbled and was covered by dust.

Through the work of Fernando Nottebohm and Arturo Alvarez-Buylla at the Rockefeller Institute, we now know that this is not the case. In the mid-1980s, Nottebohm turned the unchanging brain on its head with his studies on canaries. In the early 1970s, he mapped the areas of the brain responsible for singing in the canary. Starting with the voice box and working his way back into the brain, Nottebohm accurately determined cells in the brain that contributed to song. He and others knew that the canary could learn new songs throughout its lifetime. When the area was damaged, it impaired the canary's ability to sing.

Nottebohm, along with his student Alvarez-Buylla, looked meticulously at cell division in the canary brain after it learned.

What they found was striking. Previously, it was thought that only the brains of fish and amphibians had the capability to regenerate throughout adulthood. After Nottebohm taught the canaries new songs and then removed their brains at various time points after they died, he discovered the nuclei in the telencephalon for coding and learning new songs was enlarged. These nuclei were not enlarged in this area of the brain in canaries that didn't learn any new songs. The density of the area had changed—the brain was almost like a stuffed suitcase, swollen from exchanging a pair of pants for three more T-shirts, but still limited to the space of the suitcase.

Nottebohm expected this result when the canaries were developing, but not from just learning songs as an adult. Birds were officially added to the list of animals that could make new neurons into adulthood, and the first entirely land animal to do so. Nottebohm and Alvarez-Buylla then used Joseph Altman's model of radioactive thymidine to understand cell division. They figured if the telencephalon had more neurons, it could be due to more cell division in this area.

They found hot spots for cell division near the ventricles of the brain—the same area where cell generation occurs when we are in development. The cells in this area would explode into division when the canaries learned new songs, like a musician in a fit of creativity. But, in humans, we have the ability to create our own songs, whereas birds learn through mimicry.

The adult brain was changing, and it was likely the result of cell division. Hebb, Cajal, LTP, and all the synaptogenesis and synaptic strength theories now seemed a byproduct of new cells being created.

In the early 1980s, a new technique had been developed to study cell division. 5-Bromodeoxyuridine, simply referred to as BrdU, could be injected into the bloodstream. From there it can be accurately stained. BrdU worked in a similar manner as Thymidine by incorporating into the DNA of cells dividing at the time of injection. This method combined with fluorescence and confocal microscopy (the ability to look at cells three-dimensionally through a tissue slice to determine if the stains for

neuron and glia match up with the stain for cell division) could definitively remove unwanted and confusing background staining and more accurately determine types of cells and actual cell division.

Alvarez-Buylla found that neurons were being formed, but at a much smaller rate than nonneuronal cells. The fact that neurons were being formed solidified the idea of "adult neurogenesis." Nottebohm and Alvarez-Buylla pointed out that in the bird, the dividing cells could become neurons, but that in the mammal, emerging studies indicated that cells dividing in this area eventually settle on a glial fate. If the new cells were dominantly glia, this idea was not interesting to the field. The field lusted after new neurons.

What they discovered was similar to Altman but with better techniques. In an adult animal, new neurons and glia were formed during learning. By the late 1980s, this idea was accepted, but only believed to occur in certain areas pertaining to learning and probably not in humans. According to the accepted theory, musicians must create their songs with already established neurons. In an effort to get a closer understanding to what occurs in humans, Alvarez-Buylla decided to tackle the issue further in mammals.

By the 1990s, Alvarez Buylla was at the University of California, San Francisco. He expanded the studies they performed on canaries into mice. It had been known through Altman that cell division resulting in neurons occurred in the hippocampus and near the ventricles. Using BrdU, Alvarez-Buylla focused on the area near the ventricles. This area was also interesting because it was the same area in development that new neurons and glia are formed and where neurons contributed to song learning in adult canaries. Alvarez-Buylla was interested in what cells were dividing and where they were going.

Alvarez-Buylla went beyond what Altman noticed. Altman simply noticed that the cellular genesis occurred in the adult rodent and that a few of these cells became neurons. At the Rockefeller Institute in Nottebohm's lab, they discovered that cells divided near the ventricle in canaries learning new songs. In the mice, he found that the new cells follow a path to the olfactory bulb, the part of the brain that sticks out like two marbles behind the nose. Smell is the dominant sense in mice, and the percentage of the brain that the olfactory bulb makes up in mice is many times bigger than in humans.

Using BrdU, Alvarez-Buylla's lab could follow new cells as they traveled from the ventricle to the olfactory bulb. The cells moved by climbing fibers like children in PE class climbing a rope. The migratory stream, originally coined by Altman, is the thoroughfare; similar to the Mississippi river running through the middle of the United States, it is the main river flowing with new cells to the most important sensory area of the mouse brain. Like fish spawning up river and then swimming down to take their place downstream, cells were floating around the brain. The active moving brain, with cells dividing and migrating into adulthood, was an intense revelation.

As mice determine their environment largely through their sense of smell, the olfactory bulb is ever changing and new neurons are required to build highways to glia to understand this environment. Our smell is just sensing molecules floating around in the wind. Like sight is for light particles and hearing is for vibrations, smell is for molecules. Similar to the growth of forests and jungles after rain or the destruction in fire, masses of new cells constantly come in to replace destroyed cells or add to those currently in use to comprehend the molecules. Some of the cells that divided in the brains of the mice migrated to the olfactory bulb and changed into neurons. The new neurons laid down for smell are also tied to our memory—smelling scents linking us to the past is the equivalent to recalling how to add 2 + 2, something that goes through the hippocampus.

In the 1990s, the next thing Alvarez-Buylla and colleagues wanted to accomplish was to try to figure out what types of cells divided. Using markers for many different cell types in addition to BrdU, they found that cells dividing at the ventricle displayed characteristics of astrocytes. Soon it was understood that the dividing cells in the hippocampus were also astrocytes.

Now scientists were armed with the knowledge that astrocyte-type cells divide rapidly at the ventricle. They constantly regenerate, creating offspring like rabbits. Some of them sprout into neuronal precursor cells when necessary. When this happens, these cells migrate out to the olfactory bulb or other deep layers of the brain, to become a neuron and to lay down a highway between our reflexive senses and higher-thinking cortex.

New researchers knew hippocampus and the olfactory bulb both produce new glia constantly. Both areas are known to be areas of constant learning. However, all this research was in mice and birds. The next step was to investigate it further in humans.

In the late 1990s, Fred Gage and colleagues injected humans with BrdU and studied their hippocampuses after they died. He found new cells dividing as well, but not focusing on glia, proceeded to look only at neurons and discovered slight instances of neurogenesis in humans. The neuron-dominated ideas of Ramón y Cajal finally would believe that the adult human brain had the ability to create new cells throughout its lifetime. However, the large amount of glia produced compared to neurons was overlooked.

In 2003, Alvarez-Buylla's lab published papers about the human brain injected with BrdU. He was able to determine that the area next to the human ventricle was slightly different from the mouse, with an extra space between the dividing cells and the ventricular wall (see Figure 9.1). Cells divide in adult humans as well, and the dividing cells are astrocytes in humans. He was unable to see a migratory stream to the olfactory bulb. The human brain has tiny pockets of ventricular fluid throughout the brain, and it's possible that the olfactory bulb can take care of its own division without the main ventricular area. After we reach adulthood, our brain cells are not unchanging—they constantly divide to deal with our environment.

However, in researchers' lust for the search of neurons, they have determined that our cortex remains the same after we reach adulthood. The cortex, the area of our high-level thinking, does not form new neurons after adulthood. In primates and specifically humans, the cortex contains the majority of accessible conscious information in the brain. If new neurons can be formed in the olfactory bulb and hippocampus and neurons are supposedly responsible for our thoughts, why can't new neurons form in the cortex? This was a depressing fact for many researchers and had been believed since 1911, when Ramón y Cajal looked exhaustively at cortical neurons.

However, astrocytes divide in the human cortex throughout our lifespan.

Cell division in the adult cortex was known for some time by many in the field, but new neurons never noticed. Therefore, the research was discarded and swept under the rug. Without neurons, what was the point? The field is called "adult neurogenesis" after all. But Alvarez-Buylla's revelation that the dividing cells are astrocytes had been lost. Now that glia, and more specifically, astrocytes are known to communicate and tell neurons what to do, and they are the new cells dividing in

the adult in subcortical areas that need fast neuronal communication, and are the cells dividing *in the cortex* as well, studies of "adult gliogenesis" are coming to light.

Reprinted from *Cell Stem Cell*, Vol. 3, Issue 3, Mirzadeh, Z., Merkle, F.T., Soriano-Navarro, M., Garcia-Verdugo, J.M., and Alvarez-Buylla, A. "Neural Stem Cells Confer Unique Pinwheel Architecture to the Ventricular Surface in Neurogenic Regions of the Adult Brain," p. 274, Copyright (2008), with permission from Elsevier.

FIGURE 9.1   Astrocytes dividing by the ventricle, with cilia reaching up and floating like seaweed in the ventricular fluid (top). The astrocytes (dark cells) reach into the fluid and swing long arms to cling to blood vessels.

Cortical gliogenesis in adult humans was proven in a study published in 2006. Researchers from Sweden in collaboration with researchers from the United States and Australia used an ingenious technique to investigate cell division in adult humans. They were able to take advantage of the radioactive material that enters into brain cells as they divide, similar to how thymidine is visualized. During nuclear weapons testing aboveground between the mid-1950s and the nuclear test ban treaty in

1963, massive amounts of heavy carbon were launched into the atmosphere. By studying the brains of people who gave their organs to science and had lived during this period of time, researchers were able to look at cells that divided and incorporated the heavy carbon. There was extensive cell division. These dividing cells were then examined for whether they were neurons or glia. None of the cells became neurons. The dividing cells were glia.

They followed these studies by injecting BrdU into the bloodstream of patients dying of various forms of cancers of the body—similarly to the method used by Alvarez-Buylla. They found exactly the same result as the heavy carbon studies—constant glial growth occurs in the cortex, but no new neurons are formed.

Studies of this nature are primarily used to show that cortical neurogenesis is a phenomenon restricted to development around the birth. However, the idea of new astrocytes constantly turned over in the area of our brain being responsible for higher thought is astounding.

The formation of new astrocytes in the cortex throughout our adult life must contribute to the thoughts of human beings. This idea—combined with the knowledge of calcium wave communication and regulation of transmitters in astrocytes—leads to the theory that astrocytes are the root of thought and they can turn over constantly to keep our brains in top working order. When this constant turnover is disrupted, we begin to understand the problems that can arise. Further studies on glia illuminate the responsibility of astrocytes for the wonders of our thoughts and the causes of catastrophic disruptions to the fluid orb of will that is our brain. Strict neuronal focus in brain research cannot even begin to understand how and why we function and how to cure our most horrific brain diseases. The fact that new astrocytes continue to divide into adulthood means they attempt to form new space for the storage of information to expand thinking abilities, just as a weight lifter works his muscles to get stronger so that he can lift even greater weights. Mental exercise might be how we achieve higher intelligence and store more information. Monotonous neurons, only 10 percent of the brain and incapable of regeneration, are simply thoroughfares maintained by astrocytes to be used for the purpose of long-distance communication.

Everyone knows that learning and education increases intelligence, but where does the intelligence go? It is a definite possibility that it is

stored in astrocytes that can regenerate throughout life. Is it possible that these newly regenerated astrocytes in the cortex are replacing ones that aren't performing up to task? And in lower areas of the brain, such as the hippocampus and olfactory bulb, astrocytes can sprout into neurons to provide a fast link to glial centers when a new nugget of important information enters our environment and needs to be processed and stored by cortical astrocyte centers.

Many organs in the body create new cells throughout life—the blood, the liver, and skin. The seeming solid and unregenerative ability of the brain is due to the focus of research on neurons and not glia in the last 100 years. Cajal performed exhaustive studies of neuronal cells after his standoff with Golgi at the Nobel Prize lectures in an attempt to find some semblance of regenerative ability in the cortex. He found nothing. Alvarez-Buylla's experiments in deeper brain regions are beginning to challenge these views. Combined with the experiments that showed astrocytes communicate with themselves and neurons, we can get a grasp on the fantastic research that will soon arise in the twenty-first century when glia are no longer neglected and relegated to secondary status. The avenues to research astrocytes are numerous, and hopefully, future astrocyte research will bring to light the causes and cures for many brain diseases.

If one remembers the old Cliff Claven theory that alcohol kills brain cells, but we use only 10 percent of our brain so it was okay to kill brain cells, we were killing off the weakest. Drinking was like the survival of the fittest in the brain. The cells remaining were the strongest, so drinking heavily increased the efficiency of our thoughts. Well, it is apparent now that the 10 percent of neurons are not what we need to worry about. The health of our brain hinges on astrocyte cell division. Our brain is like a jungle, full of life and constantly growing until we die. Evidence exists for the possibility of how we control that growth, how the growth is stunted, and what happens when it is out of control.

References

Alvarez-Buylla, A., M. Theelen, and F. Nottebohm. "Proliferation 'Hot Spots' in Adult Avian Ventricular Zone Reveal Radial Cell Division." *Neuron*, 5: 101–109, 1990.

Alvarez-Buylla, A., J.R. Kirn, and F. Nottebohm. "Birth of Projection Neurons in Adult Avian Brain May Be Related to Perceptual and Motor Learning." *Science*, 249: 1444–1446, 1990.

Alvarez-Buylla, A. and J.M. Garcia-Verdugo. "Neurogenesis in Adult Subventricular Zone." *Journal of Neuroscience*, 22: 629–634, 2002.

Bhardwaj, R.D., M.A. Curtis, K.L. Spalding, B.A. Buchholz, D. Fink, T. Bjork-Eriksson, C. Nordborg, F.H. Gage, H. Druid, P.S. Eriksson, and J. Frisen. "Neocortical Neurogensis in Humans Is Restricted to Development." *PNAS*, 103: 12564–12568, 2006.

Doetsch, F., I. Caille, D.A. Lim, J.M. Garcia-Verdugo, and A. Alvarez-Buylla. "Subventricular Zone Astrocytes Are Neural Stem Cells in the Adult Mammalian Brain." *Cell*, 97: 703–716, 1999.

Gage, F.H., G. Kempermann, and H. Song. *Adult Neurogenesis*. Cold Spring Harbor, New York: Cold Spring Harbor Laboratory Press, 2008.

Lois, C. and A. Alvarez-Buylla. "Long-Distance Neuronal Migration in the Adult Mammalian Brain." *Science*, 264: 1145–1148, 1994.

Moffett, S.B. *Nervous System Regeneration in the Invertebrates*. Heidelberg, Germany: Springer-Verlag, 1996.

Nottebohm, F., T.M. Stoke, and C.M. Leonard. "Central Control of Song in the Canary, Serinus Canaries." *Journal of Comparative Neurology*, 165: 457–486, 1976.

Rakic, P. "No More Cortical Neurons for You." *Science*, 313: 928–929, 2006.

Sanai, N., A.D. Tramontin, A. Quinones-Hinojosa, N.M. Barbaro, N. Gupta, S. Kunwar, M.T. Lawton, M.W. McDermott, A.T. Parsa, J.M. Garcia-Verdugo, M.S. Berger, and A. Alvarez-Buylla. "Unique Astrocyte Ribbon in Adult Human Brain Contains Neural Stem Cells but Lacks Chain Migration." *Nature*, 427: 740–744, 2004.

10

Albert Einstein's abundant astrocytes

Hope and promise reside in glia, and now the knowledge of astrocytes as our adult stem cells gives researchers an avenue to pursue an understanding of the fundamental mysteries of the mind. The brain can be seen as a verdant entity throughout our life—constantly growing to replenish deserted areas and wastelands. It is not a static place like the moon, a rock knocked around by the bombardments of space, as previously thought, but it is like the Earth in every sense, packed with growth and changing constantly. In the cortex, this growth is the domain of the astrocytes. Neurons remain hardwired except when the astrocyte turnover becomes great enough that it requires the population to sprout a new neuron, especially in areas solidifying new memories. They are paths for quick action in our extremities and to bring and take new information from glial centers. An astrocyte controls its entire environment in the cortex and communicates with other astrocytes in the manner of calcium waves. It is a cohesive and fluid unit capable of storing complex information and recording time, but not controlled by space.

The astrocyte can be seen evolutionarily as the extension of the single cell at the start of life—it must maintain itself through interactions in the species and eventual reproduction. The neuron has evolved as the fast-acting tool at the beck of the astrocyte's will. The growth of astrocytes in areas responsible for memory controls how we survive as living beings; the astrocyte determines if something should be avoided or challenged. They are the reason we exist—our essence—and how we think is the result of our existence.

A lot has been made of synapses at neuronal connections. Synapses sprout after birth and then become more hardwired into young adulthood. However, the synapses sprout only after the peak growth of astrocytes at birth, indicating that astrocytes determine synaptogenesis.

Astrocytes can process the information that the neurons bring in from the environment through the monitoring of synapses. The amount of neural synapses is astrocyte dependent. As we age, when the less useful synapses are eliminated, the astrocyte must have a hand in this process. In children of abuse, it is believed that the synaptic elimination process is accelerated; there are less sprouts, and therefore, children do not develop properly. However, what happens to the astrocytes after the abuse is likely the key to understanding the streamlined neurons. The astrocytes take in the potent information in a heightened situation, good or bad, and then eliminate some of the synapses, streamlining the neuron—like a city removing freeway exits to help traffic move more rapidly.

Theoretically, the same would occur to a human raised in an environment that doesn't stimulate his senses. This person would develop less synaptic complexity. Because of these studies and with the revelation that children with Down's Syndrome have less synaptic complexity, it is believed that more synapses equates to higher intelligence and that to achieve more synapses is to bombard your child with as many positive learning apparatuses as possible. However, the synapses are not what need to be stimulated; it is the astrocytes. Astrocyte growth is not dependent on synapse amount. But synaptic growth and elimination is dependent on the health and growth of astrocytes.

This is the reasoning behind giving children so many things to play with, such as Baby Einstein, Legos, Transformers, He-Man figurines, Sesame Street, Cabbage Patch Kids, and Dora the Explorer. Using objects that are manipulated by the hands is important, because our hands make us distinct from other animals. Sensory interaction can create a mind that fosters neuronal connections. This is why children need to play with toys. However, the importance of glial stimulation as neuronal impulses reach the brain is paramount.

This might apply to adults as well. The growth of astrocytes in the brain might be evidence of an active brain—one always attentive, concentrating, pondering, considering, thinking, understanding. There is a reason Disney uses "Einstein" in its Baby Einstein products. It is because Einstein is synonymous with intelligence. If we think through recent history of someone who was constantly rattling his brain while trying to spring forth new ideas through imagination, we can easily agree that Albert Einstein fits this idea.

Einstein was notorious for his bouts of late-night mathematical study. His intense periods of thought resulted in the most astounding research in the area of physics in the history of mankind. He claimed that his brain was "his laboratory." But what part of his brain?

His general theory of relativity states that time and space are one and they are relative. Einstein said that the happiest moment of his life was standing in an elevator and realizing if it fell out from underneath him, he wouldn't feel his own weight. He understood that gravity was relative in our mind. This is the kind of man who used his glia.

Many dorm walls on college campuses display a poster of Einstein with the quote "Imagination is everything." And Einstein meant an active imagination, using the brain to create something complete and not thought of before, and doing this with intense concentration. This might bring some enlightenment to the purpose of astrocytes in an evolutionarily sense.

The human experience is predicated on our ability to think of something new, using tools and ideas, to keep ourselves evolving. Biologically speaking, we have evolved to the point where we can create our own evolution. Other animals are always striving to this point, to make use of their environment to survive, but only humans have reached the evolutionary point where we can simply pick up something in our environment to create complex behavior. Our conscious thought to do this is believed to reside in the cortex. The astrocyte-neuron ratio increases in the cortex up the evolutionary ladder, the highest ratio in humans.

Einstein's outward appearance was lush and rumpled like the countryside with its plush hills, creek ravines, and sugar trees sprouting in a mass of growth from glia seeds. However, his brain, like all humans, was his essence. His expression was as serene as a lake on a still June day, but his essence was as stark as a thunderstorm at night in May. He shuffled and stumbled through space like a chimpanzee, but his essence leaped like an Olympic athlete.

In the year of 1955, a wink from Einstein would be more powerful than a punch to the face from Rocky Marciano. But then he died. And his precious brain was no longer under his control. What happened is a bedtime story that all brain scientists know well. On April 17, 1955, Harry Zimmerman, the leading pathologist at Princeton University hospitals, couldn't make it down from Philadelphia for the autopsy and had

enough confidence in his understudy and former student at Yale Medical School, Thomas Harvey, to conduct it. Harvey sawed open the skull and plucked out the brain by cutting the cranial nerves, weighed it at 2.7 pounds, then plopped it in formaldehyde for preservation, finished up the autopsy (see Figure 10.1), and absconded with the brain out the door. Another doctor took off with the eyes.

Reprinted from *The Lancet*, Vol. 353, Issue 9170, Witelson, S.F., Kigar, D.L., and Harvey, T. "The Exceptional Brain of Albert Einstein," p. 2151, Copyright (1999), with permission from Elsevier.

FIGURE 10.1   Einstein's brain in 1955 after autopsy.

Harvey hung on to the brain in secret places at his home or kept it hidden in his office as the head of the university and Zimmerman demanded to know what he did with it. Harvey responded that he was preserving it for study. Their frustration grew by the day and by the year. In the meantime, Harvey had parts of it secretly sectioned into tiny slices by a lab technician, placed on slides and stained with cell-recognizing fluid similar to Golgi's stain.

While Harvey was hiding away the brain, it must have held him in utter fascination. Imagine if you could put a piece of the sun in a jar. Imagine if you could see through Da Vinci or Van Gogh's eyes and hear through Mozart's ears. Or, in Harvey's case, imagine if you had their eyes and ears in a box. Harvey must have wondered how the cogs and wheels in that pile of goo predicted that gravity would bend light. This was confirmed by Arthur Stanley Eddington (1882–1944) experimentally in 1919 during the total lunar eclipse. Einstein became an instant celebrity, even though his four seminal papers were published way back in 1905, the year before Cajal and Golgi's standoff. Surprisingly, regarding all his theories and formulas, Einstein received his Nobel Prize in physics in 1921 not for relativity, but for the groundwork that led to the notion that light is both a wave and a particle. Harvey had the goop that conjured that, too.

Harvey had a piece of matter that completely captured out of the air a notion so important to humanity that it inspired every field of study. It was a brain that could routinely cook and stir and flip the unimaginable. From the 1930s on, Einstein focused on a theory that would unify everything—a theory that hasn't come close to being solved—in addition to focusing on his nonscientific writings. In the late 1930s, his friend and former student Leo Szilard (1898–1964), who developed the nuclear chain reaction that made atomic weapons possible, came rushing out to the house where Einstein was summering in the Hamptons. Szilard was excited about the idea of how to create a super bomb, and he was terrified that the Germans might have also come up with a similar idea. He convinced Einstein to use his celebrity to write a letter to the president urging immediate research. They produced a letter to President Franklin Roosevelt, even as the government was investigating Einstein for unAmerican activities. Without the weight of his name behind the letter, the atomic bomb might never have been produced by the United States. However, Einstein claimed massive regret for signing the letter and sending it. The letter didn't deter J. Edgar Hoover from being suspicious of Einstein.

Harvey had the piece of flesh that told Einstein's neurons extending out to his hand to sign the document. Harvey might have pondered what in Einstein's brain made the decision to sign and what in that brain considered the action a regret.

The brain that signed the letter, produced the concepts, and contributed to most of the impetus of major advance in the twentieth

century was still sitting in formaldehyde somewhere in Harvey's possession at the time. However, the pressure at Princeton to give up the brain
became too much and the administration forced Harvey out of the
hospital.

Harvey took the brain with him to Missouri where he worked in family practice until he was found out and pursued by people who wanted a
piece of the brain. He uprooted numerous times, and in the early 1990s,
he was living in Lawrence, Kansas. However, when researchers requested
sections of the brain, he usually complied.

In the early 1980s, Marian Diamond at U.C. Berkeley wrote to
Harvey, requesting pieces of Einstein's brain. A few months later, she
received four pieces in a mayonnaise jar.

She compared them to 11 other similarly aged people who died from
causes other than diseases or injury to the brain. Using a method called
stereology, where researchers count cell averages at high magnification
to extrapolate how many cells are in a given area of the brain, Diamond
discovered that on average, Einstein had a higher astrocyte-to-neuron
ratio in the area of the left parietal cortex called the angular gyrus, as
shown in Figure 10.2. Einstein had so many more cells that it was "statistically significant," a scientific term to mean that it was "pretty different
enough to say that it means something."

It is possible that "applied thinking" or concentration and attention
leads to astrogliogenesis and that the more astrocytes, the more ability
for complex thinking. Einstein's active concentration and utilizing his
cortex while lost in thought might have created the growth of more astrocytes to increase his capacity for such complex thought. However, how
much this was due to his innate ability or a genetic predisposition to
astrocyte growth isn't known. He, no doubt, had an intrinsic drive that
gave him the ability to focus and think deeply. Einstein also had higher
amounts of astrocytes in the right parietal cortex and in two areas of the
front cortex. However, the only "significant" area was the left parietal
cortex.

This area is believed to be responsible for higher thought, specifically related to language, mathematics, and spatial learning. Interestingly, Einstein's parents had to take him to the doctor when he was three
years old because of his late-developing speech.

Reprinted from *Experimental Neurology*, Vol. 88, Issue 1, Diamond, M.C., Scheibel, A.B., Murphy, G.M. and Harvey, T. "On the brain of a scientist: Albert Einstein," p. 200, Copyright (1985), with permission from Elsevier.

FIGURE 10.2   The area of Einstein's brain with higher glia, the black square on the right.

Many more brains need to be studied to make a valid argument for an increase in glial cells to be responsible for more complex thought in the cortex. Eleven regular brains to one genius brain does not create the numbers scientists like to see when they are trying to find something statistically significant. However, how to acquire more brains of noted thinkers is obviously a problem to complete the study. Einstein was an obvious example. What about your next-door neighbor? Does he spend more time in active concentration and mentally strenuous activity as Einstein, but just doesn't have the work to prove it? One does not necessarily need to be a celebrity to have an increased amount of mental activity.

Another problem is how much Einstein's brain might have deterio-
rated in his old age. He seemed not to have dementia, but he wasn't
putting out papers describing the secrets of the universe anymore either.
I'm sure getting someone like Bob Dylan's brain might be interesting—
for the area responsible for songs. Maybe it would have more glial cells.
But by the time he dies, we don't know what state his brain would be in,
and researchers couldn't really whack someone in their 30s like Jack
White just to see if he has more glia, nor could they just wait behind the
Nobel Prize podium with a hatchet and a bone saw and whack scientists
after accepting the prize, and then compare the brain of the whacked
person to 11 "regular people."

Of course, the study into Einstein's brain is flawed, not to mention
that Harvey was ostracized by the scientific community and forced to
keep the brain in mayonnaise jars. In the 1994 documentary *Einstein's
Brain*, by Kevin Hull, a Japanese professor of math and science history at
Kinki University in Japan, Kenji Sugimoto, seeks out a piece of Einstein's
brain after he hears that it was preserved. He wants a piece for a souvenir
and goes to great lengths to find Harvey. When he finds Harvey's mentor
Zimmerman, he claims Harvey is dead. But Sugimoto finds him alive living near William S. Burroughs in Lawrence, Kansas. Burroughs shows
Sugimoto the movie *End of Days*, which begins with Lawrence being
wiped off the map by an atomic bomb. He gives directions on how
Sugimoto can find Harvey, "Go along the river there. And you come to
where the old cemetery used to be. That was dug up and converted into a
trailer court. The trailer court was subsequently completely destroyed in
the '81 tornado. Some said it was the judgment of the dead for being disturbed. But at any rate, there you turn left and you'll come to Stranger's
Creek. Harvey…Dr. Harvey's house is just on the other side of the creek."

Burroughs knows something about keeping an active mind into a
late age.

Harvey is surreptitious about the brain, not revealing many secrets
and unsure what to think of Sugimoto. Eventually, he brings the brain out
in a sugar jar with a clasp top. Sugimoto asks if he might have a piece.
Harvey hems, haws, and then gives him a section. Sugimoto asks again if
he might have not a section but an actual piece. Harvey laughs and real-
izes his motives are genuine and relents. Harvey then ambles over to the
kitchen and grabs a butcher knife and cutting board, pulls a piece of the

brain stem and cerebellum out of a cookie jar, likely choosing the cerebellum for its lack of interest. (The cerebellum is the back of the brain and thought to be for controlling our joints and motor coordination so we can move in 3D space. An animal with a removed cerebellum walks around like a drunk. It is an obscenely understudied part of the brain and likely not an area Harvey would receive many requests for.) He chops off a piece of the cerebellum like he's cutting an onion and hands it to Sugimoto in a prescription pill container. In the end, we learn Harvey is working as an extruder apprentice and is employee of the month at the factory.

Maybe astrocytes are responsible for Harvey's thoughts as he worked the machine and contemplated Einstein's brain in his kitchen cabinet; astrocyte calcium is in motion when Sugimoto obsessed over a piece of the brain; and Diamond uses her astrocytes while she looked through the microscope at Einstein's astrocytes. Regardless of the flaws of Diamond's study, it will be incredibly interesting if the Einstein study proves to be true. However, we still do not know because it has not been pursued. Even Diamond concluded that the glial cells only provide the neurons with more "nourishment" as the notion in 1985 was that astrocytes were support cells for the neuron.

I think we can say now that astrocytes are not simple support cells or electrical insulators. The electrical conductance of neurons is increased and insulated with myelin production. As has been shown, the predominance of neurons is rooted in the work of the nineteenth century when most work in neuroscience was performed on peripheral neurons. The discovery by Galvani of an electrical force in the periphery axon, followed by the understanding that the brain and periphery were made of single cells like the rest of the body, led to the neuron doctrine. Cajal himself said that the function of the glia cell would be illuminated as techniques get better. And now that they have, we are beginning to realize that the neuron might be subordinate to glia.

We do know four things: Astrocytes turn over in the human cortex in normal humans, which is ironically evidenced by the heavy carbon studies in the brains of people alive during the atomic testing periods. Neurons do not. Also, astrocyte turnover is associated with areas of learning as evidenced by the studies started by Nottebohm and Alvarez-Buylla in the subventricular zone and hippocampus. Additionally, Einstein had

more astrocytes in the left parietal cortex when compared to 11 "normal" brains. Lastly, we know that astrocytes communicate to each other through the fluidity of calcium waves with complete control of the neuronal synapses in their space.

The constant turnover of astrocytes occurs throughout adult life, and to accelerate it, we need to work our minds. Mental effort, like a bodybuilder lifting weights to become strong, would create greater astrocyte turnover and enable more complex thought due to more abundant astrocytes. However, the ravages of time take their toll on us biologically. The glial turnover cannot keep up, the rest of the body is bombarded by the weather of earth over time, and we perish.

Astrocytes are also the only communicatory cell in the brain that monitor and attach to blood vessels that give them the capability to bring nourishment through the blood to the brain. When we think, we can increase blood flow to the brain that can work the brain like a muscle, flexing it when we concentrate and causing more astrocyte growth. Einstein was Arnold Schwarzenegger in this sense.

In humans, we have dementia as the result of aging. At the University of Kentucky, David Snowdon studied a population of Catholic nuns in the upper Midwest. When studied for incidence of dementia, Snowdon and colleagues noticed less dementia in nuns who performed constant mental exercises, such as crossword puzzles, word games, and knitting. Using your brain staves off dementia due to aging.

This explains why Einstein had more astrocytes. Astrocytes are the thinking cell. They are the only cells that multiply in the cortex throughout our lifespans, and because cell turnover is associated with learning, this leads us to believe that working your brain will enable you to think more complex thoughts, and your brain can stave off the horrors of dementia.

The nuns Snowdon studied didn't perform strict learning tasks, but simply concentrated with their cortex. This cortical concentration could cause increased gliogenesis and might account for Einstein's abundance of glia in the left parietal cortex.

For the average person who is not Einstein, and that means everyone, there are likely two ways to increase astrocyte growth in the brain. The first would be the equivalent of environmental enrichment that is provided for children, sort of like an adult *Baby Einstein* that increases your experience of your environment through traveling, reading, seeing

as much as possible, acquiring knowledge (William S. Burroughs medicinal treatment not recommended), and working with your hands, such as mechanics, knitting, and so on. The other is to make more attempts to recall information, to flow the blood to your brain and activate astrocytes that sit dormant instead of just saying "I don't know" or simply resorting to the Internet without effort—although reading and acquiring new information through the Internet is probably a good thing.

Einstein's abundance of astrocytes could have been a genetic predisposition to producing cells or it could have been environmental. However, as we know from studies on brain aging, most destruction of the brain seems to be environmental in nature. There are some genetic causes of diseases, but usually a genetic predisposition to disease leads to early onset in the brain and the disease occurs before old age. In most brain disease, the cause is not genetic and happens randomly, indicating that you have more control over your ability to think up through your old age. Therefore, increasing your astrocyte production may be an environmental process.

The other idea is that Einstein could have had a massive growth of astrocytes at an early age instead of them growing steady over his lifetime. But either way, we know that astrocytes grow and multiply throughout life, so it is possible that Einstein had one massive moment where his astrocytes propagated and then continued at a normal pace, or it occurred gradually but at a higher rate than a normal mind.

Cell division in our brain is an asexual process; an astrocyte splits and then its daughter cell becomes a fully functioning cell, and when it is extinguished, it dies. It comes full circle, just like Einstein's brain. In his book *Driving Mr. Albert: A Trip Across America with Einstein's Brain*, Michael Paterniti writes about his drive across the country with Dr. Harvey. In the trunk of a Buick Skylark, Einstein's brain sloshed around in formaldehyde. Paterniti reveals at the end that Harvey, now in his 90s, has since given the brain to pathologist Elliot Krauss at Princeton Medical Center.

Flex your brain to increase the amount of astrocytes, the seat of imagination, creativity, and thought in the cortex. Based on the evidence that has mounted in the last 20 years, combined with the work on Einstein's brain, we have moved mightily toward understanding the brain as a more subtle structure than the neural lighting storm. It needs work like a muscle to maintain its ability and it can grow after intense thought.

And the growth and thought occur in glia in the cortical astrocyte. The glial cell turnover occurs during your whole life, and if you work your mind and keep growing new astrocytes, it keeps your mind fresh. As Bob Dylan says, "I was so much older then; I'm younger than that now."

References

Abraham, C. *Possessing Genius: The True Account of the Bizarre Odyssey of Einstein's Brain*. New York, NY: St. Martin's Griffin, 2003.

Diamond, M.C., A.B. Scheibel, G.M. Murphy, and T. Harvey. "On the Brain of a Scientist: Albert Einstein." *Experimental Neurology*, 88, 198–204, 1985.

Fields, R.D. "The Other Half of the Brain." *Scientific American*, March, 2004.

Paterniti, M. *Driving Mr. Albert: A Trip Across America with Einstein's Brain*. New York, NY: Delta, Random House, 2000.

Snowdon, D.A. "Aging and Alzheimer's Disease: Lessons from the Nun Study." *Gerontologist*, 37: 150–156, 1997.

11

I dream of glia

Emus don't get drunk and if they did, we wouldn't know why. If a bear smokes weed, we don't know what it feels while high. If you do, you assume you know what you experience. And you assume that your experiences are similar to other human beings because you are of the same species. You can communicate what you experience to other humans, as Baudelaire does in *The Poem of Hashish*, "The drunkenness, throughout its duration, it is true, will be nothing but an immense dream, thanks to the intensity of its colors and the rapidity of its conceptions. But it will always keep the idiosyncrasy of the individual. The man has desired to dream; the dream will govern the man."

Like drugs, the same also goes for dreams. Unless, that is, your parietal-occipital-temporal junction of the cortex is lesioned after an injury. Then, you will be incapable of dreaming or at least incapable of remembering your dreams. Astrocytes in this area of the cortex are abundant and produce calcium waves. This is the area of the cortex in Einstein's brain that had more astrocytes than the average person has. He must have had fantastic dreams.

From about age four on, after our explosion of astrocytes from birth, we begin to experience memories and dreams. The human dream is evidence of the sporadic ripples of calcium waves. The inner workings of the astrocyte is built in a manner to enable short puffs of calcium release. Like rain on a lake, the ripples from sporadic calcium puffs in the brain might be the seat of imagination or creativity. And therefore, it is the stuff of dreams.

When we dream, our body is thought to be resting from our intense electrical neuron firing throughout the day. Our sensory inputs and motor outputs are constantly active. One way to study them is to use the same techniques originally pioneered in the nineteenth century by

Fritsch and Hitzig to study electrical firing in the brain (without removal of the skull). For more than a century, researchers have taken their ideas to perform electroencephalographs (EEG). A researcher places electrodes on the scalp, which theoretically studies the electrical activity inside the brain. The EEG from a person sleeping falls into a monotonous predictable pattern as opposed to the sporadic EEG of wakefulness.

EEGs are a lot like the duck-billed platypus. We know they exist, but we're not sure what they mean. Dreams are thought to occur when the pattern changes in electrical firing after falling into a deep sleep. This pattern of activity might be instigated by calcium waves.

Without sensory information reaching the brain, we are able to retrieve thoughts and images. The EEG activity during sleep occurs in several different stages—one stage that has received a lot of attention is the rapid eye movement phase or REM sleep. This was previously believed to be the only time when we dream. However, now we know that dreaming can occur throughout our sleep. As we are shut off from the world, the ripples in our brain can spread and fire adjacent neurons leading to REM activity. However, the lack of integration from our senses results in the randomness and surreal nature of the experience.

Dreaming might not be as random as we think. It's possible astrocytes have been inundated with information as we make new experiences, and at night, they need to grow more cells to gain greater capacity for processing and solidify connections with their neuronal counterparts to better act on the new information the next day.

Many of us have experienced a tough day where we tire quickly after being bombarded by incessant experiences. We need to sleep, or reboot, to be fresh again for the next day. Throughout our waking state, our astrocytes could be developing in areas pertaining to our experiences. New astrocytes at night would need to make solid neuronal connections so we can act on our experiences better the next time we encounter them. The rapid eye movements seen in REM sleep could be glia experimenting with the neuronal firing to make sure their connections are solid.

Dreams follow experience. Imagine seeing a car going 50 miles per hour on a city street hit a pedestrian. The person flies halfway up the block and lands in a grotesque bloody heap, his limbs askew at awkward angles. Bystanders run in horror or stand with their mouths agape. This would leave an impression that would filter into your dreams. Just as the

instant of winning the lottery or giving birth to a child would influence your dreams.

Monotony, such as working in a plastics factory making shovel handles, computer monitors, or letter trays all day with each new piece of plastic popping out of the mold every 30–40 seconds, can seep into dreams. However, on the weekend or at night, we can break it up with activity and entertainment.

We tend to have foreboding or sad dreams if we have been paranoid or insecure that day. And if we've seen a funny movie, maybe our dreams can be more comedic. It is easier to instigate a calcium wave from a puff in a group of astrocytes that has been primed. The percolating calcium raindrops will more ready explode into a full-fledged wave traversing many astrocytes.

When we are sleeping, these waves have nowhere to go but stay in our thoughts. We can have waves corresponding to thoughts throughout our brain, but long-distance communication through neurons to muscles is impossible; all that remains is the disjointed integration we experience in dreams. We have no feedback with our senses to reassure our thoughts.

Psychologists have believed for some time that our dreams are meaningful. This might be true. They might be triggered in the waves of our most dominant astrocytes, the ones used the most from the pool of our active thought while awake. Maybe we have a recurring dream as the calcium waves from a particular population of astrocytes continually dominate the night. Or maybe astrocytes that haven't been used spark puffs and waves at night as a way to get activity when the more active astrocytes repair their machinery.

It was believed that neurons laid down new memories by making stronger connections through synaptic growth in areas that have been used more often by our brain. Strength of wiring does not occur first in the astrocyte-dominated theory of information storage. Astrocytes grow in areas that are used the most. This growth contributes to the overall pool where sporadic calcium waves occur in dreams.

If we try to retrieve information from something that happened a long time ago, we might first go through avenues in our brain we are familiar with, but when we reach the populations we are searching for, the complexity will have increased with the excess growth. There is more life in a jungle than a desert and more to growing astrocytes than the electrical wasteland of a static neuron.

Our experience in a sensory deprivation tank is more evidence for the sporadic calcium waves. Our thoughts are dreamlike, moving through surreal experiences unchecked by the outside world. This occurs with inactive neurons. Astrocytic waves flowing and crashing in our skull are responsible for this experience.

The extent of dreaming in other species is unknown. However, anyone who owns a dog who has heard the dog growl in its sleep knows that dogs sometimes seem to dream. The way the ratio of glia to neurons in the human being, the abundant astrocytes in the human cortex, and our more complex behavior could mean our dreams are more complex. However, this idea might seem attractive because we are human.

We are just tall bald bipedal rodents, our smooth bodies prancing around the planet like upright terrestrial seals. We have so much shame around our fellow species we go about gashing other animals with bloodthirsty zeal for their pelts with which to clothe ourselves. For centuries, we strutted around in rotting carcasses. Our evolution to use tools that propelled us to the top of the food chain might have simply been due to our inherent lust to massacre other animals to quench our intense desire to cover our genitals with their hides. And we sit in chairs made of cow, full of conceit at the notion of the superiority of our ideas. The thoughts of other animals almost certainly have to exist on a higher plane. If we knew how they contemplate the hominid, we would perhaps not be flattered. Then again, human beings might think on a higher level than other species. For the purpose of this book, let's just imagine that's true.

Our passive imagination, while sleeping or in sensory depravation, is a different experience than our active imagination. When we are awake and not in sensory deprivation, we also have the ability to exclude our senses. We can put ideas through logical progressions, which might illuminate a new idea related to what we already know. Or, we can ponder, wonder, and ruminate. Something can dawn on us. This is called daydreaming for a reason. It is the act of excluding the environment around us to focus on thoughts. Daydreaming is integral to the human experience and likely occurs in astrocytes. Active thought occurs at the bond between astrocytes and their connections to blood vessels. Like flexing a muscle, we can increase blood flow to our brain to nourish the calcium waves flowing to a moment of inspiration, a moment that might require us to instigate neuronal action.

The façade of dreams—macabre or wonderful, heightened thoughts, illogical, yet somehow touching on the most true and exciting elements of our nature—all reside in the abstract human mind, outside the straight-forward thinking of the practical awake, working, active, and talking person. Every night your regular normal self enters into your own psychotic world. Some people are forced to deal with this experience even while awake in the form of mental disorders.

Although most of the work related to psychiatric disorders has been geared toward the belief the problem resides in neurons, now that researchers have shifted their focus on glia and astrocytes, it should soon become obvious it will open many doors, which might illuminate the cause of these diseases.

The variegated and complex study of psychiatric disorders—as they relate to the core of human existence, our thought, imagination, and creativity—are perfect avenues for the study of astrocyte function. A study will likely reveal many astounding discoveries in the next century. Our astrocytes are who we are, and the processing of each individual must vary in some aspects. How they vary and why will be interesting to understand. One treatment that has been used for psychiatric disorders involves the long-standing relationship between lithium and bipolar disorder, formerly called manic-depression. Lithium is used as an ion to take the place of potassium and calcium, which are both ions prevalent in astrocytes. The stabilizing feature of lithium and other bipolar treatments often leads the patients to feel like "they are not themselves" and somehow have blunted their sharp existence; lithium just ain't calcium.

Also, while studying the post-mortem brains of the clinically depressed, researchers noticed the reduction in the number of cortical astrocytes when compared to the brains of people who were considered normal.

In depression, the paucity of astrocytes might likely result in the relatively few calcium waves to stimulate proper areas. The thoughts of a person might be uncontrollable, sending them into the depths of the pointlessness of existence. Whereas in mania, the calcium waves are too fluid and intense—an ocean in a hurricane state—resulting in extreme active behavior and euphoria.

Reduced numbers of astrocytes have been seen in the brains of people who have schizophrenia. The study of schizophrenia could be greatly

helped if more was understood about the disorder as it pertains to astrocytes. Disruption of serotonin, the transmitter believed to be responsible for mood, has also been reported in schizophrenia, and the action can be similar to what occurs while taking hallucinogenics. Schizophrenics are well known for their wild hallucinations. This serotonin influence causes astrocytes, which receive input from the senses to be in calcium wave activation without being stimulated by neurons.

Treatments for depression are commonly serotonin reuptake inhibitors. The theoretical idea being that serotonin is allowed to stay longer at the synapse and act on neurons for a longer period of time. Serotonin reuptake is performed by astrocytes as well, and the effect might be to stimulate receptors on astrocytes by continuing release of internal calcium stores via this pathway. Activating more astrocytes when the numbers are depleted might be the reason for the effects.

One uniquely human experience is the conscious decision to take mind-altering substances. The role of astrocytes in the processing of recreational drugs has not been adequately studied due to the relatively recent understanding of the prominence of glia in brain functioning.

However, because astrocytes express receptors and reuptake transporters for transmitters, it is believed that drugs acting specifically on transmitter receptors can instigate astrocyte activity and communication. Nicotine is known to act on the acetylcholine receptor and caffeine on the adenosine receptor. These receptors have been shown to be expressed in glial cells.

The mechanisms of withdrawal is believed to occur because constant activity on the receptor causes the cell to produce less of the receptor, which leads to a period of withdrawal symptoms off the drug where cells cannot signal as robustly until their receptor numbers are increased again. In the last 15 years, research has shown that heroin can stop cellular genesis. It seems morphine might be able to repress the action of cellular genesis, the unique process of the astrocyte. The lowering of astrocyte numbers without transmitter increases, such as serotonin, has been linked to depression. This method of depression could be the experience of withdrawal symptoms.

Just recently, exciting new research on glia from Alfonso Araque's lab has ironically come from the Cajal Institute in Madrid, named for the biggest neuronal proponent of them all, Ramón y Cajal. Araque and Marta Navarrette are giving insights into the action of marijuana on

calcium waves. Marijuana has been used for a long time in human history, and the activation and mechanisms of the drug in the brain were finally described in the early 1990s. The tetrahydrocannabinol (THC) in marijuana mimics transmitters, which have been called endocannabinoids. Because the original research was neuron-centric, endocannabinoids were shown to work as a feedback mechanism in neurons, released by a neuron to act backwards on the one that just fired to it. However, just recently it was shown that endocannabinoids can release internal calcium stores in astrocytes and cause calcium waves (see Figure 11.1).

Reprinted from *Neuron*, Vol. 57, Navarrete, M. and Araque A. "Endocannabinoids Mediate Neuron-Astrocyte Communication," p. 884, Copyright (2008), with permission from Elsevier.

FIGURE 11.1 Calcium waves in mouse hippocampus astrocytes immediately after adding a short-acting molecule that stimulates the same receptors that respond to THC, the active ingredient in marijuana.

This discovery indicates that the dreamlike state described by Baudelaire is indeed the result of marijuana causing calcium waves to ripple throughout astrocytes.

Alcohol and astrocytes have a longer history. When astrocytes are stained with antibodies to proteins related to cell structure, they show different morphology and reactivity in damaged brains. Studies have tried to determine how exactly alcohol causes brain damage by looking at astrocytes. The most intense study has only come about in the last 20 years. It seems that alcohol is able to affect calcium-binding proteins and cause calcium release from internal stores. The effects of alcohol also cause reactive oxygen species release, which can cause cell death.

Sadly, virtually nothing has been researched on astrocytes and hallucinogens such as mescaline, psilocybin, and LSD.

As pharmacology labs begin to focus on astrocytes, it will be interesting to see how the interactions of serotonin agonists, such as LSD and psilocybin, are related. The tryptamine structure of these molecules and others, such as AMT and DMT, shows they are related, but the circular thoughts and cool tones experienced with mushrooms is different from the infinity awareness and stark digitized experience of LSD.

The activation of cocaine is through the inhibition of dopamine reuptake. This is known to be an astrocyte-dependent process, but little work has been done on the astrocyte in relation to this activation and has mainly focused on neuronal circuits in reward centers of the brain. As with drugs, such as nicotine, cocaine, and so on, deep reward centers of the brain obviously play a major role, but the disregard of astrocytes in these centers, and cortical astrocytes in general, completely disrupts the understanding of human consciousness that could be achieved by studying the alterations that occur when unnatural substances bombard the brain and create such interesting and testable behavior.

The use of drugs can create dreamlike states and then affect our dreams as we withdraw. When his glial regeneration was likely stunted, Thomas de Quincey stated in *Confessions of an Opium-Eater*, "For this, and all other changes in my dreams, were accompanied by deep-seated anxiety and gloomy melancholy, such as are wholly incommunicable by words. I seemed every night to descend—not metaphorically, but literally to descend—into chasms and sunless abysses, depths below depths, from which it seemed hopeless that I could ever re-ascend. Nor did I, by waking, feel that I had re-ascended. This I do not dwell upon; because the state of gloom which attended these gorgeous spectacles, amounting at least to utter darkness, as of some suicidal despondency, cannot be approached by words."

The withdrawal symptoms infecting our astrocytes and disrupting our basic dreams is a frightening prospect. Reading Baudelaire can reassure us when he describes the less aggressive hashish, "Let it be well understood then, by worldly and ignorant folk curious of acquaintance with exceptional joys, that they will find in hashish nothing miraculous, absolutely nothing but the natural in a superabundant degree. The brain and the organism upon which hashish operates will only give their ordinary and individual phenomena, magnified. Here is the drug before your eyes: a little green sweetmeat, about as big as a nut, with a strange smell."

Our experiences reside in astrocytes. Drugs will influence and enhance them, but they are still acting on them, and they are us. When we are in a new situation and our calcium wave spreads to an area of cells responsible for a previous experience, we will have the feeling we have been here before—it's a light disruption, putting us in a reflective trance. This feeling is astrocytes on the fringe of a previously felt experience being inundated.

We do know a bear avoids eating psychedelic mushrooms. Wolves avoid them as well. But do wolves experience déjà vu?

References

Agam, G., I.P. Everall, and R.II. Belmaker. *The Post-Mortem Brain in Psychiatric Research*. Norwell, MA: Kluwer Academic Publishers, 2002.

Baudelaire, C. Trans. A. Crowley. *The Poem of Hashish*, Whitefish, MT: Kessinger Publishing, 2004.

Cotter, D.R., C.M. Pariante, and I.P. Everall. "Glial Cell Abnormalities in Major Psychiatric Disorders: The Evidence and Implications." *Brain Research Bulletin*, 55: 585–595, 2001.

de Quincey, T. *Confessions of an English Opium Eater.* Harmondsworth, UK: Penguin Books, 1995.

Domhoff, G.W. *The Scientific Study of Dreams*. Washington, DC: American Psychological Association, 2002.

Earleywine, M. *Mind-Altering Drugs*. New York: Oxford University Press, 2005.

Lancaster, F.E. *Alcohol and Glial Cells: Research Monograph 27*. Bethesda, MD: National Institutes of Health, National Institute on Alcohol Abuse and Alcoholism, 1994.

López-Ibor, J.J., W. Gaebel, M. Maj, and N. Sartorius. *Psychiatry as Neuroscience*. New York: John Wiley & Sons, 2002.

Monti, J., S.R. Pandi-Perumal, and C.M. Sinton. *Neurochemistry of Sleep and Wakefulness*. New York: Cambridge University Press, 2008.

Navarette, M. and A. Araque. "Endocannabinoids Mediate Neuron-Astrocyte Communication." *Neuron*, 57: 883–892, 2008.

Parrott, A., A. Morinan, M. Moss, and A. Scholey. *Understanding Drugs and Behavior*. San Francisco: John Wiley & Sons, 2004.

Webster, R.A. *Neurotransmitters, Drugs and Brain Function*. New York: John Wiley & Sons, 2001.

World Heath Organization. *Neuroscience of Psychoactive Substance Use and Dependance*. Geneva, Switzerland: WHO, 2004.

12

Gliadegenerative disease

Many degenerative diseases of the brain, especially Alzheimer's Disease, Parkinson's Disease, and Amyotrophic Lateral Sclerosis (Lou Gehrig's Disease) have a curious aspect. In all of them, the first thing to go is the sense of smell. Why smell? No one knows. Many reasons for this might exist—the disease somehow attacks the neurons transmitting the sense of smell into the brain. Maybe some primitive evolutionary imprint has left its mark on our nose and it just gives up when the brain begins to degenerate in any area. However, we are taught that in Alzheimer's, the point of attack is the hippocampus, which is the area responsible for forming new memories—the area cut out of Brenda Milner's famous patient HM. In Parkinson's, the debilitated area is the basal ganglia, and particularly the substantia nigra, an area that helps control movement. In Amyotrophic Lateral Sclerosis, it is the cortical motor neurons, where neurons extend long axons out of the cortex to tell our body what to do. What does the sense of smell have to do with any of this?

It turns out that, in reality, regardless of what they teach you in biology class, many of these diseases are related. Labeling the diseases undercuts the fact that they are like the color spectrum—blue and red are different but can be combined to create purple. Alzheimer's and Parkinson's are different, but a type of degenerative disease exists that is a combination of both. A doctor who specializes in treating diseases of the brain will tell you that each person is different, and someone can be classified as having Alzheimer's but can have symptoms of other diseases and so on. Again, the human desire to label and characterize to understand something can impede our understanding.

Before modern science, people with degenerative diseases were neglected, tossed aside, and allowed to die. People didn't live long enough to get diseases. If they made it to 90 and they couldn't remember

their own name, well, they had made it to 90. However, as people live longer, we feel the need to lump a group of people who can't remember anymore into a category or a group of people who have trouble moving into another category. What might have been lost in all the categorization is that an afflicted person might be experiencing a disorder similar to what other people might have, but is still unique.

It started with James Parkinson (1755–1824) who observed six people in London and wrote an article in 1817 describing "the shaking palsy." He observed in detail the tremors and the inability to start and stop movements.

In France, 60 years later, Jean-Martin Charcot (1825–1893), one of Sigmund Freud's mentors who was also an advocate of hypnotism and the main culprit in disease labeling, capitalized on Parkinson's observations. Charcot was the first proponent of describing aberrant behavior and then comparing that with the brain using the cell stains developed by Cajal and Golgi. He was prolific in naming diseases—among them, multiple sclerosis and Charcot-Marie-Tooth syndrome (the degeneration of nerves in the limbs). Charcot also coined the shaking palsy "Parkinson's Disease" based on clients he saw who resembled Parkinson's outline of symptoms in his well-known essay.

At the famous Salpétriére Hospital in Paris, Charcot didn't stop at naming diseases and created the first "neurology" clinic in a European Hospital. Perhaps his most famous finding, though, was the description of Amyotrophic Lateral Sclerosis (ALS), which is called Maladie de Charcot in Europe. In the United States, it is called Lou Gehrig's Disease after New York Yankees' first baseman Lou Gehrig. Halfway through the summer of 1938, Gehrig, who finished second in the league in hitting the year before and third in homeruns and was generally regarded the best player alive, suddenly couldn't hit at the age of 35. He finished the season with a .295 average, a good average for a normal player, but about 50 points lower than Gehrig was used to. At the beginning of 1939, he had no strength and, after previously playing 2,130 games in a row without an injury, took himself out of a game. When the Yankees were playing in Chicago, Gehrig went over to the Mayo clinic in Minnesota and was diagnosed with ALS by the famous Dr. Mayo. Eventually he had to retire, but fans were troubled by his sudden decline, from the best player in the game to an apparition of a figment of himself. He died two years later.

In degenerative disease of the brain, the complete loss of one's health and mind is the sad result. Nothing can prepare anyone for the destructive nature of the disease, especially friends and relatives of the afflicted—and in the instance of Gehrig, millions of fans who felt a special relationship with him. ALS is a particularly horrific disease. The degeneration of cortical neurons extending into the brain stem and the spine was elucidated after Charcot described the disease. The degeneration of the brain stem and the spine causes horrible pain, inability to walk, and eventually the inability to breathe.

In 1919, an Uzbek-born Russian biologist Konstantin Tretiakoff (1892–1958) noticed that patients diagnosed with Parkinson's Disease had a loss of pigmented neurons in a nucleus deep in the brain called the *substantia nigra*. Substantia nigra is Latin for "black substance," ironic in the year the Black Sox threw the World Series. It is believed the substantia nigra works with other cell nuclei under the cortex in a feedback loop to calibrate our movements.

In a section cut out of the midbrain, the substantia nigra resembles dark thumbprints. The reason for the dark coloring is melanin in the neurons, the same substance that pigments our skin. The substantia nigra is like the freckled cheeks on the face of the brain.

A German scientist using the same strategy that Charcot popularized, Alois Alzheimer (1864–1915), was the first to describe the disease of forgetfulness. Auguste Deter, a 51-year-old housewife who had developed symptoms of memory loss was recommended to him as a patient. Fascinated, when she died five years later, Alzheimer exhaustively studied her symptoms and brain with a Golgi type silver stain; he found the cortex had shrunk and looked like a walnut, and neurons had been destroyed.

The only effective treatments exist for Parkinson's. In the 1950s, Nobel Prize-winning Swedish scientist Arvid Carlsson discovered the transmitter dopamine. It was then learned that dopamine is the main transmitter in neurons signaling from the substantia nigra to other areas of the brain. By giving a dopamine depletion molecule to dogs, Carlsson showed they began to exhibit Parkinson's Disease-like symptoms. Using an analog called L-Dopa, which crosses the blood brain barrier and is converted to dopamine, researchers can immediately reverse symptoms in some patients.

This cosmetic treatment does not cure the disease. Conversely, it is believed that excessive dopamine treatment can accelerate the disease. Although it has improved the life dramatically of patients with Parkinson's in the few years after diagnosis, it does not reveal the cause of the disease.

Another current treatment in Parkinson's Disease is Deep Brain Stimulation. An electrical stimulator is placed deep in the brain in the basal ganglia, the set of nuclei that encompasses the substantia nigra. The electrical stimulation can mimic the substantia nigra firing and restore movement. As one can imagine, this treatment is cosmetic and does not cure the disease, but it has increased the quality of life in many patients much longer than they would have had without it. The difficulty is that in Parkinson's Disease, as well as other diseases of the brain, the methods of Charcot describing specific areas has proven simplistic. When, in fact, some areas might decline more rapidly at the beginning, but the entire brain of these patients, including the cortex, will eventually degenerate.

In the past 30 years, a lot of research and effort has been spent trying to connect the cause of diseases to proteins in the neurons. While studying Parkinson's, in 1912, while working in Alzheimer's laboratory, Frederick Lewy noticed that spherical protein deposits (now called Lewy Bodies) occur in neurons of people with dementia. The protein that comprises these structures has been pinpointed and is now called alpha-synuclein. It is an abundant protein highly expressed throughout the neuron and specifically in the axons and synapses. It is believed to be involved in transporting vesicles filled with transmitters for release at the synapse. As a neuron is dying, the protein begins to bind to itself. It almost works like Velcro; some minute difference in its shape causes it to clasp together. As it keeps binding to itself, like a billion magnets thrown in a room, it forms the ring-like Lewy Body.

In Alzheimer's, the proteins discovered around dead neurons after autopsy are called amyloid beta and tau. When they accumulate after the cell dies, they form plaques and tangles. In the brain, they pile up beside neurons similar to rust on a pipe.

All these proteins have been shown to be expressed in high numbers in the neuronal machinery and are some of the most abundant proteins. When the neuron perishes in the disease, it is not a surprise that the proteins build up around the cells. Proteins implicated in Parkinson's have been shown to build up in Alzheimer's and vice versa.

Genetic forms of Parkinson's Disease have all been linked to a mutation on proteins that are highly expressed in the cell, including alpha-synuclein. Mutations that cause a problem in alpha-synuclein leading to Parkinson's disease have led many researchers to believe that alpha-synuclein is the cause of the disease. However, this is like seeing a bombed-out city and blaming the ruins.

Of course, a genetic mutation in an abundant protein like alpha-synuclein is going to cause disease. In fact, this is expected. But because of its placing in the neuron, researchers have tried to see what alpha-synuclein interacts with in other attempts to understand the cause of the disease. This is scientific detective work; they see a dead body and look at what the victim associated with to find the killer. But who is the killer when everyone is dead? With mutations, people develop diseases that are more cut and dry and occur much earlier in their life than what happens to people who develop degenerative diseases of the brain as they age.

The focus on neurons in all these diseases is mainly the result of Cajal's Neuron Doctrine and electrical studies coming to prominence at the same time. Astonishingly little has been researched on glia until the twenty-first century. Researchers have simply discounted them without evidence for their insignificance. But as Willy Wonka says, "You should never, never doubt what nobody is sure about."

In 1993, researchers at Duke University Medical Center discovered a major breakthrough in Alzheimer's Disease by linking sporadic disease to the apoE gene. With more of this gene, the chance of Alzheimer's increased from 20 to 90 percent, and the average age of onset of the disease compared to people without the excess gene dropped from 80 to 68. With the gene, people were virtually guaranteed to get Alzheimer's by age 80. Previous head injury is a risk factor for all degenerative diseases of the brain. If an excess gene for the apoE protein is present and the patient had a previous head injury, she will have a much better chance of developing disease later in life. This protein is highly expressed in astrocytes. It works to shuttle cholesterol and lipids outside the cell. Recently it has been implicated in Parkinson's Disease as well.

Astrocytes and neurons work together; neurons bring information to astrocytes from the senses and execute the astrocytes on the motor level. Astrocytes maintain neurons like cities maintain roads, so that they can always perform their high-speed transmissions. Astrocyte maintenance of neurons requires them to take up glutamate—a transmitter that can be toxic if built up in the synapse. Astrocytes can also take up excess reactive

oxygen species, toxic byproducts of the energy-producing mitochondria. When unconsumed oxygen is roaming through the cell, it can become destructive and cause cell death, and this destruction is termed "oxidative stress." The dopaminergic neurons in the substantia nigra in Parkinson's Disease are more susceptible to oxidative stress than in a healthy person. There is no other explanation for this other than astrocytes not maintaining the neuron.

Astrocytes also take up excessive amyloid beta when it leaks out of the neuron. The plaques that form around neurons when they die are filled with amyloid beta. The build up of this protein might likely be because no astrocytes are available to clean them up.

Glutamate, the main transmitter released in the cortex and released by upper motor neurons, when not broken down, washes over the neurons and kills them in ALS. In 1992, at John's Hopkins, Jeffrey Rothstein showed that problems with glutamate transporters might be the reason for the beginning of ALS. It is now known that these transports reside in the membranes of astrocytes. Astrocytes take in glutamate at the synapse.

It makes sense for astrocytes to want to break down and clean up destructive molecules and proteins because they require their high-speed neuronal connections to send information long distances to have the body execute what they thought. Astrocytes don't clean up some of the excess of neuronal communication because they are subordinate—they do it because they are dominant. Just as we must maintain the roads near our cities, the astrocytes must maintain the neuron. Astrocytes have access to the blood vessels that not only provide nourishment, but can also work as a garbage dump for the waste materials that build up when the neuron fires its energy. Whether some problem with apoE functioning or the inability for astrocytes to scavenge proteins, transmitters, or by products of oxidative stress, the evidence points to astrocytes as the cause in degenerative diseases of the brain.

In another study, astrocytes and neurons were cultured together in a dish. A mass amount of amyloid beta was added to the cells. Calcium waves started in astrocytes and they killed off the neurons. Amyloid beta is normally scavenged by astrocytes, but in such large amounts, astrocytes must think the neuron is dying and prematurely euthanizes it. The brain can't have a dilapidated unfixable road. Astrocytes are all about cleaning up their neighborhoods.

The astrocyte, one of which can contact 10,000 neuronal synapses, increases up the evolutionary ladder in the cortex. They are the most

abundant cells in the human cortex; they are the only regenerative cells in the cortex; and they can communicate with each other in intricate calcium waves. They do not have time for loiterers.

In aging, it was thought that a loss of neurons was the result of our cognitive decline as we aged. After further review, neuronal number seems to remain the same as we age. However, there is a higher incidence of a phenomenon called "astrocyte reaction." A protein, called glial fibrillary acidic protein, or more commonly referred to as GFAP, becomes expressed in astrocytes in response to trauma, aging, and disease in the brain. In 1972, researchers at Stanford and the VA hospital in Palo Alto, California separated the cells and looked for immunoreaction to specific proteins that wouldn't work with neurons and found that GFAP was shown to be a marker for astrocytes. GFAP is abundant throughout the brain, including in the cortex, and is the marker that was used to demonstrate dividing astrocytes near the ventricles. Higher astrocyte reaction occurs in the substantia nigra in Parkinson's, the hippocampus in Alzheimer's, and the motor cortex in ALS—not to mention the cortex in general.

GFAP is also the protein in the cells that are multiplying and the root of cell regeneration in the brain, the same cells that constantly replenish the olfactory bulb and hippocampus. These are the same cells that multiply throughout our lives in the cortex and the only cells that are the root of cellular regeneration as we age—the astrocyte.

As it ages, the brain continually tries to regenerate its glial cells. We each have a constant turnover rate of astrocytes in our brain. That rate, over time, is unique to us. However, if that rate tapers off and astrocytes die more quickly than they are replenished, we develop a degenerative disease of the brain. As we reach our biological limits in our old age, astrocytes might multiply less robustly. This lack of an adequate turnover rate might be what leads to diseases such as Alzheimer's Disease, Parkinson's Disease, and ALS.

It is conceivable that the loss of smell at the beginning of degenerative diseases of the brain is an indicator of the cause of the disease being the inadequate turnover rate of glial cells.

The lift of the ban on astrocyte research is leading us in amazing new directions. Even in normal aged people without dementia, plaques, tangles, and Lewy Bodies can be seen in neurons in the analysis of their brains—not to the extent of a patient like Alzheimer's Auguste Deter, but enough to know it is a natural aging process. If astrocytes scavenge these

proteins, then it is possible a deficit in astrocyte scavenging is present in disease. Fewer and tired astrocytes would lead to toxic buildup of proteins and molecules released by neurons.

If Parkinson's Disease persists, the patient begins to have cognitive decline and dementia similar to what happens to Alzheimer's patients. In Alzheimer's, the movement disorder eventually develops. In both diseases, the patients have buildups of major neuronal proteins. Dementia with Lewy Bodies is a disease that begins with Alzheimer's-like dementia and then ends with Parkinson's-like movement disorder. People with Alzheimer's in reality have some Lewy Bodies, and people with Parkinson's in reality have some plaques and tangles.

In Parkinson's, it has also been shown that dopamine-expressing neurons are not the only neurons that degenerate; neurons that transmit glutamate and the transmitter GABA have also been implicated. In ALS, the main feature is a degeneration of upper motor neurons, which reach down through the brain stem. However, other areas are now known to degenerate. The same occurs with Alzheimer's; the hippocampus and cortex are the point of attack, which results in memory loss, but these are not the only areas that degenerate.

In degenerative disease of the brain, though, it is obviously true that for some people it initially attacks their movement, for some the cortex, for some hippocampus, and so on. Because it is known that most degenerative diseases of the brain are related and eventually the entire brain will degenerate, instead of lumping all Alzheimer's patients together, it might be more interesting to try and understand why one particular person might be vulnerable initially in the basal ganglia and why someone else might be vulnerable in the cortex.

In ALS, the most work has been pursued on glia because of the toxicity of glutamate, the transmitter released by neurons in the cortex, and the uptake and release of glutamate by astrocytes known due to intricate studies in the late 1980s and early 1990s. However, the focus on receptors and proteins and all things molecular might overlook a basic cellular problem: Glia just can't replace themselves as fast as they used to.

The fact that patients notice an inability to smell before they have other symptoms is telling. The cells for this area usually constantly and healthily turn over in response to the elusive ever-changing molecules floating around in our environment. Astrocytes are the cells that replenish the area. What would change if something happened to our constant

astrocytic turnover in our life? What if we work our minds like a muscle to keep the growth constant and robust, but then a tweak caused by the environment or a trigger in our bodies causes this turnover to slow down? Unlike Einstein's abundant glia, producing more astrocytes than the normal person, we might have trouble thinking and we might have trouble remembering. The transmitters fired by the neurons as information comes in from the senses might not be quenched and processed by enough glia; then problems would likely arise in our mental processing. Our brain goes from a booming mining town to a ghost town when the gold runs out. And the roads in and out of town are grown over with tumbleweed. But the roads don't cause everything to fall apart, nor does the tumbleweed. Something happened to the town, and only when we find out how to bring back the gold will the town boom again.

The evidence that suggests that glial cells can clean up the excess proteins that accumulate outside neurons might lend support to the neurocentric view that glial cells might just be support cells—the busboys cleaning up the plates after the neuron eats a steak. However, even if this is the case, it doesn't excuse the lack of research performed on glial cells.

More likely, glial cells are like a highway construction crew out there trying to fix the road when it has many potholes. They have to clean their roads so that the information they have can be acted on when they tell a neuron to send long-distance information. When the normal rate of regeneration in glia falls below normal pace, it is like an epidemic of the Black Plague has hit glial city. The glial cells will become fewer in number, unable to maintain their neural roads and potholes will develop in the form of protein buildup. Eventually the neurons will begin to die and the brain becomes full of dead glial cells and bad roads—a wasteland.

Many recent studies try to make use of neural stem cells and neural precursor cells. This has proved unsuccessful, because if more neurons are added to the brain, even if they make more connections, they still won't be able to perform properly. The glial control is not there, and they would aimlessly fire.

Injections and replacement therapy with mature astrocytes has not been attempted. Controlling astrocyte implants might serve to help us understand whether the glial cells are indeed the problem. When researchers can accurately determine the rate of astrocyte turnover in a person, then they can try to keep that rate consistent. This could block disease that resulted from astrocytes not being able to replenish adequately as we age.

Most tragic is when the cortex begins to whither. It shrinks in disease. The most numerous cell in the cortex is the astrocyte. In 1906, Alzheimer himself suggested the astrocyte as a possible cause of his disease. However, a suggestion like that was not taken seriously in 1906, the year Cajal was laying down the gauntlet at the Nobel Prize lectures.

Whether the cause of the diseases of the brain is neuronal or astrocytic in nature, studies on astrocytes are imperative. The astrocyte's known ability of scavenging abundant neuronal proteins and transmitters indicates that astrocyte research would benefit patients if not the same, then maybe even more so than research with a blind neuronal focus. If some trigger that has caused inadequate astrocyte turnover is the cause, depleting the brain of astrocytes and then resulting in neuron death, studies on astrocytes is the only way to reveal a cure.

References

Aamodt, S. "Focus on Glia and Disease." *Nature Neuroscience*, 10: 1349, 2007.

Alzheimer, A. "Uber Einen Eigenartigc Erkrankung der Hirnrinde." *Allgemeine Zeitschrift f'ur Psyciatrie und Psychisch-Gerichtliche Medizin*, 64: 146–148, 1907.

Bignami, A., L.F. Eng, D. Dahl, and C.T. Uyeda. "Localization of Glial Fibrillary Acidic Protein in Astrocytes by Immunofluroescence." *Brain Research*, 43: 429-435, 1972.

Corder, E.H., A.M. Saunders, W.J. Strittmatter, D.E. Schmechel, P.C. Gaskell, G.W. Small, A.D. Roses, J.L. Haines, and M.A. Pericakvance. "Gene Dose of Apolipoprotein-E Type-4 Allele and the Risk of Alzheimer's Disease in Late Onset Families." *Science*, 261: 921–923, 1993.

Lage, J.M.M. "100 Years of Alzheimer's Disease." *Journal of Alzheimer's Disease*, 9: 15–26, 2006.

Lees, A.J., M. Selikhova, L.A. Andrade, and C. Duyckaerts. "The Black Stuff and Konstantin Nikolaevich Tretiakoff." *Movement Disorders*, 23: 777–783, 2008.

Lobsiger, C.S. and D.W. Cleveland. "Glial Cells as Intrinsic Components of Non-Cell-Autonomous Neurodegenerative Disease." *Nature Neuroscience*, 10: 1355–1360, 2007.

Parkinson, J. *An Essay on the Shaking Palsy*. London: Whittingham and Rowland, 1817.

Rothstein, J.D., L.J. Martin, and R.W. Kuncl. "Decreased Glutamate Transport by the Brain and Spinal Cord in Amyotrophic Lateral Sclerosis." *New England Journal of Medicine*, 326: 1464–1468, 1992.

Ullian, E.M., S.K. Sapperstein, K.S. Christopherson, and B.A. Barres, "Control of Synapse Number by Glia." *Science*, 291: 657–661, 2001.

Verkhratsky, A. and A. Butt. *Glial Neurobiology*. Chichester, West Sussex: Wiley, 2007.

13

Don't insult me

Evolution has created who we are, not perfect, but simply the state we are as a species today. Some aspects of the brain—for instance, how it has folded inside the skull—and the areas of location for different functions seem completely haphazard. Little makes sense when you step back and look at it. However, it is beneficial that the brain stem is hidden at the base of the brain because we aren't going to have time to ponder how we evolved if we don't survive a head-on collision with a wall.

The brain stem is hidden deep in the base of the brain because it controls our vital functioning, such as breathing and heart rate. If you are going to commit suicide, it is best to aim for the back of your mouth instead of straight into the roof of your mouth. Otherwise, you will just blow off the front of your brain. You can lie there for a day and the paramedics might still find you alive.

Although other medical treatments from antiquity have been lost over time, we know that treatment for brain injuries likely existed as long as 10,000 years ago. Skulls with holes drilled into them (signs of trephaning) have been found as far back as the ancient Egyptians, in the ancient Incan culture as well. This surgery could also have been a cure for psychosis to relieve evil spirits, but the indications seem to be that the person might have sustained some traumatic insult.

This relief of pressure and swelling by cutting open a hole in the skull is still used by neurosurgeons today. Brain injuries come in two main types: open head injury and closed head injury. Open head injury results in a focal contusion that occurs when the brain is directly insulted because of an opening in the skull. A gunshot wound is one example. In this instance, the skull is compromised and the projectile directly damages the brain. The most obvious case of this is a widely reported event from the nineteenth century. Phineas Gage was helping repair a railroad

and slammed a spike accidentally into a bit of dynamite. This propelled the spike through the soft tissue in his cheek, behind his eye sockets, and up through his forebrain.

Amazingly, besides the exit wound at the top of his head, he experienced no other bone fractures or damage to his optic nerve. Everything was intact except the part of brain the railroad spike sliced through. As a result of this, his personality completely changed. Normally a hard worker, he became abusive and crazed and was unable to control his behaviors. The area that sustained the most damage was the amygdala and the frontal cortex, both now known to temper our personalities. Studies of open head injury have helped us understand that some areas of the brain are specialized for certain functions. A lesion in the hypothalamus can cause someone to overeat; an injury a little below that and the person is hypersexual.

The major research on open head injury has been during wars. In World War I, one of the most common injuries was a gunshot wound to the head because of the trench warfare both sides were engaged in. On the German side, they favored leaving the wound open so it could breathe, but on the British and American side, the prevailing theory was debridement, or a closing of the wound. The American and British side prevailed in this war as well, as leaving the wound open usually resulted in an infection and death.

After WWI, it became obvious that soldiers would benefit from mobile surgical units, which were put in place for WWII. With doctors arriving directly on the scene of battle, they were able to save many more lives. From the Soviet Union, Alexander Luria (1902–1977) was one surgeon who studied soldiers returning from Germany with psychiatric disorders and brain injury. An amazing short book he published in 1948, entitled *Restoration of Function after Brain Injury*, described many aspects of the injury. His research wasn't known in the West until 1963 when his book was finally translated into English. His most famous work, *The Man with a Shattered World*, was a history of an interesting case of lifelong brain injury and wasn't translated into English until 10 years after his death.

When studying soldiers, Luria determined that a secondary injury results after the primary wound. Over the cause of the next days and weeks, subsequent degeneration of brain cells occurs. This idea has

proved to be exceedingly correct and a difficult conundrum for researchers. If they can treat the primary injury, how do they also treat the subsequent secondary degeneration, which is a completely separate event? The secondary injury might result from the inability for astrocytes to help or signal to the neurons. Encouraging astrocytes to grow might counteract secondary injury.

The advances from WWI and WWII on the treatment and outcome of brain injury went stale during the Vietnam War. No new advances occurred, and in an abstract in 1971 on 2187 open head wounds in the war, the author concluded—"the previously established principles of combat neurosurgery are confirmed and their continued use recommended."

Trench warfare in WWI also created the advent of a better helmet. Bullets would ricochet off easier. However, with the helmet comes its own problems. The other type of injury, closed head injury or a diffuse axonal injury, occurs in patients who don't have a fractured skull. In 1705, a prisoner in France who was sentenced to be tortured, sprinted 15 feet across the dungeon and smashed his head into the stone wall, to commit suicide, and succeeded, dying instantly. The surgeon in charge of investigating the death, Alexis Littré (1658-1726), could find nothing wrong with the skull or the brain. This study was cited for many years, and it has only recently been understood what causes such severe damage and deficits in closed head injury patients.

The skull stays closed and the swelling has nowhere to go. It is said that you cannot receive a severe injury to the brain unless you fall from a height greater than how tall you are. But with incredibly high buildings, men smashing into each other on the football field, people driving in high-speed cars, and people riding bicycles down hills at 30 mph, it behooved people to invent the helmet.

Of course, the helmet can do only so much. As Seinfeld says about skydiving, "You jump out of that plane and that chute doesn't open, the helmet is now wearing you for protection. Later on the helmet's talking with the other helmets going 'It's a good thing that he was there or I would have hit the ground directly.'" It is true even in events less extreme than skydiving. The shaking of the brain inside the skull can cause just as much damage whether someone is wearing a helmet or not wearing a helmet. In the Iraq War, the most common effect soldiers

experience is diffuse axonal injury to the brain; with all the armor they wear, they can't help their brains from rattling around in their heads when they get tossed by an explosion.

The development of better helmet technology in football has resulted in more concussions, not less. In the early twentieth century, football was so brutal that President Teddy Roosevelt considered banning the sport. In recent years, the game has become more specialized in equipment to protect the players. However, the feelings of inhibition because of the equipment results in many more concussions than before the helmet. Severe skull fractures, though, have been minimized.

The sense of invincibility from equipment safety technology has occurred in other fields as well. In boxing, when gloves became the norm, the arm worked like an anvil slamming down a leather glove drenched in sweat that had become heavy and hard as a rock. This is the reason modern gloves are slick and waterproof.

When the brain shakes and rotates in the skull, the long axons extending out of the cortex down into the lower brain and subsequently the spinal cord are sheared and stretch. The stretching can cause some adverse impairment. Our astrocytes come to the rescue. The astrocytic response in the white matter is extensive. When someone suffers from a coma, he rarely comes back like in the soap operas. Most people are debilitated for the rest of their lives. In rare cases, they can come back and talk or maybe walk, but usually they are never the same.

The first research on closed-head injuries by French military surgeon Jean-Pierre Gama (1775-1861) involved putting jelly in a jar with wires and shaking it up to see how the wires (white matter) and jelly (grey matter) moved around. This was an early nineteenth century attempt to understand how our brain moved in our skull under fast impact. However, a jar of jelly certainly didn't tell us about the extensive glial reaction to the wound.

Most research on brain injury is an attempt to find out how to protect the neurons. Equations to determine the amount of force and speed the brain undergoes and amount of neuronal degeneration that results are studied thoroughly. The key to understanding how to help brain injuries might be in the astrocytes and how they repair the neuron. First, protection of remaining neurons immediately after injury would be essential. Then, the only way to stop subsequent secondary degeneration of neurons would be to influence astrocytes to become more robust and

beneficial by manipulating their growth and regenerative properties to repair areas of damage.

In the event of a gunshot wound to the head, astrocyte therapy might be the only avenue to regrow areas of the brain. It is known that astrocytes cause a scar to occur in the brain after an injury. Astrocyte scarring can be considered a good thing, like after injury to the muscle. The goal should be how to reconstruct the part of the brain lost to the destructive force that injured it.

In brain injury and stroke, astrocytes light up when the tissue is stained for GFAP (glial fibrillary acidic protein). Around the area affected, many spider-shaped astrocytes come to the call of duty. Since the 1970s, not long after GFAP was discovered, astrocytes have been known to proliferate when they are near an injured area. One interesting aspect of research is to look at whether two markers occur at the same time. For instance, researchers looked at GFAP to see if it was expressed in the same cells that were marked with thymidine, cells that are dividing to form new cells. This way, they could tell if astrocytes divided and compare them to neuron markers. Neurons do not divide. But researchers noticed that astrocytes proliferate in an attempt to replace the cells in this area and eventually create a scar.

However, this evidence did not satisfy researchers at the time to continue to study how to get astrocyte growth to protect the brain. At the time, in their blind lust for neurons, the researchers were not impressed and decided not to pursue that avenue, but instead looked for a way to create neurons. It is known that we can create neurons in a dish with embryonic stem cells, and researchers thought that implanting these cells in the brain would regrow neurons. This has produced little noteworthy results to date.

However, an attempt to understand why astrocytes would proliferate near destroyed brain tissue might bring us insight into how to help the brain survive and regrow. We now know that astrocytes are the adult stem cells that eventually lead to neurons in some areas and turnover to replace themselves in all areas. After injury, if it is possible to protect neurons initially, then harnessing innate astrocytic regenerative ability could lead to brain injury treatments that are effective.

It is still currently the belief that astrocyte scarring is an impediment to growth. Cajal would take cats, brutally lesion their brains, let the cat survive for a while longer, then take the brain out and analyze it. Cajal

noticed that neurons were not able to grow past a scar that the glia formed. His conclusion was not that glia are trying to save the brain, but that glia are somehow impediments to neuronal growth necessary to repair the brain. However, because his torturous slice through the cat brain was too destructive to replace, Cajal didn't realize that glia do beneficial services.

Placing neuronal stem cells in the brain does not help it grow past an astrocyte scar either. Somehow the astrocytes cause the neuroblasts not to grow into the area of wound. However, if one thinks about scarring on our skin, the clotting material does exactly that: It repairs the wound.

If you lose the area in your brain that contributes to speech, it is a bit like having a leg amputated. For humans, attempting to regrow a large swath of brain is as challenging as trying to regrow an arm or leg. Some invertebrate animals can do it, such as the starfish, earthworm, or the leech, but we cannot.

Astrocyte turnover contributes to our ever-changing information and thoughts in our brain; as the seat of our imagination and creativity, they are the quintessential cells that are responsible for repairing the damage that occurs in the brain. This constant turnover, likely increased in areas of injury, repairs small rifts that occur in the brain over time. However, a traumatic event like a gunshot wound or railroad spike that rips through the brain like a tornado can take some time to repair.

One of the things known about glial cells is that they respond to almost any insult, as shown in brains of alcoholics. Someone who drinks alcohol heavily, when their brain is autopsied, will have many GFAP-expressing cells. Eventually, like in Parkinson's disease and Alzheimer's disease, degeneration of the brain will occur in the brain of someone who abuses alcohol over many years in immense amounts. However, the glial reaction might be astrocytes trying to replace sacrificed members of their families in the war against the alcohol invasion.

After the astrocytes are disrupted, cognitive problems happen, and then the neuronal roads have nothing to maintain them and they will start to deteriorate. Alcohol attacks an area in the brain called the mammillary bodies, which are aptly named because of their resemblance to two breasts sitting on top of the brain stem. They seem to control function related to vision and cortical integration of information. When many of the cells have died off, severe alcoholics develop Korsakoff's syndrome, in which patients exhibit behaviors similar to Alzheimer's patients.

The same might happen with a brain injury; the astrocyte that reacts in areas that are injured could try to replace fellow astrocytes that have been destroyed because it is true that if astrocytes are healthy, neurons are healthy.

In a stroke, a clot in a blood vessel in the brain causes the lack of oxygen to get to cells surrounding the area of the clot. Astrocytes in the area die and other astrocytes outside the zone of oxygen depletion react trying to replace astrocytes in that area. But even in a stroke, where this is a known event, much of the research and response work centers around neuronal replacement stem cell therapy. Obviously, in the case of stroke or brain injury, it is helpful to protect the neurons as well. But for regrowth and replacement of cells that are more able to contribute to the overall recovery from injury or stroke, the focus should most definitely be on astrocytes.

One of the main tenants of injury research is Wallerian degeneration—as axons are stretched and destroyed, the far end of each axon degenerates away and the end nearest to the cell body sits there in a stump. The nerves that extend from the spinal cord out toward the muscles grow back at a snail's pace and will eventually extend back out after damage.

In the brain, the axons do not regrow. When axons are cut or sheared in diffuse axonal injury, they degenerate and the cell dies. Proteins that comprise the bulk of the machinery in the cell can accumulate in the stump closest to the brain cell. One of the main proteins that builds up is APP. APP, when cut in two, creates Amyloid Beta, the protein implicated in Alzheimer's Disease. This protein occurs in such massive amounts that if it isn't taken up by the glia, it forms plaques in the cell and is one of the main components transported down the axon in a healthy cell.

Brain injury has been linked to degenerative disease. The prevailing theory is that the insult or injury to the neurons somehow starts a process that over time evolves into Alzheimer's or Parkinson's. This is thought to be because brain injury causes reactive oxygen to be released and oxidative stress. Reactive oxygen is destructive to the cell. Also, extracellular calcium can enter the neuron and destroy the cell.

We know that brain injury causes oxidative stress, and astrocytes are the cells that counteract this stress. We also know that dead astrocytes leave a calcium mark afterwards. Reactive oxygen species float out of cells with nowhere to go, and calcium slithers around without any

purpose. This can be the result of dying astrocytes as well. Neurons have no way to cope with the reactive oxygen species and excess calcium if astrocytes are not present, and they subsequently die. Neurons die because astrocytes die.

If astrocytes cannot replace themselves fast enough and some die, then the reactive oxygen species will kill all the neurons in the area. Therefore, brain injury leading to neurodegenerative disease can be prevented if astrocytes are replenished. However, almost all the research on oxidative stress focuses entirely on neurons and how to save neurons from this process. Without astrocytes, the neurons are doomed. They have no reason to function. Similar to a broken conveyer belt at the factory assembly line after everyone has been laid off (you might be able to get the conveyor belt magically working), no one will be there to run it.

That is the difficulty with most studies on injury, stroke, and disease in the field at the moment. So much evidence has mounted for the importance and possible dominance of the astrocyte, but every study is undertaken with the idea that neurons should be the focus. It's like standing on your head to take a drink of water.

Brain injury research is messy business; the models to undertake the studies vary between a piston type machine that slams directly onto the brain of a rat or mouse after the skull plate has been removed to a huge anvil that slams onto a massive tube filled with saline, like a syringe that is the size of a barrel of a baseball bat. The experimenters can calibrate the machine to determine how much fluid they want to squirt out. They cut out the skull, drop the anvil, and water sloshes onto the brain, compressing it and causing injury. Both of these models were developed by the automobile industry in the 1970s to better understand what happens to its customers when they drive at 55 mph into a brick wall.

Both of these models produce open-head injury contusions. Closed head injury is achieved by dropping a brass weight onto a metal plate affixed to the top of the skull of the rat brain. These models have provided a variety of cellular information on how to protect axons in the brain.

Another model that looks at rotational forces in the closed head is to put the head of a large animal in a vice and shake it vigorously. Experiments of this type have been unofficially banned because of an incident where researchers were taped performing them on monkeys. Watching

this in action if you are not desensitized as the experimenter can lead to complete disgust. However, much of what we know now about the brain after injury, for better or worse, comes from these studies. With these messy models, research on injury is a slow process and compounded by lack of glial research as well.

The studies of cellular genesis have been the most interesting. Many reports have shown that glial cell division eventually results in new neurons in the brains of rats and mice that have been given a contusion injury. A study has yet to determine the amount of astrocyte replacement that occurs after injury in the brain.

Children and infants who experience more brain tumors and astrocyte growth than adults have better recovery from brain injury. If adults could experience similar regeneration, they might also recover better. They might not be able to acquire information from the past, have different personalities, and have to relearn everything they know, but they would have the ability to do so with astrocytes available.

The implications for controlling increased intrinsic cellular genesis is immense. If researchers could somehow determine the responsible mechanism that creates astrocytes to turn over in this manner, they could feasibly repair the brain.

At this point, the idea of recreating neurons with embryonic cells is the prevailing notion instead of trying to understand how to replace astrocytes or influence more constructive astrocyte growth. In the near future, as more studies on astrocytes reveal the nature of their purposes during an insult to the brain, researchers can hopefully bring to light cell-based beneficial treatments for patients.

References

Adams, J.H., D.I. Graham, L.S. Murray, and G. Scott. "Diffuse Axonal Injury Due to Nonmissile Head-Injury in Humans—an Analysis of 45 Cases." *Annals of Neurology*, 12: 557–563, 1982.

Adams, J.H., D. Doyle, I. Ford, T.A. Gennarelli, D.I. Graham, and D.R. McLellan. "Diffuse Axonal Injury in Head-Injury—Definition, Diagnosis, and Grading." *Histopathology*, 15: 45–59, 1989.

Blonstein, J.L. and Clarke, E. "The Medical Aspects of Amateur Boxing." *British Medical Journal.* 2: 1523–1525, 1954.

Borgens, R.B. *Restoring Function to the Injured Human Spinal Cord: Advances in Anatomy Embryology and Cell Biology*. NY: Springer, 2003.

Carey, M.E. "The Treatment of Wartime Brain Wounds: Traditional Versus Minimal Debridement." *Surgical Neurology*, 60: 112–119, 2003.

Duhaime, A.C., S.S. Margulies, S.R. Durham, M.M. O'Rourke, J.A. Golden, S. Marwaha, and R. Raghupathi. "Maturation-Dependent Response of the Piglet Brain to Scaled Cortical Impact." *Journal of Neurosurgery*, 93: 455–462, 2000.

Feinsod, M. "A Flask Full of Jelly: The First In Vitro Model of Concussive Head Injury—1830." *Neurosurgery*, 50: 386–391, 2002.

Gennarelli, T.A., L.E. Thibault, J.H. Adams, D.I. Graham, C.J. Thompson, and R.P. Marcincin. "Diffuse Axonal Injury and Traumatic Coma in the Primate." *Annals of Neurology*, 12: 564–574, 1982.

Haas, L.F. "Phineas Gage and the Science of Brain Localization." *Journal of Neurology, Neurosurgery, and Psychiatry*, 71: 761, 2001.

Hammon, W.M. "Analysis of 2187 Consecultive Penetrating Wounds of the Brain from Vietnam." *Journal of Neurosurgery*, 34: 127–131, 1971.

Hughes, J.T. "Hugh Cairns (1896-1952) and the mobile neurosurgical units of World War II. *Journal of Medical Biography*, 12: 18–24, 2004.

Latov, N., G. Nilaver, E.A. Zimmerman, W.G. Johnson, A.J. Silverman, R. Defendini, and L. Cote. "Fibrillary Astrocytes Proliferate in Response to Brain Injury—Study Combining Immunoperoxidase Technique for Glial Fibrillary Acidic Protein and Autoradiography of Tritiated-Thymidine." *Developmental Biology*, 72: 381–384, 1979.

Luria, A.R. *Restoration of Function After Brain Injury*. London: Pergamon Press, 1963.

Luria, A.R. *The Man with a Shattered World: The History of a Brain Wound*. Cambridge, MA: Harvard University Press, 1987.

Marmarou, A., M.A.A. Foda, W. Vandenbrink, J. Campbell, H. Kita, and K. Demetriadou. "A New Model of Diffuse Brain Injury in Rats: Pathophysiology and Biomechanics." *Journal of Neurosurgery*, 80: 291–300, 1994.

Rogers, L. "The History of Craniotomy." *Annals of Medical History*, 2: 495, 1930.

Stone, J.R., S.A. Walker, and J.T. Povlishock. "The Visualization of a New Class of Traumatically Injured Axons Through the Use of a Modified Method of Microwave Antigen Retrieval." *Acta Neuropathologica*, 97: 335–345, 1999.

Stritch, S.J. "Shearing of Nerve Fibers as a Cause of Brain Damage Due to Head Injury." *The Lancet*, 2: 443–448, 1961.

Zoroya, G. "Key Iraq Wound: Brain Trauma." *USA Today*, March 4, 2005.

14

The seething breeding glioma

Sustaining adequate astrocyte turnover leads to a healthy brain. If astrocytes cannot replace themselves fast enough, a wasteland of ineffective cellular communication occurs and reveals itself in the form of neurodegenerative disease. This wasteland cannot provide an adequate level of consciousness when handling the environmental cues sent to it by the neurons. Astrocytes' calcium puffs spur the imagination sparkling in our brains. Extra concentration, learning, and thinking might create full calcium waves and spawn additional astrocyte growth. More cells contribute to the ability to handle more complex ideas and process the environment on a higher level. More astrocytes also help a person create more new ideas, like a muscle that can lift more weights because it has been used so frequently.

However, when a trigger causes excessive astrocyte growth—unchecked and robust—a brain tumor results. Like a biblical scourge of pestilent insects, the astrocytes end up destroying everything in their paths. Cells in our brain are asexual like amoebas that breed with themselves. They need energy and nourishment and care for nothing else. The insidious cells multiply like a pile of gremlins tossed in Lake Huron.

Tumors on our body usually originate from cells that are not static, but work to produce fluid or constantly regenerate while dealing with the environment. For instance, breast cancer and testicular cancer arise from cells that produce milk and sperm. Ovarian cancer arises from an organ that produces eggs. Prostate cancer is so prevalent that it is believed that it will occur in any man if he lives long enough. The prostate is an incredibly active gland creating massive amounts of seminal fluid. Two areas that have to regenerate cells to handle the environment most notably are the colon and the lung. High incidence of malignant cancer can form in these two tissues. In the lung, the dirty air

means that constant turnover of cells is needed because of the bombardment they receive from dirt and debris. Similarly, cancer originating in the brain comes from two main types of cells: cells producing fluid and cells that regularly turn over.

About 60 to 70 percent of brain tumors are of astrocyte origin. The other 30 to 40 percent come from the meninges, the cells that produce the ventricular fluid the brain is encased in, the same ventricular fluid used by astrocytes to divide during development and into adulthood. The cells in the meninges turn cancerous because they work like a prostate. Astrocytes produce tumors because they constantly divide and are more likely to have a glitch that would result in the onset of cancer. A tumor comprised of neurons is as rare as being hit by a meteor. The miniscule amount of neuronal-based tumors mainly occurs in the spine and on sensory ends like in the ear. When it happens, there are also glial cells present in the destructive mass. Ependymal cells lining the blood vessels and ventricles form some tumors, but astrocytes are also frequently present in these tumors. Similar to oligodendroglioma, where oligodendrocytes go rabid, astrocytes are frequently mixed in. Tumors in the brain are called gliomas for this reason.

The main malignant brain tumor is called the glioblastoma multiforme. This tumor is a wildly dividing astrocyte-comprised mass that is incredibly destructive. The most egregious aspect to the neuronal focus in the last 100 years has been the complete lack of understanding of the cause of brain tumors. Like all cancer, brain tumors remain incomprehensible. Cancer is a nasty disease, and there is absolutely no cure, but at least in other cancers, the nature of the cell that has morphed into a carcinoma is clear. This was not the case in the brain until recently.

In the early 1980s, glial fibrillary acidic protein (GFAP), the marker for astrocytes, was used in a set of patients with tumors. It was discovered that GFAP labeling existed in glioblastoma multiforme large cells and other tumors of the brain. During injury and disease, increased expression of this protein is noticed. Although the reasons why this protein is expressed are not certain, it might provide some function when astrocytes attempt to divide and proliferate. Glioblastoma multiforme was previously believed to be comprised of embryonic neoplasms—a fancy way of referring to cells that stay with us from the womb, an incredibly bizarre support of Cajal's idea that the brain stopped dividing after we reach adulthood.

It wasn't until the World Health Organization's conference to classify tumors in 1993 that it was generally accepted that astrocytes were likely the main cell that morphed into the large cells in the glioblastoma multiforme tumors. It is known that astrocytes are the main components in these malignant tumors, as well as the second most prevalent tumor, the astrocytoma.

Astrocytomas occur mainly in the cortex. Astrocytes comprise the bulk of tumors in other parts of the brain as well, but research has yet to discover what sets off the transformation process from normal, healthy, pondering astrocyte to rabid, insane, seething, breeding astrocyte.

Without knowing the reason astrocytes become cancerous in the brain, a limited amount of therapy is available. The first treatment is to just cut it out. For instance, Ted Kennedy had a tumor and they just cut it out. If the surgeon is able to get the entire tumor out of the brain, the patient is able to survive for years afterwards. The cells need to be eliminated or they will continue to grow and multiply in the brain. Dracula would have better temperament in a blood bank than a cancerous astrocyte does in your brain.

Some evidence exists that one has a higher chance of developing a glioma if there has been previous instance of brain cancer in your family. However, as far back as the 1950s, a link in families has been discarded as nonexistent. No molecular genetic link has been adequately described, and studies claiming an increase of instances of brain cancer in families might be attributed to the fact that people in the same family are raised in the same environment, and therefore an environmental cause might be the culprit.

One of the creepiest things that occurs when astrocytes are cancerous is angiogenesis, the increase in formation of blood vessels so they can supply themselves with nourishment. Like a guerilla army setting up shop in your skull, the glial cells wrap themselves around warped, newly formed blood vessels and consume all the energy and oxygen meant to keep your brain healthy. The two most common forms of brain tumors—glioblastomas and astrocytomas—have interesting times during the lifespans when their incidence is the highest. Astrocytomas peak in childhood, and the incidence stays steady for the rest of the lifetime through adulthood. Glioblastomas occur at the same time in the lifespan as heart attacks. They begin to become a problem when people turn 30 years old and then the incidence rate increases steadily throughout their life.

The relative paltry research on brain cancer and the cause, combined with a complete focus on neurons in much of the field of brain research, has led to a complete lack of understanding of the disease. Little funding is given to study brain cancer, with more effort and funding put into understanding degenerative diseases. To understand degenerative diseases, one must understand why cells like astrocytes can suddenly freak out and start growing like Jack's beanstalk.

In the last 20 years, the protein O6-methylguanine-DNA methyltransferase, or MGMT, was discovered to perform the function of gene repair. Gene repair enables cells to be more resistant to death and better able to divide. In the late 1980s, it was shown to exist in the brain and is now known to be expressed in astrocytes and completely absent in neurons.

One of the problems with glioblastoma multiforme is its resistance to chemotherapy and radiotherapy. However, when researchers noticed when the MGMT gene was silenced, they were able to effectively treat the tumor and get much better long-term outcomes in patients.

MGMT seems to be expressed in normal astrocytes and is highly expressed in cancerous astrocytes. The protein repairs the DNA as the cells rapidly divide. With this protein actively maintaining the cells' capabilities to continue to divide, treatments are fated to pretend.

Consciousness and cognition can be severely disrupted by a brain tumor. Although the increase in astrocytes—the pondering imaginative thinking cell in the brain—might be beneficial in the case of healthy cells, after the cells turn into little gremlins, they do not function as a cohesive calcium wave unit. They also push aside the neural roads they need to use to transfer information long distances for action, destroying and mashing everything in their wake. If a brain tumor could increase our intelligence through the increase in astrocytes, everyone with a tumor would be walking around like John Travolta's character in the movie *Phenomenon*.

Cognitive problems in patients with brain tumors differ based on where their tumors reside. A tumor can occur almost anywhere in the brain. An obvious place is the walls of the lateral ventricles where dividing astrocytes can morph and invade the cortex. Tumors in this area can strain the optic nerve and cause visual problems, including blindness. Headaches and seizures are also common problems that people with tumors can experience.

To determine the location of a tumor, doctors use imaging equipment to take pictures to pinpoint the location before performing the tricky task of removing it from the slop of the brain, the teeming mass that is responsible for their patients' thoughts and dreams. Anything can happen afterwards—personality changes, a vegetative state, or death. The most dreaded area is called Broca's area, which is the left temporal cortex where the speech area resides. Tumors in the temporal cortex look a like a fist sitting in the side of the brain. For humans, speech is the most important function that we possess. Without speech, we are unable to communicate with other people or intelligently pass information to other people. Damage to this area also disrupts nonverbal communication; a hearing-impaired person who communicates through sign language would be impaired and unable to communicate as well.

The other concern that frightens doctors is if the medulla is under strain. If the tumor is a medullablastoma or the tumor disrupts the medulla—the area that is responsible for breathing and other involuntary functions we need to live—it is difficult to perform surgery. The surgery becomes a life-or-death situation. Sometimes, the tumor can reach out like a spider, almost looking like a giant astrocyte. In this case, it is difficult to remove the malignant cells and the tumor can make a comeback. Some tumors in the base of the brain starting in the area of the substantia nigra are responsible for Parkinson's Disease and can create a butterfly pattern in the brain, with wings reaching up into each hemisphere.

Doctors publish short case histories when they encounter something interesting or different. One case was the result of a patient who had been diagnosed with Parkinson's Disease for 14 years. As his symptoms began to increase, he saw little green and orange monkeys jumping across the room. The patient then reported seeing men in green uniforms marching around, on top of dreams that he was fighting *Braveheart*-type bloody battles and being tortured by aliens.

After an MRI was taken, it showed that the poor patient didn't have Parkinson's Disease at all, but a massive butterfly tumor covering much of his brain (see Figure 14.1). Because it is known that Parkinson's Disease can lead to some hallucinations in patients, the doctors had difficultly pinpointing the problem because the patient's hallucinations were much more aggressive than someone with the disease. For a time, they had diagnosed him as being psychotic.

Reprinted from *The Lancet*, Vol. 370, Issue 9598, Guptha, S.H., Han, T., Arafat, Q., and Deyo, O. "Orange and Green Monkeys Jumping Around the Room," p. 1588, Copyright (2007), with permission from Elsevier.

FIGURE 14.1   MRI of butterfly tumor spreading in the brain of a patient originally diagnosed with Parkinson's Disease.

One of the most curious cases occurred in a housewife in Innsbruck, Austria. She had a tumor in her left parietal cortex. After removal, researchers noticed she had difficulty calculating numbers. She could memorize a math problem, but couldn't understand how to multiply or divide. This is the same area in which Einstein had excess glia. However, in the woman's case, she didn't become a math genius; she suffered the inability to think on a higher mathematical level. Sadly, researchers do not know if she had deficits before the surgery. The problem in mathematical conceptualization instead is most definitely the result of taking out an area of the brain responsible.

In another patient, the tumor caused him to experience sensations of déjà vu and of watching a bright movie, with images moving in front of a bright light, like dancing figures before a hatch opening in an illuminated spaceship at night. After surgery, the patient experienced the overwhelming sensation of someone nearby looming over his shoulder. When

the patient was lying in bed, it felt like someone was in bed with him (not such a bad thing, if it is Natalie Portman or Christina Ricci, but very troubling if it is someone who isn't there). This sensation can best be described as something akin to when you are working late at night and it feels like there is a ghost in the room. The tumor was in the area near the amygdala in the base of the brain. People have claimed this feeling when receiving an electrical stimulus to the amygdala, the area responsible for emotional modulation.

Other strange cognitive problems that arise warp visual images. Patients experience tracking of images like they have taken hallucinogens, but the images still leave an after-print of an object immediately in the vicinity, similar to a bird flying through the air that passes by and seems to leave a cartoon afterimage.

In another case, a patient with a tumor in the left temporal lobe near Broca's area, the valuable area for speech, couldn't remember names and dates. He had absolutely no problem cognitively in any other aspect of his thinking. He just simply couldn't remember his telephone number, address, and dates—random important numbers that had been etched in his brain.

In another wild sensation with astrocytomas in the cortex, one of the phenomena occurs with tumors in the right cortex. The result is the feeling of multiple selves in the room with you, called polyopic heautoscopy. Patients think more of them are walking around the room, as though they have been cloned. There might be five of them, as if someone had thrown a rock against a mirror and the other bodies exploded out of it and were just hanging around. The experience isn't like multiple separate personalities, but actually the belief that several people, all you, are existing simultaneously in the same space and time as you.

All these cases point to possible evidence for astrocytes functioning in warped behavior as the tumor grows. At a certain point, they become so destructive that they eliminate functioning in the area they have invaded. However, when it is initially beginning, astrocytes can give the feeling of multiple selves or déjà vu, possible evidence for astrocytes as the seat of thinking and information in the brain. In the problem of a tumor in Broca's area that destroys a person's communication ability, it would be interesting to know what exactly the patient experienced. However, they would be unable to perform that unique human trait of complex verbal communication. In mice and rats, naturally occurring glioblastomas do not seem to

occur; astrocytomas are the most prominent tumors. In dogs, tumors similar to those found in humans form as they age. In dogs, astrocytomas are the most prominent, oligodendrogliomas the second most prominent, and glioblastomas, the most common in humans, are the third most common.

Incidence of brain tumors has also been reported in horses, cows, sheep, goats, and pigs. The occurrences in animals are extremely low; however, these animals do not usually live out their entire lifespans and might not have the opportunity to develop brain cancer. The prevalence of tumors in dogs was also much higher than what was seen in cats. Boxers, Boston terriers, and bulldogs were the breeds with the highest incidence of brain tumor development, indicating a genetic factor at work at least in dogs.

In humans, it is telling that tumors comprised of astrocytes occur separate from degenerative diseases of the brain. Doctors will not see them both in the brain at the same time except in cases of multiple sclerosis. Multiple sclerosis is unique compared to other diseases of the brain. In multiple sclerosis, it seems that the immune system from outside the brain attacks the myelin on neuronal axons. Astrocytomas and glioblastomas can occur in these patients; it is possible multiple sclerosis triggers the astrocyte response of growth. This growth might be a glitch in the astrocyte's eager response to save its degenerating neuronal roads by regenerating itself, which is like the massive effort to repair a bridge after it collapses.

It is possible that astrocytes have the capability to go one direction or the other, either as rabid dividing gremlins, causing cancer or dying off without replacement and causing an astrocytic wasteland, which results in degenerative disease. The normal turnover of astrocytes in the brain is a simple and natural process (see Figure 14.2). Like cells in the lung, the astrocytes deal with our environment by monitoring the blood flow to the brain and processing information brought in by the neurons from the senses.

When the trigger sends astrocytes to insanely divide, they become invasive and concerned with one thing: taking all the energy in the vicinity to facilitate more growth. They push on to other areas of the brain, which causes the cells to rupture and die. That's the drawback of living on the planet earth where everything is intertwined with growth. Plants grow and are eaten by animals that grow and are eaten by animals that grow and die and are used by plants that grow. In growth, sometimes there's too much and sometimes there's too little.

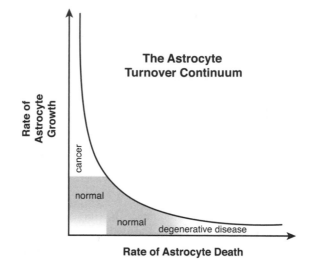

FIGURE 14.2   The astrocyte continuum curve—a balance of astrocyte death and growth—is required for a normal, healthy human brain.

As we work our brains to create more beneficial astrocytes to counteract those that are lost as we age and to keep our mind young, sometimes the brain short-circuits and cells become cancerous. However, neurons rarely turn cancerous. Neurons are simply the glue that enable astrocyte communication. Astrocytes constantly change, grow, and move. Subordinate neurons exist because of astrocytes. Astrocytes contain our thoughts and reasons for existence. The motivation of astrocytes is our motivation. Our bodies are vessels to support their existence; the body has evolved to surround these cells that are responsible for growth and have existed since the dawn of life.

References

Brugger, P., O. Blanke, M. Regard, D.T. Bradford, and T. Landis. "Polyopic Heautoscopy: Case Report and Review of the Literature." *Cortex*, 42: 666–674, 2006.

Delazer, M. and T. Benke. "Arithmetic Facts Without Meaning." *Cortex*, 33: 697–710, 1997.

Folkman, J. "Angiogenesis in Cancer, Vascular, Rheumatoid and Other Disease." *Nature Medicine*, 1: 27–31, 1995.

Gupta, S.H., T. Han, Q. Arafat, and O. Deyo. "Orange and Green Monkeys Jumping Around the Room." *Lancet*, 370: 1588, 2007.

Hegi, M.E., A. Diserens, T. Gorlia, M. Hamou, N. de Tribolet, M. Weller, J.M. Kros, J.A. Hainfellner, W. Mason, L. Mariani, J.E.C. Bromberg, P. Hau, R.O. Mirimanoff, J.G. Cairncross, R.C. Janzer, and R. Stupp. "MGMT Gene Silencing and Benefit from Temozolomide in Glioblastoma." *New England Journal of Medicine*, 352: 997–1003, 2005.

Kleihues, P., P.C. Burger, and B.W. Scheithauer. *Histological Typing of Tumors of the Central Nervous System.* World Health Organization International Classification of Tumors. Berlin: Springer, 1993.

Nakasu, S., T. Fukami, K. Baba, and M. Matsuda. "Immunohistochemical Study for O6-Methylguanine-DNA Methyltransferase in the Nonneoplastic and Neoplastic Components of Gliomas." *Journal of Neurooncology*, 70: 333–340, 2004.

Ohgaki, H. and P. Kleihues. "Epidemiology and Etiology of Gliomas." *Acta Neuropathologica*, 109: 93–108, 2005.

Schiffer, D. *Brain Tumors: Pathology and Its Biological Correlates.* Berlin: Springer-Verlag, 1993.

Solleveld, H.A., D.D. Bigner, D.R. Averill, S.H. Bigner, G.A. Boorman, P.C. Burger, Y. Gillespie, G.B. Hubbard, O.D. Laerum, R.D. McComb, J.T. McGrath, K.T. Morgan, A. Peters, L.J. Rubinstein, B.S. Schoenberg, S.C. Schold, J.A. Swenberg, M.B. Thompson, M. Vandevelde, and S.A. Vinores. "Brain Tumors in Man and Animals: Report of a Workshop." *Environmental Health Perspectives*, 68: 155–173, 1986.

Tascos, N.A., J. Parr, and N.K. Gonatas. "Immunocytochemical Study of the Glial Fibrillary Acidic Protein in Human Neoplasms of the Central Nervous System." *Human Pathology*, 13: 454–458, 1982.

15

Cities and highways revisited

As researchers scour the highways in the land that is our brain, they examine all the potholes and roadside trash as if it exhibits significant meaning. The baked and deteriorating pavement for the transport of electrical signals long distances was believed to contain all the information in the brain. Now, as researchers turn their microscopes and equipment to the astrocytes, the cities in this land, they are beginning to realize where the information in our brain lies and how it is created.

It has been more than 100 years since Cajal gave Golgi a beating in Stockholm. However, just because Cajal beat Golgi doesn't mean he's right. When Mike Tyson slaughtered Spinks and his ridiculous socks 20 years ago in 91 seconds, it didn't mean Tyson had triumphed viscerally or that his boxing philosophy was some tenant of truth—it just meant he was the strongest. In the mid-1980s, glia was becoming understood to be much more important than Cajal's brother Pedro thought.

However, at that moment in 1906, the year the forward pass was invented, a year after Einstein's miracle year, the same year Sherrington coined the synapse, Cajal was strongest. He was a more dedicated scientist than Golgi at the time and displayed it with ironclad intelligence. Although he knew glia might have an important function, he saved his reputation for future generations by hanging his lame idea related to glia on to his poor brother Pedro—a despicable act by a controlling man. Golgi's notion of a syncytium was completely obliterated and the Neuron Doctrine became the rule and the law. One didn't question it unless they wanted to commit scientific suicide.

So astrocytes are getting their day in the sun now. Hopefully, researchers will find ways to treat diseases with the newfound renaissance in the world of brain science. The most abundant cell in the brain is no longer just putty, glue, or support; it is an active cell that contributes

to our thoughts. It is no wonder no cures exist for brain diseases when the most abundant cell in the brain was completely neglected for so long.

The neuron-glial dichotomy is like the chicken and the egg. What came first? It's hard to know if you study only the egg. Maybe 100 years from now, when a person visits the neurologist or walks by the neuroscience department, she will ask why it is called neuroscience when our thought has been proven to reside in our astrocytes. The use of "neuro" will be a nice antiquated term and an interesting story, such as why Iceland is called Iceland and Greenland is called Greenland.

Besides the obvious implications in disease treatment, as researchers delve more into the astrocyte, another enormous implication is the understanding of consciousness, creativity, and imagination. The astrocyte is more abundant in the human cortex than in lower animals, and the astrocyte turnover in lower animals is known to occur in places such as the olfactory bulb.

The turnover of astrocytes might be the quintessential cornerstone for our human information storage. As the mouse needs to understand its environment through its nose, maybe humans have evolved to process information from all senses on a higher level and the astrocyte turnover in the cortex is an integral part of this processing. This might be similar to how the shark's skin has evolved to increase its swimming speed, to make it a better killing machine as it slices through the ocean searching for a meal. What makes humans special is the turnover of astrocytes, the best on the planet evolutionarily for the understanding of the environment.

Human social behavior evolves when we break the barrier of time and understand the calcium flow in our astrocytes. Next time you come up with an idea or look at a piece of art, hear a good song, watch a fantastic movie or cartoon, think about where it burgeoned. A calcium puff sparked a wave through astrocytes in an area that possesses information corresponding to the framework of the creative idea. As you ponder what you imagine, more calcium waves flow, creating more astrocyte growth. When you decide to act on it, the astrocytes correspond with adjacent neurons and whoosh—off it goes down to your muscles.

The neuron web, like the Internet, zooms information electrically back and forth; however, information is stored in computers by people. Although information in the brain is sent quickly along neurons, the information is stored and controlled by the astrocytes.

Calcium is one of the most volatile ions on the planet. It is sequestered in compartments in astrocytes. The astrocytes receive information from the senses through the neurons and the waves of calcium ions flow from astrocyte to astrocyte. The calcium puff is the beginning of creativity, and the man behind the computer talks fluidly with other people like the calcium waves in the astrocytes, and information is sent again down the Internet.

Who knows? The root of thought might be in our electrons or protons or quarks or gluons. However, the cell needed to understand whether this is true is in the astrocytes.

We assume what we know is true, but how we know it might prove false. For instance, the notion started by Cajal that solidified synapses are how we learn might have little to do with the beginnings of information processing. When astrocytes determine the amount of synapses, the synapse number no longer becomes important except as a consequence of astrocyte activity. The fact that the synapse number is controlled by astrocytes means to study the synapse number without astrocytes is like studying soldiers in a war without trying to understand the motives of the generals and commanders.

Synapses are just exits off the neural freeway. Neuronal action is like sex with no foreplay. It alone involves reflex and base thought—just taking in sensory information without processing. Glia are the pondering cell—the cities where the information resides. The rumination over the senses and effective action gets done when glia tell the neurons what to do.

The secret murmurings in the back of labs about the pointlessness of neuronal focus have been coming out in the last 20 years in a few brave papers by fearless scientists. The repression lasted for so long because of the nature of the Neuron Doctrine. It had infiltrated every facet of brain science. Any class on the subject completely discounted the most abundant cell in our brain by saying that their role is "to support neurons." Because of the money it takes to run a lab, research on glia became impossible. Funding wasn't typically given out for glial projects, so there was no incentive to spend a large amount of time applying for a grant to study glia when it was obviously going to be rejected. Glia was seen as a waste of time.

The prevailing thought was that if the people in charge of funding want to hear about neurons, we'll give them neurons. Following the

latest trend in the neuron black hole could reward a researcher with a hefty grant to lure them down the path of Cajal servitude. Cajal ruled his world with a clenched fist long after he died.

Thankfully, this is changing and the Cajal grip is loosening. The secret that they won't tell you in biology class is that at most brain scientists agree that glia are equal or more important than the neuron. Science can be a religion in certain aspects and all things believed today can turn out of favor tomorrow. There are an infinite number of avenues to pursue, shrouds to lift, and worlds to discover. Discovery is fun, good, and fantastic; however, no matter what we believe today, always somewhere below lies the truth.

It is good to be cautious about what is absolute truth. Science constantly changes as the equipment changes. It was difficult to study glia with the techniques available during the time of Cajal. It was also difficult to study neurons. However, with the discovery of electricity and the electrical body, more could be inferred.

It is astonishing that so much has been placed on the neuron. It is now blatant this focus has resulted in stunted knowledge of many aspects of human thinking and cures for human diseases. Because when something is discovered, it always leads to the next thing to be discovered. And that next thing might negate much of what preceded it. As brain science exists now, the dominance of the neuron is under review, and we can hope as the community focuses on astrocytes that it will be more fruitful in the understanding of brain disease and injury.

So enjoy the waves, but watch out for the sharks.

Acknowledgments

This book materialized from four places. The first one was a lecture by Dr. Arturo Alvarez-Buylla for Dr. Paul Collodi's neuroscience seminar at Purdue University in the Fall of 2002. It opened all of our eyes.

Then, after sharing glial cell research ideas and lamenting the impossibility of glial cell research funding with fellow graduate student Peter Cormie over beers at Harry's Chocolate shop on a random Tuesday afternoon while trying to avoid lab work, and more specifically the torture of rats, Pete said something when we were walking out of the bar after we had about five Guinness while listening to the entire Appetite for Destruction CD on the jukebox, "What if glial cells hold all the information in the brain?" And we both stopped in our tracks.

In the Spring of 2004, I was in the Las Vegas airport during the NCAA tournament. I was upset that the DePaul game went over, when I came across the *Scientific American* article "The Other Half of the Brain," written by R. Douglas Fields about Einstein's brain and glial cells. The article blew me away not just because of the subject but because of the way it was presented.

Lastly, while gathering information for this book, I noticed a recently published little green book called *Glial Neurobiology: A Textbook*, which is a fantastic resource by Alexei Verkhratsky and Arthur Butt. In the preface, they state, "In a way, the binary coded electrical communication within neural networks may be considered as highly specialized for rapid conveyance of information, whereas astroglial cells may represent the true substance for information processing, integration, and storage." If you are interested in learning more about the glial cell, this book is the place to start.

First, I'd like to thank my wife, Lisa, who has been part of this from the beginning. It's been fueled by chicken cutlets.

My parents, and especially my brother Alex, for checking out all the books at the University of Iowa. It's his passion.

I would also like to thank my editor Amanda Moran. She is fantastic to work with and has been incredible throughout the whole process.

Thanks to my graduate advisor, Dr. Richard Ben Borgens, a wonderful combination of Mark Twain and Teddy Roosevelt and the perfect mentor. Dr. Borgens is someone who understands the art of science. His enthusiasm is unmatched. If it weren't for him, I'd be out in a field somewhere left for dead.

I also want to thank Dr. Thomas Klopstock and Dr. Andreas Bender, for bringing me to Munich to work on fascinating projects, and suffering through times when my mind is out to lunch.

And special thanks to Jodie Rhodes, who was the reason this book materialized.

About the Author

Andrew Koob is currently researching brain disease at the University of Munich, Germany, where he continues to trumpet subversive glial theories. Previously, he has worked as a postdoctoral research fellow in pediatric neurosurgery at Dartmouth College and was a postdoctoral fellow for research in Parkinson's Disease at the University of California, San Diego.

Index

W-X-Y-Z

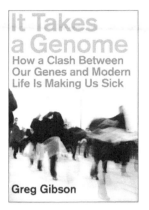

Greg Gibson

FT Press

It Takes a Genome: How a Clash Between Our Genes and Modern Life Is Making Us Sick

Greg Gibson

013713746X / 9780137137466
Available now

Read the following excerpt from
It Takes a Genome...

Human beings have astonishing genetic vulnerabilities. More than half of us will die from complex diseases that trace directly to those vulnerabilities, and the modern world we've created places us at unprecedented risk from them. In *It Takes a Genome*, Greg Gibson posits a revolutionary new hypothesis: Our genome is out of equilibrium, both with itself and its environment. Simply put, our genes aren't coping well with modern culture. Our bodies were never designed to subsist on fat and sugary foods; our immune systems weren't designed for today's clean, bland environments; our minds weren't designed to process hard-edged, artificial electronic inputs from dawn 'til midnight. And *that's* why so many of us suffer from chronic diseases that barely touched our ancestors.

Gibson begins by revealing the stunningly complex ways in which multiple genes cooperate and interact to shape our bodies and influence our behaviors. Then, drawing on the very latest science, he explains the genetic "mismatches" that increasingly lead to cancer, diabetes, inflammatory and infectious diseases, AIDS, depression, and senility. He concludes with a look at the probable genetic variations in human psychology, sharing the evidence that traits like introversion and agreeableness are grounded in equally complex genetic interactions.

It Takes a Genome demolishes yesterday's stale debates over "nature versus nurture," introducing a new view that is far more intriguing and far closer to the truth.

- See how broken genes cause cancer
  Meet the body's "genetic repairmen"—and understand what happens when they fail
- The growing price of the modern lifestyle
  Why one-third of all Westerners have obesity, Type 2 diabetes, or other signs of "metabolic syndrome"
- The Alzheimer's generation
  Why some of us are predisposed to dementia
- What's really normal: the deepest lessons of the human genome
  The remarkable diversity of physical and emotional "normality"

The adolescent genome

genetic imperfection   Disease is a normal and inevitable part of life
that arises from the way that organisms are put together.

unselfish genes   The way that different flavors (*alleles*) of thousands
of genes work together establishes how an organism looks or behaves,
or how healthy it is.

how genes work and why they come in different flavors
We all differ from one another at millions of places in the genome.

three reasons why genes might make us sick   Rare alleles that
have a large impact, common alleles that have a moderate one, or
hundreds of alleles with very small effects can all contribute.

a unified theory of complex disease   The combination of rapid
human evolution and recent cultural change has pushed us out of a
genetic comfort zone, predisposing many more people to disease.

the human genome project   Public and private efforts have jointly
produced a complete sequence of the human genome that lays the
foundation for a century of medical research to come.

genomewide association   The scalpel that will be used to isolate
most of the major disease susceptibility alleles for complex disease of
the next few decades.

genetic imperfection

Of all the paradoxes in the world, surely one of the most absurd is that the very same genome that gives us life inevitably also takes it away. Even when they aren't killing us, our genes are generally making existence more difficult than seems absolutely necessary. Very few people escape this world having avoided a bout with cancer or diabetes or asthma or depression, and those who do often end up too senile to remember much of the journey anyway. What good reason could there possibly be for so much suffering and disease?

Maybe there is no good reason, other than that genetic disease is an unavoidable byproduct of the way organisms are assembled; **disease arises because humans, like all other species on the planet, are an unfinished symphony. Perhaps we are even more unfinished than most, thoroughly out of equilibrium with the modern world, and even a little bit uncomfortable in our own skin.** In short, we possess an adolescent genome.

This notion may seem counterintuitive, because we are so conditioned to think in terms of perfection. A simplistic way to think about biology is to imagine that every species is perfectly suited to whatever ecological niche it occupies. Its genome has evolved to ensure that each individual is made to be as close as possible to the optimum shape and set of functions that a perfect member of the species would have. Adaptation to a dragonfly is having exquisitely refined lace wings, to an orchid it is pitching the lips of its pouting petals at just the most attractive angle, and to a human it is whatever it takes to live a long and comfortable life. Maybe no one individual is ever truly cast as the ideal that defines the species, but all approximate the optimum.

If an individual doesn't quite define perfection, it is either because optimality actually comes in a variety of shapes and sizes, or because forces are conspiring against the person. Debating whether humanity is more closely realized in the form of Colin Powell or Tiger Woods, Jennifer Lopez or Hillary Clinton, we would no doubt agree to disagree on what attributes are desirable in a person. We would, however, likely find common ground when it comes to health, concluding that some not-so-optimal types of genes floating around make us hypersensitive to pollen, push us to eat too much, or make us prone to mental illness. So the question is, why are such bad influences tolerated in the gene pool?

As the book unfolds, we will look closely at six different types of disease, each given its own chapter. It is first necessary to lay the foundation, so I have three goals in this opening chapter: first, to disavow you of any sense that there is such a thing as a "disease gene;" second, to lay out the general theory of complex disease that I enunciate as the book unfolds; and third, to explain how contemporary geneticists go about finding the genes that influence susceptibility to illness.

unselfish genes

Telling someone that she has the gene for Parkinson's or the gene for restless leg syndrome is a bit like telling her that her house has termites or sits on a toxic dump. It implies that her misfortune is that she has something that most people don't have, and further that all would be well if only she could get rid of the termites or toxins.

Genes are not like that, though. They are not things that some people have, and others do not. Approximately 23,000 genes are in the human genome, and all of us have pretty much the same number, give or take a few dozen. What we actually have are different flavors of genes. The technical term for a gene flavor is *allele*, pronounced *ah-lee-el*: Whenever you read the word "allele," think of chocolate and vanilla ice cream. Alleles are different versions of the same gene, just with different spelling and slightly different function.

In fact, in many cases, when a gene is associated with a disease it is because the gene is in some way broken or missing. Just getting rid of the gene would not help. A better house analogy than termites and toxins might be damp foundations, or cheap window frames. The house is basically the same as everyone else's, but problems arise because it just wasn't built as well as it should have been. Generally in such cases, many other things also are likely to go wrong and in this sense, too, the analogy with complex disease is improved.

Similarly, it seems that almost daily we read proclamations that scientists have discovered the gene for stroke or the gene for homosexuality. In almost every case, what they really mean is that the scientists have discovered a particular variant of a gene that slightly increases the likelihood that some people will suffer strokes or prefer their own sex. Sometimes the headlines replace "the" with "a," which is definitely better but still conveys the impression that the purpose of such

genes is to cause the disease or trait. Actually, the genes universally promote what we colloquially refer to as normality. They come in different alleles, and under some conditions particular alleles promote disease, or conditions we choose to label abnormal.

Contemporary genetic research is focused on finding these alleles and is as much about basic understanding of what they do as it is about finding cures for specific diseases. This is because there is little prospect of finding new cures for cancer until we understand why tumor cells grow out of control in the first place, and the next drugs for treatment of depression won't arrive until we appreciate what is wrong deep inside the brains of the chronically sad. This makes sense if you consider that most of us would prefer that our automobile mechanic understand how the engine works, rather than just try the same old fixes he's always used in the past.

The advantage that a mechanic has is that humans made cars, so we know not just what every part does but also what its purpose is and how it interacts with all the other parts. Biomedical researchers now have a pretty complete parts list and a fair idea of where each part goes, but there is still much to be learned before we know what all the parts do and how they fit together to make a healthy person.

Much genetic research involves pulling apart and putting back together model organisms that we can manipulate, like mice and rats and zebrafish, and even flies and nematodes. Increasingly the tools are at hand to do it with humans directly—at least, the pulling apart bit. Also, for just about every gene, somewhere in the world there is a person with an allele that does not work, and many thousands of these are responsible for rare syndromes. They are teaching us a lot about how things function, but for the most part don't explain the common diseases that afflict us all.

To this end, a parallel mode of genetic analysis is much less familiar to most people and yet influences all of our lives on a daily basis to a much greater extent than the genetics that we learn in school. Variously referred to as *quantitative genetics*, or by phrases such as *complex disease*, *multifactorial trait*, or *polygenic disorder*, it is the study of how common variants in many genes interact with one another and with the environment to produce the biological variation that surrounds us. Genes are fundamentally interactive entities, working together, adjusting to the

environment around them, molding organisms but not determining their destiny. For anything the least bit complicated, it truly takes a genome.

Most of the differences between species are of this type, as are the attributes that make us unique, from body shape and facial features to metabolism and even aspects of temperament. So too are the diseases that touch every one of us directly or indirectly as they afflict friends and family: cancer, diabetes, cardiovascular disease, asthma, and depression. The language associated with quantitative genetics switches from the imagery of control, determination, and causation, terms popularly associated with genetics, to the less strident tones of susceptibility, influence, and contribution. This book is predominately about the genetics of complexity.

Perhaps another analogy might make the distinction clearer. All of us are probably painfully aware of the impact that one individual can have on a business. If the CEO, or CFO, or CSO, or Director of IT, or head housekeeper for that matter, stops working or starts making bad decisions, the company can deteriorate rapidly. Yet it is the more subtle failings or distractions of multiple employees that most often disturb the health of the company even in good times. Two co-workers are going through a divorce, a supervisor is having an affair, the junior VP for marketing is caring for her ailing mother, and one of the bookkeepers has repetitive strain injury. Nothing is particularly unusual about any of these circumstances, and each of them is almost to be expected in even a moderate-sized group of people. For the most part organizations can and do deal with them, but mix them together in certain combinations and pretty soon potential dissipates, opportunities are lost, maybe employees start leaving, and things can fall apart. Such is also the fate of our genomes: Genes are ultimately individuals that have to work together, but they're not perfect, and sometimes the pieces just don't mesh.

Far from being selfish robots, genes are in fact little molecular existentialists. Contemporary molecular biology is about relationships and networks. It is the context within which a gene is used that defines what it does and what it is. Sure, certain genes are essential for the development of the eye or the heart, but these same genes do other things in different contexts. Think not of genes as dictators, but rather as a parliament of constituents—a parliament that on the whole does a pretty decent job, but sometimes messes up, with dire consequences for the health of the organism.

how genes work and why they come in different flavors

Even if you haven't asked yourself why it is that genes makes us sick, perhaps you have wondered why it is that your sister has legs up to her ears and piercing blue eyes that haven't been seen in the family since Great-Aunt Bessie, while you seem to have inherited a horrible mix of dad's stockiness and mom's frumpiness? And what's up with your brother's moroseness: Where did that come from?

It is not much of an explanation, but the straight answer is that **genetics is a lot more complex than the idea that there's a gene for every trait.** Most traits, or attributes, are regulated by many genes, not just one. Furthermore, while it is a nice abstraction to suppose that genes come in normal, or good, versions and mutant, or bad, ones, the reality is that there are always multiple different flavors of normal. The gradation from the most common allele to various types of normal alleles to abnormality is continuous. Just having certain alleles is insufficient to predict whether a person will get a disease.

Crucially, too, the environment has a pervasive effect on the way our genes function. "Environment" means much more than the temperature outside or the nutritional content of the food we eat. It also includes influences as diverse as a mother's health during pregnancy and the pressure that peers and society put on us to behave in certain ways. As we shall see, in many cases environmental interventions are likely to have a much greater impact on public health than pharmaceutical ones. Unfortunately, most of us find it easier to pop a pill than to buck a social trend, so drugs are likely to have an ever-increasing role in disease control.

Without going into any mechanistic details, it is helpful to recognize that genes function on two levels, the biochemical and the biological. The biochemical is hidden to most observers, and therefore typically excluded from general conversation. The biological is what we actually see.

Each of the 23,000 or so genes scattered along our chromosomes encodes the information to perform a specific biochemical function. Less than a third of these genes function in every cell in your body to provide the basic building blocks and to generate energy—they are the bricks and mortar, if you like. Another third of our genes makes every one of the hundreds of different cell types in your body different. Neurons need proteins that process electrical signals, muscle cells are

full of actin and myosin that make them stretch and contract, and white blood cells carry around the components of your immune system. These are the doors and windows and furniture and appliances. The final third of our genes is responsible for regulating which genes are used when and where and in what amount. Turning on hair keratin in your pancreas wouldn't be good, and light receptors have no place in your heart, so development and physiology are highly regulated processes. These genes are the architects, foremen, and designers.

We hear and read about genes for cancer and for autism, or are given to believe that there is an aggression gene or a blonde hair gene. The reality is that these attributes are many steps removed from the molecular functions that the genes perform. If a gene contributes to cancer, it is because it normally performs a role in making sure that the right number of cells are produced at the right time and place. The reason there may be a genetic contribution to spirituality is not because some genes function to ensure that we have a belief in God, but rather because there are genes that affect how the neurons are wired together and the strength of signaling across synapses.

Fly geneticists like to name genes after the way flies look when the gene is mutated. *Antennapedia* flies have legs on their heads, *technical knock out* ones fall over when you bump their heads, and *shaven baby* embryos don't have any hairs. It is an amusing, but unfortunate habit, because it reinforces the notion that there are genes for traits. Time after time it turns out that the same gene does completely different things in different contexts. A favorite example of mine is *staufen*, which is required both for sperm development and for memory. It is not that male flies think with their penises, but rather that both of these attributes turn out to depend on a biochemical process called intracellular RNA localization, which *staufen* is involved in. Almost without exception the biological functions of genes are not written in the DNA, but rather emerge from the network of biochemical interactions within cells, and in turn the manner in which cells work together to build tissues and organs.

It follows that the reason we are all a little different from one another is because these interactions occur between ever so slightly different copies of the genes. Each gene comes in multiple different flavors—I mean, alleles—that have cropped up during the evolution of the species. These different alleles have their origin in the process of

mutation, which is basically what happens to genes when you leave them out in the sun or exposed to poisons.

Mutations are ultimately the source of all things good, but for the most part are harmful, tending to break genes. Every one of us has a few mutations that neither of our parents had, simply because mistakes are made every time the genome is copied. (But don't get too upset about this: The error rate is only about one in a billion letters in the DNA. Most of us would be thrilled to make a mistake only once in every hundred times we do something.) Mutations are also so plentiful that we all carry several of them that would kill us if we got the same one from both parents.

Mutations are so plentiful in fact that there is no way that natural selection can possibly purge them all. Obviously alleles that would tend to kill a person will not generally last long in the gene pool, and similarly ones that would tend to make us sick should not fare well either. But all new mutations are extremely rare when they appear, and nature has bigger fish to fry. It is more concerned with common alleles that affect the fitness of a large percentage of the population, so the fate of new mutations is largely governed by chance. Consequently, some mutations manage to drift around for a while and can even become reasonably common before they start having a noticeable effect on public health. The process is called *mutation-selection-drift balance*, which is a fancy way of saying that a lot of bad things happen to genomes, and evolution deals with them, but it is so busy that some of the bad things hang around for a while.

Some mutations are also good for you. Maybe they offer protection from diabetes; maybe they make a person more fertile. These tend to be favored by natural selection, but before they become the standard allele, they necessarily share real estate in the genome with the original allele. Typically it takes thousands of generations for one allele to replace another, so in the meantime you have variation. Sometimes the new allele will be better under some conditions, while the ancestral one is better under others. Maybe they have different effects in men and women, or in rural and urban settings. In such cases, geneticists speak of *balanced polymorphisms*, the classic case being sickle cell anemia, which is bad under some circumstances but protects a person from malaria in others.

You will also see it argued that many of the bad effects are actually offset by some absolute good that they do. Perhaps at a different stage of life they are sufficiently beneficial that natural selection overlooks their contribution to disease. Or perhaps at some earlier phase of human evolution they were the right gene in the right place at the right time. It is easy to get carried away with devising clever stories along these lines. Some, particularly in the domain of psychology, are even tempted to postulate that promoting disease is in itself advantageous to the selfish genes, but it really stretches credulity to suppose that there is some benefit to having genes that make us suicidal. We won't go down that road. Rarely is it necessary anyway.

It turns out that as species go, humans are actually among the least variable, at least at the level of their DNA. Nevertheless, the average person has a few million differences between the copy of his genome received from his mother and the copy received from his father. Somewhere among all those differences are the genetic variants that are responsible for all genetic diseases, but no more than a couple dozen have a big enough impact on any particular disease for us to have any hope of finding them. Finding a few dozen out of a few million is a genuine needle-in-a-haystack problem.

three reasons why genes might make us sick

The upshot of all this is that there are basically three ways that genetic variation can influence disease susceptibility. These are called the *rare alleles*, *common variant*, and *small effect* models. I will briefly describe each and then in the next section present a unified framework that iterates throughout the remaining chapters.

The simplest model is that a disease can be traced to one badly disrupted gene. This is pretty much the case for cystic fibrosis, and for thousands of other rare conditions. Around 1 in 100 of us carries a mutated version of the *CFTR* gene without any ill effects, but if two carriers marry, their children have a 1 in 4 chance of getting both bad copies and consequently having cystic fibrosis. The incidence in the general population is only about 1 in 10,000, most of which is due to a few mutations that have been around for centuries, but actually hundreds of other mutations can be found in the gene as well. Whether the disease is so severe that it claims the life of an infant, or mild enough

that a person can live to adulthood and maybe receive a life-saving lung transplant, is in part a function of which mutations they have, in part of the rest of their genome, and in part their upbringing.

Single genes can also cause diseases in other ways. Muscular dystrophy is often due to a gene, *dystrophin*, that is so big that it picks up mutations often enough that most new cases arise in the individual who has the disease. Another small set of genes has an odd feature that makes them mutate at an unusually high rate, leading to the paralysis or ataxia observed in Fragile X syndrome and Huntington's disease. For the most part, though, single gene diseases are rare.

Large-effect mutations also do not generally explain common diseases, those seen in five percent to ten percent or more of people. Really the only way they could is if there were hundreds of genes that cause a syndrome that we choose to think of as a single disease. Schizophrenia might be in this class, as might the wide spectrum of cardiovascular conditions that lead to heart attacks and stroke. It is possible that these rare mutations interact with one another, so that a person needs two or three of them in any condition to be predisposed to the disease. Unfortunately geneticists have not yet devised a systematic way to discover such mutations.

Currently the most popular model is called the common disease-common variant, or CD-CV, hypothesis. It is the idea that if there are diseases found in ten percent of the population, then there ought to be alleles at about the same frequency that are found in these people, but not in "normal" people. This sounds reasonable enough, so millions and millions of dollars are being spent in pursuit of these alleles, each of which contributes about five percent to ten percent of the risk of illness. So far, Crohn's disease, an inflammatory bowel syndrome, is the poster child success story, except that it is not actually a common disease. However, ten or so genes have been discovered that contribute to Crohn's, each with correspondingly common risk alleles. Diabetes and prostate cancer also show signs of following the CD-CV model, but the jury is out on whether this will really be a common explanation for disease.